Waiting for the Sun

Strange Days, Weird Scenes and the Sound of Los Angeles

BARNEY HOSKYNS

with photographs from the Michael Ochs Archives

St. Martin's Press
New York

WAITING FOR THE SUN: STRANGE DAYS, WEIRD SCENES AND THE SOUND OF LOS ANGELES.
Copyright © 1996 by Barney Hoskyns. All rights reserved. Printed in England. No part of this book may be used or reproduced in any manner whatsoever without written permission except in the case of brief quotations embodied in critical articles or reviews. For information, address St. Martin's Press, 175 Fifth Avenue, New York, N.Y. 10010.

The acknowledgements on p. xii constitute an extension of this copyright page

ISBN 0 312 14444 X

First published in Great Britain by Viking, 1996.

Library of Congress cataloging-in-publication data available upon request.

First US Edition
10 9 8 7 6 5 4 3 2 1

For my son Fred

Contents

A message from James Ellroy...

Prologue:
Apocalypse Now! (We Love It!)

There is no culture here in California, only trash. The West Coast has no tradition, no dignity, no ethics – this is where that monster Richard Nixon grew up. One must work with the trash, pit it against itself . . .

> Philip K. Dick, in a letter to Stanislaw Lem, September 1973

And if California slides into the ocean,
As the mystics and statistics say it will,
I predict this motel will be standing
Until I've paid my bill . . .

> Warren Zevon, 'Desperadoes Under the Eaves', 1976

When Randy Newman proclaimed 'I love LA!' back in 1983, he was doing no more than a thousand LA 'boosters' have done over the course of this century: he was celebrating the mindless golden wonder of Southern California. Yet, Newman being Newman, he couldn't resist sticking 'I Love LA' on an album called *Trouble in Paradise*. And Newman being Newman, he couldn't conceal the tongue planted firmly in his cheek.

'I Love LA' is still an oddly exhilarating record, its power undiminished by what has happened in Los Angeles in the subsequent decade. I remember watching the video on MTV when I was living in the city at the time of its release and revelling in the way its boosterist message was so brilliantly undermined by Newman's music. All the love-hate I came to feel for the place was embodied in lines such as: 'Everybody's very happy, coz the sun is shining all the time/Looks like another perfect day . . . I love LA!' As one of many thousands of Englishmen in temporary Californian exile, I was only too alert to the ironies of the troubled paradise, and relished the thrilled ambivalence that Newman's song conveyed.

Ten years earlier, another Englishman had come to LA – come to make a BBC documentary and do his boosterist bit for the city. The result was *Reyner Banham Loves Los Angeles* (1972), a film based on the bushy-bearded professor's classic study of Southern Californian buildings, *Los Angeles: The Architecture of Four Ecologies* (Penguin, 1971). Banham's boosterism may look a little glib and outdated today, but basically he was doing what Newman was doing, which was *celebrating the reviled.*

Furthermore, his attraction to Los Angeles paralleled my own and that of countless Europeans who, on the run from the old world, had ended up in the city.

'I have to admit that I do miss the casual kerbside encounters with friends and strangers to which I am accustomed in other cities,' Banham had written in *Los Angeles*. 'But I am happy to be relieved of the frustrations and dangers of the congested pedestrian traffic of Oxford Street.' For Banham, as for Brits from Isherwood to Idol, LA (and Southern California in general) seemed to represent an escape from the rain-sodden, class-ridden claustrophobia of old Europe. The very dryness of the semi-desert air was like a release from England's fetid dampness.

Twenty years on, it is less easy to love LA as the place everyone is supposed to loathe. For starters we've all, at one time or another, 'loved' LA as the plastic paradise where the American Dream has most obviously run riot: there's nothing terribly radical about a Banham-esque pro-Bad Taste stand on the issue, however much our yoof TV presenters would like to think otherwise. Indeed, we Brits have done more than anyone to overdetermine the cultural meaning of Los Angeles – 'the most mediated town in America,' as Michael Sorkin has said – recycling its hackneyed mythologies to the vanishing point of pure redundancy.

Secondly, the riots, scandals and natural disasters of the nineties have made it impossible to shut Los Angeles reality out of the 'hyper-real' Hollywood LA in our minds, try as we might to turn these spectacles into the quasi-apocalyptic climax to some epic movie. Los Angeles may sometimes resemble a cyberpunk summer blockbuster starring Ice Cube and Arnie Schwarzenegger, but that don't mean doodley-squat in Compton.

None the less, I still love LA enough to want to write about it – specifically about the history of Los Angeles as a music town, and what that music tells us of the phenomenon of the place itself. This book has been germinating in me ever since I lived in the city ten years ago, a period when a debilitating struggle with drug (ab)use was periodically punctuated by interviews with LA entertainers as different as Donna Summer and Black Flag. The seductive sickness of the place began to fascinate me at that time, and has never left me. Indeed, what Mike Davis has characterized as a sunshine/*noir* dialectic could have been summed up by the gulf between Donna Summer and Black Flag. Yet even that would have been too simplistic, as one listen to Donna Summer's 'Sunset People' reveals.

What I'm really attempting in *Waiting for the Sun* is a study of the peculiarly Californian interplay between light and darkness, or good and evil. If the history of the LA music scene can be traced partway along a line that stretches from Doris Day to Charles Manson via Day's son Terry Melcher and his sometime-surfer pals the Beach Boys, then the book's aim is to explore the reasons why such an unlikely chain of relationships should unfold there. It will become clear as the narrative progresses that my own LA heroes are the ones whose music most obviously combines the light with the dark: the Brian Wilsons and Phil Spectors and Arthur Lees of the world. The fact that I've borrowed both my title and my subtitle from the Doors should not be construed to mean that I rate Jim Morrison alongside such figures. But then old Jimbo did have a certain way with words: 'The west is the best/Get here and we'll do the rest . . .' Perhaps the question now is: If Los Angeles the apocalyptic dystopia is as much a *mythological site* as the edenic LA utopia of old – thanks to Nathanael West, Kenneth Anger, Joan Didion, James Ellroy and Niggaz With Attitude – what do we still hope to find there? Or are we all just queueing up for more violence and insanity?

Among the people who've pondered these questions with me – and shared their versions of the LA story – I am especially indebted to the following: Lou Adler, David Anderle, Peter Asher, Eve Babitz, Richard Berry, Rodney Bingenheimer, Dan Bourgoise, Jackson Browne, Denny Bruce, Peter Case, Ed Cobb, Buddy Collette, Stan Cornyn, Jim Dawson, Pamela Des Barres, Henry Diltz, Doctor Demento (Barry Hansen), Todd Everett, Donald Fagen, Perry Farrell, Art Fein, Kim Fowley, Pleasant Gehman, Rick Gershon, Jeff Gold, Carl Gottlieb, William Gibson, Sid Griffin, Matt Groening, Rick Harper, Richie Hayward, Bones Howe, Danny Hutton, Rickie Lee Jones, Bob Keane, Nick Kent, Martin Kibbee, Harvey Kubernik, Arthur Lee, Darlene Love, Michael McDonald, Maria McKee, Cyril Maitland, Joni Mitchell, Paul Moshay, Walter Mosley, Randy Newman, Gene Norman, Michael Ochs, Van Dyke Parks, Bill Payne, John Platt, Iggy Pop, Kid Congo Powers, Cheryl Rixon-Davis, Elliot Roberts, Henry Rollins, Linda Ronstadt, Metal Mike Saunders, Greg Shaw, Kirk Silsbee, Pat Smear, Terry Southern, Ronnie Spector, Penelope Spheeris, Gary Stewart, Mike Stoller, Ron Stone, Donna Summer, Derek Taylor, Russ Titelman, Gregg Turner, Nik Venet, Tom Waits, Paul Wasserman, Bill Wasserzieher, Jimmy Webb, Ian Whitcomb and Bobby Womack.

On the pictorial front, a major debt of gratitude is owed to Michael Ochs, Helen Ashford, Jonathan Hymes and Robbi Seagal at the Michael Ochs Archives; and to Harvey Kubernik, who undertook the heroic labour of gathering the photographs. In addition, I should like to thank the following for helping me in numerous different ways during my research: Barry Adamson, Robert Asher, Frank Beeson, Harold Bronson, Roy Carr, Barbara Charone, Alan Clayson, Anton Corbijn, John Crace and Jill Coleman, Chris and Steve Darrow, Paul Du Noyer, Mark Ellen, Pete Frame, Mick Houghton, Mike Howard, Lindsay Hutton, Jim Irvin, Rayner Jesson, Laura Lamson, Andrew Lauder, Muir Mackcan, Lee Ellen Newman, Philip Norman, Andy Preverser, Tom Reed, Sally Reeves, Johnny Rogan, Jon Savage, Steve Sheperd, Mat Snow, Derek Taylor, John Tobler and Rod Tootell. For other favours past and present, thanks to Richard Gehr, Annene Kaye, Jim Sclavunos and Davitt Sigerson. Thanks finally to Jonathan Riley, who green-lighted the book before leaving Viking; to Tony Lacey, who shepherded it through the final stages; to Richard Duguid; and of course to my agent, Tony Peake.

A particular debt of thanks is owed to Avik and Elaine Gilboa, for their endless patience and message-taking during my stay in Hollywood. As for the support of my wife, Victoria, words are quite inadequate to convey the depth of my gratitude to her.

Acknowledgements

Grateful acknowledgement is given to the following for permission to reproduce photographs:

The Michael Ochs Archives, for all photographs apart from the following: p. 11 – Kirk Silsbee; p. 15 – Buddy Collette; p. 77 – Derek Taylor; p. 135 – Chris Darrow; p. 216 – Denny Bruce; p. 250 – Rik Walton; p. 252 – Cyril Maitland; pp. 286, 287, 289, 307 – Jenny Lens; p. 297 – Rick Gershon; p. 309 – Ed Colver; p. 320 – Ken Sharp. The photographs on pp. viii, xiv, 4, 6, 36, 68, 78, 89, 91, 108, 148, 165, 186, 194, 222, 240, 282, 327 and 340 are the author's own.

Grateful acknowledgement is given to the following for permission to reproduce lyrics:

'Desperadoes under the Eaves' by Warren Zevon. Copyright © 1996 Warner-Tamerlane, Dark Room Music. Warner/Chappell Music Ltd, London W1. Reproduced by permission of International Music Publications Ltd.

Los Angeles

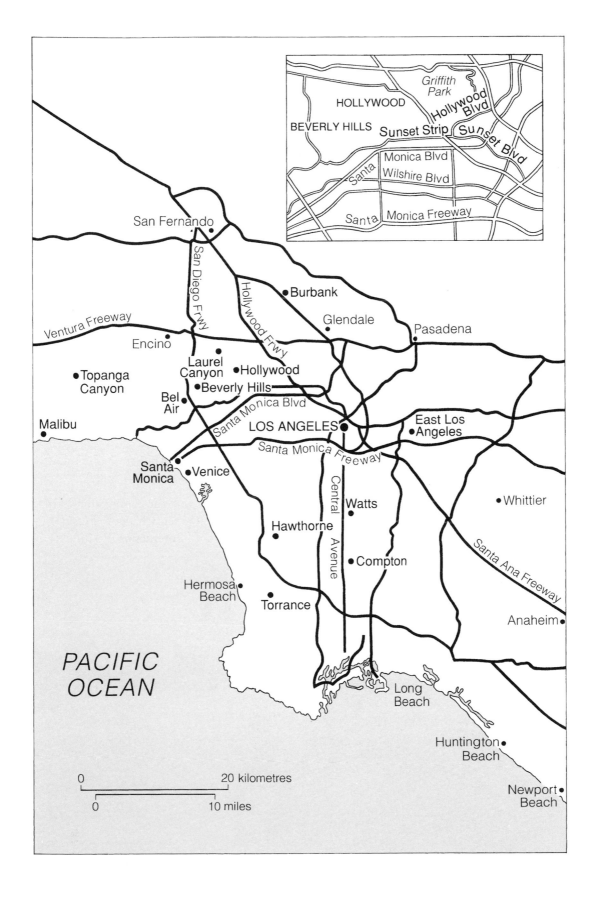

Griffith Park

HOLLYWOOD
Hollywood Blvd

BEVERLY HILLS Sunset Strip Sunset Blvd

Santa

Monica Blvd

Wilshire Blvd

Santa Monica Freeway

San Fernando

Burbank

Ventura Freeway

San Diego Frwy

Hollywood Frwy

Glendale

Pasadena

Encino

Topanga
Canyon

Laurel
Canyon

Hollywood

Beverly Hills

Bel
Air

Santa Monica Blvd

LOS ANGELES

East Los
Angeles

Malibu

Santa
Monica

Venice

Santa Monica Freeway

Whittier

Watts

Hawthorne

Central Avenue

Compton

Santa Ana Freeway

Hermosa
Beach

Torrance

Anaheim

PACIFIC
OCEAN

Long
Beach

Huntington
Beach

0   20 kilometres

0   10 miles

Newport
Beach

After the Goldrush, or Los Angeles Without a Star Map

Millions of ugly WHITE PEOPLE. Under an ugly WHITE SKY. White sand, white sky, white folks.

Richard Meltzer on Newport Beach, 1980

Los Angeles never actually had a gold rush, but you might be forgiven for thinking that gold alone could have brought people to Southern California in such droves after 1880. In fact, it was a combination of oil, railroads, sunshine, real estate and bogus folklore that lured millions of middle Americans to the shimmering edge of the Pacific Ocean – a folklore concocted by boosters and entrepreneurs whose commercial interests should have been only too clear to everyone.

The selling of Southern California to the world as a paradise of blue skies and orange groves was achieved partly through the crudest rewriting of history. A quaint mythology of noble Mission priests and docile Indians – epitomized by Helen Hunt Jackson's hugely popular novel *Ramona* (1884) – subtly obscured what had been the almost total eradication of native Americans in the area, as well as the brutal treatment of indigenous Mexicans. Underlying the cult of the Missions, moreover – and even the cult of sunshine itself – was an implicitly racist programme of white supremacy. Charles Fletcher Lummis, editor of the magazine *Out West (Land of Sunshine)*, believed that the power of sunshine would 'reinvigorate the racial energies of the Anglo-Saxons', while Abbot Kinney, who built the Californian version of Venice just south of Santa Monica, crusaded simultaneously for Mission Indians and for racial purity through eugenics. Topping both men was Joseph Widney, the University of Southern California president who argued in *The Race Life of the Aryan Peoples* (1907) that Los Angeles would one day be 'the Aryan capital of the world'. (If only he could have seen the city in 1995.)

All of this makes perfect *California über alles* sense in a land promoted – in Mike Davis' words – as 'a sunny refuge of White Protestant America in an age of labour upheaval and the mass immigration of the Catholic

Chandler Boulevard, North Hollywood, 1993.

and Jewish poor from Eastern and Southern Europe'. It is also what lies behind the cult of golden-skinned surfers that produced the Beach Boys and a hundred other surf bands in the early sixties. Indeed, the whole phenomenon of Los Angeles pop is predicated on a certain WASPy whiteness, from 'cool' West Coast jazz to the Beach Boys, the Byrds and the Eagles.

'California is a queer place,' wrote D. H. Lawrence. 'In a way, it has turned its back on the world and looks into the void Pacific.' For the Midwestern Protestants who poured into the LA flatlands in the twenties, the town meant a new beginning, a break with the old world of the East Coast and Europe. Tycoon Henry Huntingdon called the Pacific 'the ocean of the future', and the future looked good to the hordes of Iowans and Nebraskans who came to prosper among the palm trees. It even looked good to some of the exiled European intellectuals who settled in the city in the thirties and forties. As it was to be for Reyner Banham thirty years later, Los Angeles for Aldous Huxley and Christopher Isherwood was a place of release and freedom, a place where one could shake off one's European identity. Even Thomas Mann, who thought Hollywood shared something of the sickness of his *Magic Mountain*, found in Santa Monica what he'd 'always wanted': 'The light; the dry, always refreshing warmth; the spaciousness, the ocean...'

The trouble was that the 'boostering' of Los Angeles was too successful by half: by the thirties, the influx of migrants was relentless. Now everyone wanted a chunk of the Californian dream, including those Depression-crazed Okies immortalized in Steinbeck's *Grapes of Wrath*. The resulting maladjustment – divorce, suicide, mob violence – testified to the overwhelming sense of betrayal experienced by those who'd uprooted themselves only to find the same poverty awaiting them.

This was the dark flipside to the picture-postcard fantasy of California, one which gave rise not only to the *noir* LA of Raymond Chandler and James M. Cain but also to the apocalyptic ruminations of numerous non-crime writers. 'California will be a silent desert again,' wrote J. B. Priestley. 'It is all as impermanent and brittle as a reel of film.' Hanns Eisler declared that 'if one stopped the flow of water here for three days the jackals would reappear,' while his collaborator Bertolt Brecht wrote of 'luxuriant gardens/with flowers as big as trees, which of course wither/Unhesitantly if not nourished with very expensive water'. 'God never meant man to live here,' thundered Thornton Wilder like some hellfire preacher. 'Man has come and invaded a desert, and he has tortured this desert into giving up sustenance and growth to him, and he has defeated and perverted the purpose of God.'

This apocalyptic mindset – reinforced by earthquakes, brush fires, mudslides and howling Santa Ana winds – finds its apogee in Nathanael West's celebrated if decidedly overrated *Day of the Locust* (1939), in which 'the never-ending, enervating sunshine wasn't enough' for the 'masqueraders' who'd reached the promised land. Like many writers forced to make a living in the Hollywood studio system, West harboured a deep desire to destroy LA, and had Tod Hackett, his studio artist hero, paint an apocalyptic scene entitled 'The Burning of Los Angeles'. When, at the end of the novel, a hysterical flatland rabble rampages through the streets of Hollywood, it is as though Hackett's painting has come to life. The crowd is made up of the bitter and the betrayed – the hordes for whom the glimpse of a movie star gliding into a premiere can't compensate for the fact that the city has cheated them.

As they were in West's novel, the movies were for all these writers a key element in the apocalyptic scenario. The fact that Hollywood, while concealing under its glittering surface all manner of sins and perversions, pumped out the heartwarming fictions by which Middle America lived, made it irresistible as a place of disjuncture. Despite pleadings such as those of MGM studio chief Dore Schary, who insisted that 'the entire working personnel' of the dream factory should not be condemned on the basis of a handful of degenerates, Hollywood was always destined to serve as Sodom and Gomorrah for prurient Middle America, which had as little use for a 'clean-living' Tinseltown as Kenneth Anger had when he came to write his classic *Hollywood Babylon*. The birth of the scandal industry in the early 1950s made it impossible for Hollywood to pretend any longer that it wasn't hopelessly immoral. 'This is what comes of taking vulgarians from the gutter and making idols of them,' the boyfriend of Fatty Arbuckle's victim is quoted as saying in *Hollywood Babylon*, and it's a judgement which could be said to sum up the whole history of Hollywood as Babylon, a place where the disease of fame destroys all but the noblest of God's creatures.

'I used to like this town,' muses Chandler's Philip Marlowe as he drives west on Sunset with Dolores in *The Little Sister* (1949). 'Los Angeles was just a big dry sunny place with ugly homes and no style. Now we've got the big money, the sharp shooters, the percentage workers, the fast-dollar boys, the hoodlums out of New York and Chicago ... the flashy restaurants and nightclubs they run ... the riffraff of a big hard-boiled city with no more personality than a paper-cup.'

By the time *The Little Sister* had been published, the 'big hard-boiled city' was already a swinging music town, thanks to the last of the great internal migrations to Southern California. Whether its personality was as meagre and soulless as Marlowe claimed is, to say the least, debatable.

The Capitol mural, Hollywood. Left to right: Chet Baker, Gerry Mulligan, Charlie Parker, Tito Puente, Miles Davis, Ella Fitzgerald, Nat 'King' Cole, Shelly Manne, Dizzy Gillespie, Billie Holiday, Duke Ellington.

1 On the Avenue: West Coast Cool, California Crazy

Some call it the land of sunshine,
Some call it old Central Avenue.
I call it a big old country town,
Where the folks don't care what they do.

Crown Prince Waterford, 'LA Blues' (1947)

California was wide open – an experimental, innovative, and exceptionally creative environment. People felt free to try new ideas, anything at all. This kind of atmosphere produces its share of kooks, weirdos, and psychotics, but it also produces brilliant concepts in science, art, business, education, and spiritual matters ... released from ties to Europe's conservative, rationalistic past, Californians delved into new dimensions.

Paul Horn, Inside Paul Horn (1990)

I

As Mike Davis observed in his justly praised *City of Quartz* (1990), it is a striking fact that Bertolt Brecht, who'd dreamed in faraway Europe of a magical America, never bothered to explore the 'real-life Mahagonny' that was on his doorstep when he lived in Los Angeles. Peremptorily dismissing the city from the comfort of his expensively nourished garden in Santa Monica, the playwright and polemicist never saw the Boyle Heights dancehalls, Wilmington honky-tonks and Central Avenue jazz joints which made up its teeming musical nightlife.

Curiously, the most vibrant of these musical subcultures was to be found in the black ghetto which had sprung up along Central Avenue, running due south from downtown LA; curious, because Los Angeles had been a bedrock of racism and bigotry ever since the days of its support for the Confederacy during the Civil War.

The first blacks had come out to Southern California on the first major wave of migration in the 1880s, yet there were still only 75,000 African-Americans in Los Angeles County in 1940. Watts (or 'Mud Town') was established as a semi-rural black neighbourhood by the early twenties, when migrants drifted in from the deep south and started small businesses on Central Avenue – men like Elihu 'Black Dot' McGhee, who came in from El Paso in 1926, opened a barbershop, and later controlled the neighbourhood's lucrative numbers racket. Also making a living on the Avenue in the twenties were the jazz musicians Kid Ory, Dink Johnson, Mutt Carey, Buddy Petit and the Black and Tan Band, most of them originally from New Orleans. The legendary Jelly Roll Morton was playing piano in a downtown whorehouse as early as 1918 and recorded in the early twenties for Johnny and 'Reb' Spikes' local Sunshine label, the first black record company of any note in Los Angeles.

An early 'mayor' of Central Avenue was bandleader Curtis Mosby, who owned a store at Central and 23rd Street and founded the Apex Club, heart of black nightlife. By the thirties, the Apex had become the Club Alabam, and Cadillacs would line up outside on the street every night. Here the new black bourgeoisie mingled with gangsters and racketeers, providing a non-stop night parade of fur and fob-chains, pinkie-rings and pompadours – double-breasted ghetto chic at its finest. Next door to the famous Dunbar Hotel, where visiting celebrities stayed, boxer Jack Johnson owned a club called the Showboat. Even the matinée idols of Hollywood made tracks to 'darktown' to check out floor shows featuring the comedian Eddie 'Rochester' Anderson, dancers such as the brilliant Nicholas Brothers, and the ever-curvaceous assortments of 'Original Creole Cuties'. Hampton and Basie and Lunceford were in and out of

Central Avenue's Dunbar Hotel, where all visiting black stars stayed in the thirties and forties.

Los Angeles every other month, and Ellington's ground-breaking *Jump for Joy* revue was a smash hit in the city. The place was cooking.

War equalled boom time in the forties, and Southerners of all descriptions poured into Los Angeles. Whites settled in the San Fernando Valley north of the city (and much further north in towns like Bakersfield, where a strong country music scene developed); blacks, at a rate of almost 5,000 a month, followed their predecessors into the 'south-central' areas of Watts and Compton. From 1940 to 1945, when the city became the foundry of the American war effort and jobs in the munitions industry were going begging, the black population of Los Angeles doubled. By the war's end, it comprised one of Southern California's biggest ethnic groups.

Duelling tenor men Wardell Gray (left) and Dexter Gordon.

As this population grew, so Central Avenue became more bustlingly alive. At night it was hard to move for the crowds promenading and filing into clubs like the Plantation, the Downbeat, the Savoy, Lovejoy's, the Memo, and sometime Ellington singer Ivie Anderson's celebrated Chicken Shack. Here was the whole gamut of nocturnal life, from the swankiest vaudeville theatres to the dingiest poolhalls. Here was the 'sea of opulence' Art Pepper recalled from his teenage days in Lee Young's Alabam house band; here also were the cheap Chinese diners and chicken-wire dives where vicious-looking men sat around plotting heists and hijackings.

Somewhere between the two extremes were the innumerable 'after-hours' joints which littered the Avenue like rats' nests: places like Brother's, the Turban Room, Jack's Basket Room, Johnny Cornish's Double V, Stuff Crouch's Backstage. These were open-house, bring-a-bottle, leave-your-piece-at-the-door establishments where you heard the best music of all: raucous jump-blues singers such as Big Joe Turner, tenor 'cutting contests' between hard-blowing young lions Wardell Gray and Dexter Gordon. In the earliest of Walter Mosley's excellent Easy Rawlins novels, *Devil in a Blue Dress* (1990), after-hours clubs are places where 'you could come now and then and remember how it felt back home in Texas, dreaming of California'.

Black club-owners were quick, too, to move into the 'Little Tokyo' area from which LA's Japanese community had been so summarily expelled after the Pearl Harbor attack. Here, north of the main Avenue scene, one found places like the Rendezvous, the Cobra Room and Shepp's Playhouse, where a young Sammy Davis Jr sang and the audience sometimes included Howard Hughes. At the Club Finale on First Street, exiled New Yorker Howard McGhee led LA's first real bop band.

The wartime boom did not mean that blacks were any more readily accepted by white Angelenos. In a city where there was strong Ku Klux Klan activity, and where blacks were continually being driven out of insulated white neighbourhoods, it was never easy for African-Americans to embrace the Californian dream in the way whites did. 'Black LA is a place where people came to realize their dreams,' says Walter Mosley, who grew up in Watts during the fifties. 'Many people did realize them,

The effortlessly debonair Nat 'King' Cole, who had crosses burned on his Hancock Park lawn.

but many were trapped in the image they brought with them from the South, and all of that was informed by the racism of whites, or of blacks towards themselves.'

Even black stars as big as Nat 'King' Cole and Hattie (*Gone With the Wind*) McDaniel suffered violent harassment from whites. After Cole's purchase of a mock-tudor home in swanky Hancock Park in 1948, wealthy white neighbours not only refused to speak to him but burned crosses on his lawn. Bandleader Roy Porter recalled police having to escort him back to Pico Boulevard after a show in Hollywood, and pianist/vocal coach Eddie Beal was asked to sit at a separate table from a white colleague when he went to hear Count Basie at Culver City's Cotton Club in 1949. The LAPD were themselves on a crusade against any kind of miscegenation in the city, especially when it was a case of white (or at least light-skinned) girls – like Moose Malloy's Velma in Chandler's *Farewell, My Lovely* – hanging around the Avenue. Pianist Hampton Hawes recalled that 'on any weekend night on Central Avenue in the forties', it was not unusual for a whole clubful of mixed-race couples to be frogmarched down to the Newton Street station for inspection.

The rage of black musicians like Charles Mingus – who once tore down the black jockey statuettes on the lawns of Rossmore Avenue because he detested their antebellum associations – found its voice in Chester Himes' searing 1945 novel *If He Hollers, Let Him Go*, which straddled the worlds of Watts and the educated black bourgeoisie. 'If you couldn't swing down Hollywood Boulevard and know that you belonged,' fulminated Himes's hero Robert Jones; 'if you couldn't make a polite pass at Lana Turner at Ciro's without having the gendarmes beat the black off you for getting out of your place; if you couldn't eat a thirty-dollar dinner at a hotel without choking on the insults, being a great big "Mister" nigger didn't mean a thing.' Himes himself encountered the ingrained racism of Hollywood after Jack Warner stipulated that he 'didn't want no niggers' on the Warner Brothers lot, even if they could write screenplays. 'Under the mental corrosion of race prejudice in LA,' Himes wrote, 'I became bitter and saturated with hate.'

Among the many jazz clubs in Hollywood in the forties – the Ubangi, the Century, Shep Kelley's, the Swanee Inn, the Rum Boogie, Jimmy Otto's Steak House – a few made a point of welcoming integrated audiences. One such was Billy Berg's, a one-storey stucco building at 1356 North Vine Street where a Greyhound bus station now stands, bringing in all those starstruck dreamers and runaways from the boondocks. It was here, significantly, that modern jazz first hit Hollywood with the full force of the East Coast bebop revolution in late 1945.

When Billy Berg asked Harry 'The Hipster' Gibson to recommend some New York acts for the club, Gibson had no hesitation in urging him to book the all-star Dizzy Gillespie sextet, featuring the one-man whirlwind of Charlie 'Bird' Parker. Although it hardly did great business, perplexing punters used to the Hipster and Slim Gaillard, the sextet's eight-week stint at Berg's had an immediate impact on such local heroes as Hampton Hawes and Teddy Edwards, who could scarcely believe what they were hearing. 'Not everybody embraced it, but it was incredibly exciting if you were 22,' says Buddy Collette, one of the few players from that era to survive in LA with his health and sanity intact. 'Gillespie and Parker came in with a completely new way of storytelling – new notes and lines, flat ninths. When those scales and chords came in, it was hard to hear them, you had to know what they were. So it got more technical, rather than just being a case of finding some notes and playing around the blues.'

Charlie Parker at Capitol Studios, 1946.

Charlie Parker was predictably elusive in LA, constantly disappearing in search of heroin that was far more expensive than it was in the east, but he was at least together enough to cut sides for tiny labels like Bel Tone. After Dizzy returned to New York, moreover, Parker stayed on, landing a gig with Howard McGhee's band at the Club Finale and cutting such famous sides as 'Ornithology' and 'Night in Tunisia' for Ross Russell, an ex-marine who ran a record store in Hollywood and issued records on his little Dial label.

Bird's main preoccupations in LA were more accurately reflected by 'Moose the Mooche', inspired by a crippled dope dealer who peddled his wares from a shoeshine parlour on Central Avenue. The heroin habit proved increasingly debilitating: after the Finale's temporary closure, Bird ended up living in a garage, all but penniless. In July, on the night he recorded the heartbreaking ballad 'Lover Man' at C. P. MacGregor's studio on Western Avenue, he nodded out in a hotel and set fire to his mattress – a typical junkie tale, but one which landed him in the nut ward at Camarillo State Hospital for six months. The stay probably saved his life. Certainly he was in better shape when he emerged in January 1947 to take up a residency at the Hi-De-Ho Club with Howard McGhee and Hampton Hawes. By the time he returned to New York in March, he'd cut further electrifying sessions for Dial (including the drolly titled 'Relaxin' at Camarillo') and left a mark on West Coast jazz that was virtually indelible.

Bird's later claim that no one on the Coast understood what he was doing may just have been the standard New York contempt for California; he can hardly have failed to be aware of the manifold influences, both musical and narcotic, that he'd had on the LA scene. By the same token, his denunciations of Ross Russell – who moved his Dial operation to New York after Bird had returned there – were probably the standard grouching of a musician. 'Quite a few people took the opposite line and said Ross Russell was a saint,' says jazz writer Kirk Silsbee.

Russell certainly managed to record some important LA musicians before he moved east. In the wake of MGM film editor Norman Granz's seminal 'Jazz at the Philharmonic' 'sax battles' between Lester Young and Coleman Hawkins (and Illinois Jacquet and Flip Phillips), Dial issued sides like the seven-minute Dexter Gordon–Wardell Gray classic 'The Chase' and the Gordon–Teddy Edwards 'The Duel', thrilling bop jousts between men whom Hampton Hawes called 'the keepers of Bird's flame'. Gray, who'd come to LA with Earl 'Fatha' Hines and usually had the edge over Gordon, would spar with the latter at the Downbeat, then schlep up to joints like Jack's Basket Room, where the music became rawer and wilder by the hour. To the old bandleaders of the swing era they posed a clear threat, but to their fellow players they were the new rulers of the jazz scene.

By the time Gray and Gordon were duelling for Ross Russell and the after-hours club-owners, Central Avenue was already coming to the end of its boom period: Russell himself wrote that 'the high point was reached in the spring of '46, after which wartime prosperity subsided into saner, squarer modes of life.' The big spenders had gone, and only the established clubs were surviving. Elihu 'Black Dot' McGhee, who managed the Downbeat, laid the blame on blacks who were moving away from the Avenue to assimilate into white LA. Bandleader Johnny Otis argued that the return of white soldiers from the war had displaced blacks from the employment they'd enjoyed. Whatever the precise reasons, the decline set in, and it hit the jazzmen hard. 'All the hip cats on the corner/They don't look so sharp no mo',' sang Jimmy Witherspoon on his 1947 side 'Skid Row Blues', 'Coz all the good times is over/And the squares don't have no dough.'

II

By the early fifties, the Avenue was almost dead, leaving only a few diehards – Hampton Hawes, Sonny Criss, Harold Land, Curtis Counce – to carry the torch into the next decade. Addiction put Dexter Gordon's career on hold for close to a decade, and it killed Wardell Gray. Men like Mingus went east and stayed. Simultaneously, a new West Coast sound took root among white players who'd come off the road after stints in the big bands of Stan Kenton, Woody Herman and Charlie Barnet. Eventually dubbed the 'cool' sound of sunny Southern California, it took its cue not from the breathless bop runs of Bird but from the dreamy, wistful phrasing of Lester Young and the neo-classical constructions of pianist Lennie Tristano. Above all, it was anchored in the seminal *Birth of the Cool* sessions of 1949, when Miles Davis had teamed up in New York with Gil Evans, Gerry Mulligan and others to push jazz beyond bop into a new era of composition and arrangement.

Although the *Birth* sessions weren't properly released until 1957, the Davis Nonet held great appeal for the formally trained white players who'd settled in Los Angeles in the late forties: men such as Shorty Rogers, for example, who'd arrived in 1946 and joined Kenton's LA-

Shorty Rogers, linchpin of West Coast Cool.

based Innovations in Modern Music Orchestra two years later. In the Orchestra, Rogers wrote for the players who would form the bedrock of West Coast jazz in the fifties – Art Pepper, Bud Shank, Bob Cooper, Shelly Manne – and forged close friendships with all of them. For him as for many of them, LA was a place of warmth and comfort, a place to put down roots and bring up kids. Furthermore, with work in the film studios, there was for the first time the real possibility of long-term financial security.

Rogers, aided by his new cohorts, effectively put West Coast jazz on the map with *Modern Sounds* (1952), an album featuring such Kentonesque instruments as the tuba and the French horn, new sounds far removed from the raw improvisation of bop. By the time he'd decided to quit the road for good and put together an 'All-Stars' band for Howard Rumsey's Lighthouse club, West Coast jazz was a reality. 'Shorty told me that all his kids had been born nine months after Christmas,' says Kirk Silsbee. 'That was the only time he'd ever got to see his wife, and he was tired of it. So he grabbed the chance to play for Rumsey. The money was chump change,

The Lighthouse All-Stars, Hermosa Beach, August 1952. **Left to right:** *Shorty Rogers, Jimmy Guiffre, Shelly Manne, Rod Bacon, Howard Rumsey.*

but it sharpened his writing skills considerably, and that was very important.'

The Lighthouse at 30 Pier Avenue on Hermosa Beach, with its 180 seats and kitsch Polynesian decor, quickly became the laboratory of 'cool' white jazz. Ironically, the first bands Rumsey hired for the club had featured the cream of the Central Avenue survivors – Teddy Edwards, Sonny Criss, Hampton Hawes – and there may have been an insidious racism at work in their gradual replacement by Rogers and his Kentonite cronies. Certainly the black players regarded the 'writing skills' of Shorty Rogers with scepticism. 'Shorty *was* a great writer,' says Buddy Collette, 'but I'm not sure that he was a great *jazz* writer, in the sense of someone who came up with new sonorities or encouraged his players to come up with new sonorities.'

The prevailing view of the West Coast from New York's *down beat* circles tended to take the same line, stereotyping the cool sound as cerebral, filleted, bloodless. If it wasn't quite that simple, since the Lighthouse's famous Sunday afternoon jam sessions were often dominated by exuberant improvising, it's true that Rogers and his acolytes increasingly eschewed blues and saxophones for flutes and oblique neo-classicism. 'Being a jazz musician, you got full of curiosity to see what you could make of something,' Bud Shank recalled; 'we rose to those challenges and then moved along to something else.' Pianist Lou Levy conceded that West Coast was 'a little bit lower-keyed', adding that 'it *was* just a little bit whiter than black' but arguing that there was 'nothing wrong with that'.

Bolstering the work of Shorty Rogers were more recent arrivals in Los Angeles. The emaciated baritonist Gerry Mulligan, already a hardened junkie, hitchhiked across America in 1952 and landed a Monday night gig at a converted bungalow on Wilshire Boulevard called the Haig Club. Alongside him was 22-year-old trumpeter Chet Baker, an Oklahoman who'd already made an impact that year playing with Charlie Parker, plus a rhythm section comprising drummer Chico Hamilton and bassist Bob Whitlock. This was the famous pianoless quartet, Mulligan's monophonic attempt to free jazz from the limits imposed by chords. It had its critics, who derided its sound as 'neo-Dixieland', but like Rogers' *Modern Sounds* it was a key influence on the kind of restrained 'chamber jazz' later heard in the work of tenorman/clarinettist Jimmy Giuffre and in Chico Hamilton's own groups. This was contrapuntal cool – quintessential West Coast.

Mulligan was still playing John Bennett's Haig club when the brilliant altoist Lee Konitz – another alumnus of the *Birth of the Cool* class – joined the lineup in early 1953. The group's riveting treatments of standards like 'Lover Man', 'These Foolish Things' and 'Too Marvellous for Words', released by Richard Bock's fledgling Pacific Jazz label, remain outstanding examples of the Cool sound, fascinating in their very abstraction. After getting banged up on a dope charge that summer, however, Mulligan

Chet Baker, junkie icon of West Coast Cool.

decided he'd had enough of California.* Like Charlie Parker and Howard McGhee before him, Mulligan disavowed the West Coast connection once he was back in New York. 'My bands would have been successful anywhere,' he claimed. 'I had very little contact with anything that was going on out there.'

One musician who didn't – couldn't – put on these airs was native Angeleno Art Pepper. 'Pepper was a rare example of the homegrown LA musician,' says Kirk Silsbee. 'He was a guy whose conception of the horn was formed during the swing era, but who developed independent of New York influence. He had to deal with bebop as everybody else did, but like Chet Baker he essentially made an end-run around Charlie Parker.' Pepper was one of the real stars of the West Coast sound, and everyone wanted his iridescent lyricism on their sessions. 'Art to me *was* the sound of West Coast jazz,' said arranger-bandleader Marty Paich. 'It was a melodic style rather than the hard-driving New York style a lot of the players had adopted.'

Art Pepper: 'Art to me was the *sound of West Coast Jazz...'*

Unfortunately, Pepper also fell victim to the same narcotic temptations which had ensnared Gerry Mulligan and so many others. Turned on to heroin during a Stan Kenton tour in 1950, Pepper spent much of the subsequent decade behind bars, his infamous life becoming a kind of squalid flipside to the 'cool' jazz world of cocktails, sports slacks, and continental coupés. This was the grimy James Ellroy reality behind the façade created by William Claxton's photographs and Bob Guidi's designs for West Coast album covers — particularly those on Contemporary releases. By 1954, Art was incarcerated in the grim, aptly named Terminal Island, overlooking the San Pedro of his miserable childhood.

If there was one label-owner who held the key to the West Coast sound of the fifties, it was Contemporary's sainted Lester Koenig, who'd been director William Wyler's assistant at Paramount before falling foul of Joe McCarthy's House UnAmerican Activities Committee. Koenig not only kept faith with hopeless addicts of the Art Pepper variety, he gave the stars of the Lighthouse bands free rein with their experiments. 'We were immersed in jazz twenty-five hours a day,' said Shorty Rogers. 'When I was in the Lighthouse band with guys like Giuffre and Shank, we'd write music during the day and drive down there and play it all night.' If many of the All-Stars recordings weren't exactly challenging, there were always enough interesting players on them to make the experiments worthy of investigation. As forums within which these players could develop, the Contemporary sessions were unparalleled.

---

* It was down to Gene Norman, an influential promoter and disc jockey for whom he'd cut some tentette sessions, that Mulligan got out. 'I often used to get musicians out of the Honor Farm,' says Norman, who still runs his GNP-Crescendo operation from an office above a Sunset Boulevard hotel. 'Mulligan, Wardell Gray, Frank Morgan, Stan Getz, you name them. I had some clout because I used to plug things for the Sheriff on my radio show!'

True, the Bud Shank/Bob Cooper *Flute'n'Oboe* album could be said to have taken the cool tendency too far, and when MGM staffer André Previn had a million-selling album in 1956 with a cool-jazz treatment of the *My Fair Lady* soundtrack there was clearly an argument for flushing the whole thing down the toilet. By any other name, this stuff was Muzak. But it was harder to dismiss recordings by, say, the Chico Hamilton Quintet, who incorporated Fred Katz's slithering cello into an ensemble featuring Buddy Collette and guitarist Jim Hall. 'Chico was the leader of a trailblazing group,' wrote Paul Horn, Collette's replacement in the quintet in 1956. 'In a sense, he lived in a middle ground, a kind of no-man's-land between black jazz, which springs from the heart of America's black culture, and white jazz, influenced by European classical music, perhaps especially as written by Fred Katz. Chico led this group because he *liked* blending straight-ahead jazz with classical music.' Horn here sums up the acquired-taste appeal of West Coast jazz, which of late has come in for some long-overdue reassessment. Once dismissed as 'a neatly packaged soundtrack for the Cold War', the cool style now has begrudging admirers among those who wouldn't have been caught dead listening to a Shorty Rogers album.

Chico Hamilton was one of the many artists recorded by Lester Koenig's chief rival, Dick Bock, the man who signed Chet Baker shortly after the young trumpeter's unceremonious dismissal by Gerry Mulligan in the summer of 1953. Baker's 1953 recordings with sidemen like Shelly Manne, pianist Russ Freeman, and altoist Herb Geller were among the best West Coast jazz of the time, and the following year Bock even persuaded Baker to sing, thus making him an honorary member of the vibratoless 'vo-cool' school established by Anita O'Day and June Christy. If Baker's cheekbones helped him turn into the Jimmy Dean of jazz, his smack habit made him almost as much of a junkie icon as Billie Holiday.

Interestingly, although his vo-cool classics typify the breezy style of the white West Coast, Chet Baker was one of the players who helped mount a revolt against that laid-back sound with a band he called 'The Crew'. The spur for this neo-bop 'hard' sound of the mid-fifties was the astounding group formed in LA by East Coaster Max Roach. Roach had drummed with the Lighthouse All-Stars for six months, relishing the club's drug-free atmosphere, but in the spring of 1954 he responded to Gene Norman's requests for shows by bringing the brilliant young trumpeter Clifford Brown over from Philadelphia and pairing him with such practitioners of 'hard' jazz as Teddy Edwards, Harold Land, Herb Geller and Joe Maini – all players holding fast to the spirit of bop. The furious splendour of the Roach/Brown band on pieces such as 'Parisian Thoroughfare' and reworkings of standards like 'I Get a Kick Out of You' almost blew the cool school out of the water.

The following year saw similar manifestations of the 'hard' sound in the work of Hampton Hawes, who spoke of retaining a certain 'funk' in the face of cerebral white jazz. Also briefly on the same scene again was Dexter Gordon, making up for his lost years in the pen with recordings for the Bethlehem label. Yet the bleak truth is that most of the black players who chose to stay in LA were neglected. 'If you didn't get exposure back east,' said Harold Land, 'you were written off.' Which isn't to say that Land or Edwards or Hawes or Sonny Criss would necessarily have fared any better in New York; only perhaps that had they been as versatile as a man like Buddy Collette they might have got more work in the studios. Doubtless

Buddy Collette with harpist Corky Hale (centre) *and Billie Holiday at Hollywood's Jazz City, 1958.*

it was envy which prompted a certain scorn for the Collettes of the world. 'He used to really play, but Whitey scared him white inside,' wrote Charles Mingus of Collette in *Beneath the Underdog*, although he went on to advise Lucky Thompson not to try to 'cut Buddy in his own bag': 'Everybody in the studio clique tried it. He plays flute, clarinet, everything – just like the white man says you're supposed to and a little fuller.'

Collette, who knows that his jazz reputation suffered even as his coffers were swelled by Hollywood studio work, remembers Charlie Parker saying to him in 1952, 'I wish I could be like you, with a nice apartment and a brand-new car and a chicken dinner with all the trimmings.' 'See, I don't care who you are,' Collette says today, 'it's lonely when you're not working. Parker didn't play any doubles, so he didn't get the studio calls I got. That was why me and a bunch of guys went to music school and studied woodwind after the war ended. I was looking into the future, and I didn't see a decent living in the clubs. You couldn't necessarily play what you wanted to in the clubs anyway. Half the people who hired you just wanted to hear "Stardust" or "Over the Rainbow".' Buddy says that while he himself was raking in $130 for a three-hour shift on *The Groucho Marx Show*, Bird was lucky to total $200 *a week* in a club.

It was Collette who, with Mingus and others, helped bring about the merging of the separate black and white musicians' unions in Los Angeles. 'It took about three years of hard work,' he says. 'Really, it came out of a date Mingus played with Billy Eckstine at the Million Dollar Theater, where he was the only black guy in the band. He brought me down to the theatre to show them I could play, and the white drummer Milt Holland came up to us and said, "I hear you guys want one union – I have some friends who feel the same way."' Despite the opposition of a separatist black faction, who felt they wouldn't have an equal say in its affairs, Local 47 was a single union by 1953.

The merging of the unions did not significantly alter the disparity between studio opportunities for white players and those for blacks. The lucky ones – like Collette, Red Callender, Marl Young – found TV and film work, but most of the black musicians who couldn't 'double up' had a lean time of it. 'Let's just say that people hire their friends,' says Kirk Silsbee. 'That's what the studio system is all about. You had to be approved and led in by the hand. Once you'd proved yourself, you were in. On the other hand, there were lots of very capable musicians who were not allowed in, and when you look at their worldwide reputations you wonder why.' Sonny Criss, dubbed 'the fastest alto player alive' by Ornette Coleman, claimed he'd never seen the inside of a film studio in LA, yet he was working on a film within two weeks of arriving in Paris.

Out on the street, the name of the game was still raw survival. And as the fifties went on, the street got tougher by the month. Central Avenue was now the haunt of junkies and muggers, many of them musicians from the Avenue's glory days. 'The casualty list in the fifties,' wrote Hampton Hawes, 'started to look like the Korean War was being fought at the corner of Central and 45th.' In *White Butterfly*, set in 1956, Walter Mosley writes of 'Bone Street', four long and jagged blocks just west of Central near 103rd Street: here, he notes, there were no more Cadillacs, no more foxy ladies in furs, only weeds pushing up through the cracked sidewalks. 'The jazzmen had found new arenas,' reflects Mosley's private eye Easy Rawlins. 'Many had gone to Paris and New York. But the blues was still with us. The blues would always be with us.'

To Art Pepper, who fell on such hard times that he was obliged at one point to work as a door-to-door accordion salesman, the clubs grew 'smaller and sleazier' as the decade wore on. Even when he did get a break, recording once again for Lester Koenig, he managed to sabotage the opportunity to change. Unhappy in 'this false paradise I'd carved out for myself in Studio City', he helped two Chicano junkies break into a club next door to his apartment, and by 1961 was banged up in San Quentin. But then Pepper's is a singularly sad and ignoble story: there is never even the sense that the music was any kind of compensation for all the squalour and violence. 'As a person, he was one of the most loathsome, horrible human beings anybody can imagine,' says Kirk Silsbee. 'And yet he was capable of playing as well as anybody in jazz. What can you say?'

There were a few last gasps of the West Coast scene which had bloomed in the forties. The four albums cut by Shelly Manne's Men at San Francisco's Black Hawk proved there was still fire in even the most seasoned studio cats, while albums by Harold Land, Curtis Amy and Teddy Edwards gave the lie to the stock notion that the LA 'hard' school was irreparably burnt out. Manne even managed to keep his Hollywood club the Manne-Hole going for the fourteen years between 1960 and 1974, though he made his bread-and-butter wages alongside old pals like Shorty Rogers and Bob Cooper in the movie studios.

But by the same token Chet Baker, a hopeless addict by the early sixties, was reduced to cutting sub-Tijuana Brass albums for Liberty. 'Chet was unravelling hard and heavy,' says A&R man and producer Nik Venet, who worked with him briefly at World Pacific. 'People like him were starting to get a look in their eyes I'd never seen before, a look of desperation. A lot of them started experimenting with soundtracks and pop shows, and it was disastrous.' Baker's fellow junkie Hampton Hawes met a similar fate when he wound up on the cocktail-lounge circuit. Playing Mitchell's Studio Club in Hollywood in 1965, Hawes felt like it was 'the final act, the last gig of its kind – those straight-ahead improvising jobs where you could stretch out and burn all night'.

One atypical figure had emerged out of the LA jazz scene in the fifties and inadvertently signalled its decline. Ornette Coleman had come west with urban bluesman Pee Wee Crayton in 1950 but only settled in California four years later. Virtually self-taught, and ignoring the standard rules he did know, he quickly became a laughing-stock among the Lighthouse and Central Avenue regulars, who assumed he couldn't play. In fact, Coleman was attempting to take jazz out of the tonal system altogether, opening the way for the 'free jazz' of the sixties. And fortunately, before he could get too disheartened, he connected with a group of young players who weren't yet completely set in their musical ways.

Local boy Don Cherry, who'd grown up on Central Avenue, first heard the sound of Coleman's white plastic alto coming from a record store one afternoon in August 1956. 'I could hear him a block away, and it was something like a horse whinnying,' he recalled. Musicians like Cherry soon recognized that Coleman was an original. When the two men hitched themselves to a group led by Paul Bley at the Hillcrest on Washington Boulevard, a landmark avant-jazz unit was born. Not that you'd have known it from the reaction of the club's patrons, for whom the 'out-of-tune' caterwauling was too much to take. 'The audience literally walked out of the club every time we played,' remembered Bley's then-wife Carla.

Predictably, Lester Koenig was the only man prepared to take a risk with this radically free sound, though Coleman tempered his wilder instincts on the comparatively accessible Contemporary debut *Something Else!*, cut in February 1958. The following year, Atlantic's Nesuhi Ertegun brought Coleman and band to New York, where they were an immediate *succès de scandale* at the Five Spot in November 1959. 'To Ornette, LA was a sort of laboratory, as it had been to Mingus, and to the Mulligan/Baker band, and to some extent to Eric Dolphy,' says Kirk Silsbee. 'So often Los Angeles has served as a laboratory for musicians, and of course once they've gotten themselves together they go to the marketplace.' Ted Gioia reaches a similar conclusion in his excellent book *West Coast Jazz*, adding that 'as with Dolphy and Mingus, the West Coast proved it could develop an avant-garde but was capable neither of appreciating it once it came to be, nor of establishing it as a legitimate form of jazz worthy of close attention, widespread dissemination, and emulation.'

'Time has not treated these men badly,' wrote Richard Williams when the re-formed Lighthouse All-Stars (Rogers, Cooper, Shank, Levy, et al.) played London's Royal Albert Hall in November 1991. 'Rogers, 67, sails his boat out of Marina del Rey, where he has an oceanside condo ...' Ah yes, but what of all those fallen heroes? What of the 'big old country town' where men in spats and double-breasted suits had stepped out of Cadillacs and floated through the doors of the swankiest clubs in California? Where did it all go?

III

So rigid is the stratification into which historians organize their accounts of musical evolution that one might be forgiven for assuming that 'jazz' and 'rhythm and blues' were entirely distinct musical spheres. But the fact is that in Los Angeles as elsewhere, there was continual interchange between the two spheres. If rhythm and blues, the label pinned on to 'race' music by *Billboard* writer Gerald Wexler in 1949, was a cruder, more populist version of jazz, that didn't stop a host of jazz musicians from dabbling in it. Hardcore bop freaks might have castigated R&B (or 'jump' blues) as 'cornbread' music, but many of their heroes were perfectly happy to muddy the fine line between 'art' and 'entertainment'. 'Blues was basic music, and we'd all grown up with it,' says Buddy Collette. 'It's almost like you grow up with home cooking, and then you get to the point where you're eating caviar. But you can always go back to home cooking. You can always go back to the blues.'

Johnny Otis, the original 'White Negro'.

Blues tunes had been a staple part of the repertoires of big bands in the Southwest ever since the thirties, when singers such as Jimmy Rushing, Walter Brown and Julia Lee roared over blaring saxophonists and churning rhythm sections. For all the instrumental virtuosity of the great swing-era players, people still came to see these bands in order to dance, drink and flirt. By the early 1940s, in the novel atmosphere of wartime prosperity, there was a huge demand for the 'territory' bands which traversed the Southwest and usually ended up in LA: bands with formidable singers like Big Joe Turner and Eddie 'Cleanhead' Vinson, with hard-blowing tenormen like Illinois Jacquet and Eddie 'Lockjaw' Davis. It was these bands, moreover, that paved the way – and provided much of the personnel – for the smaller-scale jump-blues combos that dominated the rest of the decade.

'All of us came from a big-band environment,' said Johnny Otis, the Greek-born Negrophile who in 1942 was drumming with Harlan Leonard's

Kansas City Rockets at Central Avenue's Club Alabam. 'When I formed *my* band, I still wanted my five reeds, four trumpets, and the trombones – I wanted to hear that in my ear. But I couldn't have that, because the big bands were breaking up and nobody could afford to keep them going. So when I got my first job, I had a baritone and a tenor, a trumpet and a trombone. That was my reed section and my brass section!'

Otis's experience was typical of the many big-band sidemen who found themselves playing in smaller units of the kind standardized by Louis Jordan's Tympany Five (which actually numbered seven) and tailoring their music to the needs of Central Avenue's less sophisticated denizens. 'Some so-called jazz musicians, the bush leaguers,' Otis told Don Snowden in 1982, 'considered people like Sonny Thompson, Roy Milton or myself traitors to the jazz cause. I might take that seriously if I'd been a great instrumentalist, a man who created deathless art, but I never was. I was kind of a nice drummer, and later I dinged on the vibes and boogied three- finger-style on the piano.'

The 'bush leaguers' would probably have concurred with Otis's humble self-assessment, but there were more talented musicians who were not averse to simplifying their technique in the service of musical excitement. Singers like Helen Humes, Jimmy Witherspoon, Nellie Lutcher and Ernie Andrews all combined jazz technique with the gusto of jump-blues, while players of the calibre of Teddy Edwards and Buddy Collette frequently took jobs with R&B bands. Indeed, the whole 'honking' tenor sax school came directly out of the big bands, which by the early forties had all but formularized the kinds of 'duels' which led to the Dexter Gordon/Wardell Gray classic 'The Chase' (and later to Gordon's and Teddy Edwards' 'The Duel'). Illinois Jacquet's famous solo on the 1942 Lionel Hampton recording 'Flying Home' is often referred to as the first R&B sax solo; he was also the wild soloist on a key recording – known as 'Blues, Part Two' – from Norman Granz's first 'Jazz at the Philharmonic' show in July 1944. This new kind of squalling, pumped-up solo was nothing more than a showbiz trick designed to liven up audiences, yet its influence on West Coast R&B was almost immeasurable. By the time of Wild Bill Moore's solos on Helen Humes' 'Be-Baba-Leba' (1945), the fine line between 'jazz' and what the world knows as 'rhythm and blues' had been decisively crossed. 'There was a new kind of frenzy and extra-local vulgarity to rhythm and blues that had never been present in older blues forms,' wrote LeRoi Jones in *Blues People* (1963). 'Suddenly it was as if a great deal of the Euro-American humanist façade Afro-American music had taken on had been washed away by the war.

It is a curious fact that for years the importance of Los Angeles as a hotbed of rhythm and blues was overlooked in favour of cities like Memphis, Chicago and New Orleans. Two principal reasons accounted for this: first, the comparative cultural isolation of Los Angeles until the 1950s, and second, the fact that LA's thriving R&B scene failed to produce any major stars in the rock'n'roll era. But it has also been difficult for rock historians to conceive of LA as a black environment, even with the knowledge that thousands of blacks migrated to the West Coast from Texas and Oklahoma. The whole idea of California as a funky rhythm and blues town seems like a contradiction in terms, particularly when the great days of Central Avenue are so long gone.

Despite this, there is a case for arguing that LA can boast a more important R&B heritage than almost any other American city. 'The first big surge of R&B was on the West Coast in LA, not in New York,' said Ralph Bass, while Mike Stoller asserts that 'LA really was the hub of R&B labels, far more so than anywhere else.' It is certainly true that there were more independent R&B-oriented labels in the city than in, say, New York or Chicago, and this at least partly reflected the greater number of R&B acts there. With Central Avenue flooded by affluent nightlifers and

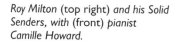

Roy Milton (top right) *and his Solid Senders, with* (front) *pianist Camille Howard.*

demobbed GIs searching for good times, there was an ever-increasing demand for the post-swing marriage of blues and rhythm, whether it manifested itself in the raucous after-hours music of Roy Milton's Solid Senders or in the melancholy piano blues of Johnny Moore's Three Blazers.

'Roy Milton and I are accused of starting the whole R&B thing,' said Joe Liggins, whose massive 1945 hit 'The Honeydripper' really established the new sound. 'It was the rhythm that kicked off R&B here in the forties – it's still blues, but it's dance blues with an earthy feel in the melody, phrasing and stories.' For Johnny Otis, the style was 'a hybrid of big-band jazz and bebop, small group and good-time swing, country blues and basic boogie-woogie ... amplified and squashed down for public dancing'. 'Squashed down' gets it nicely, as one listen to the sassy small-combo sound of 'The Honeydripper' or Roy Milton's 'RM Blues' makes clear. This was Texas/Oklahoma cornbread blues relocated in smoggy, sunburned Watts.

By the time Milton's record was nudging No. 1 on the 'race' chart in April of 1946, there were already a handful of important independent labels in Los Angeles, all of them rushing to capitalize on the majors' slowness to pick up on the new trend. It's true that Capitol Records, founded in Hollywood in 1942, had signed Nat 'King' Cole and T-Bone Walker, but the more established, New York-based majors (Columbia and RCA-Victor) wouldn't touch Milton or Liggins with a bargepole. 'They weren't interested in us small-fry,' said Johnny Otis. 'It was like, "Who are they and what is this bastard product with two saxes and a trumpet?" We couldn't even get auditions.'

Ultimately, it was down to the likes of Leon and Otis Rene, Creole brothers who'd come out to LA from Louisiana in the thirties, to take a risk with this 'jump-blues' sound. Having written Louis Armstrong's 'When It's Sleepytime Down South' and the Ink Spots' 'When the Swallows Come Back to Capistrano', Leon Rene was dismayed to find that he couldn't get more of his material recorded by major labels. As a result he founded the Exclusive label in 1942, his brother Otis following close behind with Excelsior.

Early in 1945, Leon Rene got wind of a song – a fifteen-minute brag-a-thon known as 'The Honeydripper' – which Joe Liggins and his band were performing nightly at the Samba Club on 5th Street. Evolving out of a dance called the Texas Hop, and based around Liggins' insistent boogie piano riff, 'The Honeydripper' was tearing the house down every night, epitomizing the 'squashed-down' combo style described by Johnny Otis. By the late summer, on Exclusive, it was blaring out of every black record store in America. Liggins stayed at No. 1 on the black chart for eighteen straight weeks.

But if there was one record which could really be said to have galvanized the independent record business in LA, it would have to be Private Cecil

Gant's 'I Wonder', cut in late 1944 in a garage belonging to former pressing-plant worker Cliff McDonald. 'I Wonder' was the obverse of the jump-combo style of Liggins, a mournful pop-blues ballad that came all the way down the line from Leroy Carr via Nat Cole and Charles Brown, striking a deep nerve in sweethearts separated by the war and establishing the so-called 'sepia Sinatra' style of piano-accompanied blues balladeering. Released on the Gilt Edge label, 'I Wonder' took off after Gant persuaded the US Treasury to let him sing at a downtown Los Angeles war-bond rally on Broadway and 9th Street. Within weeks he was the 'GI Sing-sation' of the country and the record was at No. 1, the first major black hit on an independent label.

'The Rene brothers said, "What the fuck do you *need* in order to be a record company? All you got to do is to get a record, get it pressed and put it out!"' recalled Johnny Otis, whose 'Harlem Nocturne' – a typical jazz-into-R&B transitional record from 1945 – was a minor hit on Excelsior. 'Of course, once all these labels set up, they had to find product. They couldn't get Basie or Duke because they couldn't afford 'em, and they couldn't get Big Bill Broonzy 'cos they were in the wrong part of the country. So what was left to them was T-Bone Walker, Joe Liggins, Roy Milton, and the rest of us.' A crucial factor in the success of the new labels was the work of independent distributors such as Jack Gutshall, who was able to exploit the contacts he had in other cities to secure orders for records like Roy Milton's 1946 side 'RM Blues'.

With the exception of Jack Lauderdale's Swingtime, Al Patrick's Supreme, Jake Porter's Combo, and the Renes' labels, the majority of the independent companies were Jewish-owned, just as they were in New York or Chicago. 'Whether there was a real affinity between Jews and blacks, or whether it was simply a case of Jewish neighbourhoods gradually becoming black neighbourhoods, there was definitely an intermingling in those days,' says Mike Stoller, himself a Jewish songwriter who came to Los Angeles from New York. 'Unfortunately, in the last decade or so, there seems to have been a terrible schism between blacks and Jews.' The novelist Walter Mosley, who is that rare thing a black Jew, recalls harmonious relations between Jewish merchants and the black community from the Watts of his childhood, pointing out that 'you shouldn't ever confuse resentments caused by capitalism with bad relations between the races.' Undoubtedly, as Jews have steadily been assimilated into mainstream white culture in America, the affinity they once shared with blacks as a fellow oppressed minority has dwindled. Yet there remains a strong relationship between black artists and Jewish entrepreneurs in the record industry, as Matt Dyke and Mike Ross of Delicious Vinyl – described by music mogul Lou Adler as 'the rap Leiber and Stoller' – could attest.

The two most important independents founded in 1945, a pivotal year in the musical life of Los Angeles, were both Jewish-owned. Modern Music was the name of the company formed in March by Jules, Saul and

Joe Bihari, sons of a Lebanese grain merchant who'd come to LA only four years earlier and entered the restaurant and jukebox business. Helped out by their sisters Florette, Roz and Maxene, and a fourth brother, Lester, the Biharis' operation was an old-style family business on a grand scale. The prime mover was Jules, who'd worked the jukeboxes around Central Avenue and had a genuine love for black music.

Early in 1947, after recording a variety of jazzmen – Illinois Jacquet and Wardell Gray among them – Modern took over an old American Recording Artists plant on Robertson Boulevard in Culver City, then hit paydirt with female boogie pianist Hadda Brooks' 'That's My Desire'. Subsequently they picked up the cream of the local blues/R&B talent, in addition to licensing masters from labels as far away as Houston and Detroit. 1948's 'Boogie Chillen' was the first big hit for the inimitable John Lee Hooker, and there were equally successful sides by Smokey Hogg ('Long Tall Mama'), Pee Wee Crayton ('Blues After Hours'), and Little Willie Littlefield ('It's Midnight'). In the words of Jimmy Witherspoon, who signed to the label after his 1949 smash 'Ain't Nobody's Business', 'Modern Records – Jules Bihari – discovered more blues singers than any other record company in history.'

Philo was a label formed in 1945 by the brothers Leo and Eddie Mesner, who ran the Philharmonic Music Shop downtown on West 5th Street. Like Modern, they kicked off with an impressive roster of jazz artists (Jacquet, Lester Young, Jay McShann, even Billie Holiday for a handful of releases), but quickly imprinted their seal on the new jump-blues sound with the classic Helen Humes side 'Be-Baba-Leba'. Humes had been a Basie fixture in the late thirties, but here she sang in the piercingly girlish voice which Little Esther would later make her own, cutting through the red-hot bop sound of Bill Doggett's Octet and sparring with tenorist Wild Bill Moore. For R&B scholar Jim Dawson, 'Be-Baba-Leba', cut in August 1945, was just one example of the new sound brewing in Los Angeles. 'People talk about East Coast records like Hal Singer's "Corn Bread" or Paul Williams's "The Hucklebuck" as ground-breaking R&B,' he says, 'but if you go back and listen to them, they're really not that wild. "Be-Baba-Leba" really is wild.'

Early in 1946, Philo became Aladdin Records, a label which proceeded to chalk up an impressive run of hits by Texan boogieman Amos Milburn and by Charles Brown, who signed to the Mesners after quitting Johnny Moore's Three Blazers in 1948. Here again were the two sides of LA's R&B sound: the earthy, rolling piano blues of Milburn (from 'Chicken Shack Boogie' to the succession of booze anthems which commenced with 1950's 'Bad, Bad Whiskey') and the mournful balladry of Brown, whose 'Trouble Blues' – an R&B No. 1 for fifteen successive weeks in 1949 – must have struck some deep chord in depressed post-war black America. For Jerry Wexler, writing in his autobiography *Rhythm and the Blues* (1993), the Charles Brown of 'Trouble Blues' shared a West Coast

Charles Brown, whose melancholy piano blues brought him several big R&B hits in the late forties and fifties.

blues sensibility with the T-Bone Walker of 'Stormy Monday Blues' and the Percy Mayfield of 'Please Send Me Someone to Love' – 'a sensibility that was smooth and salty at once, sweet but anguished, simple yet profound'. The post-war Southern California blues, noted Wexler, had 'a mystique all its own, refined and relaxed'.*

The Mesners, operating from their offices at 4918 Santa Monica Boulevard, were lucky enough to have a tenacious A&R man in Sammy Goldberg (another black Jew) and an inspired arranger/bandleader in Maxwell Davis, one of the key figures in the sound of LA rhythm and blues. 'Maxwell Davis was a major unsung hero,' says Mike Stoller. 'He really was Mr Rhythm and Blues in LA.' Most of Aladdin's rivals boasted similar behind-the-scenes figures, some more renowned than others: men such as Johnny Otis (Modern, Savoy), Ralph Bass (Black & White, Savoy, Federal), Bumps Blackwell (Specialty), Lloyd Glenn (Swingtime), and a group of freelance heavyweights that included Rene Hall, Ernie Freeman, Red Callender and H. B. Barnum.

Johnny Otis managed to do very well for himself, especially after opening the Barrelhouse club on Wilmington and 116th Street, just a few blocks south of Sabato Rodia's Watts Towers. If 1948 was a tough year for Central Avenue as a whole, it was kind enough to Otis. With sawdust strewn on the floor, barrels for tables, and cartoons projected on to the walls, the Barrelhouse was the hottest joint in Watts. 'The club held about a hundred people, with a dancefloor in the middle,' remembered Ralph Bass. 'It featured all kinds of acts and gimmicks of the Moms Mabley and Pigmeat Markham variety.' Bass recalled that he and Otis would 'steal all their fucking tunes' from the church next door, which doubtless served them well when they were producing records for the infamous Herman Lubinsky.

Bass was himself a good example of a man who surfed the transition from jazz to jump-blues in LA. As an A&R man for Paul Reiner's Black & White label, he cut former Hampton tenorist Jack McVea on the jump-blues novelty song 'Open the Door, Richard', only to find it becoming *the* sensation of 1947. 'I produced it by accident,' he recalled. 'We were doing some blues because I'd gotten bored with everything else sounding alike. I'd seen him do "Richard" live, so I said what the hell, let's cut it.' To fully appreciate 'Richard', you had to be in on Dusty Fletcher's slapstick

* A singer who took his cue from the style of Charles Brown and other 'sepia Sinatras' was Ray Charles, who signed to Jack Lauderdale's Swing Time label in 1949 and recorded in LA with Johnny Moore's Three Blazers. (Both 'Baby Let Me Hold Your Hand' and 'Kiss Me Baby' were Top 10 R&B hits on Swingtime.) After two years on the road with Lowell Fulson, first as a mere sideman and then as Fulson's musical director, Charles split to do his own thing. By 1953, having incorporated the influence of gospel music into his R&B songs, he had signed to Atlantic Records in New York. The rest is history that doesn't properly belong in this book, although Charles returned to LA after being busted for heroin in 1958, and then defected from Atlantic to the Hollywood-based ABC-Paramount label.

Johnny Otis (centre) introduces Specialty duo Don and Dewey.

comedy skit about drunks coming home late and knocking on Richard's door – the obvious innuendo-laden question being, what was Richard *doing* in there?

Once he'd realized that 'this shit made money', Bass proposed that he and Johnny Otis make some records for Savoy, Herman Lubinsky's New Jersey-based label. Neither man had to search very hard to find artists: Big Jay McNeely, king of the homegrown honkers in LA, regularly played the Barrelhouse, while talent shows such as those at the nearby Largo Theater brought in an abundance of new faces. 14-year-old Esther Mae Jones had only been in LA a few months when Otis caught her at the Largo, intoning her idol Dinah Washington's recent hit 'Baby, Get Lost' and walking off with the $10 prize money. Bowled over, Otis soon had 'Little Esther' singing at the Barrelhouse. When her recording debut, the merrily flirtatious 'Double Crossing Blues', suddenly took off early in 1950, Bass and Otis drove all the way out to Pasadena in the middle of the night to get contracts signed by her mother. Esther subsequently became an integral part of Otis's Rhythm & Blues Caravan, her kittenish voice and Dinahesque phrasing making her one of R&B's most distinctive singers. In the process, she also picked up a bigtime heroin habit.

The pubescent Little Esther, star of Johnny Otis's Rhythm and Blues Caravan.

After success with Esther, Big Jay McNeely, the Robins and Otis himself, Bass quit to head Federal, a new subsidiary of Syd Nathan's King Records. From an office on 'Record Row', a section of Pico Boulevard where most of the independent record distributors were based, he managed to woo Little Esther away from his old boss Lubinsky but otherwise did much better with such non-LA vocal groups as Billy Ward and the Dominoes, Hank Ballard and the Midnighters and – later – James Brown and the Famous Flames. Otis, meanwhile, went from Savoy to Mercury and finally, in 1954, to the Houston-based Peacock label.

With the success of Modern and Philo/Aladdin came new labels, new competition. When Art Rupe, born Arthur Goldberg in Pittsburgh, failed to break into the movie business after studying at UCLA, he instead became a partner in Robert Sherman's Atlas Records, which at one time had Nat 'King' Cole on its books. The label's collapse in 1943 left Rupe with just enough capital ($600) to start his own Jukebox label, whose first release, the Sepia Tones' 'Boogie No. 1', managed to sell 70,000 copies in California and confirmed Rupe in his pursuit of the new urban blues sound of LA. 'The majors kept recording country blues, but the black people I knew never lived in the country,' he told Arnold Shaw. 'They looked down on country music, called it "field nigger" music. They wanted to be citified.'

Rupe approached his 'neglected market' with hard business acumen, trying to discern a formula for hits. Concluding that the secret lay in 'a big band sound, expressed in a churchy way', he checked out the after-hours clubs and eventually found Roy Milton and his Solid Senders. 'Milton played regular hours in a white club,' Rupe recalled. 'Then he went down to Watts and played for the black people.' Milton's 'RM Blues', recorded in December 1945, was an infectiously mellow small-combo blues, with a walking mid-tempo beat, a repeated horn riff, and the free-ranging piano fills of Ms Camille Howard: not exactly remarkable, but a big hit in the spring and a blueprint for many more over the course of the next seven years.

Milton, mainstay of Rupe's operation after Jukebox was renamed Specialty Records in late 1946, also provided the snappy beat on his pianist Camille Howard's hit instrumental 'X-Temporaneous Boogie', recorded in the final minutes before the Musicians' Union recording ban of 1948. By 1950, Rupe had a roster which included Joe Liggins and his Honeydrippers, who were at No. 1 with 'Pink Champagne' for almost as long as they'd been there with 'The Honeydripper', and blues-balladeer Percy Mayfield, whose moodily beautiful songs ('Please Send Me Someone to Love', 'Strange Things Happening', and others) gave him a distinct edge over the other melancholic 'sepia Sinatras'. Rupe had also moved into the gospel field, signing quartets like the Pilgrim Travellers, the Chosen Gospel Singers, and of course the Soul Stirrers, from whose ranks sprang Sam Cooke. A key figure in the Specialty setup was Robert 'Bumps' Blackwell, who'd studied composition at UCLA and was equally adept at producing gospel and R&B.

It wasn't long before Rupe was following the lead of Lew Chudd, the former NBC radio executive who'd formed Imperial Records in 1947. After making inroads into Mexican and country music, Chudd had entered the R&B field, even looking beyond Los Angeles for black talent.* Establishing a relationship with bandleader/arranger Dave Bartholomew in New Orleans, he signed Fats Domino in 1949, eventually turning 'the fat man' into one of the major rock and roll stars of the fifties. Nor was it just Chudd who was cashing in on the south: Modern had begun making field trips in 1948, with Lester Bihari appointing Ike Turner the label's Memphis talent scout in 1950.

Rupe's decision to visit New Orleans reaped almost instant rewards when Lloyd Price's 'Lawdy Miss Clawdy' went to No. 1 on the R&B chart in May 1952. Thanks to local scout/promo-man Johnny Vincent, moreover, Specialty had an even bigger New Orleans hit with Guitar Slim's deliciously drawling 'The Things That I Used to Do' (1954), as arranged by Ray Charles shortly before his signing to Atlantic. But neither Price nor Slim could have held a candle to Rupe's biggest Crescent City catch: the one and only Little Richard, whose 'Tutti Frutti' hit the world in late 1955.

IV

The fact that companies like Imperial and Specialty had to go to New Orleans to find their new stars tells us something about the decline of LA's own R&B sound. Just as Central Avenue jazz had foundered towards the end of the forties, so West Coast rhythm and blues was starting to lose its edge in the mid-fifties. 'Our musicians were getting a little bit glib, and either I needed a change or they did,' said Art Rupe. 'I didn't feel the original spontaneity anymore.' Yet amidst the general decline there were signs of fresh life, most obviously in the work of two Jewish teenagers who'd moved to California from the East Coast.

When Mike Stoller arrived from New York in July 1949, Jerry Leiber was at Fairfax High, a veritable breeding-ground of Jewish music-biz talent. Six weeks older than Leiber but a year ahead of him educationally, Stoller graduated from Belmont High after one semester and moved on to LA City College, downtown on Vermont. 'I missed 52nd Street, but I found LA very exciting because of the cultural mix,' says Stoller. 'In New York, most of my high school friends had been white and middle-class, whereas here the majority of the students were Mexicans, Orientals, and some blacks. Black culture wasn't foreign to me: what was foreign was the admixture.'

---

* Imperial's subsequent abandonment of its Mexican artists was the cause of much bitterness. 'Those guys made a fortune,' recalled Lalo Guerrero, one of the label's early Mexican stars. '[But] after they got the black groups, they went higher and they dropped all the Latinos and Chicanos. Then they sold the label to, I believe it was Liberty first and eventually it ended up with Capitol, and they sold it for a million dollars – something that started with us Chicanos [in a] little hole on Western Avenue.' See Steven Loza, *Barrio Rhythm: Mexican–American Music in Los Angeles*, pp. 77–8.

Outside Atlantic's LA office in 1957: Jerry Leiber, Lester Sill and Mike Stoller, with Lou Krevetz in the foreground.

At City College, a drummer from Fairfax High heard Stoller fooling around at the piano and suggested he make contact with Leiber, then working after school at Norty's Record Shop on Fairfax Avenue. Norty's, in the heart of the Jewish district, was hardly a blues or R&B outlet, but the seventeen-year-old shop assistant was already a fanatical lover of black music. 'We found we had some common ground in the blues,' remembers Stoller, 'and we started to frequent a lot of the clubs here. We'd go down to the Club Alabam, see Johnny Otis or Roy Milton or Joe Liggins. We were welcomed in general, I think, and certainly we were never in fear of physical violence.' One place the two boys were always welcome was the house of black law student Jimmy Talbot on 31st Street near Western, especially after he'd put on Friday night shows with front lines consisting of Wardell Gray, Dexter Gordon, Art Farmer and Frank Morgan.

Stoller and Leiber were soon writing together, Stoller at the piano and Leiber plucking droll couplets out of the air. One afternoon, Modern Records salesman Lester Sill walked into Norty's and wound up listening to Jerry Leiber singing 'That's What The Good Book Says' – in Leiber's words 'a kind of fucked-up blues and gospel number and really not much of either' which the Robins cut for Modern in late 1950. Sill was instrumental in introducing the duo not only to Modern but to powerful men like Gene Norman, at one of whose 'Blue Jubilees' Jimmy Witherspoon sang the Leiber and Stoller song 'Real Ugly Woman'. At Modern, the teenagers were lucky enough to receive free tutelage in arranging and producing from Maxwell Davis, whom the Biharis had poached from Aladdin.

Sill's belief in his protégés led in turn to meetings in 1952 with Ralph Bass and Johnny Otis, the result being a series of songs for the likes of Little Esther ('Mainliner', 'Saturday Night Daddy') which showed the duo inching towards their trademark wit and panache. After chalking up their first real hit – with Charles Brown's last, the despairing 'Hard Times' – Leiber and Stoller were introduced to Willie Mae 'Big Mama' Thornton, a six-foot, 300-pound lesbian whom Peacock Records had sent from Texas to receive the Johnny Otis treatment. After an initial encounter at Otis's house, Jerry and Mike wrote 'Hound Dog' and presented it to the 'pretty salty' giantess, who 'started to sing the words and put in some of my own, all that talkin' and hollerin''. Recorded in August 1952, the record went on to become one of the bestselling black hits of 1953 – and, three years later, a huge hit for Elvis Presley.

Leiber and Stoller, still only twenty years old, learned their first real music-biz lesson when Peacock's Don Robey characteristically omitted to put their names on 'Hound Dog'. In late 1953, in a somewhat misguided attempt to protect their interests, they formed Spark Records with Lester Sill, opening a cramped storefront office north of 'Record Row' on Crenshaw Boulevard. 'My dad and a friend of Lester's put up about $1,800 each to start a record company, a publishing company and a sales company!' laughs Mike Stoller. 'Of course we were under-capitalized and couldn't get paid by the distributors.'

The Coasters, a first vehicle for Leiber and Stoller's pop satire. Left to right: Cornell Gunter, Will 'Dub' Jones, Billy Guy, Carl Gardner, Adolphi Jacobs.

Spark's first releases appeared in the spring of 1954, most of them recorded at Abe 'Bunny' Robyn's Master Recorders on Fairfax Avenue and featuring such illustrious sessionmen as Shorty Rogers, Shelly Manne and Jimmy Giuffre. The contribution of engineers like Robyn and Val Valentin at Radio Recorders to LA rhythm and blues was incalculable. Robyn in particular – nicknamed Bunny because of his protruding front teeth – was prepared to experiment with sound, splicing tape and playing with sound effects such as the sirens and gunfire on the Robins' brilliant 'Riot in Cell Block No. 9'.

Distributed by Abe Diamond and played to death by Hunter Hancock on KGFJ, Spark's releases did well in LA but 'couldn't get past the Rockies' – an old problem for West Coast indies. 'Lester could have done it if he'd had the budget to travel,' says Stoller. 'But we just didn't have the money.' In the end, in November 1955, it was Atlantic's Nesuhi Ertegun who came to the rescue, picking up the last Spark release (the Robins' 'Smokey Joe's Cafe') and offering the duo an almost unprecedented production deal which eventually took them to New York.

By the time they were producing the first Coasters hits for Atlantic subsidiary Atco – 'Down In Mexico', 'Searchin'', 'Young Blood' – Leiber and Stoller had honed their writing skills to the point of great art, bringing a degree of wit and sophistication to R&B which it had never had before. 'The material we were writing was more complex,' said Leiber. 'There were four or five people in the group, and we gave lines to the bass singer, first tenor, second tenor and baritone. It needed split-second timing because the songs were based on punch lines and jokes.' Combined with Stoller's exotic, sinuous rhythms, these clowning vocal arrangements helped establish the Coasters as America's premier black satirists.

Or were the group just Uncle Tomming? There were detractors who claimed they objected to the racial stereotyping of blacks in Leiber and Stoller songs. Johnny Otis even maintained that he'd 'taken some stuff out of "Hound Dog" that black people would have found offensive', though this may simply have been a pretext for adding his name to the song credits. Mike Stoller is adamant that denigrating blacks was the farthest thing from his or Jerry Leiber's mind: 'I remember someone saying that our songs had too many references to drinking and gambling, but if you look at the history of black popular music and the blues, it's filled with references to those things. Our only intention was to be historically accurate.'

Leiber and Stoller finally packed their bags and split for New York in October 1957, by which time they'd produced most of the soundtrack to *Jailhouse Rock*, recording Presley at the Radio Recorders annexe. 'Jerry was really the catalyst in the move back to New York,' said Lester Sill. 'He was the one who felt they could accomplish more in New York, and who wanted the kind of exposure you could get there. And they were both Easterners by culture.' Sill later kicked himself for allowing the duo to buy out his 25 per cent share in the publishing company, claiming rather tersely that 'they were ruthless when it came to business'.

V

Just as the Coasters records which Leiber and Stoller produced in New York reflected the transition from black rhythm and blues to white rock'n'roll, so in Los Angeles rhythm and blues became increasingly teen-oriented through the fifties. If labels such as Modern kept faith with the likes of Helen Humes, Roy Hawkins and Jimmy Witherspoon, and (on its RPM subsidiary) updated Delta blues with the hugely successful B. B. King, they were more than ready for rock'n'roll with, for example, the Teen Queens and the Cadets (a.k.a. the Jacks). Hits like the Jacks' 'Why Don't You Write Me?' (1955), the Teen Queens' 'Eddie My Love' (1956) and the Cadets' 'Stranded in the Jungle' (1956) gave Modern a rock'n'roll profile, just as Little Richard did Specialty and Fats Domino Imperial. Aladdin, too, enjoyed crossover hits with Shirley and Lee's 'Let the Good Times Roll' (1956) and Thurston Harris's exuberant 'Little Bitty Pretty One' (1957), prior to being acquired by Imperial.

At the centre of this new vocal-group sound, which spawned a flood of LA doo-wop quartets, were such key individuals as Richard Berry, Jesse Belvin, Bobby Day, Eugene Church, Obie 'Young' Jessie, Gaynell Hodge, Ray Agee and H. B. Barnum. 'LA boiled with cliques of black talent,' wrote Bill Millar. 'They rehearsed together, swapped songs, and sang on each other's records in a loose and informal manner with scant regard for contractual agreements.' Richard Berry, who'd supplied the ice-cool, proto-rap narration on the Robins' 'Riot in Cell Block No. 9', was also the male voice on Etta James's 1955 Modern hit 'Wallflower', and a ubiquitous presence on the scene. Jesse Belvin, whose soulful 'Goodnight, My Love' (1956) was yet another hit for the Biharis, wrote dozens of songs for groups like the Sheiks, the Shields, and the Cliques, and was even substantially responsible for what is arguably the most famous doo-wop song of all time, the Penguins' 'Earth Angel'.

Although Belvin was a mentor to many – 'we'd go over to his house just to sit there on the floor and listen,' says Richard Berry – he also epitomized the disposable, fly by night quality of the LA scene in the fifties. A native Angeleno, he'd sung with Big Jay McNeely at the age of sixteen, then become a prodigious supplier of pop ephemera to the countless independent labels which now infested Los Angeles. 'Jesse could go into a studio with a few musicians and compose on the spot,'

Shorty Rogers supervises a doo-wop session at Radio Recorders in 1959. Left to right: Shorty Rogers, Jesse Belvin, Gaynell Hodge, Buster Williams, Alex Hodge.

Walter 'Dootsie' Williams (right) presents KFOX DJ Johnny Otis with a copy of 'Earth Angel', 1955.

recalled Rene Hall, who often accompanied Belvin on his rounds. 'He'd just pull the tunes out of thin air, and if he didn't like a song, he'd run it down again and change the song completely.'

Gaynell Hodge of the Turks was more blunt: 'Jesse could hypnotize people with his voice because he had such a strong effect when he sang. But after he left with his money, the people would realize the song had been all Jesse, and all they were left with was smoke.' So omnipresent was Belvin on the scene that his contribution to the music has obscured that of singers like Bobby ('Rockin' Robin') Day or Eugene ('Pretty Girls Everywhere') Church.

Doo-wop Central in Los Angeles was undoubtedly Dootone Records, formed in 1954 by Walter 'Dootsie' Williams, a former bandleader whose Harlem Dukes band had been a regular attraction at the Club Alabam in the forties. Williams was still leading a band at the Brown Sisters' Harlem Club down on 118th Street when he noticed that the younger crowd seemed to prefer the sound of the new vocal groups. With a porch-front office on Central Avenue at 95th Street, he began cutting groups such as the Medallions in a garage studio at 2190 West 30th Street. When the Penguins' 'Earth Angel', a wistful ballad in the vein of Jesse Belvin's earlier 'Dream Girl', went to No. 1 on the R&B chart at the end of 1954 it opened the doo-wop floodgates.

Among the other LA doo-wop outfits of the time (some recorded by Dootsie Williams and others by John Dolphin of the Central Avenue record store Dolphin's of Hollywood) were the Dootones, the Meadowlarks, the Squires, the Jewels, the Titans, the Crescendos, the Jaguars, the Cubans, the Gassers, the Silks, the Up-Fronts, the Calvanes and the Cuff-Linx, not forgetting crossover successes like the Platters or considerably more 'schooled' groups like Rex Middleton's Hi-Fis. Most of them came out of high schools like Fremont, Belmont and Jefferson, and all of them stemmed to some extent from the influence of the Robins, or from early fifties groups like the Flairs, the Flamingos and the Hollywood Flames.

The Penguins, whose 'Earth Angel' remains the most beloved of all doo-wop records.

Few of the groups boasted exceptional singers, but that was at least a part of their charm. 'Even my dear friends the Penguins and the Medallions sounded horrible,' remarked Johnny Otis, who'd never rated the Robins too highly, either. What they lacked in vocal finesse they made up for in raw excitement – in Dave Marsh's words 'a singular drive and bounce, a salacious craziness, a willingness to go for any effect so long as it worked'. Frank Zappa, whose 1963 song for the re-formed Penguins, 'Memories of El Monte', was a celebration of LA's doo-wop golden age, maintained that the California groups had a better sense of humour than their East Coast counterparts. 'The ghetto situation in LA wasn't as nasty as it was in Harlem,' the head Mother theorized, 'so it developed a different aura.' By this he meant the aura of Leiber and Stoller's early classics and, later, of hits such as the Olympics' 'Western Movies' (1958) and the Marathons' 'Peanut Butter' (1961), both produced by ex-Robin H. B. Barnum.

The 'El Monte' of the young Zappa's song – a nostalgic checklist of fifties doo-wop favourites – referred to the El Monte Legion Stadium in East LA, where 'weekend dances' hosted by DJs such as Hunter Hancock, Art Laboe and Dick 'Huggy Boy' Hugg would pull in teenagers, mainly whites and local Chicanos, by the thousand. Earlier in the decade, the stadium had staged wild shows by such tenor-sax honkers as Joe Houston and Chuck Higgins, who scored big local hits with 'All Night Long' and 'Pachuco Hop' and drew Zoot-suited pachucos thrilled by their crazed antics. The ultimate squawking showman was Cecil 'Big Jay' McNeely, who would lie on his back kicking his legs in the air, then jump into the audience and walk through the crowd wailing away on one note. On one occasion, McNeely and Huggy Boy were arrested for 'exciting Mexicans' after racing around on roller skates in costumes borrowed from the MGM epic *Ben Hur*.

Big Jay McNeely, the honking sax man who drove Chicano zoot-suiters wild in El Monte.

Now El Monte was ruled by doo-wop idols like Cleve Duncan of the Penguins and Vernon Green of the Medallions, who inspired the slow dancing known as 'scrunching', and by Chicano heartthrobs like L'il Julian Herrera, whose 'Lonely, Lonely Nights' was another LA favourite. Eventually, the stadium was closed to live music when the powers-that-be took exception to the concentration of racially mixed teenagers at the shows. Although Hunter Hancock rounded up an industry group that included Art Rupe and Johnny Otis to oppose the ban, there were no more shows there. Hence the nostalgia for El Monte after Art Laboe had instigated his 'Oldies but Goodies' revival of the early sixties.

This seems as good a place as any to give credit to the LA disc jockeys who played such a part in the R&B/rock'n'roll revolution: it was Art Laboe, for example, who was largely responsible for making the Chords' 'Sh-Boom' (sometimes cited as the first rock'n'roll record) an LA No. 1 in 1954. Black music had first been heard on a white LA station when Al Jarvis played a Louis Armstrong record during his KFWB show 'Make Believe Ballroom'. 'Jarvis was known as the dean of DJs here,' recalled Johnny Otis. 'It was he who broke the ice, so that by the time Hunter Hancock came along there was no big stink about black music on the air.'

The southern-born Hancock's 'Harlem Matinée' show made its KFVD debut in May 1943. 'Let's go a huntin' with Hunter,' went the opening announcement, 'huntin' around for some of the very best popular Negro musicians, singers and entertainers in the world. You'll hear music that runs the gamut from bebop to ballads, swing to sweet, blues to boogie …' By 1948, 'Ol' H. H.' was providing an 'exclusive diet' of the music that was soon christened 'rhythm and blues'. 'As long as I was on the air,' he reminisced years later, 'I was either the top R&B jockey in LA or next to the top man, from 1948 to 1968.' One of the many white kids to tune into Hancock's mid-fifties shows on KGFJ was a young Phil Spector, who waxed nostalgic about 'Ol' H. H.' when he inducted the Platters into the Rock'n'Roll Hall of Fame in 1990.

Hunter 'ol' HH' Hancock, deacon of R&B DJs in LA.

Despite the breakthrough, there weren't too many other jocks playing blues or R&B in the forties, and the only black DJ of real note was Al Jarvis protégé Joe Adams. 'When I first met Jerry Leiber,' remembers Mike Stoller, 'the black music of the time was only played on stations that were beamed into the ghetto.' One important development in the early fifties was the employment of DJs by Dolphin's of Hollywood, which had them broadcasting live on KRKD from its shop window on Central at Vernon Avenue. John Dolphin, a local mogul who once said that 'If blacks can't go to Hollywood, I'll bring Hollywood to the blacks,' employed Hunter Hancock, 'Huggy Boy' and Charlie 'C. T.' Trammell to give his store that extra edge, the ploy working so well that even white teenagers made the trek down to the Avenue. This grated with Chief William Parker's LAPD, who did their best to scare whites away from the area. Dolphin responded in late 1954 by organizing a protest by 150 black businessmen against the harassment of his customers.

Unfortunately, Dolphin was as much of a cigar-chewing shyster as the names of his various record labels – Cash, Money, Lucky – implied. His slogan was 'We'll record you today and have you a hit tonight' (as played on KRKD), but he conspicuously failed to deliver on the second half of the promise – despite recording such venerable figures as Pee Wee Crayton, Percy Mayfield and Jimmy Witherspoon, and doo-wop entities fronted by Jesse Belvin and Bobby Day. In February 1958 he was shot dead by one Percy Ivy, a songwriter who'd come to collect royalties from the Dolphin's of Hollywood office on South Berendo Avenue.*

If doo-wop was partly a black response to the white commercialization of R&B after Presley, it wasn't enough to halt the gradual decline of black music in Los Angeles; if anything, it accelerated the process of attrition. As long as the majors were paying it no attention, R&B had flourished in the city. Now, as the end of the fifties neared, the big companies were eager to buy up and dilute everything that had been great about 'race music', to the extent of getting Pat Boone to cover Fats Domino, or Georgia Gibbs to cover Etta James. And some black artists were willing to play ball, as RCA's transformation of Jesse Belvin into a Nat Cole-style supper-club singer demonstrated. 'By the end of the fifties, everyone was *trying* to be swallowed up by the mainstream,' says writer Jim Dawson. 'That's where the money was.'

If a maverick like Ray Charles managed to stay ahead of the game by ceaselessly reinventing himself, the original heroes of Los Angeles rhythm and blues – the Roy Miltons, Charles Browns and Amos Milburns – got lost in the rock'n'roll shuffle. 'Don't forget that it wasn't just the *Los Angeles* R&B sound which petered out,' says Mike Stoller, who had himself already dabbled in teen rock'n'roll by writing the Cheers' 1955 Capitol hit

---

* Witnesses to the shooting included two white kids who'd ventured down to Central Avenue to play Dolphin one of their songs. One of them was future Beach Boy Bruce Johnston, the other Sandy 'Let There be Drums' Nelson.

'Black Denim Trousers' with Jerry Leiber. 'Whatever the precise amalgam of urban and southern small-town blues that West Coast R&B was, it and all the regional sounds disappeared in the growing homogenization. There was financial gain in this for the successful performers and writers, including ourselves, but there was also a loss of distinct flavours. More to the point, the small companies fell by the wayside or were gobbled up as catalogue by bigger labels. Today, there are almost no record companies that reflect the peculiar tastes of their owners.'

Ultimately, rock'n'roll was the beginning of the mass youth culture we know too well today, bulldozing the little differences that made West Coast R&B so special. In the words of writer Jim Burns, 'there was no longer much room for R&B artists who needed a sense of identification with the community as a whole.'

For white America, meanwhile, LA was about to become *the* pop city.

The Gardner Street house in which Phil Spector and Marshall Lieb wrote 'To Know Him is to Love Him'.

2 *Boys of Summer*

This was the blond, fair-haired breed of the steel-blue eyes, which stood to him for the pure, the blithe, the untroubled in life; for a virginal aloofness that was at once simple and full of pride...

Thomas Mann, 'Tonio Kröger'

It was all more sullen and boring and small and vile. You know, barfing and stuff, making fun of ugly people. There wasn't any of that fairyland stuff that I've been seeing. It was social castes, where you ate your lunch, standing around looking tough, or whatever the fuck you were supposed to do.

Randy Newman, 1975

I

If the pop historians are to be believed, the White American Teenager was born in 1955. Nicholas Ray's *Rebel Without a Cause*, released that year on the very eve of the Presley explosion, might almost have been called *Rebel Without Rock'n'Roll*. All hyped-up with nowhere to go, and no soundtrack to give vent to his rage, James Dean's Jim Stark was just waiting for an Elvis to happen.*

With a fine irony, the White American Teenager defined his rebellion through black rhythm and blues, just as suburban white punks of the early nineties defined theirs through gangsta rap. By 1955, more and more white kids were pitching up for Californian shows by Johnny Otis's Caravan of R&B stars, along with a smattering of Chicanos from East LA. And Otis noticed that the more he and his artists hammed up the black aspects of the music, the more whites loved the show: it was minstrelsy reborn with tenor saxophones.

As it turned out, Johnny Otis was lucky to squeeze even one hit – the ever-popular and much-covered 'Willie and the Hand Jive' (1958) – from the subsequent rock'n'roll boom. Few of his peers from the great days of

---

* *Rebel Without a Cause*, of course, turned out to be a classic case of Hollywood Babylonia. James Dean died before the film was even released; Nick Adams, star of the subsequent TV series *The Rebel*, overdosed in 1968; Sal Mineo was stabbed to death in 1976; Natalie Wood drowned in 1981; both Nick Ray and Dennis Hopper struggled with drug problems. Was this film cursed or what?

Teenagers flock to a 'record hop' with KPOP's Art Laboe.

Central Avenue would be *that* lucky, what with the steady dilution of black rhythm and blues by the burgeoning pop industry. By the early 1960s it was all up for Otis, too. 'Somebody once booked me at a place and I showed up with my little blues band,' he recalled. 'When I asked where the piano was, the guy bawled me out, saying, "Who the hell needs *pianos*, nobody plays those anymore!" '

In Los Angeles, as in most other American cities in the mid fifties, teenagers drank malt shakes, stuck nickels in jukeboxes, necked during drive-in horror flicks, and observed the new rules of juvenile style. At Scrivner's Drive-In Restaurant at Sunset and Cahuenga, KPOP's Art Laboe staged regular after-school broadcasts or 'record hops', attracting thousands of ducktailed, pink-peg-slacked boys with their pony-tailed, pedal-pushing dates. Laboe's show was soon the highest-rated on LA radio, an obligatory stopping-off point for all hit acts.

The difference in Los Angeles was that these kids were growing up in a place which instantly took teen trends and turned them into movies. Scarcely had Elvis erupted on *The Ed Sullivan Show* than Hollywood went into delinquency overdrive with a flood of cheapo-cheapo, rush-released juve pix, most of them from the stables of Sam Katzman and Sam Arkoff's American International Pictures. It was pure drive-in heaven, with endless trash like *Rock, Rock, Rock* periodically redeemed by such superior vehicles as *The Girl Can't Help It* or even *Jailhouse Rock*. Maybe if you were growing up pimply in Long Beach, then Hollywood seemed as far away as it did to any other American teens; any closer and the thin line between reality and celluloid illusion quickly blurred.

Given that Hollywood helped to spread rock'n'roll on a global scale –
even *black* artists got a look-in, though only as entertainers – it was almost
inevitable that the place would eventually produce its own rock'n'roll star.
Eric Hilliard 'Ricky' Nelson, all of sweet sixteen in 1957, was the perfect
post-Presley adolescent – except that he lived most of his life on TV, as
the cute younger son in his dad's sitcom *The Adventures of Ozzie and Harriet*.
Indeed, it was Ozzie Nelson himself, a bandleader from the thirties, who
perceived the obvious benefits of turning his son into a pop star. Prior to
recording his version of Fats Domino's 'I'm Walkin'', Rick evinced little
interest in rock'n'roll, though supposedly he bragged to girls that he could
sing better than Elvis.

*Ricky Nelson (right) receives a
gold disc for 'Be Bop Baby' from
Imperial's Lew Chudd.*

One man who sat up and took notice when 'I'm Walkin'' became a
Top 20 hit in May 1957 was Lew Chudd of Imperial Records: hardly
surprising, since Imperial had released the Fats Domino original of 'I'm
Walkin'' earlier that year. For Chudd, who'd seen Pat Boone clean up
with Domino's 'Ain't That a Shame' two years earlier, the Nelson kid had
an authentic teen appeal that Boone would never have. Moreover, if the
Elvis Presleys of the world really were taking over from the black
originators of rock'n'roll, it was probably time to think about adding some
white pop acts to the Imperial roster.

Although it took being sued by Norman Granz of Verve Records to
do it, Lew Chudd landed himself a genuine star when he signed Ricky
Nelson. In the hands of uncredited producer Jimmie Haskell, moreover,
Nelson managed to record a slew of almost improbably exciting records –
especially 'Believe What You Say' (1958), written by transplanted southerners Dorsey and Johnny Burnette and featuring a stupendous solo by
transplanted Louisianan guitarist James Burton. The quality of Nelson's
records had a great deal to do with the work of Bunny Robyn. 'Bunny
was an incredibly talented mastering engineer,' says Bones Howe. 'It got
to the point where Bunny's masters were twice as loud as, say, RCA's,
and people would come in to see me at Radio Recorders and ask if I could
duplicate his sound.'

'More than anything else, I wanted to be Carl Perkins,' Ricky claimed,
and it was this fantasy which kept him from falling into the teen-idol
sappiness of most of his peers. Stifled by the parallel life of the TV
Ricky – his family's *Adventures* lasted till 1966 – he found an exhilarating
release through rock'n'roll, just as he had through hanging out with car-
club greasers when he was at Hollywood High. Although he was more
than a little responsible for inspiring the wave of scrimped pretty-boys-
next-door who combined to put out the fire of rock'n'roll as the fifties
turned into the sixties, he was far from happy about it.

'I was very jealous that Rick Nelson got to be Elvis and I didn't,' said
John Stewart, who'd hung around Johnny Otis's studio as a kid and lived
on a strict diet of rhythm and blues. Later a member of pop folkies the
Kingston Trio, Stewart was just one of many LA teenagers who dreamed

Hollywood's very own Elvis, rockin'
Ricky Nelson, onstage in 1958.

of becoming The Next Elvis. Slightly more credible than Ricky as a 'Hollybilly' rocker was Eddie Cochran, raised on dyed-in-the-wool country music in backwoods Minnesota before moving to the Okie-infested Los Angeles suburb of Bell Gardens in 1953. In Cochran, a kind of processed Jimmy Dean of rock'n'roll, sullenly lusty teen America found its true post-Presley voice. The mighty 'Summertime Blues', a Top 10 hit in August 1958, was a howl of adolescent angst, a perfect anthem for Californian youth which summed up the feelings of all those teenagers who didn't conform to the jock mentality of the Great American High School – misfits like Brian Wilson, Phil Spector, Randy Newman and Frank Zappa. 'Where I went to school,' recalled Randy Newman, 'everyone liked the surfers, the guys who were good at pool, the football players. I never had a hero, and I don't like them.'

The blurring of reality and TV illusion created a certain disjuncture in teenagers generally, but particularly in those born in sunny Southern California. 'As much as I loved my parents, I sometimes wished I had a mother like Donna Reed, or been part of the Nelsons, or been Jerry Mathers in *Leave It to Beaver*,' says Harold Bronson, who grew up in suburban Westchester and later founded LA's Rhino Records. 'There was a definite separation between the idyllic life you saw on those shows and what you were actually living.'

It has been the self-imposed mission of writers such as James Ellroy to deconstruct – even dismember – the cosily nostalgic Ozzie'n'Harriet picture most people have of Los Angeles in the fifties. The city of Ellroy's bravura 'LA Quartet' is a hellish metropolis of white-trash psychosis, Mexangeleno sleaze, *Grand Guignol* gouging, and HUAC hysteria – Chandler eat your heart out. Ellroy strips fifties LA of the sanitized, pacifying kitsch in which we've coated it for thirty-odd years, turning it back into the home of Kenneth Anger and the cold-turkeying Art Pepper. For Ellroy, haunted by the memory of his mother's murder in 1958, there *were* no *Happy Days* in Los Angeles.

Summertime blues: Eddie Cochran in LA, 1958.

II

Lew Chudd's signing of Ricky Nelson was symptomatic of the change in the LA record industry of the late 1950s, which was starting to buzz with the possibilities of pop. Just as independent labels had homed in on black artists in the forties and fifties, so now a new breed of hustlers was out to milk white rock'n'roll for all it was worth. 'The basis of music in Los Angeles was little labels like Allied Records,' says long-time mogul Lou Adler, reclining in his Malibu offices as the afternoon sun sparkles on the Pacific through the windows. 'It was guys like John Dolphin, who gave away Cadillacs rather than royalties. But that all started to disappear towards the end of the fifties, because three things happened to black music in LA. One, there was a Muslim movement that divided blacks. Two, a lot of great singers like Jesse Belvin died. And finally, rock'n'roll was moving into the nightclubs, on a big level with Bobby Darin, on a smaller one with guys like Donnie Brooks.' By the time Donnie Brooks – a typical one-hit teen wonder of the period – was hot with 'Mission Bell' in July 1960, Los Angeles was, in Adler's words, 'pretty much a pop/rock'n'roll town'.

   Adler was himself one of the many hustlers who began making waves at the turn of the decade. For young cats like Lou and his partner Herb Alpert, LA was wide-open, capitalism a go-go, a town where anyone with *chutzpah* could barge into the offices of an independent company and announce that they had the future of pop in their hands. 'In 1960, the record business was contained between the intersection of Selma and Argyle and the parking lot at Hollywood and Vine,' says perennial Hollywood hustler Kim Fowley, seated in rather less salubrious sur-roundings than those in which Lou Adler grants his rare audiences. 'You could sell any tape for $100, and there was no playing clubs for guys in suits. We were kids running amok in studios like rappers do now, except the rappers have attorneys. We were all thieves – there was no bullshit about art or integrity or sensitivity. People were willing to pay us to do shit and keep doing it, and we were addicted to the process.'

   In their different ways, both Fowley and Adler were attempting to get one over on the big companies, several of which were divisions of the major film studios. 'The music business here was always a bastard child of the movie industry,' says Fowley. 'It was only in later years that they became equal, and you had the situation where MTV was free advertising for the latest Schwarzenegger movie.' MGM Records, for instance, had been launched back in 1946, and in 1960 happened to be very hot with the unstoppable Connie Francis. Fed with such cutesy juvenilia as 'Frankie' and 'Stupid Cupid', the Italian-born Connie was the biggest female pop star of the era, rivalled only by Decca's Brenda Lee. Another studio-affiliated label was ABC-Paramount, then enjoying a run of hits by the sappy Paul Anka. The fact that ABC-Paramount had filched Ray Charles from Atlantic was not enough to redeem the label's taste, especially when it went on to sign Brian 'Sealed With a Kiss' Hyland, and managed into the bargain to turn Charles into a kind of cod country & western MOR singer.

Last off the blocks was the Warner Brothers label, founded in March 1958 as an outlet for the musical endeavours of such starlets as Connie Stevens, Tab Hunter and Edd 'Kookie' Byrnes, the jive-talking parking-lot attendant from television's *77, Sunset Strip*. Byrnes, the Hollywood archetype of Southern Californian youth, rose all the way to No. 4 on the pop chart by singing about his comb – in 1959's 'Kookie, Kookie (Lend Me Your Comb)' – to Connie Stevens.* Warners' first real music act was the Everly Brothers, who came from Cadence in 1960 and hit immediately with the No. 1 'Cathy's Clown'. But the Everlys weren't enough to stop Warner Brothers Records losing approximately $3m a year in its first four years of operation, a state of affairs which almost forced the studio chiefs to close it down. Joe Smith, the man who'd been made the label's national promotion director in 1961, had to think fast. 'I had no idea,' he claimed later, 'that what Warners really wanted to do was get out of the record business.' Had it not been for Albert Grossman, the fearsome New York manager who convinced the label that his folk-pop trio Peter, Paul and Mary could outsell the Kingston Trio, Warner Bros Records might have gone down the tubes there and then. By 1963, the label was so profitable that it could afford to buy Frank Sinatra's company Reprise, which came complete with Sinatra, his 'Rat Pack' cronies, and the company's brilliant accountant Mo Ostin.

'Most of the record companies were very WASPy,' says Nik Venet, a Greek-American who'd come to LA from Baltimore in 1958 and later signed the Beach Boys to Capitol Records. 'I could never understand how this great group of Jewish movie people had come to pick the most

---

* The relationship between young pop and movie stars, an ongoing feature of Sunset Strip nightlife in the nineties, dates back to this period. In 1959, there was less of a 'wannabe' aspect to the phenomenon. 'You could come to Hollywood and socialize with movie stars and musicians, but they'd never work together,' recalls Kim Fowley. 'We'd all go to the same parties, Eddie Cochran and Tuesday Weld and so on. They thought we were cool, and we thought they were cool, but that was as far as it went.'

WASPish place in the world as the home for their industry. I mean, Warners was like Hitler's Aryan dream come true: do you realize that up until about 1964 there wasn't anybody but *blond men* under contract to the label? It was all Edd Byrnes and Troy Donahue – Hitler's favourite look!'*

It was poignant that Alan Freed – the disc jockey who'd popularized the currency of the term 'rock'n'roll' and then been had up on payola charges – chose in 1960 to come to LA in search of a new beginning. The inescapable fact was that the Alan Freed era was over and the Dick Clark era – that limbo-zone of twisting, teen idols and teddy-bear Elvis – in full swing. Although Art Laboe got him a break on KDAY, Freed could never establish a foothold in LA. 'In the bright sunshine of California, Alan's show sounded silly,' recalled Joe Smith. 'He clicked on a winter's night in the east, but not in LA with the beach and the surfboards.' The last year of the rock'n'roll pioneer's life was abject in the extreme: indicted for income-tax evasion in 1964, he was often to be found slouched at the bar in Martoni's on Cahuenga, then the principal music-biz watering-hole in Hollywood. In 1965 he died of uremic poisoning in Palm Springs.

In a way, it was inevitable that Hollywood would start to challenge Philadelphia as the mecca of the Teen Idol business. As Greg Shaw put it in *The Rolling Stone Illustrated History of Rock And Roll*, 'what chance did a Jodie Sands or a Claudine Clark have against Disney's Annette, the winsome Mouseketeer whose developing bustline had been measured daily by every young male in the country?' Indeed, cutesy Annette – later Annette Funicello of beach-party flick fame – notched up no fewer than five Top 40 hits (including 'Tall Paul' and 'O Dio Mio', both Top 10) in an eighteen-month period between 1959 and 1960, and all on Disney's own Disneyland and Vista labels. In much the same manner, *77, Sunset Strip* gave the world Edd Byrnes and Connie Stevens, and *The Donna Reed Show* gave it Shelly Fabares and Paul Petersen, both the latter on Don Kirshner's Colpix label.

III

The real birth of the Los Angeles music business had occurred about twenty years earlier, with the formation of Capitol Records. The label was the brainchild of the great Tin Pan Alley songsmith Johnny Mercer, in conjunction with ex-Paramount movie producer G. B. 'Buddy' De Sylva and tenacious music-store owner Glenn E. Wallichs. With start-up capital of just $17,000, most of it raised by De Sylva, Capitol's first offices consisted of a small room above Wallichs' Music City store on Vine Street at Sunset. *Variety* predicted that the label stood little chance of competing

---

* But then America's white-picket-fence values were really the values of such Jewish moguls as MGM's Louis B. Mayer, who'd talked of 'a unity of ancient bloods' and opined that 'we are not here as Protestants or Jews but as *Americans*.'

The man who built Capitol: Nat 'King' Cole at a recording session in Hollywood.

with the big three companies of the time – Columbia, RCA-Victor, and Decca – but it failed to take into account the respect the three men commanded in Hollywood. By August 1942, despite the wartime shortage of shellac, Capitol had itself a hit with Freddie Slack's 'Mr Five by Five', followed immediately by his boogie-piano-driven, western-themed 'Cow Cow Boogie', sassily sung by Ella Mae Morse. The label also signed T-Bone Walker, father of the electric blues guitar.

With the signing of Nat 'King' Cole in 1944, Capitol soon grew into the pre-eminent Los Angeles record label, its impressive jazz/swing roster boasting names such as Andy Russell, Jo Stafford, Kay Starr, Paul Whiteman, Benny Carter, Stan Kenton and Johnny Mercer himself. A& R man Dave Dexter, previously the editor of the East Coast jazz journal *down beat*, added R&B acts Julia Lee and Nellie Lutcher to the list, as well as producing numerous jazz releases. In the early 1950s the label resurrected the career of the washed-up Frank Sinatra, producing the series of sublime long-players which commenced in 1953 with the 10″ *Songs for Young Lovers*. It was Sinatra's success, augmenting that of Nat 'King' Cole and company, which enabled Capitol to commence work on the famous thirteen-storey 'Stack o' Records' building in 1954. When the ailing Buddy De Sylva persuaded his partners to sell to Britain's EMI the following year, the label was valued at $8.5m.

Despite the signing of Gene Vincent by Ken Nelson, the label's man in Nashville, Capitol were slow to recognize the true impact of rock'n'roll. Reflecting the taste of its original owners, the company remained cool towards a youth phenomenon it regarded as faddish and ephemeral, choosing instead to concentrate on soundtracks (*Oklahoma*, *Carousel*) and country stars such as Tex Ritter, Ferlin Husky, Sonny James, Hank Thompson and Merle Travis. The anti-rock'n'roll stance of Capitol's resident satirist Stan Freberg perhaps betrayed the label's true ethos, leaving the way open for a multitude of smaller independents to scoop up neglected Los Angeles talent.

The main rivals to Capitol's supremacy on the Coast were Liberty, formed by Si Waronker and Herb Newman in 1955, and Dot, whose Randy Wood shifted his base from Tennessee to LA in 1956. Liberty got off to a rocky start when Herb Newman departed to form Era Records, but kept its head above water via distribution deals with the Demon and Dolton labels. After hiring Mississippian promo man Al Bennett, the company was soon chalking up its first hit, Julie London's classic 'Cry Me a River', in 1955. 'Liberty was a hot label and a very aggressive group of guys,' recalls Russ Regan, himself a legendary promotion man of the period. Among their successful artists were Patience and Prudence, Eddie Cochran, Jody Reynolds, Martin Denny, Dick and DeeDee, and David Seville and the Chipmunks, whose ghastly 'Witch Doctor' was a No. 1 in 1958. The less successful included Jett Powers, a moody rock'n'roller who later metamorphosed into the infamous P. J. Proby.

Al Bennett functioned as Liberty's A&R head until the arrival in 1959 of a lanky Texan named Tommy 'Snuff' Garrett. Formerly a disc jockey in Lubbock, Garrett had been a friend of Buddy Holly's – which was probably why he made it his first job to pick up where Holly had left off before his death, updating the string-accompanied pop style of his last hit 'It Doesn't Matter Anymore' on a series of hits by the vapid Bobby Vee. In supervising Vee's career, starting with the 1960 hits 'Devil or Angel' and 'Rubber Ball', Snuff proved himself a master of LA teen-dross – the first real Name Producer the city had produced, with a track record to match. The fact that he managed to make pop singers of Dorsey Burnette, a veteran Memphis rockabilly reduced to the fluff of 'You're Sixteen' (1960), and Gene McDaniels, a fine black baritone who'd recorded with vocal group the Sultans on Duke in 1954, was testament to his commercial pragmatism. McDaniels' elaborately arranged 1961 hits 'A Hundred Pounds of Clay' and 'Tower of Strength' were as close as Los Angeles came to the New York black pop sound of the Drifters.

Dot, boasting such execrable artists as Pat Boone, Tab Hunter and the virginal Gale Storm, has always been regarded as one of the chief culprits in the white dilution of rock'n'roll. Boone's endless string of fifties hits, including his desecration of two certified Little Richard classics, was bad enough: add to those such grotesqueries as Storm's cover of Smiley Lewis's 'I Hear You Knocking' (1955) and heartthrob Hunter's 'Young Love' (1957) and you've got the perfect argument for inducting Randy Wood and his musical director Billy Vaughn into a new Rock'n'Roll Hall of Infamy. Few could argue with the commercial logic, though: when Wood sold Dot to Paramount in 1965, he pocketed a tidy $5m for his troubles.

'The way the independent companies were lined up on Sunset Boulevard reminded me of gumball machines,' recalled Salvatore Bono of the Hollywood record industry of the late fifties. 'All you had to do was put in

Ritchie Valens with Del-Fi's Bob Keane on the TV show Pik-a-Platter.

the right coin and they were ready to pay off.' In 1956, 'Sonny' Bono was working for a meat company, making deliveries on Sunset so he could drop his teen-dream songs in to companies such as Frankie Laine's Crystal Records. Among the other indie labels tasting success at the time was Herb Newman and Lew Biddell's Era, which had struck gold almost immediately with Gogi Grant's 'Suddenly There's a Valley' (1955), capitalizing on it with her No. 1 'The Wayward Wind' the following year. Then there was Challenge, a label launched in 1956 by

sometime singin' cowboy Gene Autry, which made the charts two years later with the Champs' Mexican-flavoured instrumental 'Tequila'. Art Laboe's Original Sound, founded in 1957, hit in 1959 with Sandy Nelson's 'Teen Beat' and Preston Epps' 'Bongo Rock'. And Bob Keane's Del-Fi cleaned up in the Hispanic market after the signing of Ritchie Valens, a squat Mexican version of Buddy Holly from the north Valley *barrio* of Pacoima.

Los Angeles by this time was already the largest Mexican city in the world after Mexico City itself, and the impact of Mexican culture on West Coast rock'n'roll could be heard in everything from 'Tequila' to the Coasters' 'Down in Mexico'. Ever since the Mexican 'Zoot Suit' riots of June 1943 – the result of white thugs attacking blacks and Mexicans – teenage *pachucos* had embraced R&B and rock'n'roll as the sound of their rebellion. Now Mexangelenos had their own rock'n'roll star in Valens, with his hits 'Come On, Let's Go', 'Donna' and the anthemic 'La Bamba'. For some years after Valens' death in the plane crash that killed Buddy Holly, young Latinos trooped in and out of Del-Fi: Chan Romero with his 'Hippy Hippy Shake', L'il Ray with 'I (Who Have Nothing)', along with the Fantastics, Ronnie and the Pomona Casuals, Rene and Ray and more. Only Eddie Davis's Faro Productions rivalled Del-Fi as a Latino outlet.

Lined up alongside the other 'gumball machines' on Sunset was Art Rupe's Specialty, still comparatively hot in 1957 with Little Richard, Larry Williams and other artists who'd managed to survive the transition from rhythm and blues to rock'n'roll. Unlike Lew Chudd, Art Rupe chose not to keep up with the times and sign white pop acts; if anything, he was resigned to winding down his operation, switching to movies and property instead. Rupe was even reticent about grooming his one real asset, Sam Cooke, as a black teen idol. 'Lovable', the pop single Cooke had released under the name Dale Cook in 1956, was one thing; going secular as Sam Cooke was something else again, as the singer himself eventually found out when he incurred the wrath of the gospel faithful. But Cooke and Specialty's in-house producer 'Bumps' Blackwell – the man responsible for all of Little Richard's great hits – were adamant that the risk had to be taken, especially with a song as strong as the wistful 'You Send Me'.

It was Sonny Bono's good fortune to be in the Specialty office just as the argument over the secularization of Sam Cooke was coming to a head. 'You're fired!' Rupe barked at Bumps Blackwell before turning to Bono with the words: 'You're hired!' Bono, who'd managed to sneak a couple of his compositions on to Larry Williams b-sides, promptly gave up the meat-packing gig and joined Specialty on the modest salary of $75 a week, his first assignment – with a fine irony – being to exploit the hell out of 'I'll Come Running Back to You', the only Sam Cooke pop side left in the Specialty catalogue.

Supposedly, Art Rupe let Bumps Blackwell walk off with Cooke and 'You Send Me' in lieu of $15,000 he owed the producer. Whatever the truth behind the bust-up, Bumps and Sam wound up signing with a

Sam Cooke, the great black hope of Los Angeles.

Hollywood label called Keen, and in September 1957 had a No. 1 hit with 'You Send Me'. The record made the irresistibly handsome Cooke an overnight star and led to eight more hits, including 'Only Sixteen', 'Wonderful World', and 'Everybody Likes to Cha-Cha'. Few of these retained the feel of Cooke's awesome gospel recordings with the Soul Stirrers, however immaculately they were sung, but he and Blackwell were responding to the decline of rhythm and blues in the only way realistically that they could: with quality black pop.

They were hardly unique in doing this, as the work of men such as Rene Hall, Ernie Freeman, Harold Battiste and H. B. Barnum demonstrated. Just as the Platters had allowed white impresario Samuel 'Buck' Ram to mould them into an updated version of the Ink Spots, so the likes of Blackwell and Barnum were moving away from their R&B roots towards the kind of pop which was beginning to get vital radio play and equally vital TV exposure on Dick Clark's *American Bandstand*. 'You wouldn't want to call it selling out, because it was just a case of going where the work was,' says West Coast R&B authority Jim Dawson. 'But one of the things that doesn't come out very often about Bumps Blackwell was that he really wanted acceptance in the white world. So I guess it was natural for him to gravitate towards Hollywood.'

Perhaps this was why Blackwell signed up the two Jewish kids who kept pestering him at the Keen office on Hollywood Boulevard early in 1958. 'Herbie and I spent the first four months just trying to *find* Bumps,' recalls Lou Adler, who co-wrote Sam Cooke's 'Wonderful World' with Herb Alpert under the pseudonym 'Barbara Campbell'. 'What he did do was give us an education in almost every area of the record business – producing, publishing, arranging, A&R-ing. He was a teacher, and since neither of us knew anything, we were prime subjects for what he wanted to do.' Just as much of a teacher was Sam Cooke himself, who not only taught Adler how to communicate with musicians in the studio but primed him on the black culture of Los Angeles. 'I roomed with Sam for several months, in which time I learned more about the music and the people than I'd ever known. It was my introduction to gospel – to the Soul Stirrers, to J. W. Alexander and Lou Rawls in the Pilgrim Travellers. Nor did I ever experience one bit of racial intolerance. They just took me in like I was one of them.'

To Adler's dismay, it wasn't long before Sam took off for the more exalted climes of RCA, who figured – correctly – that they could mould him into some dapper hybrid of Harry Belafonte, Sidney Poitier and Cassius Clay. The company had already attempted this with former doo-wop king Jesse Belvin, whose 1959 album *Mr Easy* presented Jesse as a youth-oriented version of the old 'sepia Sinatras'. 'We felt a great career had been launched,' remembered Marty Paich, Belvin's RCA arranger; 'if he'd lived, I feel Jesse would have been the consummate black artist of our time.' Tragically, Belvin was killed in a car crash in February 1960, when his junkie chauffeur

Zola Taylor of the Platters with DJ Art Laboe (centre) *and Sam Cooke.*

Herb Alpert and Lou Adler, a decade after discovering Jan and Dean.

nodded out at the wheel on a southern chitlin'-circuit tour of the kind Sam Cooke also liked periodically to undertake. When Cooke came in as Belvin's replacement, he immediately hit with the infectious 'Chain Gang', only to be saddled thereafter with all manner of easy-listening abominations. It said everything about the impasse in post-rock'n'roll pop that a singer as great as Cooke was expected to sing such tripe, and that he didn't question it. Caught in the limbo between early fifties R&B and mid-sixties soul, Sam was really a man out of time. Occasionally, arrangements by Rene Hall offset the orchestral saturation of the RCA sound; more often, the likes of Hugo Peretti and Luigi Creatore were allowed free rein.

Lou Adler and Herb Alpert were too hungry and restless to remain at Keen for long. 'We were learning very quickly,' says Adler, 'and we had aspirations towards being more than A&R staff.' After an introduction to Jan and Dean – blond WASPs who played volleyball on State Beach when they weren't studying at UCLA and USC – Alpert and Adler produced the duo's 'Baby Talk', a Top 10 hit for Herb Newman's Era subsidiary Doré in August 1959. Another pair of young street hustlers were on the music-industry map.

'In retrospect, it was very exciting, like the beginning of any industry,' says Adler. 'There were lots of hustlers around Vine Street. We knew we were independents, and that there were no rules. When Doré put "Produced by Alpert and Adler" on a record, it was the first time you saw the names of anyone but A&R men on an LA label. Radio was open to us, because now they had guys who were right down the street having coffee with them, instead of being on the East Coast. We'd tried to deal with Capitol and Columbia, but there was such a structure of A&R men, guys matching songs to artists, whereas we were trying to come up with street acts.' For Herb Alpert, the joy lay in the speed with which one could operate: 'In those days, for a couple of hundred bucks, you could make a record, have it pressed, stick a label on it, and put it out. If somebody bit, you either turned it over for distribution or tried to hold it for yourself and get paid by the distributors, which was pretty impossible. But you got the thing out.'

Getting the thing out: it was what LA was all about at the turn of the decade. Where the movie studios spent months grooming their celluloid heartthrobs, the indie hustlers merely rounded up kids on the street, herded them into garage studios, and hit the 'Record' buttons. With thirty-six indie distributors in town, and new producers beginning to challenge the union stranglehold on recording sessions, LA was opening up to embrace any two-bit cowboy who was prepared to chance his arm at this game. Hustlers were 'teenage pukes' like Kim Fowley, Sandy Nelson and Bruce Johnston, who played together as the Sleepwalkers at University High and continued to interact throughout the evolution of LA's music industry. This was the nerd's revenge against the jocks and bullies: the chinless, asthmatic Phil Spector putting together the Teddy Bears and scoring a No. 1 with the sepulchral 'To Know Him is to Love Him' (1958); the stick-insect polio victim Kim Fowley taking his first production, the Renegades' 'Charge', and flaunting it in front of every schoolkid who'd ever teased him; desert weirdos Frank Zappa and Don Van Vliet cutting Little Richard's 'Slippin' and Slidin'' at Zappa's little studio out in Cucamonga and having Dot Records turn it down 'because the guitars are too distorted'.

Hustling was getting in between the cracks and taking chances on the trash the majors (and even minors like Capitol and Liberty) wouldn't touch. It was Fowley and Sandy Nelson, drunk as skunks, who bashed empty bottles and wastepaper baskets while Gary Paxton drawled out the lyric to Dallas Frazier's flagrant Coasters ripoff 'Alley-Oop', a No. 1 for the Hollywood Argyles in 1960. 'Just like rap, rock'n'roll had a criminal background,' says Fowley. 'We'd steal golf clubs from rich neighbourhoods and sell them in the black ghetto. We'd make demos by finding the ugliest kid in school and staging drunken sessions in his house while his dentist father and breast-cancer mother were in Palm Springs.' Like Phil Spector, Fowley learned how to make records by hanging out at Gold Star, a studio on Vine Street opened in 1950 by Stan Ross and Dave Gold. 'That's how I learned to record drums, how to arrange, how to mix. I almost cry now, because I was an ugly, uneducated kid who, though I'd been around Hollywood, hadn't done *this*. And these were hillbillies, black people, New York Jewish people, and they were letting me sit there and learn. You can't do that anymore.'

Other hustlers on the make included our old friend Sonny Bono, sacked from Specialty after moonlighting on sessions with a boffin-like arranger named Jack Nitzsche. Nitzsche himself wasn't long off the bus from Michigan, but his lead sheets were soon in demand by everyone from Frankie Laine and Dorsey Burnette to Doris Day and her would-be teen idol son Terry. While Bono himself was vainly attempting to launch the Gold and Rush record labels, Nitzsche was writing his first arrangements for Phil Spector. Early in 1962, Bono and Nitzsche co-wrote the classic 'Needles and Pins', complete with Spectoresque timpani and a catchy guitar counter-melody, for Imperial artistc Jackie DeShannon. Although the song wasn't a big hit until 1964, when it was covered by the English group the Searchers, it was enough for Bono to exploit the Nitzschean connection and badger Spector himself for a job.

Off the bus and in demand: Jack Nitzsche.

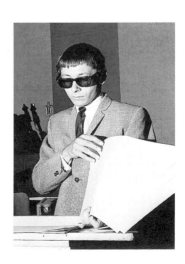

The Teddy Bears: Phil Spector (left), Annette Kleinbard and Marshall Lieb.

IV

By the summer of 1962, Harvey Phillip Spector was already a music-biz whiz-kid. An obsessive dweeb with a Jewish Mother From Hell and a father dead by his own hand, little Phil was possessed of an outsize ego. With his taller, better-looking chum Marshall Lieb – 'I was really Phil's first bodyguard' – he'd formed the Teddy Bears and hit very big with 'To Know Him is to Love Him', a throwaway b-side cut at Gold Star in July 1958. 'You never saw such a complete change in a little fuckin' Jewish kid,' grouched Lew Bedell, the crusty co-owner of Doré Records, but the truth was that Phil had mapped out his pop destiny long before the Teddy Bears.

By the time Lew Chudd had signed the Teddy Bears to Imperial Records for three flop singles and one thoroughly icky album, Spector was a magnetic presence on the LA scene, attracting such disciples as future Warners honcho Russ Titelman and sometime Mother/Magic Band member Elliott Ingber to his side. Moreover, he was already experimenting in the studio, 'bouncing' tracks and stacking vocals to build up his primitive pop sound. 'The Teddy Bears were one of the first hit groups out of LA,' says Lou Adler. 'They were sort of the beginning of the West Coast pop business.'

Following the dissolution of the Teddy Bears in the spring of 1959, Spector approached ex-Spark Records partner Lester Sill for advice on his next move in the music business. Sill had been impressed watching Phil at work in Master Recorders the year before, and offered to take the superbrat to Phoenix to meet Lee Hazelwood, with whom he'd briefly run Atlantic's unsuccessful East-West label in 1957–8. In Hazelwood's Ramco studio, where Duane Eddy had cut a string of instrumental hits for Jamie Records, Spector observed the creation of Eddy's famous guitar 'twang' with the aid of a storage-tank echo chamber. Unfortunately, Hazelwood found Spector almost as obnoxious as Lew Bedell had done, so Sill packed him off to New York to serve a rather different apprenticeship with Jerry Leiber and Mike Stoller.

New York taught Spector everything he needed to know about pop. Not only did he learn from Leiber and Stoller themselves – co-writing Ben E. King's 'Spanish Harlem' with Leiber in the process – but he produced a handful of sessions by artists on Atlantic and other labels (including, on Musicor, Gene Pitney's orgasmic 'Every Breath I Take'). Yet his biggest hit in 1961 was cut back in LA after Lester Sill had asked him to fly home and produce a trio called the Paris Sisters. The group's 'I Love How You Love Me', which reached No. 5 in October, was almost as sickly-sweet as 'To Know Him is to Love Him', but it gave the twenty-year-old Spector sufficient confidence to propose the formation with Sill of a new record label, eventually christened Philles. Back in New York, he found the Crystals through publishers Hill and

Range and earmarked them for his label. Then – on the recommendation of Snuff Garrett but to the surprise of most onlookers – he took a $25,000-a-year job as Liberty's man in New York. Garrett was to rue the day he persuaded the company to hire the kid he called 'Spec', because the megalomaniac whiz-kid did little for five months except bide his time behind a vast conference table playing air hockey.

Phil Spector's great period really started the week he quit Liberty and flew back to LA with the demo of a Gene Pitney song Snuff was saving for Mexican singer Vicki Carr. Recorded in July 1962 at Gold Star – by now relocated to a seedy business stretch of Santa Monica Boulevard – 'He's a Rebel' brought together some of the celebrated musicians who'd come to be known as the 'Wrecking Crew': bassist Ray Pohlman, saxophonist Steve Douglas, guitarist Tommy Tedesco, bassist Jimmy Bond and drummer Hal Blaine. It also cemented the crucial partnership between Spector and arranger Jack Nitzsche, who knew most of the 'Wrecking Crew' musicians and recommended the trio who depped as 'the Crystals' for 'He's a Rebel': lead singer Darlene Love and fellow Blossoms Fanita James and Jean King.

Spector had come close to creating his famed 'Wall of Sound' in New York with the Crystals' 'Uptown', a wonderful Barry Mann/Cynthia Weil paean-to-Manhattan that provided Philles with its first hit. But the superbrat had tired of the condescension of East Coast sessionmen, and now welcomed the chance to work with the younger, hipper musicians of Hollywood. Where the New York session mafia viewed the foppish, fob-chained Spector as a freak, the West Coasters found him at once intriguing and inspiring – to the point of overt emulation, at least on the part of Nitzsche, Nino Tempo and sometime percussionist/aide-de-camp Sonny Bono. 'He had his nose up Phil's ass a mile,' recalled Lester Sill of Bono, who would dutifully haul himself out of bed in the middle of the night whenever the maestro asked him to drive to Canter's for coleslaw.

'He's a Rebel' was the first true blast of the Wall of Sound, as patented in the stifling summer heat of Stan Ross's studio. It was teen trash raised to the level of heroic art, a cavernous mesh of vibes and pianos, booming drum rolls and fuzzy saxophones, bearing aloft the rich, assured voice of Darlene Love. Spector wanted huge excitement, a stampede of devotion, and at Gold Star he got it. 'To me,' he said later, 'the cloudier and fuzzier a record is, the more honesty and guts it has.' To other producers, Spector broke all the rules: pushing volume levels way into the red, packing the studio with musicians and instruments, devoting hours to each song. He also broke some of the rules of the business: just as he'd taken Liberty's money and run, so he forced out Lester Sill in late 1962, fobbing him off with a promise of $60,000 severance pay and becoming a tycoon as a result. Spector, wrote Nik Cohn, 'was a walking, talking, V-sign millionaire'.*

* Lester Sill died in 1994. Post-Spector, he was an executive at Screen Gems and Jobete Music.

Spector at the controls: but the days of the teen symphony were numbered.

1963 was Spector's classic year – the year of the great Jeff Barry/Ellie Greenwich confections 'Da Doo Ron Ron', 'And Then He Kissed Me' and 'Be My Baby', all recorded in LA. As his ego swelled, so did the size of the sessions. To the core of the musicians who'd played on 'He's a Rebel', he added the likes of Glen Campbell (guitar), Leon Russell (piano), Larry Knechtel (keyboards, bass), Jim Gordon (drums), Carol Kaye (bass), Billy Strange (guitar) and Harold Battiste (sax), together with full orchestral string sections.

Sessions kicked off at 4 p.m. and dragged on till breakfast. Musicians doubled, tripled and quadrupled up so that there were often two drummers, three pianists, and four guitarists on one track, all of them blending into one blast of noise. 'A lot of the time we had three piano players going at once,' Jack Nitzsche recalled. 'Phil knew the way he wanted the keyboards played, and it wasn't much of a problem who played them. Leon was there for the solos and fancy stuff, but the pianos would interlock and things would sound cohesive.' Drummer Hal Blaine was encouraged, in his own words, 'to do fills that were total lunacy', while Sonny Bono supervised crates of percussion instruments: bells and bongos, congas and castanets.

Enter the fabulous Ronettes, three streetcorner mulattos from Spanish Harlem who looked more vixenish than they were but turned out to be the ultimate vehicle for Phil's 'teen symphonies'. 'Be My Baby', cut at Gold Star exactly a year after 'He's a Rebel', showed just how colossal the Wall of Sound had become. This was Wagner for teenyboppers, a cacophonous pop army rampaging for three breathless minutes while Veronica let loose her inimitable vibrato whine. By the autumn, when his adulterous relationship with 'Ronnie' was an open secret, the cult of Phil Spector was in full swing. Ensconced in Gold Star for the six punishing weeks it took to complete *A Christmas Gift for You*, Spector flaunted all the quirks and affectations that caused Tom Wolfe to dub him 'The Tycoon of Teen'. Here was pop's first great *auteur*, a visionary of sound, a new Charles Foster Kane. 'In its urgent solipsism, its perfectionism, its mad *bricollage*,' wrote Evan Eisenberg in *The Recording Angel*, 'Spector's work was perhaps the first fully self-conscious phonography in the popular field.'

Behind the megalomania, however, lay profound insecurities. When Lou Adler brought a black vocal quartet called the Alley Cats down to Gold Star to record for Philles, he immediately sensed competition from Spector. 'Phil could never accept anybody being on a level with him,' recalled engineer Larry Levine. And when Spector's two Italian lieutenants, Nino Tempo and Sonny Bono, were successful in their own right – Tempo's and April Stevens' 'Deep Purple' was a No. 1 hit in December 1963 – Phil felt profoundly threatened.

V

Lou Adler by this time was heading the West Coast office of Aldon Music, the New York publishing company owned by Al Nevins and Don Kirshner. It was significant that Aldon had opened an LA office in the first place: tacit acknowledgement, perhaps, that California was beginning to compete with the New York foundry of teen pop. As Kirshner's man on the Coast, Adler not only fed Aldon songs to the likes of Snuff Garrett – Bobby Vee's Goffin/King-penned 1961 No. 1 'Take Good Care of My Baby' being a perfect example – but he signed young LA-based writers like P. F. Sloan and Steve Barri, who proceeded to churn out songs for Connie Stevens, Ann-Margret, Betty Everett and Adler's sometime companion Shelly Fabares. 'That was really my education in the publishing business,' says Adler, who managed to continue his association with Jan and Dean during this period.

'Lou had a good sense of songs,' says Bones Howe, who began engineering for him at this time. 'He knew how to cast particular songs for particular artists. He wasn't technically minded and he wasn't a musician, but he knew what he wanted a record to sound like.' During Adler's two or three years with Aldon, the company chalked up over thirty Top 10 records, only for Nevins and Kirshner to sell out to Columbia-Screen Gems for $2m in April 1963.

Although Adler continued his association with Jan and Dean, he parted company with Herb Alpert. According to Dean Torrence, Alpert thought Jan and Dean were finished and wanted to go in the direction of instrumental records. Adler, meanwhile, wasn't impressed by the tepid, pseudo-Mexican trumpet material Alpert was producing in his makeshift garage studio in West Hollywood and bid him *adios*. This left Lou free to concentrate on publishing and Herb to hook up with Bronx-born promo

The perfect combination: Herb Alpert (left) and Jerry Moss of A&M, early seventies.

man Jerry Moss, with whom he proceeded to form the tiny Carnival label. Carnival had a minor local hit with Charlie Robinson's 'Tell It to the Birds', then turned the record over to Dot and cut Alpert's own 'The Lonely Bull (El Solo Toro)' with the proceeds. Thus, in 1962, was born the mighty empire of A&M Records, home to MOR and LA soft-rock through to the mid seventies. 'Jerry and I never had this master plan of starting a record company,' Alpert claims. 'It just sort of happened that way.'

While Lou Adler was signing West Coast songwriters to a New York-based company, companies such as Liberty were developing their own publishing stables. Metric Music, the Liberty publishing arm headed by Aaron Schroeder, was a hotbed of LA pop, home to writers such as Sharon Sheeley, Jackie DeShannon, Leon Russell, David Gates, P. J. Proby and a young UCLA graduate called Randy Newman. Sheeley, the fiancée of the late Eddie Cochran, had not only written 'Something Else' for Cochran but penned 'Poor Little Fool' for Ricky Nelson and 'Hurry Up' for Ritchie Valens.* After recovering from her injuries in the crash that had killed Cochran, she teamed up with DeShannon to write hits for Brenda Lee ('Dum Dum', 'Heart in Hand') and the Fleetwoods ('The Great Impostor').

Sharon Sheeley, writer of pop classics, girlfriend of Eddie Cochran.

DeShannon herself, a pretty blonde who'd come out to LA from Illinois after being told by Eddie Cochran 'You *are* a California girl!', was really one of the original 'singer-songwriters'. But she had to be content with the classic sessions produced by Jack Nitzsche and Sonny Bono until the concept of a female singer-songwriter became acceptable to her label, Imperial. '"Needles and Pins" and "When You Walk in the Room" really carved out a particular way of recording in LA,' she says. 'Jack understood me, and we shared similar tastes in music. When we were working together, he was so in tune and so sensitive to what I did.' Interestingly, both records anticipate the folk-rock sound of mid-sixties Los Angeles, with DeShannon's strong, countrified voice suggesting a kind of campus version of Brenda Lee.

Another writer with whom DeShannon collaborated was Randy Newman, who'd signed to Metric as a teenager in 1961. Music was in Newman's blood, since his uncles Alfred and Lionel were renowned Hollywood soundtrack composers, but the boy's first recorded song was the trite, undistinguished 'They Tell Me It's Summer', flipside of the Fleetwoods' 'Lovers by Night, Strangers by Day' (1962). 'My first songs were bad rock'n'roll, typical Shirelles stuff,' he recalled. 'At Metric we were a kind of poor man's Carole King and Barry Mann and Neil Sedaka.' Rather better than 'They Tell Me It's Summer', or his own 'Golden Gridiron Boy', were the songs cut by such Liberty/Imperial artists as Gene McDaniels ('Somebody's Waiting', the b-side of Top 40 hit 'Spanish

Jackie DeShannon: 'You are *a California girl!'*

* In the late fifties, the twin hubs of the Hollywood songwriters' scene were Sheeley's mother's apartment on Fountain Avenue and the Park Sunset Hotel at 8462 Sunset, at both of which Cochran, Nelson and the Burnette brothers would often congregate. In the late summer of 1959, a psychopathic man wandered in off Fountain Avenue and attacked Nelson, only to be wrestled to the ground by the Burnettes. Living in the apartment below was none other than Kim Fowley, who made himself highly unpopular by calling the press about the incident. At the time, teen-idol Ricky was squiring a beatnik chick called Leslie Petit, who'd come out to Tinseltown from Greenwich Village with one Dennis Hopper. Permanently attired in black, Petit was a habitual user of heroin, something she apparently managed to keep from Nelson. So who says James Ellroy's version of Los Angeles is overwrought?

Lace') and New Orleans soulstress Irma Thomas ('While the City Sleeps' and 'Baby Don't Look Down').

VI

Liberty was one of the big record companies forced to respond to the increasingly popular sound of surf music in the early sixties. By the time a bunch of faceless session hacks recorded the Marketts' 'Surfer's Stomp', a Top 40 hit for the label in February 1962, surf was *the* teen sound of southern California. The following year, the newly signed Jan and Dean had a No. 1 hit on the label with Brian Wilson's 'Surf City', the national anthem of this souped-up, super-white musical form. 'Putting Brian and Jan Berry together was real important for West Coast music,' says Lou Adler. 'After those surf records broke through, New York and the industry looked up and said, "Maybe there *is* something out there." '

Surf pop had its roots in instrumental groups such as Johnny and the Hurricanes, whose guitar/sax/organ sound on 'Red River Rock' (1959) spawned countless imitations. A bigger influence still was the reverbed,

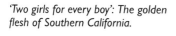

'Two girls for every boy': The golden flesh of Southern California.

tremolo'd guitar twang of Seattle's Ventures, as heard on their big 1960 hit 'Walk, Don't Run'. Down in the coastal baby-boom 'burbs of southern California, dozens of little instrumental combos popped out of the woodwork, most of them with matching suits and Fender Stratocasters. 'It doesn't have a nose or a mouth or eyes,' former Pixie and southern California native Frank Black says of surf pop. 'It's something else, like amps and guitars. It's totally egoless and anonymous.'

Prime movers in this new Pacific wave of instro-pop were groups such as the Belairs, who played in Redondo Beach and hit locally with 'Mr Moto', and Dick Dale and his Del-Tones, led by guitarist Dale, a.k.a. 'The Pied Piper of Balboa Beach'. Applying his sliding chromatic runs to an eclectic assortment of tunes – blues, mariachis, even old Arabic songs recalled from his childhood in Beirut – Dick Dale was soon pulling in upwards of 4,000 kids to shows at Balboa's Rendezvous Ballroom, where Stan Kenton had held court in the early years of the war. Signed to a local label, the band was soon at No. 1 in LA with 'Miserlou' (1961), following up with the equally exciting 'Let's Go Trippin''. (It's said that a young James Marshall Hendrix would often catch the Del-Tones at the Rendezvous while stationed at the Air Force base in nearby San Pedro.)

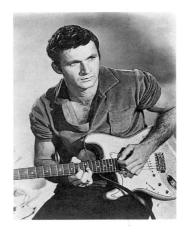

The Pied Piper of Balboa Beach: surf guitar demon Dick Dale.

It was only a matter of time before this spacey, staccato music became inextricably entwined with the cult of Californian beach life. Surfing had been popular in southern California since the early years of the century, but the modern type of fibreglass-encased surfboard was only five years old. By 1961, the region's beaches were attracting around 30,000 surfers every weekend, many of them kids who – after a day spent riding the waves – required Saturday-night entertainment. For Dick Dale, it was only too easy to make the connection between surfing and rock'n'roll. 'When I got that feeling from surfing,' he said, 'the whitewater comin' over my head was the high notes going *dikidikidiki*, and then the *dungundungun* on the bottom was the waves, and I started double-picking faster and faster, like a locomotive, to feel the power of the waves.'*

The instro-surf sound pioneered by Dale reached its apex in records such as the Chantays' 'Pipeline' and the Surfaris' 'Wipe Out', both big national hits in 1963. By then, surf culture had permeated America, with surf records emerging even from such landlocked environments as Colorado (the Astronauts), Minnesota (the Trashmen) and Michigan (the Rivieras). For teenagers all over America, California became a promised fantasy land of woodies and wetsuits, baggies and bikinis – of golden flesh and innocent sex. It was just how LA's founding fathers had always wanted southern California to be seen: as Myra Breckinridge reflects in Gore Vidal's once-notorious novel of the same name, 'it is fascinating

---

* Dale became something of a cult star in the mid nineties after Quentin Tarantino used 'Miserlou' – or, more correctly, 'Misirlou' – in the opening credits to that quintessential LA movie *Pulp Fiction*.

how, in a single generation, stern New England Protestants, grim Iowans, and keen New York Jews have become entirely Tahitianized by that dead ocean with its sweet miasmic climate in which thoughts become dreams while perceptions blur and distinctions are so erased that men are women are nothing are everything are one . . .'

Once again, Hollywood assisted in fashioning a fantasy which blurred into Californian reality. The rock'n'roll rebel boom was over by now: teenagers preferred bland suburban fun, with a tincture of angst and heartache. 'Our audiences welcome clean sex,' said American International Pictures director William Asher. 'They're bored with juvenile delinquency.' If the proto-surf-flick was *Gidget* (1959), starring sexless Sandra Dee and rent-a-dreamboat James Darren, it was Asher who was responsible for the series of beach-party movies featuring Frankie Avalon and Annette Funicello. 'Never outside *Playboy* has such sick plastic sex been seen,' wrote Richard Staehling of these films in *Kings of the Bs*, but malt-slurping drive-in teenagers all over America loved them. 'In the Beach Party movies, everyone was dancing and playing and looking for fun and romances and kisses in the dark,' wrote film-maker/performance artist Annie Griffin, who grew up in Buffalo in the sixties. 'For my sister and I, growing up was the dream of becoming a teenager. Anything beyond that was inconceivable.'

'The dream of becoming a teenager': for Brian Wilson, growing up in the barren, treeless tracts of Hawthorne, there *was* only the dream. The eldest of three brothers raised by the rage-a-holic Murry Wilson, Brian was an all-American misfit, a reluctant jock who quit his high school football team and didn't surf at all. (When, years later, John Belushi 'arrested' Brian for never having surfed in a famous *Saturday Night Live* sketch, it was excruciating to watch the nervous, overweight genius being forced into the Pacific.) It is one of the great ironies of Californian pop that its sunniest teen anthems – from 'Surfin'' to 'California Girls' – were written by a gawky, introspective geek who couldn't relate to the opposite sex.

What isn't pointed out so often is that the surfing lifestyle was a beach-party fantasy to all three Wilson brothers. 'They were pure white trash, West Coast hillbillies,' says Nik Venet, who signed the Beach Boys to Capitol. 'At that time, even Dennis didn't surf – they got most of it from the movies.' Granted that Dennis eventually acted out Brian's teenage dreams – became, indeed, the very personification of T-shirted Californian maleness – the fact remains that the Beach Boys were as much an illusion as anything churned out by Hollywood.

Here, then, is Elvis Costello's 'The Other Side of Summer': scratch the bronzed surface of the Californian dream and all you find is a severely dysfunctional family, terrorized by a pipe-smoking ogre of a *paterfamilias*. Yet what idyllic pictures Brian Wilson painted of the Pacific, of those endless teenage summers. 'I don't think that the Californian myth, the dream that a few of us touched, would have happened without Brian,' says the songwriter Jimmy Webb, who first heard Jan and Dean's 'Surf City' while working on his dad's farm in Oklahoma. 'But I don't think Brian would have happened without the dream.'

Wilson's melodic genius, almost unparalleled in the history of pop, was fashioned as much by Gershwin's *Rhapsody in Blue* as by the close-harmony singing of groups such as the Four Freshmen: from an early age, his taste inclined towards the complex, the ambitious, the operatic. But little brother Carl turned him on to Chuck Berry guitar riffs, and his well-off cousins the Loves converted him to the R&B on Johnny Otis's KFOX show – the 'magic transistor radio' of the fairy-tale song 'Mount Vernon and Fairway'. Out of these different tributaries came the cheap, garagey sound of the Pendletones, later rechristened the Beach Boys. 'Really, they were the first garage band, and the first innocent band,' says Nik Venet. 'They had none of the musical aspects I'd been trained to look for!'

The early Beach Boys with regulation 'woodie'. Left to right: Brian Wilson, Mike Love, Carl Wilson, David Marks, Dennis Wilson.

In September 1961, the odious Murry Wilson took the group to Hite and Dorinda Morgan's Guild Music on Melrose Avenue, where a month later they cut the very primitive 'Surfin''. When the record was released on the Candix label in December, promo man Russ Regan suggested the band change its name. They agreed, and KFWB and KDAY played the record enough to make it a local hit. Ironically, the whiter-than-white group played its first major show in front of a predominantly black audience, bottom of the bill at the Ritchie Valens Memorial Dance in Long Beach.

After Candix declined to release another record by the group, Murry Wilson took a four-song Beach Boys demo to Nik Venet at Capitol. The 21-year-old Venet had come out to LA from the East Coast in 1958, learning about 'taste, style, history, and turtleneck sweaters' from Dick Bock at jazz/beatnik label World Pacific. After trying to make it himself as a teen-idol type, he'd been hired by Capitol as the first of a new breed of young gunslingers. 'At the time I went to work for Capitol, there wasn't a producer in Los Angeles under the age of forty,' says Venet, who had an office on the top floor of the 'stack o' records' building and took to driving around town in a dirt-encrusted Land Rover with a surfboard strapped to its roof. 'I was the first one to be given legitimate money and allowed to develop acts that weren't already established. I also tried to promote the idea of longevity by not releasing too many singles from albums, which helped to open up the West Coast scene for everybody we know. Otherwise it would have remained one-shot polka-dot bikini bullshit, where the artist didn't mean anything.'

Venet's immediate problem was that Capitol, slow to pick up on new youth trends, hadn't had a Top 10 single since the pop-folk Kingston Trio's 'Tom Dooley' in 1958. As a tentative move in the direction of Tom Wolfe's 'teenage netherworld', he signed a Four Freshmen-style white harmony trio called the Lettermen, quickly guiding them into the Top 10 in late 1961 with a Capitol classic, Nat Cole's 'When I Fall in Love'. 'I didn't wanna give the label a cultural shock,' says Venet. 'Our promo men hadn't even been to the radio stations for two years, so I couldn't send them out there with something off-the-wall. What I was going after was the audience that went to see Troy Donahue movies.'

All this while, Venet had his ear pinned to the ground, listening out for grassroots pop activity. One of his favourite Hollywood hustlers was Kim Fowley. 'It was Kim who kept me in touch with the suburban white teen thing, the world that was only being shown in AIP movies,' says Venet. 'He took me out to a soda fountain in Pacific Palisades and said we were going to watch the kids who came in and listen to the records they played on the jukebox.'

Brian Wilson, all-American misfit.

Venet watched and listened, and not long afterwards had his first encounter with Murry Wilson. The four songs Murry played him – 'Surfin' Safari', 'Surfer Girl', '409' and 'Judy' – were enough to convince Venet that he'd struck teenage gold. A natural pop theorist, he saw the Beach Boys in terms of the kind of West Coast Pop Art being produced by Ed Ruscha, Craig Kauffmann, Billy Al Bangston and Larry Bell, artists whose work was like an avant-garde refraction of surf and Hot Rod subculture.* 'I instantly knew that I'd found my group,' he says. 'I also knew that if I could keep them away from the glitter – let them *dream the glitter* – then we were in business. Let them sing about things they *think* happened.'

Appropriately enough, 'Surfin' Safari' actually broke in Phoenix, Arizona, where – in Venet's words – 'they *needed* the AIP fantasy'. Most of the Capitol executives had dismissed the Beach Boys as suburban hicks, but 'Safari' climbed all the way to No. 14 in September 1962, the first real vocal hit to come out of the surfing craze. During the sessions for their first album that summer, Venet was putatively at the controls, but says his main task was keeping Murry away from Brian: 'My job was to let Brian write and arrange, to keep his theories alive.' After the sessions were over, Brian finally left home, rooming with songwriter Bob Norberg in an apartment in Inglewood.

---

* Mike Davis in his *City of Quartz* deplored the way most of these artists merely reflected 'the mesmerizing vision of a white kids' car-and-surf-based Utopia', but he praised Edward Keinholz's disturbing 1964 piece *Back Seat Dodge-38*, in which dead lovers embrace in a real 1938 coupé. For Davis, the work suggested 'Frankie Avalon and Annette Funicello petting after the Holocaust'!

It was almost certainly Norberg who turned Wilson on to the productions of Phil Spector, records which would come to haunt Brian over the next three years. In the meantime, surf-pop grew into a nationwide beach-party cult, with every pop hustler and record company in town fighting to cash in. 'Teen-surf California was all things bright and beautiful,' says Pamela Des Barres. 'I was in high school then, and it was like we *claimed* that music. It made us somebody, it helped us to invent ourselves as Angelenos.'

After the Beach Boys had united the entire nation with 'Surfin' USA' in April 1963, Jack Nitzsche went Top 40 with the orchestral 'The Lonely Surfer' on Reprise; P. F. Sloan and Steve Barri teamed up as the Fantastic Baggys and sang 'Tell 'Em I'm Surfin''; Bruce (Johnston) and Terry (Melcher) cut 'Summer Means Fun'; Bobby Darin and Jim McGuinn, no less, became the City Surfers for 'Beach Ball'; and future Bread frontman David Gates recorded an absurd song called 'The Okie Surfer'. Jazz master-drummer Shelly Manne was responsible for 'The Monster Surfer', while session guitarist Al Casey twanged out 'Surfin' Hootenanny'. This is without mentioning the Surf Mariachis' *Surfin' South of the Border*, the Bongo Teens' *Surfin' Bongos*, the Avalanches' *Ski Surfin'*, the Crossfires' 'Santa the Sidewalk Surfer', and the King Records compilation *Look Who's Surfin' Now*, featuring contributions from such notable tube-shooting enthusiasts as James Brown, Albert King and Little Willie John.*

In his room: the boy wonder at work.

There were just as many motorcycle/Hot Rod combos, from Ronnie and the Daytonas ('Little GTO') and Bruce Johnston and Terry Melcher's Rip Chords ('Hey Little Cobra') to the Hornets, the Risers, the Scramblers, the Kickstands and the Kustom Kings. Several bands covered both bases, as the title of the T-Bones' *Boss Drag at the Beach* attests. The Beach Boys sang '409' alongside 'Surfer Girl', while the anonymous session group who cut 'Surfer's Stomp' as the Marketts went on to record Hot Rod numbers ('Let's Go' and 'Stingray') as the Routers. In Jack

* When Nik Venet, Gary Usher and Roger Christian later put together the cretinous *Sounds of the Silly Surfers* albums for Mercury, Venet stuck a sign on the recording booth saying that this was 'the last tired effort of a producer who once did something finer and better ... with apologies to F. Scott Fitzgerald'. Brian Wilson, dropping by, saw the sign and asked: 'What does this Fitzgerald guy play and what did Venet do to him?'

Arnold's *The Lively Set* (1964), bands such as the Surfaris performed dragster songs penned by the unlikely writing team of Bobby Darin, Randy Newman and Terry Melcher.

The poignant reality behind Brian Wilson's 'two-girls-for-every-boy' beach fantasies came through on the extraordinary 'In My Room', flipside of the nauseating 'Be True to Your School'. Written with Hawthorne neighbour Gary Usher, who was five years older than Brian and *au fait* with the world of the Brill Building, the dreamy ballad belied the agoraphobia and solipsism that informed many of Wilson's later songs. The irony of the surf poet too paralysed by shyness to emerge from the womb-like safety of his room was numbingly obvious: the famous Guy Peellaert image of Brian at the piano in *Rock Dreams*, his bedroom flooded by the orange of a Pacific sunset, captures the introspection Gary Usher intuited in the song's melody. As John Rockwell noted, the picture 'suggests that Hollywood is a fantasy, not only for the rest of the world but for the very people who fuel the fantasy'.

When, one wonders, did Capitol realize that in Brian Wilson they had a musical prodigy on their hands? *Did* they realize, or did it only occur to them when Derek Taylor declared that Brian Wilson was a genius in 1966? Hell, as long as the kid was knocking out things like 'Shut Down' and 'Little Deuce Coupe' – scribbled over hot fudge sundaes with KFWB deejay and part-time lyricist Roger Christian – Capitol didn't care much either way. Yet for all the success he was having with his surf anthems, Wilson viewed his competition as Spector and Tamla Motown, not the Chantays and the Surfaris – nor Jan and Dean, who followed up the No. 1 'Surf City' with 'Drag City', 'Dead Man's Curve', and 'The Little Old Lady from Pasadena'.*

Wilson's *rite de passage* was marked by his refusal to use the big Capitol studios, where Cole, Sinatra and all the label's other great artists had recorded. Wanting something closer to Spector's setup at Gold Star, he persuaded Capitol's Voyle Gilmore that Studio 3 at Western Recorders was more likely to give him 'the bright, high sound' he required for songs like 'Surfin' USA'. As engineered by Chuck Britz, the Beach Boys' 1963 sessions defined their double-tracked, meticulously synchronized harmonies. 'They used very little vibrato and sang in very straight tones,' says Jimmy Webb, who made it his business to study Brian's production techniques. 'The voices all lie down beside each other very easily – there's no bumping between them because the pitch is very precise.'

Brian's obsession with Phil Spector grew almost daily. 'Be My Baby', in the charts at the same time as 'Little Deuce Coupe', shook him to the

---

* Jan and Dean's somewhat cynical riding of the surf wave was evident in remarks they made in 1965 to *Atlantic Monthly*, to the effect that 'we intend to be around earning a good living long after this surfing stuff has been forgotten'. The following year, Jan Berry was nearly killed after losing control of his Corvette Stingray on a bend very similar to the one in 'Dead Man's Curve'.

core – so much so that he even put together his very own surfer-girl group, the Honeys, and used 'Wrecking Crew' musicians Hal Blaine, Steve Douglas and Glen Campbell to record the trio's sides. Consisting of Gary Usher's ex-girlfriend Ginger Blake, and Marilyn and Diane Rovell – nice Jewish girls whose house in LA's Fairfax district was to become Brian's second home – the Honeys never had any hits, but they did re-form later as the excellent American Spring.

'I was unable to really think as a producer until the time where I really got familiar with Phil Spector's work,' Wilson said later. 'That was when I started to design the experience to be a record rather than just a song.' Brian even crossed Spector's path on several occasions: once in the summer in Lou Adler's office, then again during the Christmas-album sessions at Gold Star. If it was really a case of Spector flaunting his power to the awkward *goy* from the beach-city boondocks, that didn't matter to

Brian. By the end of 1963, Wilson was finally making the music he heard in his head, spending most of his time in the studio and the rest of it with the Rovells. In the name of fun, fun, fun, it was all work, work, work.

While Brian holed up in the studio, the other Beach Boys made hay in the California sun. Exploiting the teen-girl mania which greeted them everywhere they went, hoodlum Dennis picked fights with the boyfriends of fans, David Marks caught VD, and even dumpy little Carl lost his virginity. Brian had already started skipping odd live dates, but an Australasian tour in January 1964 saw him increasingly alienated by the puerile pre-

The boys who loved California girls. Clockwise from top left: Mike Love, Brian Wilson, Carl Wilson, Dennis Wilson, Al Jardine.

occupations of the others. And when the group returned to LA in February, what did he find awaiting him but the seismic shock of the Beatles.

In retrospect, it was remarkable just how long the surf craze lasted.* Given the mayfly lifespan of today's musical trends, the fact that two Phil Spector henchmen, Pete Anders and Vinnie Poncia, were able to make

---

* But then Hollywood could still crank out a movie like *Don't Make Waves* as late as 1967. This fatuous romantic comedy, directed by Alexander (*Sweet Smell of Success*) Mackendrick of all people and 'introducing' the lovely Sharon Tate as 'Malibu', employed every known Californian cliché, from its Byrds theme song right down to its closing image of a swimming pool collapsing in a mudslide.

the Top 40 with the surfer's lament 'New York's a Lonely Town' as late as 1965 was astonishing. But by the end of that summer – the summer of 'California Girls' – the surf sound was on its last legs. When Tom Wolfe met his 'Pump House Gang' down in La Jolla, he found surfers who were already bordering on a communal hippie lifestyle, smoking grass and driving VW vans.

Of course, the resonance of Californian surf mythology can still be felt in such cultural artefacts as the TV series *Baywatch* (a.k.a. *Boobwatch*, *Buttwatch*, etc.). This Malibu lifeguard drama serves as the perfect excuse to present weekly parades of pneumatic golden flesh, while virtually ignoring minorities or homeless bums of the kind one finds on most Californian beaches. Such is the continuing legacy of southern California's Aryan fantasy that when Englishman Richard Rayner experienced the beach life of Los Angeles in the 1980s he concluded that 'it was LA, not Hitler's Germany, which had given the world a master race' – the children and grandchildren of 'the strongest, fittest and most beautiful people' who'd come to make it in movies and had then interbred, creating a generation of 'bikini stormtroopers and surf Nazis'. Not much has changed since the days of Wolfe's Pump House Gang, when Windansea Beach was '*verboten* for fifty-year-olds' and you could look down on the beach and see 'nothing but lean, tanned kids'.*

VII

In *City of Quartz*, Mike Davis noted that the white kids' 'endless summer' – the idyllic 1959–65 period – was experienced by blacks as a winter of discontent. While there were jobs aplenty for white Angelenos in construction and in aerospace, black unemployment skyrocketed from 12 per cent to 20 per cent, rising to 30 per cent in Watts. Significantly, this coincided with the near-total drying-up of the city's once fertile black music scene. Once rock'n'roll had been co-opted by white teenagers, the music industry forgot about black performers.

Richard Berry, author of that white garage-band perennial 'Louie Louie', is hardly alone in noting the irony in Brian Wilson's lifting a Chuck Berry riff for 'Surfin' USA'. 'I think it's a joke that somebody took a Chuck Berry song and turned it into a surfing song, when you never saw any black dudes on those surfboards!' For Berry, the gradual phasing-out of black acts by the LA record industry was shameful. 'I think the prejudice within the LA record business was the most despicable form of prejudice,' he says. 'To hide behind liberalism is the worst thing. I have more respect

* There is yet more irony in the fact that surf culture is historically Hawaiian/Polynesian. As black writer Lenwood O. Sloan observed, 'The culture of the beach and the barbecue and the surfboard is Polynesian, but if you stopped a blond-haired, blue-eyed surfer on the beach and told him he was a Hawaiian Polynesian, he'd bust your teeth out.'

for a southerner who says he don't like niggers than for the person who whispers: "Let's move, here he comes." In the south, they put the sheet over their heads, but in California they did it more subtly, and we *knew* it. And if you look at the mess California is in now, it shows what their stupidity and laid-backness and Beach Boys mentality produces.'

Whether or not there was a conscious decision by white-run record labels to ignore black talent, the dearth of any kind of 'soul' scene in Los Angeles remains striking – even if some of the blame must fall on the shoulders of the black community's own entrepreneurs. 'There was still a lot of black talent here in the sixties and seventies,' says writer Kirk Silsbee. 'Why it didn't coalesce into something more than all the two-bit hustlers out for themselves, I don't know. I can only speculate that there were so many Dolphins and Dootsies out there that everyone was very shortsighted. They never realized how big this stuff was going to get.'

Of course, there *were* black records being made in LA in the early sixties. H. B. Barnum arranged classic sides by Irma Thomas, including the 1964 Imperial hit 'Wish Someone Would Care' and the majestic 'Anyone Who Knows What Love Is'. Maxwell Davis oversaw soul sessions by the likes of Z. Z. Hill for the Bihari brothers' Kent label. A young

H. B. Barnum (left) supervises a recording session by Muhammad Ali and Sam Cooke.

Sam Cooke in the studio, 1963.

Barry White arranged sides for Eddie Davis's Rampart label and played piano on Bob and Earl's 1963 classic 'Harlem Shuffle'. Jimmy Holiday, who later co-wrote 'Put a Little Love in Your Heart' with Jackie DeShannon, hit with 'How Can I Forget' (1963). Producers Fred S. Smith and Cliff Goldsmith formed Keyman Records and produced hits for the Olympics, Jackie Lee and others. Jewel Akens hit with 'The Birds and the Bees' on Era, as did Leon Hayward with the Motown-derivative 'She's With Her Other Love' on Imperial. Brian Wilson and Gary Usher, no less, produced black singer Betty Willis as 'Rachel and the Revolvers' on the Goffin/King song 'Revolution' (Dot, 1962). Former Four Preps bass singer Ed Cobb produced Ketty Lester's brooding 'Love Letters', and was also at the board on some of the first West Coast sessions for Motown, which opened a small Los Angeles office in 1965. Meanwhile, singers like Lou Rawls and O. C. Smith took 'soul' into the supper clubs, forging what – in the hands of, for example, the Fifth Dimension – was to become an indissoluble link between R&B and MOR in LA.

It was the voice of Lou Rawls which one heard providing the vocal counterpoint on Sam Cooke's soulful 1962 hit 'Bring It On Home to Me'. In many ways, Cooke himself was the great black hope for Los Angeles. Despite recording all manner of pop trifles for RCA, the suave golden boy of the gospel circuit was doing his bit for black pride via the mini-empire he'd founded early in 1960 with his manager, J. W. Alexander. The 'empire' consisted of Kags Music, SAR Records, the affiliated Derby label and Malloy Music publishing arm, and even SAR Pictures, with an artist roster consisting of the Soul Stirrers, Mel Carter, future Stax singer Johnnie Taylor, the Simms Twins, the Valentinos and a barely pubescent Billy Preston. Next to most of Sam's own records, SAR was pretty black, hitting the R&B chart with the Simms Twins' Cooke-penned 'Soothe Me', the Valentinos' gospely 'Lookin' for a Love', and Mel Carter's 'When a Boy Falls in Love', all featuring the famous AFO band out of New Orleans.* In 1963, shortly after Allen Klein had renegotiated his contract with RCA, Cooke declared that his future lay 'more in creating music and records than in being a nightclub performer'. None the less, he liked nothing better than hitting the road with a little touring band and shaking the chitlin' circuit with the kind of raw, sanctified display captured on his *Live at the Harlem Square* album.

Despite three comparatively soulful albums (*Mr Soul, Night Beat* and *Ain't That Good News*) in 1963 and early 1964, Sam still viewed his summer residency at New York's ritzy Copacabana nightclub – trumpeted by a 70-foot billboard in Times Square – as the pinnacle of his career to date. A year later and he would probably have been recording in Memphis, but he never got to see the Soul era he did so much to foster. On 10 December

---

* When Harold Battiste of the AFO band developed the idea of a network of 'soul stations' – musical centres for disadvantaged black youth – Sam paid the rent on a storefront on Vermont and 37th Street near the University of Southern California.

1964, two nights after sitting in on a Johnnie Taylor session at the RCA studio, the 33-year-old singer picked up 22-year-old Elisa Boyer at Martoni's and drove in his $14,000 Ferrari to a fleabag motel on South Figueroa Street called the Hacienda. Boyer claimed that Cooke tried to rape her, and that he then chased her as she fled from the room. Manageress Bertha Lee Franklin said she shot him three times after he broke down her office door. Whatever the truth – and the whole thing has all the ingredients of a set-up, fuelling endless speculation that vested music-business interests had decided to cut this 'uppity nigger' down to size – Sam Cooke was dead, and with him died most of the hopes for black music in LA.

The first posthumous Sam Cooke release was the funky 'Shake', coupled with 'A Change is Gonna Come', the latter as close to black protest as it was possible to get in early 1965. 200,000 people filed past his body in LA, and then in his birthplace, Chicago. Sadly, J. W. Alexander was to fall out with Sam's widow Barbara, who only three months after the funeral married Bobby Womack of the Valentinos. The result was that Alexander shut down SAR and sold Allen Klein his half of the Kags Music catalogue. So much for the dream of black pride.

Cooke's Hollywood Babylonian death was an early indication that all was not so idyllic in the pop paradise of Los Angeles. The Beach Boys notwithstanding, Nathanael West's version of the city still held good. Kenneth Anger himself sowed seeds of darkness in the kingdom of sunlight and 'bushy, bushy blonde hairdos': his short films *Scorpio Rising* and *Kustom Kar Kommandos* were startling subversions of pop iconography, verging on porno-kitsch, emanating from the seamy underside of Hollywood.

In his Anger-esque *City of Night* (1963), the gay writer John Rechy depicted an LA 'nightworld' of fringe deviants decidedly at odds with the bright fantasyland of Hollywood. 'Southern California,' he wrote, 'is a giant sanatorium with flowers, where people come to be cured of life itself in whatever way … this is the last stop before the sun gives up and sinks into the black, black ocean, and night – usually starless here – comes down.'

3 Sunset Nights, Jingle-Jangle Mornings

It happened to be the ripe, or baroque, phase of LA's relations
with rock'n'roll, which had swept in on what Zoyd Wheeler, with
his surfer's eye, judged to be a twenty-year cycle – movies back in
the twenties, radio in the forties, and now records in the sixties.

Thomas Pynchon, *Vineland*

We don't want any poor Englishmen hanging around Hollywood.

Sir Ambrose Abercrombie in Evelyn Waugh's *The Loved One*

I

The Sunset Strip had been a major centre of Hollywood nightlife long
before the dawn of pop music. Back in the forties, celluloid heroes and
villains filed into Ciro's and the El Mocambo, caroused in Preston Sturges'
Players Club, and whored the night away at discreet establishments in the
Hollywood Hills above. The Chateau Marmont hotel was a glitzy palace
of sin, and Schwab's drugstore was where every starlet perched in hopes
of catching the eyes of movie scouts.

In the fifties, with jazz thriving at the Renaissance and the Crescendo,
beatniks congregated in coffeehouses such as Pandora's and the Sea Witch.
The real beat scene was down in Venice – a haven even then for dropouts
of every description – but Hollywood produced its own showbizzy variant
on the theme. James Dean, for instance, used to hang out at Googie's
coffee bar with a crew of cronies led by ghoulish television hostess
Vampira. Playing twisted mind games and spouting cod versions of
existentialism, 'The Night Watch' (as they called themselves) liked to
imagine the Strip was their very own North Beach or Greenwich Village.

A little later, a favoured topic in such bars was the overthrow of
capitalism. 'I remember a bunch of women in leotards discussing Marx
and the Industrial Revolution,' says Van Dyke Parks, who played the
coffeehouse folk circuit around Hollywood in the late fifties. 'People
smoked cigarettes and were very intense, and sometimes I was aware of
the subtle encroachment of a narcotic atmosphere.' According to fellow

The ultimate teen hangout: Canter's Deli on Fairfax Avenue.

Tinseltown troubadour David Crosby, you could have arrested every pot smoker on the Strip by planting an undercover cop at Wil Wright's Ice Cream Parlor.

By the end of the fifties, Sunset between Highland Avenue and Doheny Drive was also Mecca for Los Angeles youth of the clean-living, crewcut-and-varsity-sweater variety. Edd 'Kookie' Byrnes of television's *77, Sunset Strip* epitomized this species of Californian teen, and had a smash hit record ('Kookie, Kookie') into the bargain. After taking in a KRLA Teen Hop at the Red Velvet, you grabbed a shake and a burger at the Carolina Pines on Sunset and Highland, then headed down Fairfax Avenue for coffee and bagels at Canter's deli. Slowly but surely, even the old Beat-infested coffeehouses gave way to the kids. In 1962, disc jockey Jimmy O'Niell took over Pandora's, where bongo man Preston Epps had been the resident entertainer, and turned it into a teen stronghold of hot chocolate and iced tea – the perfect venue for the Beach Boys, who played there that October.

'At that time, the Strip was just guys in matching suits and pompadours playing generic Top 40 stuff,' says LA producer/manager Denny Bruce. 'It was like going to Australia or some place where there are no black people and hearing covers of "In the Midnight Hour".' At P.J.'s on Santa Monica or Gazzari's on La Cienega, acts such as Pat and Lolly Vegas, or the early Standells and Walker Brothers, churned out bleached versions

The 'human jukebox' that was Johnny Rivers, live at the Whisky a Go Go.

of rock'n'roll and Motown songs for the entertainment of undemanding nightlifers. Later, P.J.'s and the Red Velvet were the kind of clubs reviled by the Sunset Strip in-crowd: in a 1966 piece for the *LA Free Press*, Frank Zappa called the Red Velvet 'the HQ for the plastic and pompadour set'. The Mothers of Invention song 'Plastic People' was about club-owners who wanted nothing but regurgitations of 'Louie Louie'.

But the real 'human jukeboxes', as these acts came to be known, were men such as Trini Lopez, a Mexican pop folkie from Dallas whom Don Costa signed to Warners' Reprise label in early 1963 and whose *Trini Lopez at P.J.'s* (featuring a hit version of Pete Seeger's 'If I Had a Hammer') was on the charts for a staggering forty-eight weeks. The king of them all was John Henry Ramistella, a.k.a. Johnny Rivers, a Baton Rouge singer-guitarist who'd survived uneventful stints in New York and Nashville only to join a growing procession of southerners who were heading out to California. In 1963, Rivers was offered a spot at Gazzari's and began playing R&B and rock'n'roll numbers such as Chuck Berry's 'Memphis' and Tommy Tucker's 'Hi Heel Sneakers', dressed in a tuxedo and backed only by drummer Eddie Rubin.

One night, Lou Adler was strolling down La Cienega Boulevard with some time to kill and decided to wander into Gazzari's. 'I saw something I hadn't seen in LA before, which was adults dancing to rock'n'roll,' he recalls. 'I'd seen the Twist in New York and Philly, but this guy Rivers was playing straight-ahead country-blues rock'n'roll.' Well, he was and he wasn't: Rivers certainly had country-blues roots, but what he was providing in Hollywood was really a sort of cleaned-up 'discotheque' rock'n'roll, stripped of soul and free of jarring regional inflections. Which was why it went down so well when Adler introduced him to Elmer Valentine, a sometime Chicago vice cop in his mid-thirties who'd just opened the Whisky a Go Go at 8901 Sunset. Sometimes described as American's first discotheque, the club was based on the original Whisky a Go Go in Paris.

With bassist Joe Osborn added to the lineup, Johnny Rivers and his red Gibson EB-335 quickly became *the* sound of the Strip in the spring of 1964 – so much so, indeed, that Lou Adler had the bright idea of cutting a Trini Lopez-style 'live' album at the Whisky with the aid of a mobile recording unit belonging to Wally Heider. (The record was about as live as a Memorex tape: by everyone's admission, it was doctored by Adler and his favourite sessionmen, with a bunch of high-school girls bussed in to supply background chat and handclaps.) The surprising thing was that every label, including Don Kirshner's Colpix, turned the album down, deeming its rock'n'roll covers to be dated and anachronistic. Adler's instincts were vindicated only after Bob Skaff of Imperial got the go-ahead to release the album on the label which had been home to many of Rivers' own New Orleans heroes. By July 1964, *Johnny Rivers at the Whisky a Go Go* was at No. 12, with the chugging, infectious 'Memphis' at No. 2 on the singles chart.

Johnny Rivers accepts a gold record for 'Memphis', with Lou Adler (right) and Dunhill Records co-founder Bobby Roberts.

The Strip was already buzzing by the time the Beach Boys announced that they were searching for 'a new place where the kids are hip' in 'I Get Around' that summer. At the Whisky, the 'Go-Go girl' was born when the club's female DJ – suspended in a cage above the dancefloor – began dancing to the records she was spinning between Johnny Rivers sets. Not long afterwards, Gazzari's moved to the Strip and began booking the likes of Jackie DeShannon and the Dalton Brothers, the latter featuring future Walker Brothers Scott Engel and John Maus. Coffeehouses such as Fred C. Dobbs' and Tiny Naylor's teemed with teenage life, and Beatlemania was everywhere. 'The sixties really began with Kennedy's death,' says Kim Fowley, who'd produced the Murmaids' girl-group classic 'Popsicles and Icicles' at the time of the assassination in late 1963. 'America needed someone to love after Kennedy died, so it got to love the Beatles. That was Brian Epstein's great stroke of luck.'

The week 'Popsicles and Icicles' slipped out of the Top 10, in January 1964, the Beatles' 'I Want to Hold Your Hand' went to No. 1. 'They snuck up on all of us, because we didn't see it coming,' says Fowley. 'We'd seen *Expresso Bongo* and jacked off to Diana Dors, but we just didn't know.' The great days of the girl groups, dominated by mini-moguls like Spector and renegade hustlers like Fowley, were about to end. After the Brit invasion began, indeed, Fowley did the logical thing and split for London, where he wore a silver suit, road-managed the pony-tailed P. J. Proby, and swanned in and out of the Ad Lib with a Hollywood fruitcake called Bongo Wolf.

II

All this while, folk music had been as integral a part of the Los Angeles music scene as it had been of the scene in New York or London. In the late fifties, folk acts old and new played to rapt audiences at the Ash Grove on Melrose and Doug Weston's Troubadour on La Cienega, as well as at all the Hollywood coffeehouses. At the Ash Grove, you'd see old-time mountain musicians like Clarence Ashley, or dusted-off blues veterans like Sleepy John Estes; at the Troubadour, the bill would be more likely to feature black folk songstress Odetta or the motley all-stars of the New Christy Minstrels. 'The Ash Grove was a sedate, historicity-obsessed bastion,' says Van Dyke Parks, 'whereas the Troub was more eclectic and experimental.'

The schism between 'historicity-obsessed' purists and commercial folkies was a nationwide affair, but it was especially pronounced in Los Angeles, where Capitol's Kingston Trio had given folk music a new lease of commercial life with their 1958 No. 1 hit 'Tom Dooley'. The trio's success had prompted the formation of countless softly harmonizing frat-house trios and quartets on the campuses and coffeehouse circuits of

A young Van Dyke Parks (right) on the coffeehouse folk circuit with his brother Carson, 1961.

America – groups such as the Limeliters, the Brothers Four, the Greenbriar Boys and ultimately the million-selling Peter, Paul and Mary. Hits like the Rooftop Singers' 'Walk Right In' made it difficult to argue that folk was a real alternative to the fluff of Fabian and company: in Paul Nelson's words, folk-pop 'simply added a Four Freshmen-cum-Weavers regularity to the Southern Mountain sound, refined the gold from them thar hills, and laughed all the way to the top of the pop charts'. There was even a weekly folk music show on television, the much-derided *Hootenanny*, featuring only the most inoffensive, politically uncontentious groups. 'Folk was getting very commercial and cellophane-packaged,' recalled Roger McGuinn. 'It was a low-quality product, and I wanted to get into something else.' Ironically, the Kingston Trio themselves wanted to pursue a less pop-oriented direction, but were discouraged by Capitol from attempting anything overtly political. This was, after all, the tail-end of the McCarthy era.

Pop-folkies the Kingston Trio. Left to right: Nick Reynolds, John Stewart, Bob Shane.

By the time the Troubadour had moved in 1961 to 9081 Santa Monica Boulevard – where it survives to this day as a minor bastion of heavy metal – the club's famous Monday night 'hootenanny' was where every two-bit folkie in town had his or her turn in the spotlight. Biggish names (Judy Collins, Phil Ochs, Judy Henske) often played there, but the Troub's real contribution was to nurture the artists who were to become the leading lights of LA's folk-rock boom: singers such as David Crosby, Gene Clark and Jerry Yester, along with a variety of jug and bluegrass bands. 'You'd see ten to fifteen acts on Monday nights,' recalls Henry 'Tad' Diltz of the Modern Folk Quartet. 'The place would be absolutely packed with agents and managers and record company people.'

Other folk venues where these singers got breaks were the Ice House out in Pasadena and the Unicorn, owned by two brothers who'd come out to the Coast from the Bronx. It was at the Unicorn that young David Crosby, an arrogant rich kid possessed of an ethereal tenor voice, met Jim Dickson, a producer then working for Dick Bock at World-Pacific Records. Dickson had previously been involved with jazz and beat recordings – among other things, he'd produced the great Lord Buckley – but by 1962 he was checking out the folk scene with a view to forming a publishing company with accountant Eddie Tickner. In 1964, when he met Crosby, Jim Dickson was as hip as anyone on the Sunset Strip, a man who'd hung out with James Dean and Dennis Hopper and was more than comfortable with the aroma of good Mexican reefer.

Crosby by this time had struck up an acquaintance with Jim McGuinn, late of the Chad Mitchell Trio, and Gene Clark, fresh from a Canadian tour by the New Christy Minstrels. McGuinn wasn't too enamoured of the cocky young Crosby, who'd served his own pop-folk apprenticeship as one of Les Baxter's Balladeers, but the two men were able to bond through an admiration for the Beatles that was frowned upon even at the Troubadour. 'One of the first indications of the changes in store,' says

Henry Diltz, 'was Jim McGuinn showing up at the Troub one night and singing Beatles songs all by himself.' This tacit acceptance of pop had quiet support throughout the LA folk community, even among some of the Ash Grove crowd. 'The people who sent off for Library of Congress tapes had no truck with it,' says Barry 'Doctor Demento' Hansen, an Ash Grove regular at the time, 'but some of my other friends were impressed by the Beatles. These were people who'd given up on rock'n'roll after the Fabians and Frankie Avalons took over but now came back to it and discovered the Beatles and Tamla Motown. They were impressed by *A Hard Day's Night* on a cultural level.'

It was after seeing *A Hard Day's Night* in the summer of 1964, indeed, that David Crosby, Jim McGuinn and Gene Clark first discussed the idea of forming an electric band. Under Jim Dickson's patronage, the trio had already cut some acoustic sessions at the World-Pacific studios, but the influence of the Beatles was hard to shake off. 'They were looking to be the American Beatles,' recalled Jim Dickson, who was equally fascinated by the Liverpudlians. 'As we worked on the process, we found our own way to go with a combination of folk and rock'n'roll.' It was Dickson who brought bassist Chris Hillman into the fold, since he'd recorded Hillman's bluegrass outfit the year before. Then it was simply down to Crosby making contact with Michael Clarke, a pretty-boy drummer he'd met up in Big Sur. Shortly afterwards, McGuinn acquired the first of his famous twelve-string Rickenbackers and Crosby bought a Gretsch. Michael Clarke noted the make of kit Ringo Starr played in *A Hard Day's Night* and persuaded Eddie Tickner to stump up the cash for some Ludwig drums. They called themselves the Jet Set.

After some shambolic rehearsals through the late summer, the quintet recorded their first single – the forgettable 'Please Let Me Love You' – under the laughably Anglophile name the Beefeaters. Released on the New York folk label Elektra, it was hardly an auspicious debut, especially since it wasn't even a band performance, featuring instead such renowned sessionmen as bassist Ray Pohlman and drummer Earl Palmer. The obvious ineptitude of Michael Clarke and shakiness of most of the others was still a problem when Jim Dickson got the band signed to Columbia in November. Assigned to new staff producer Terry Melcher, their first sessions highlighted the transition from pop to rock, producers to bands, slick sessionmen to rough-edged DIY. Melcher, already a pop veteran of the teen-idol/surf era, and the son of Columbia artiste Doris Day, wanted to junk the whole group. Even Jim McGuinn, whose jangly twelve-string picking was the trademark of the resulting 'Mr Tambourine Man', was lucky to be included on the session alongside Hal Blaine (drums), Larry Knechtel (bass), Leon Russell (electric piano), and Jerry Cole (rhythm guitar).

Actually, it was remarkable enough that Columbia had even signed the band who now called themselves – with cute Beatles-style misspelling – the Byrds. The monolithic New York label was on the verge of decline,

'They were looking to be the American Beatles': The Byrds in early 1965. Left to right: *Chris Hillman, David Crosby, Michael Clarke, Jim McGuinn, Gene Clark.*

with the MOR era of Mitch Miller, Ray Coniff and Percy Faith distinctly on the wane and only Streisand and Andy Williams still shifting vinyl in any real quantities. A&R legend John Hammond had shown great perspicacity in signing the young Bob Dylan, but he was a lone voice in the company. On the West Coast, things were no better, save for the fact that 33-year-old ex-actor Billy James had recently joined the staff. 'The one Columbia executive who seemed to feel the change coming was Billy,' recalled Clive Davis, the corporate lawyer who'd just been made the company's Administrative V-P. 'He was a writer, a publicist and a creative spirit who roamed the West Coast listening to artists and issuing clarion – and unheeded – calls that times were indeed changing.'

Billy James was certainly one of the few record company hirelings on the LA scene who understood the rationale behind Jim Dickson's strategy for the Byrds. As all halfway-decent managers in the rock era have done, Dickson worked on seducing the in-crowd and creating a buzz around the band. In March 1965, he booked the Byrds into the newly renovated Ciro's, which had been a ritzy watering-hole-to-the-stars in the forties before falling out of favour in the late fifties. The timing was perfect: galvanized by the pop revolution of the Beatles and the Rolling Stones, LA's baby-boomers were mobile, getting around, looking for action. And

Billy James, the Columbia press officer who was instrumental in the career of the Byrds.

now they were joined by the hip elite of Hollywood itself, from Sal Mineo and Peter Fonda to junkie comic Lenny Bruce. Among fellow musicians, a key Byrds supporter at this early stage was Jackie DeShannon, whose 'Don't Doubt Yourself, Babe' was included on the *Mr Tambourine Man* album and whom Jim Dickson recalled as 'the first professional person in rock'n'roll to risk her credibility by saying the Byrds were great'. 'We had all the up-and-coming elite who wanted to know what was going on,' boasted Dickson. 'All the young Hollywood people came there ... it was too big an event to miss.'

Particularly crucial to the scene was the roving troupe of self-styled 'freaks' led by ancient beatnik Vito Paulekas and his trusty, lusty sidekick Carl Franzoni. 'Vito was in his fifties, but he had four-way sex with goddesses,' says Kim Fowley, who'd just returned from his sojourn in England. 'He held these clay-sculpting classes on Laurel Avenue, teaching rich Beverly Hills dowagers how to sculpt. And that was the Byrds' rehearsal room. Then Jim Dickson had the idea to put them on at Ciro's, on the basis that all the freaks would show up and the Byrds would be their Beatles. And the theory proved exactly right.'

Fowley, who quickly latched on to Vito's crowd because of the array of pussy on offer, remembers the early Byrds shows as almost orgiastic affairs: 'You'd leap into the middle of the room and begin dancing like an Indian or something, virtually having sex on the dancefloor. A band didn't have to be good, as long as the dancers were there.' Among the other dancers in this Warholesque crew were Emerald, Butchie, Beatle Bob, Linda Bopp, Errol Flynn's six-foot daughter Rory, and the wonderfully nicknamed Karen Yum Yum.

As it happened, the Byrds *weren't* terribly good, their live shows invariably sounding as chaotic as their early World-Pacific sessions. But Fowley was right: it didn't matter. When the dreamy, narcotic version of Dylan's 'Mr Tambourine Man' was released in May, these 'five bland Apollonians' – in the words of Sandy Pearlman – caught the pulse of the times and made 'folk rock' a reality. Aiming for what he described as 'a wispy kind of freaked-out vocal treatment', McGuinn sounded like some imaginary cross between Dylan and John Lennon, and the Wrecking Crew sessionmen drove the song brilliantly behind him. With Dylan himself scandalizing the purist diehards by going electric at the Newport folk festival in July, the jingle-jangle dawn of sixties rock had arrived. Coming through LA that summer, the scrawny messiah even bestowed his seal of approval on the Byrds, joining them onstage at Ciro's.

III

In her famous rock encyclopaedia, Lillian Roxon wrote that '*Newsweek* called the Byrds "the Dylanized Beatles", when the whole point was that they were Beatlized Dylans.' Whichever way round it was, there was neat synchronicity in the fact that Beatles press officer Derek Taylor moved to Los Angeles that spring and began doing the Byrds' publicity. Asked to form a press agency by Bob Eubanks of *The Dating Game*, who'd promoted the Beatles' Hollywood Bowl shows, Taylor's arrival symbolized the synergy between swinging London and happening Hollywood. And with 'Mr Tambourine Man' climbing all the way to No. 1 in both America and Britain, he quickly became *the* LA pop publicist.

Derek Taylor (centre) *backstage at the Hollywood Palladium with Byrds Gene Clark* (left) *and Chris Hillman in September 1965. 'I was considered to be hip just because I was English. They didn't know what an ugly bunch of shits we were!'*

'I didn't even know that much about pop,' confesses Taylor in the London offices of Apple, where he still works a couple of days a week. 'I knew about the Beatles, but basically I was a provincial journalist. Suddenly, there I was in the 9000 Sunset building with a press agency and a drink problem! Initially, I was given Dick and Dee Dee and the Standells and all kinds of stuff I knew wasn't suitable for my mentality. When I heard "Mr Tambourine Man" on an acetate, I knew this was for me, so I left Eubanks and took the Byrds with me. And I didn't really have to do a lot for them, in all honesty. Billy James had done most of the work, but he was such a generous soul that he just said, "Over to you". Then I started smoking dope and became sort of hip. I never really *was* hip, but I was considered to be, just because I was English. They didn't know what an ugly bunch of shits we were!'

Hollywood had always been infested with Brits, so Taylor's arrival was hardly revolutionary. For umpteen actors, writers, artists and common-

Music-biz hive the 9000 Sunset building, seen from Santa Monica Boulevard.

or-garden escapees, Los Angeles was the cultural polar opposite of grey-green, rain-sodden Blighty. Settling here was for them a kind of colonialism, with weird religious sects instead of punkah-wallahs. 'We limeys have a peculiar position to keep up, you know,' Sir Ambrose Abercrombie tells the hapless Dennis Barlow in the opening scene of Evelyn Waugh's Hollywood satire *The Loved One* (1948). 'They may laugh at us a bit – the way we talk and the way we dress . . . they may think us cliquey and stand-offish, but, by God, they respect us.'

Brits had always exploited the rampant Anglophilia of Hollywood, and it was no different in the record business. The following year, an Englishman who took over the management of flower-powerized garage band the Seeds dubbed himself 'Lord' Tim Hudson. The cachet accorded Taylor and Hudson was also enjoyed by such transplanted limeys as Jack Good, producer of the TV pop show *Shindig* – not to mention the Beatles, the Stones, old Andrew Loog Oldham and all. 'Any group that came from England, everyone went to see them and wanted to talk to them,' says Danny Hutton, a Hollywood scenester who became pally with the Beatles. 'It was like, we're kind of cool, but they're *really* cool.'*

It was the British invasion groups who proved to be the targets for the very first LA groupies that summer. 'By 1965, any English-looking boy with long hair was considered worth chasing down Sunset,' says writer Eve Babitz. 'There were A- and B-list groupies. My sister was A-list – you had to be a size 3 or under to be in that crowd. There were a lot of rabidly ambitious 20-year-old boys around, and *our* only ambition was to stop them complaining.' According to Kim Fowley, whose authority in such matters cannot be doubted, the first real *groupie* as such was a redhead named Liz – 'the first bitch to show up at a hotel for the express purpose of fucking a musician' (in her case Manfred Mann's Paul Jones).

The first groupies were really just teenyboppers who'd decided to take things the whole way. In a 1967 piece in *Cheetah*, Tom Nolan said that most of them were 'pretty young things' from Glendale and Pasadena and Pacoima who'd seen the Beatles at the Coliseum and 'just learned to love their mod-bods, tanned and lean and budding'. For Pamela Des Barres, fresh out of the Valley at sweet sixteen, it wasn't enough to sit and listen to these groups in clubs. 'I wanted to meet them, that's all it was,' she says. 'Luckily the proximity made it possible. Ciro's was just over the hill, so I knocked on the backstage door and the Byrds let me in! That's how it happened. I sat there and watched them all smoke pot and thought I'd really made it to the in-crowd. And no one believed me at school.'

Sixties Brits were just as smitten with Los Angeles – with the sheer plasticity of the place – as Angelenos were with Brits. For David Hockney, who was in town when the Beatles played the Hollywood Bowl for the first time, southern California was veritably the Aryan paradise of the

---

* It was perfect somehow that 'Lord' Tim Hudson ended up providing some of the Scouse and Cockney voices for the vultures in *The Jungle Book*.

Beach Boys' surfing anthems, a 'strange big city' full of beautiful blond boys such as Bobby Earles, a Laguna Beach go-go dancer who later died of a drug overdose. Hockney's famous paintings of Beverly Hills swimming pools and vacuous art collectors were an ironic celebration of the city's mid-sixties affluence – a bright new 'pop' California of the kind discussed in Reyner Banham's *Los Angeles*. In fact, 'A Bigger Splash' (1968) was *the* image of pop LA, its perfectly contained explosion suggesting to art historian Hugh Honour a kind of 'brand new world'. As Georgina Howell noted in a recent *Vogue* profile, 'for me and millions of others, [Hockney] is the man who invented California.'

Reyner Banham applauded the 'eager guilelessness' that was for him the key to LA's ethos and aesthetic. 'By comparison with the general body of official culture, given over to facile, evasive, and self-regarding pessimism,' he noted, 'it can be a very refreshing attitude to encounter.' Banham's 'love' for Los Angeles was itself a variation on the joy Brits such as Aldous Huxley and Christopher Isherwood had taken in the transience and artifice of Californian life. For both men, in their different ways, southern California was a place of mystical naivety, refuting European cynicism and encouraging rebirth through cinema, new religions, and psychotropic drugs. Even the city's suburban homogenization – decried by Europeans and East Coasters alike – was for them more honest than the class-governed hierarchies of London, Paris or New York. As Peter Conrad noted in his *Imagining America*, LA provided an escape from 'the ancestral and the familial', because it was 'a place of motorized transience, where not only relationships but even the landscape was fickle and unenduring'. Isherwood resented the old-world Catholic snobbery which fuelled Evelyn Waugh's mockery in *The Loved One*: for Peter Conrad, Isherwood's screenplay for Tony Richardson's 1965 film of the novel, written with Terry Southern, 'sabotaged' Waugh, celebrating 'the Californian accord between mysticism and mechanism' instead of satirizing it.*

While Richardson filmed scenes from *The Loved One* at Forest Lawn cemetery – that extraordinary theme park of death – the British pop

* It was interesting how the Steve Martin film *LA Story* – directed by Hollywood limey Mick Jackson – used Brits to address the sunshine/*noir* dialectic. In the film, Richard E. Grant's character takes the old Nathanael West line – sneering that 'if they turned the sprinklers off, [LA] would revert to desert' – but his wife, played by Victoria Tennant, falls in love with the city. We are only too obviously encouraged to take her view, moreover: he is creepy, misanthropic, unwholesome, whereas she is made for California – blonde and starry-eyed with wonder. Meanwhile the Steve Martin character (a native Angeleno) also falls in love with his own hometown, rescuing it from the cynicism of Euros like Grant. As Martin sleeps, the flicker of freeway headlights plays magically over him. When he drives, a sign declares that 'LA WANTS TO HELP YOU'. Finally, united with Tennant (Martin's then real-life spouse) he tells us he's 'learned that romance *does* exist deep in the heart of LA' – and all this to the accompaniment of an Enya soundtrack! The whole thing is a sort of insidious pop promo for the city, strewn with stereotypes, teeming with tropes.

invasion was gathering pace. Into the city poured all manner of English-men, from ex-public schoolboys Peter and Gordon to chirpy Mancunians Freddie and the Dreamers. 'Coming from England, of course, it was extraordinary,' says Peter (Asher), who with Gordon (Waller) was still enjoying Top 20 American success after their Lennon and McCartney-penned No. 1 'A World Without Love' (1964). 'There we were, renting a Mustang convertible and driving down Sunset, picking up beautiful blonde girls. I mean, it was a fairly decent introduction to *anywhere*! If anything, I got an overly golden impression of Los Angeles at that point.'

Peter Asher (right) with Gordon Waller. *'There we were, driving down Sunset, picking up beautiful blondes…'*

Observing Asher behind an enormous desk in his luxurious Doheny Drive office, one wonders just how tarnished the 'overly golden' LA dream could possibly have become. 'Well, Brits *were* treated like gods,' he admits. 'The miraculous thing is that they still are, although less so. When you think about the awful contempt the British hold for America, actually making fun of their virtues – their generosity and hospitality – it's amazing that people here still think a British accent is rather interesting.'

Another public schoolboy come good in pop Babylon was the preposterous Ian Whitcomb, who rose to the giddy heights of No. 8 in June 1965 with his cod-Mod travesty 'You Turn Me On (Turn On Song)'. Whitcomb still lives out in Pasadena (not far from the local 'Olde English Tea Shoppe') and is still happy to play the resident pop fogey for anyone who's got an hour or two to spare. 'I found it magical here, and I *still* find it magical,' says the man whom Christopher Isherwood and David Hockney befriended at the Troubadour back in 1966. 'People here still say, "Go for it!", whereas in Britain all you ever get is, "Oh, it's been done before." Brits always knock America for being homogenized, but it's *Britain* that's homogenized. In Los Angeles, every suburban house is different!'

If all this is starting to sound a mite familiar, bear in mind that it wasn't only Brits who found LA a magical place in 1965. Teenagers were flocking in to the Sunset Strip from all over America that summer, most of them in search of the groovy, cerebral spirit they picked up from 'Mr Tambourine Man'. 'The whole scene was still very sweet and innocent at this point,' says Linda Ronstadt, who moved to LA after hearing the Byrds on the radio in her native Tucson. 'It was all about sitting around in little embroidered dresses and listening to Elizabethan folk ballads, and that's how I thought it was always going to be!'

'I was astonished not only by the money and fame and glamour,' says Greg Shaw, who came down from San Francisco and later founded Bomp Records, 'but by the fact that a stupid-looking kid like me could end up at Sonny and Cher's house with all these gorgeous actresses. It really was wide-open. It wasn't just a culture celebrating itself, it was a whole *industry* celebrating itself! The music was inextricably tied up with the industry, with money, with the self-awareness of incipient stars, and there was something fabulous about it.'

Also from the San Francisco area came a nerdy-looking kid named Rodney Bingenheimer, who got to hang out with the Byrds at Ben Frank's coffee shop and 'became the talk of the town because I had the perfect Brian Jones 'do'. Rodney was so ubiquitous that actor Sal Mineo eventually dubbed him 'The Mayor of Sunset Strip', a title the diminutive scenester retained right up until the closure of his celebrated glam-rock English Disco in 1975. Catch Rodney at the so-called 'Rock and Roll Denny's' on Sunset these days and you'll find the same ageless pageboy in a corner, scoffing porridge and giggling like a strange, retarded child. If you're lucky, he'll take you round the corner to the apartment he's lived in for seventeen-odd years, a personal pop shrine stuffed with relics and souvenirs, its walls lined top to bottom with pictures of Rodney and Brian, Rodney and Bowie, Rodney and Spector, Rodney and Jagger, Rodney and Lennon – even Rodney and *Elvis*. The man still exudes the gossipy ingenuousness of an Andy Warhol, except that he isn't gay – far from it, indeed. 'Tiny guys like Charlie Chaplin and Mickey Rooney have always gotten laid in Hollywood,' says Kim Fowley, the Sunset Strip vampire Bingenheimer befriended on his arrival in Hollywood. 'But Rodney fucked movie-star bitches you would not believe. He got so much cunt that in his early thirties he had a stroke. Allegedly, Led Zeppelin paid the hospital bill – a hundred thousand dollars – because he had no insurance.'

The arrival in LA of teen scenesters such as Bingenheimer seemed to coincide with a concerted Californian response to the British pop invasion. With the help of Jim Dickson, Billy James and Derek Taylor, the Byrds had got the ball rolling; now a real LA pop scene began to flourish. 'The Beatles and the Stones had had a huge effect, because they'd demonstrated that you didn't have to be Bobby Vee, you could be a band and *get somewhere*,' says Greg Shaw. 'The Beatles were a prototype, just as Elvis had been. But the backlash was "Who are these foreigners coming over here and stealing our girlfriends? We'll show 'em!" And that inspired a lot of people to get out there and do it.'

Van Dyke Parks remembers living under a billboard that proclaimed 'THE BEATLES ARE COMING!' and sensing that 'a plague with vast cultural implications' was on its way. When it did come, he became aware of 'a severe competitive atmosphere' among new Los Angeles acts. 'We somehow wanted to wrest this trophy back from the English who'd preceded us,' he says. 'It was as though we'd neglected our own goods – no one had thought of Buddy Holly for a while. So the British reminded us of who we were.'

The first LA act to pick up the 'folk-rock' baton from the Byrds was that unlikely duo Sonny and Cher, who'd already recorded without notable success for Vault Records as Caesar and Cleo. Sonny Bono had hustled his way through 1964, playing Spector sessions and moonlighting for such indies as Charger. But after he was foolish enough to agree with a KFWB disc jockey's opinion that the Ronettes' 'Walkin' in the Rain' sounded

Sonny and Cher, king and queen of pop Hollywood.

'kinda tired', he got his marching orders from Gold Star. 'Sonny Bono will never know what happened when it's all over,' Spector said later, with gratuitous venom. 'He'll never know why it happened because he didn't know what happened to make it happen, so he won't know what happened to make it fail.'

Freed from Spector's overbearing influence, Bono observed the rise of the Byrds with interest. Hip to the burgeoning sound of folk-rock, and to the sartorial revolution taking place on the Strip, he signed to the management team of Charlie Greene and Brian Stone and turned Caesar and Cleo into the king and queen of Pop Hollywood, hippie clowns in opossum vests and leopard-skin ponchos. Playing on bills with such second-division Brits as Herman's Hermits and the Dave Clark Five, they caught the attention of Mo Ostin at Reprise, who issued one single ('Baby Don't Go') in early 1965, and then of Ahmet Ertegun at Atlantic.

Signed to Atlantic's pop outlet Atco, Sonny and Cher finally hit very big with 'I Got You, Babe', cleverly arranged by former AFO member Harold Battiste. 'Sonny seemed to know only two chords on the piano,' recalled Mac Rebennack, who'd followed Battiste to Hollywood from New Orleans. 'Harold took these songs and heroically made them sound like real music.' Now a golden oldie to end all golden oldies, 'I Got You Babe' perfectly bridged the gulf between Phil Spector and the Byrds, the old pop and the new rock. It was Spector-meets-Dylan in a pair of hiphugger bellbottoms, complete with oboe and harpsichord: MOR folk-rock, to be precise. Singing it on *Shindig* that summer, they looked and sounded so phoney that the act worked: a diminutive Sicilian dwarfed by his deep-voiced, half-Cherokee wife, shaking a leg with the new love generation. Cher herself became such a pop icon that Imperial Records not only signed her as a solo artist but – to the indignation of the Byrds, who themselves released the song as their follow-up to 'Mr Tambourine Man' – put her in the Top 20 that August with Bob Dylan's 'All I Really Want to Do'.

For their troubles, Sonny and Cher were pilloried as 'freaks' and 'hippies' by middle America; Bono was called a 'fag', Cher a 'hooker'. When Sonny and Rodney Bingenheimer went to Martoni's for lunch they were asked to leave, prompting Sonny to pen the instant protest song 'Laugh at Me'. Risible he was, but more for his blatant opportunism than his sartorial daring. 'Under all the hair and hype,' swiped Nik Cohn, 'Sonny and Cher emerged as pop-age answers to Jeanette McDonald and Nelson Eddy.'

Another act who took a Dylan song into the Top 20 that summer was the Turtles, who'd begun life as surf combo the Crossfires and had recently landed a two-month residency at disc jockey Reb Foster's Rebellaire Club in Manhattan Beach. Foster managed the band, which was led by twin frontmen Mark Volman and Howard Kaylan, and signed them to White Whale, a new label formed by ex-Liberty distributors Lee

The Byrds return from the UK, September 1965. Left to right: McGuinn, Hillman, Clark, Crosby, Clarke.

Laseff and Ted Fagan. There they swiftly transformed themselves into the Turtles, recording Dylan's 'It Ain't Me, Babe' and playing Pasadena's Rose Bowl on a bill headlined by Herman's Hermits. The single, the first production by master engineer Bones Howe, went all the way to No. 8 in August.

When the Byrds returned from a summer tour of Britain which saw them overhyped by promoter Mervyn Conn as 'America's Beatles', there was a distant sense that Sonny and Cher and the Turtles had stolen the band's folk-rock fire, commercializing it to the point of redundancy. Despite the presence of the Vito and Peter Fonda crowds at a 'Welcome Home'-style Palladium show in September, the gig was hardly a sellout. Moreover, factions were forming within the group, with increasing tension developing in the studio between Jim Dickson and Terry Melcher. After Melcher hired Jack Nitzsche to produce a Byrds version of Dylan's 'It's All Over Now, Baby Blue', he discovered that Dickson and the band were redoing the track behind his back. Not long afterwards, he was fired as the Byrds' producer, though not before putting the band back on the pop map with a classic version of Pete Seeger's 'Turn! Turn! Turn!' – their second No. 1.

But if there was one record which epitomized the blatant LA commercialization of folk-rock that summer, it was ex-Christy Minstrel Barry McGuire's 'Eve of Destruction'. Once again, the ever-shrewd Lou Adler had managed to tap into the pop *zeitgeist*, manufacturing a prime piece of 'protest' by Trousdale staff writer P. F. Sloan. Adler, Sloan and Steve Barri had seen McGuire at Byrds shows on the Strip, and signed him to the new Dunhill label. Written after Lou pressed a copy of 'Like a Rolling Stone' into Sloan's hands, 'Eve of Destruction' was almost as phoney as 'I Got You, Babe' – and almost as successful, hitting the No. 1 spot in August. It was the sound of the New Christy Minstrels meeting the Fantastic Baggys, or protest a-go-go. Fittingly, when Dylan brought his new electric show to the Hollywood Bowl in September, he gave Phil Sloan the icy treatment he'd meted out to Donovan in London earlier in the year. Alas, this didn't stop Sloan following up with similar protest-by-rote numbers such as the Turtles' 'Let Me Be' and the Searchers' 'Take Me for What I'm Worth', as well as his own Dunhill album *Songs for Our Times* (1965).

In his book *Rock Odyssey*, Ian Whitcomb called Dunhill a 'protest factory', which wasn't quite fair but wasn't that wide of the mark. Canny enough to realize that the conveyor-belt pop era of Don Kirshner and the Brill Building was almost over, Lou Adler merely employed Sloan and Barri to simulate the style of folk-rock singer-songwriters. 'When Dylan plugged in his guitar, he took a lot of people from the folk field into rock'n'roll,' says Adler. 'Simultaneously, the Beatles validated rock'n'roll: people could listen to them knowing they were really writing their songs, as opposed to Jan and Dean or Spector's artists.' If it wasn't quite as ludicrous as Dino, Desi and Billy cutting 'Chimes of Freedom' for Reprise, 'Eve of Destruction' said everything about Dunhill, which had recently taken on the aggressive Jay Lasker as head of sales, as well as an all-purpose office boy in the form of public-school-Brit-about-town Andy Wickham.

The success of the long-haired, fur-clad Barry McGuire was just one more feather in the cap of Lou Adler, who impressed writer Nik Cohn as 'the runaway winner' in the 'image race' of Californian pop. For Cohn, Adler embodied the essence of mid-sixties Hollywood cool, a mode of behaviour in which 'the etiquette was crippling' and clumsiness of any kind unpardonable. With a succession of movie actresses on his arm, and a pronounced taste for expensive clothes, cars and wines, Adler was clearly a mogul-in-the-making. 'He was rich, wore interesting hats, and didn't give a lot of clues to his innermost being,' wrote the lissome Michelle Phillips, who developed a crush on Adler after the Mamas and the Papas hit the big time.*

If Dunhill was guilty of passing off conveyor-belt pop as home-cooked folk-rock, at least Adler was moving in the direction of hipness. Over at Liberty, Snuff Garrett was doing exactly what he'd done with Bobby Vee, except now he was doing it with a Beatles-style 'band' called Gary Lewis and the Playboys. Somehow, it made perfect Hollywood sense that Gary, the group's drummer-singer, was the son of

Leon Russell (left) and Snuff Garrett inspect their hit productions of Liberty artists Bobby Vee and Gary Lewis and the Playboys.

* Clearly, Adler's ice-cool demeanour was *de rigueur* at Dunhill. When Nik Cohn came to see Johnny Rivers, the singer 'gave me the toughest interview I ever did in my life ... slouching, shrugging, and looking only at Lou Adler'. Cohn observed exactly the same 'deadpan and remote' stance in the Byrds.

comedian Jerry Lewis, as did the fact that the group had played numerous teen dances at Disneyland. Basically, they were the worst kind of teenage pap, but the combination of Garrett and arranger Leon Russell – abetted by all the usual session stalwarts – worked commercial miracles, netting the band seven consecutive Top 10 hits in the eighteen-month period between January 1965 and May 1966. Some of these were good pop records – the version of Sammy Ambrose's 'This Diamond Ring', pianist Glen D. Hardin's 'Count Me In' – but others were just sub-surf piffle. 'Things were set up where Snuff Garrett was in absolute 100 per cent control of everything,' Lewis himself recalled. 'Many times I would just be called to come in and sing.' The Playboys' winning streak soon came to an end after Garrett quit Liberty in the summer of 1966 to form Viva Records with Jimmy Bowen of Reprise.

IV

The success of acts as different as the Byrds and Gary Lewis and the Playboys was helping to turn Los Angeles into the new epicentre of American pop. Charlie Gillett has computed that in 1963, records made in New York were at No. 1 for twenty-six weeks, while those made in Los Angeles accounted for only three. But in 1965, LA jumped to twenty weeks, with New York plummeting to just one (the McCoys' 'Hang On, Sloopy'). Part of the reason for this was that stringent new cabaret laws in New York City were making it hard for club-owners to risk booking unsigned acts, prompting the exit of a large segment of the Greenwich Village folk scene. But equally important was the fact that Los Angeles had become synonymous with change, open-mindedness, and the good life in the sun. It was significant that Bob Dylan met with a far less hostile reaction to his newly electrified sound when he played the Hollywood Bowl in September 1965.

Without the weight of the Tin Pan Alley/Brill Building tradition on their shoulders, LA bands and producers unhesitatingly jumped on the British Invasion bandwagon and took the pop initiative away from New York. By the same token, groups such as the Stones acknowledging the genius of movers and shakers like Phil Spector and Jack Nitzsche, to the extent of featuring both men on their records. It was ironic that 'Satisfaction', perhaps *the* anthem of 'Swinging London', was recorded on Nitzsche's advice at the RCA studio on Sunset, using Sam Cooke's old engineer Dave Hassinger. By May 1965, when that session took place, the Stones were so *au fait* with the Hollywood music business that they could even take a potshot at it in the memorable 'Under Assistant West Coast Promotion Man', a tribute to those old-school hustlers whom Nik Cohn stigmatized as 'all toupée and seersucker suit'.

The new prominence of Los Angeles as a pop capital was reflected by the fact that *American Bandstand* host Dick Clark shifted his empire to the West Coast, even launching a new TV show there called *Where the Action Is*. In October 1964, the *Teen Age Music International (TAMI) Show* – staged at the Santa Monica Civic Auditorium with Jack Nitzsche as its musical director – brought together under one banner all the different strands of pop, from surf (Jan and Dean and the Beach Boys) to Motown (the Supremes and Marvin Gaye) to the Brit Invaders (the Stones and others) to the incomparable James Brown. The first great pop performance film, it was tantamount to a state-

Terry Melcher in the studio with Paul Revere and the Raiders, 1966. Left to right: Mark Lindsay, Paul Revere, Melcher (seated), Philip Volk.

ment of the LA industry's power. And now *Where the Action Is* (on CBS), *Shindig* (ABC), and *Hullabaloo* (NBC) helped to bolster that impression, beaming out weekly images of LA teenagers doing the latest pop dance. In the words of writer Carl Gottlieb, 'California culture was becoming the national standard.'*

Dick Clark claimed he'd moved his operation to LA because it was 'the most youth-oriented city in the nation'. Still smarting from the blow to his teen-idol empire that was the British Invasion, the ageless puppeteer now had camera crews out canvassing LA's freeways and taco stands in a desperate search for teen action. 'I don't think Hollywood knows any kids,' he sighed to one interviewer; 'by the time they get here they aren't kids anymore.' Just as pop mogul Don Kirshner had kept his foot in pop's door by supplying Screen Gems songs to producers like Phil Spector, so Dick Clark did everything he could to stop pop running away from him. He even managed to turn a punkish, garage-style band called Paul Revere and the Raiders into an outfit more akin to Gary Lewis and the Playboys than to the Rolling Stones.

Before he hired them to be the house band on *Where the Action Is*, the Raiders were just one of the many raw bar bands from the Pacific

* The acknowledgement that California had become something more than a celluloid Lotusland can be felt in East Coast novels such as Alison Lurie's *The Nowhere City* (1965). In Lurie's novel, New Englander Katharine Cattleman doesn't like 'the sun shining all the time in November and the grass showing ... as if we were all shut up in some horrible big greenhouse away from the real world and the real seasons'. Her husband Paul, however, falls in with a group of Beatniks in Venice and experiences a new lease of life. Albeit rather dated, Lurie's novel marks a turning-point in the perception of the 'brand new world' on the coast.

Northwest who'd performed (and, in their case, recorded) Richard Berry's 'Louie Louie'. But after their disc jockey manager Roger Hart wangled the band on to the bill at the Rolling Stones' landmark Long Beach Auditorium shows of 1964, they not only signed to Columbia Records but auditioned for the new Dick Clark show. If only they'd stuck to recording: produced by Terry Melcher, still wrestling with Jim Dickson and the Byrds, the Raiders' first singles had all the sneering energy of Them and the Animals, or of such celebrated 'garage' bands as the Seeds and the Shadows of Knight. 'Steppin' Out' and 'Just Like Me' were classic proto-punk, with singer Mark Lindsay howling the get-off-my-case lyrics in a voice which anticipated everyone from David Johansen to Feargal Sharkey. Even 'Kicks', an anti-drug sermonette by Screen Gems writers Barry Mann and Cynthia Weil that made the Top 5 in March 1966, had its roots in the northwest sound of the Sonics and the Wailers. (Ironically, just as he'd done with the Byrds, Terry Melcher drafted in Leon Russell and Hal Blaine for the band's sessions, along with such new faces as guitarist Ry Cooder and keyboard player Van Dyke Parks. Yet they still sounded like a 'garage' band, almost justifying Dave Marsh's contention that Melcher was 'the most underrated Hollywood producer of the sixties'.)

The sentiments of 'Kicks' were doubtless music to Dick Clark's ears, but they were as much at odds with the Raiders' punky-rebel sound as the absurd American Revolution jackets and britches they were obliged to wear on *Where the Action Is*. Suggesting a somewhat jingoistic resistance to the British Invasion, the 'Spirit of '76' outfits only succeeded in making the band terminally unhip. By 1967, they were, from one perspective, hopelessly outmoded by the likes of Love and the Doors; and from the other, comprehensively outflanked by the Monkees.

Not that Dick Clark was the only man clinging to a safe, hygienic conception of pop culture. LA was full of record company executives and producers resisting the movement from pop towards rock. As Charlie Gillett noted in *The Sound of the City*, 'it was a paradox of the period that while the creative impetus shifted from the East to the West Coast, several of the biggest LA-based artists (e.g. the Byrds, Sonny and Cher, and later, the Doors) recorded for New York-based companies ... only Liberty, Imperial, and Dunhill showed more than average initiative, while Capitol, Warner-Reprise, and A&M missed much of what was going on.'

It said a lot about Capitol, for example, that although it had first option on the Beatles, being a subsidiary of EMI Records, the label initially passed on them. Only after considerable pressure from EMI did Capitol agree to release 'I Want to Hold Your Hand'. And even when they launched Tower Records in late 1964, it was only as a kind of dumping ground for such inferior Brit invaders as Ian Whitcomb and Freddie and the Dreamers: as far as nurturing local talent went, Capitol seemed happy to entrust matters to the likes of Mike Curb, a millionaire brat from the Valley who packaged soundtracks for American International Pictures

The famous 'Stack o' Records'
Capitol building in Hollywood.

featuring such spurious outfits as Davie Allan and the Arrows. Curb was
a typical Hollywood operator, and ideologically unsound to boot. Despite
cashing in with soundtracks for such AIP exploitation classics as *Riot on
Sunset Strip* and *Wild in the Streets*, he was a staunch Nixon supporter who
in 1970 – as the 26-year-old president of MGM Records – purged that
label of all known drug users.

It wasn't, after all, as if Capitol was completely lacking in the hipster
department. Their in-house *Teen Scene* magazine, for instance, was edited
by the goatee-bearded Earl Leaf, whose 'My Fair and Frantic Hollywood'
column gave teenypunters the lowdown on the activities of the Beach

Brian Wilson with Earl Leaf, editor
of Capitol's in-house Beach Boys
fanzine The Teen Set.

Boys. Tower even signed the Standells, revamped by producer Ed Cobb as the bad-boy garage punks of 'Dirty Water' and 'Sometimes Good Guys Don't Wear White'. But the fact that the Capitol executives – whiling away their time on the top floor of the famous tower as black waiters padded around with silver pitchers – all but dispensed with the services of Nik Venet was a clear indication of how out of touch they were, or how content to sit back while their coffers were swelled by the Beatles and Brian Wilson. By the end of the decade, the only new rock act they'd managed to break with any success was The Band.*

The innate conservatism of the majors on the West Coast had its counterpart in pop radio, especially after KHJ began its notorious 'playlist' system in 1965. KHJ had been fighting a losing battle against rivals KRLA and KFWB for nearly ten years when they approached former country DJ Bill Drake and asked him to repeat the success he'd had with independent Top 40 stations in Fresno and San Diego. As programme director, Drake ran countless competitions, inserted KHJ jingles into the format at every available opportunity, and cut the freewheeling raps of DJs such as the Real Don Steele and 'Humble' Harve Miller. More damagingly, he tightened the playlist to thirty-five rotated hits, eliminating anything marginal or experimental. 'Much more music!', boasted the station's principal jingle, but it was actually a case of *more of less*. Not that this seemed to bother the majority of KHJ's listeners, because the play-safe approach rapidly made it the No. 1 station in LA. By the summer of 1966, Bob Krasnow could surmise that giving the first play of Ike and Tina Turner's 'River Deep, Mountain High' to KRLA rather than KHJ was the beginning of its undoing.

                                    V

Despite the stranglehold of the playlist format, and the power of the Dick Clarks and Don Kirshners, the grassroots club scene continued to thrive along the Sunset Strip. As 1965 drew to a close, the Byrds, the Turtles and the Lovin' Spoonful all held court at Ciro's and the Whisky a Go Go. The hottest venue of all was Elmer Valentine's new club the Trip, which had moved into Gene Norman's old jazz joint the Crescendo in the spring. Across the street at 8585 Sunset was Ben Frank's, rapidly becoming *the* hip eatery: Arthur Lee met Byrds roadie Bryan MacLean there and

* Nik Cohn was almost as impressed by Nik Venet as he was by Lou Adler. 'Dark and florid and flash inside camel-hair coats,' Cohn wrote in *Awopbopaloobop Awopbamboom*, 'Venet looked the eternal operator, a B-feature heavy, and he talked entirely in declamations, slogans, odd little sayings.' Sitting in a café near Venice Beach, the affable, big-hearted Venet tells me that he and Bobby Darin deliberately dressed over-the-top for Cohn. 'We put him on something terrible,' he says with a fruity smoker's laugh. 'I don't know how much I impressed him, but he even changed the spelling of his name!'

Ben Frank's, hippest of the Sunset Strip coffee shops.

proposed the formation of the band that would eventually become Love. Equally popular was Fred C. Dobbs, where Phil Spector rendezvous'd with Bob Dylan in the fall, and where Dean Stockwell, Eve Babitz and a young Toni Basil sat around listening to 'Earth Angel' on the jukebox. 'Fred C. Dobbs had been, like Ben Frank's, a late-night hip-beat hangout on the Strip,' recalled actor Richard Blackburn. 'Then, practically overnight, all the bohemians in their cord coats with the big pockets and the knit-ties were suddenly pushed aside by the incoming hippies.'

Although the real in-crowd tended to see bands on weekdays, the Strip was none the less an awesome sight at weekends. Carl Gottlieb recalls that on a Friday or Saturday night it could take as long as four hours to navigate the mile and a half from Beverly Hills city line to Schwab's. The sidewalks were jam-packed with girls in boots and bellbottoms, and with boys in tunics and white Levi's. The girls all looked like Cher, and the boys like Brian Jones. 'It was a little like the Village on a Saturday night, a total love scene,' says Henry Diltz, whose Modern Folk Quartet had – like everyone else – 'gone electric' that summer. 'There was a tremendous awakening in the air, and mind-expansion was becoming very important. We started playing places like the Trip and the Action as the MFQ, doing fifteen-minute jams so that the love children could dance around with their eyes like saucers.' As 1965 melted into 1966, acid became more and more prominent on the scene. By February, San Francisco consciousness had penetrated LA to the point where Ken Kesey could stage an acid test near Watts, just two blocks from the motel where Sam Cooke had been killed.

Even folk clubs like the Troubadour and the Ash Grove were adapting to the folk-rock revolution. Doug Weston at the Troub had baulked when the Modern Folk Quartet first turned up at the club carrying amplifiers, but it wasn't long before he was claiming he'd invented the term 'Folk Rock' and billing a new band called the Association as 'America's First Folk-Rock Group'. At the hole-in-the-wall Sea Witch on Sunset, the management ditched folk duo Lyme and Cybelle – one half of which was a very young Warren Zevon – and replaced them with an early version of garage-psych legends the Seeds. Perhaps most radically of all, that bastion of tradition known as the Ash Grove began booking a new electric band called the Rising Sons.

The great should-have-beens of the mid-sixties Los Angeles scene, the Rising Sons were remarkable not simply for being, as many people put it, 'the Rolling Stones to the Byrds' Beatles', but for being an interracial pop group at a time when such a thing was unthinkable in California. Fronted by the giant Taj Mahal, a Harlem boy by way of the folk-blues scene in Cambridge, Massachusetts, the Sons played a raw electric version of country blues which briefly made them the hottest thing in Hollywood. Mahal had come west with fellow folkie Jesse Lee Kincaid in late 1964, hooking up shortly afterwards with bassist Gary Marker, bald-headed jazz drummer Ed Cassidy and Kincaid's guitar prodigy acquaintance Ryland Cooder. The teenage Cooder was already something of a legend on the folk/blues circuit, having been hired by Ed Pearl at the Ash Grove to back Jackie DeShannon, then going through her own folkie phase. As a blues devotee, he was a distinct anomaly at Santa Monica High, where he was still studying in 1963. 'If anybody there even thought about music, they probably thought about surf music,' he recalled. 'They had surfing

The Rising Sons, 'the great should-have-beens of mid-60s LA'. Left to right: Taj Mahal, Ry Cooder, Kevin Kelley, Gary Marker, Jesse Lee Kincaid.

and records and dances and a certain style of clothes, and they were sort of acknowledging that music existed, but I could see it was a low-grade experience for them.' When Taj Mahal started pitching up at the Ash Grove, Cooder instinctively bonded with him. 'He was real raggedy and I was real raggedy, so we went to the Teenage Fair in Hollywood and played Delta blues in the Martin Guitars booth. The Byrds were the big thing at the time, so it was different. And all of a sudden we had a blues band.'

Signed by Columbia at the prompting of Billy James, the Rising Sons were inevitably assigned the red-hot Terry Melcher as their producer. The trouble was, Melcher wasn't too sure what to do with the band. Asking him to repeat the success of the Byrds seemed like a tall order. 'The thing about the Byrds was that they were all going in the same direction,' he recalled. 'Here you had guys who should have been in two different groups. If I had to do it over, I would have found some Beatles-type band and put Kincaid in there, and then had another group with Ry and Taj.'

What actually happened was that Melcher tried covering both bases, with Taj singing rocked-up versions of Blind Willie McTell's 'Statesboro Blues' and Sleepy John Estes' 'If the River was Whiskey' and Jesse Lee Kincaid singing his own poppier songs, such as 'The Girl With Green Eyes' and 'Sunny's Dream'. In desperation, Melcher even turned to the pop fount of Gerry Goffin and Carole King, whose made-for-the-Monkees 'Take A Giant Step' was recorded in March 1966. For the purist Cooder, this was all too much: Mahal was an energetic frontman, and Cooder was already a virtuoso slide guitarist, but even when they played straight blues Ry – ever the perfectionist – didn't think the Sons were up to scratch. He was having a better time with lucrative session work for Melcher's other charges Paul Revere and the Raiders.

'On a good night, the Sons were terrific,' says Barry Hansen, the Ash Grove habitué who co-arranged 'Take a Giant Step'. 'They could also be sloppy and disorganized, because they weren't the most compatible of groups personally and it would show. I think it would be generally agreed that they never quite equalled the sum of their parts, and certainly the existing recordings lack the dynamics they had live. Also, once they'd played together for a few months, they never really progressed beyond the level they'd established.' Ed Cassidy, who'd left the band before the first Columbia sessions because he'd damaged his wrist, felt the Rising Sons had 'lost a lot of what I'd seen in it at the beginning, which was a very progressive blues group that was into a lot of different trips'. When the smoke had cleared, all the band had left to their name was a single comprising Skip James' 'Devil's Got My Woman' and the Rev. Gary Davis's 'Candy Man'. 'It's really hard to say what the Rising Sons achieved, other than to set a kind of standard,' says David Anderle, head of A&M's West Coast A&R department. 'The problem was that they were one album short of being Love. But they were strong enough and visual enough that a lot of people got some heat off them.'

Among the folkies flocking into Los Angeles as the Rising Sons had their fifteen minutes of in-crowd glory was a quartet of Greenwich Village refugees led by John Phillips, who'd first recorded with a Four Freshmen-esque group called the Smoothies back in 1960. The tall, gaunt Phillips was married to Holly Michelle Gilliam, a radiant vision of Californian loveliness who'd lured him away from his first wife and children. They'd met Denny Doherty on the New York Hootenanny circuit in the fall of 1963 and a year later were singing with him and Cass Elliot (née Naomi Cohen), an obese Jewish girl from Baltimore with a booming contralto voice legendary in Village folk circles. On acid, appropriately, the foursome had first hung out together in a run-down Lower East Side crashpad, singing songs Phillips had written over the course of several months. One of them was 'California Dreamin'', partly an expression of his wife's yearning for home as she sat in freezing Manhattan – a homesickness made worse by the fact that some of the group's closest friends had already split for California.

After two months of playing together and getting stoned on the Virgin Island of St Thomas, the quartet returned to the America of 'Mr Tambourine Man', 'Eve of Destruction' and the Lovin' Spoonful's 'Do You Believe in Magic?'. These were records by the very friends who'd quit New York: McGuire and McGuinn, Clark and Crosby. Denny and Cass had even sung in the Mugwumps with John Sebastian and Zal Yanofsky of the Spoonful. The message was clear: it was time to stop dreaming about California and get out there.

In August 1965 Cass flew west while the others drove cross-country with 'Tambourine Man' and 'Eve of Destruction' buzzing from their tinny car radio. When they arrived they moved into the Landmark Hotel on Franklin Avenue and quickly set to work exploiting their connections. Kim Fowley, who has claimed a piece of everything in his time, says he urged Gene Norman of GNP-Crescendo to sign the group, but Norman 'didn't want to shell out $250 a month or some pathetic sum'. Instead, Fowley referred them to his old friend Nik Venet, who auditioned the quartet at his North Canyon View Drive house up in Laurel Canyon. At that point, Fowley claims, an 'interception' occurred whereby Barry McGuire – asked by the group to score them some grass – steered them over to Western Recorders to see Lou Adler. 'The upshot,' says Fowley, 'was that they sang for Lou, and Lou did a deal with them right there and then for $3,000. See, when Lou heard my name in connection with that group, he couldn't stand it any more. When he and Herb Alpert covered me with the Dante and the Evergreens version of "Alley-Oop", we kicked their ass on the charts, so this was his revenge.'

Cut from the frozen-dinners-and-porn-mags scenario of the Fowley lair off Hollywood Boulevard to the immaculate Malibu offices of Lou Adler, high above the glittering Pacific. 'Kim Fowley claims to have discovered every group and every person in Los Angeles, including me,'

Adler smiles indulgently. 'I once made him open his briefcase and there was nothing in it, which about sums him up. He *was* outrageous and he *was* a great character — you could walk into the Whisky a Go Go and out of the crowd of dancers would emerge this tall string-bean of a guy, jumping up and down. But some of the stuff he comes up with! I mean, I never felt the competition, despite "Alley Oop".'

The truth is, it was just another case of Lou Adler having his finger firmly on the pulse of the times and responding to the glorious four-part sound and Hollywood hippie vision of the group who dubbed themselves the Mamas and the Papas. 'I really *couldn't* believe my eyes and ears when McGuire brought me the Mamas,' he says, referring to the title of their first album. 'They had just come down off about eighty acid trips, they were funky and dirty and grizzly, and yet they sang like absolute angels.'

Greenwich Village refugees the Mamas and the Papas gaze out across the promised pop land of California. Clockwise from left: John Phillips, Denny Doherty, Cass Elliot, Michelle Phillips.

Taking their name from Hell's Angels terminology, the quartet were quickly promoted from being background singers on Barry McGuire's second album to being Dunhill artists in their own right. Bringing in super-engineer Bones Howe, arranger Gene Page, and a band comprising Glen Campbell, Joe Osborn, Larry Knechtel, and the ubiquitous Hal Blaine, Adler cut the classic singles 'California Dreamin'' and 'Monday, Monday', along with the rest of *If You Can Believe Your Eyes and Ears.* When 'California Dreamin'' made the Top 5 in February 1966, LA pop had reached its zenith. The record was a love song to the West Coast, a joyous cascade of harmonies rounded off by a sort of funky-MOR flute solo by jazz veteran Bud Shank. With Phillips' lyric trumpeting the new golden dawn of California, summoning the youth of America in their beads and bells, the group became LA royalty.

Behind their image, with its central juxtaposition of the enormous Cass Elliott and the California-cute Michelle Phillips, lay all kinds of messy complications. An affair began between Michelle and Denny, for whom Cass lusted; when it was over, Denny and John raised bachelor hell on Woods Drive while Michelle lived alone on Lookout Mountain Road. By May, when the group was at No. 1 with 'Monday, Monday', Michelle was seeing Gene Clark of the Byrds, drugs were being consumed in prodigious quantities, and hundreds of dollars were being frittered away on the latest hippie regalia. Cass, embraced by pop America's freaks as their very own Earth Mother, bought a Porsche she couldn't fit into. From Lower East Side squalor to Laurel Canyon shenanigans in less than a year was upward mobility with a vengeance.

Once again, Lou Adler was able to have his cake and eat it. It was a testament to his opportunistic savvy that the Mamas and the Papas were at once hip and hugely successful, autonomous and studio-honed – a bunch of dopers who sold records to America's suburban squares. This was Hollywood to a T. But the real secret of Dunhill's success was that Adler was canny enough to hover on the margins of pop's street life, watching and digesting the changes on the Sunset Strip. In contrast, a producer like Phil Spector was almost as threatened by the post-Beatles pop scene as the Dick Clarks of the entertainment industry.

VI

1964 hadn't, in any case, been a good year for Phil Spector. None of the Ronettes' follow-ups to 'Be My Baby' had so much as made the Top 20: not even the mighty Mann/Weil-composed 'Walking in the Rain', a Ronnie wail-a-thon complete with full thunderstorm effects. The fear that the maestro was losing his touch, or that America had lost its appetite for

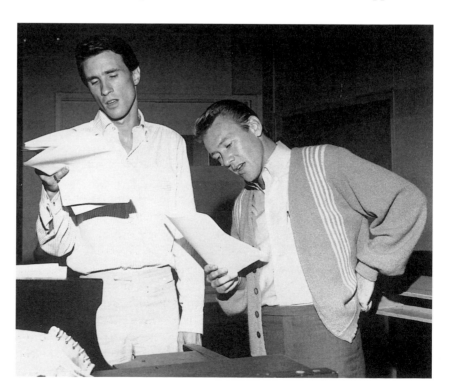

Bill Medley (left) and Bobby Hatfield: the Righteous Brothers.

the epic scale of his 'teen symphonies', was creeping in. Just then an unlikely blue-eyed soul duo came to Spector's rescue.

Bill Medley and Bobby Hatfield were R&B-loving strangers in a strange land – the white Republican stronghold of Orange County. (It was black sailors at the El Toro marine base who'd dubbed them 'the righteous brothers'.) Spector loved their pseudo-black voices and figured he could use them to take pop back to the R&B roots he loved. Which made it doubly ironic that after he signed the duo in October 1964, he amassed his biggest wall-of-sound pop army to date for their first session at Gold Star.

Desperate for a hit, Spector flew Barry Mann and Cynthia Weil out to Hollywood and put them up at the Chateau Marmont, where a piano had been specially installed for their use. Inspired by the Four Tops' 'Baby, I Need Your Loving', a Top 20 hit that summer, the husband-and-wife team came up with an almost grief-stricken song about the slow death of a love affair. Medley and Hatfield were unconvinced when they came by the hotel to hear Mann and Spector intoning 'You've Lost that Lovin' Feelin'' in their thin, reedy voices. To Medley's ears, it sounded like a song for the Everly Brothers, but lowered to his baritone range it came to life as an orgasmic howl of pain.

With Jack Nitzsche hard at work on the *TAMI Show*, Spector brought in Gene Page to arrange the date. Also unavailable were Hal Blaine and his 'monster drum kit', so Earl Palmer came in to power the formidable rhythm section. To give some indication of the scale of the production, there were no fewer than three bass guitars on the session, with jazz guitarist Barney Kessel coming in on a six-string instrument alongside Ray Pohlman and Carol Kaye. For Kessel, who'd encountered Spector as a teenager, the sound was 'swimming around like it was all down a well', yet he couldn't help but feel impressed watching Phil, resplendent in waistcoat and watchchain, at the eye of this hurricane of passion. With its swelling strings and vast, cathedral-like choir, 'Lovin' Feelin'' was 3' 50" of heartstopping *sturm und drang*, and it deservedly rose to No. 1 at the very end of 1964. Against the grain of Beatles-style pop, Phil had defiantly reasserted his claim to pop's throne.

Remarkably, Spector was able to continue in this vein with the Righteous Brothers for the whole of 1965, producing further epics of MOR-pop in the form not only of Goffin and King's 'Lovin' Feelin'' rehash 'Just Once in My Life', but of such Tin Pan Alley standards as 'Unchained Melody', 'Ebb Tide', and 'The White Cliffs of Dover'. These were superlush, dizzyingly *kitsch* – all crashing drums and swirling violins. Adult counterparts to his Girl Group classics, they were a logical progression from 'Lovin' Feelin'', anticipating the sort of OTT arrangements Jimmy Webb would later write for Richard Harris and even Frank Sinatra's 1966 No. 1 hit 'Strangers in the Night'. They also coincided with a pronounced increase in Spector's megalomania, which at times seemed to verge on

madness. By the fall of 1965, when he not only set up Phil Spector
Productions in a penthouse at 9130 Sunset but bought his very own
Beverly Hills version of Xanadu at 1200 La Collina Drive, he was assuming
the airs of a Hollywood sultan, tooling around town in a $100,000 Rolls-
Royce with a retinue of blondes and bodyguards.

For guitarist Howard Roberts, who'd given him guitar lessons back in
the fifties, Phil Spector quickly 'slipped into that Never-Never land of
Hollywood success and really strange weirdness' – an impression, of
course, that Spector was himself only too happy to encourage. A famous
Tom Wolfe article, 'The First Tycoon of Teen', had appeared in the New
York *Herald Tribune* in February, giving America the lowdown on this
neurotic, dandyish Mozart of the pop world, with his terror of flying and
his contempt for the 'cigar-chewing fatties' who controlled the record
industry. For Ronnie Spector, Phil 'became a replica of what he read
about himself' in such pieces. If they proclaimed him a genius, she said
in 1991, he became a genius; if they said he was a *mad* genius, that was
what he became.

Spector became increasingly obsessive as 1965 drew to a close. There
were the repeated viewings of Welles' *Citizen Kane* which Ronnie had to
sit through, as well as the sound of Wagner's 'Ride of the Valkyries'
booming through the house. Often Spector would spend hours simply
playing pinball, already a semi-recluse. 'In New York, I could always get
him out,' recalled Vinnie Poncia, a Philles staff writer and aide-de-camp.
'In LA, I was losing him.' Then there was Lenny Bruce, the brilliant junkie
comic with whom Phil in some way seemed to identify, and whom he
adopted as his principal cause and crusade that year. Spector's records
meant *zilch* to Bruce, but the semi-ostracized legend knew a good squeeze
when he saw one, especially when the producer offered to release an
album on Philles and finance a residency at a little theatre called the Music
Box. Spector refused to admit that Lenny was washed up, spitting poison
at everyone who'd turned away from the comedian, but the shows were
catastrophically bad. For Bruce had lost the plot completely, spending his
last months scuffling for smack and poring over endless legal briefs. In
August 1966, he overdosed and died in a house on Sunset Plaza Drive,
just above the Strip.

Not long after Bruce's death, stories started filtering out that Spector
had paid an LAPD detective $5,000 for pictures of his friend with the
needle still dangling from his arm. Phil claimed he'd bought the pictures
to prevent them falling into other hands, but people close to him suspected
a more morbid interest. 'There was a time when I wanted to believe him,'
said Danny Davis, the business manager of Phil Spector Productions. 'I
guess I still try to cling to it.'

Spector's various obsessions were really just distractions from the
central fact, which was that his quasi-Wagnerian conception of pop was
slowly going out of style. Not even four Top 10 hits by the Righteous

Lenny Bruce, Spector's great cause in the months before the comedian's death in August 1966.

Brothers could mask the fact that by this stage Philles Records *was* the Righteous Brothers, or that what was really happening out there in Popland was the Beatles and the Byrds. 'He'd say, "That's what we gotta do, we gotta get back to just guitars",' recalled Vinnie Poncia. 'Yet he'd be contradicting that all the time, with his own sound going through the roof. That was the only identity he had left.' The trouble with self-contained groups, of course, was that working with them entailed a major reduction in his control over a record. Although he went to see both the Lovin' Spoonful and the Young Rascals with a view to signing them, he hated what they represented.

In the fall of 1965, Spector actually found a group for Philles. 'We'd heard that Spector was looking for a folk-rock band,' says Henry Diltz of the Modern Folk Quartet. 'The word was that he really wanted the Lovin' Spoonful, but he couldn't get them. So he came down to see us instead.' So close did Spector come to the 'band' ethos with the MFQ that he even jumped onstage at the Trip with a twelve-string guitar and sang 'Spanish Harlem' with them. But what appealed to Phil about the group was their very malleability: there weren't any John Sebastians in the lineup, and that was just the way he wanted it. And when it came to recording, the pre-production for the sessions seemed even more elaborate than the preparation for 'You've Lost that Lovin' Feelin''.

'We started going up to Spector's house every day,' recalls Diltz. 'We'd spend two hours waiting around before he even appeared, and there were all these karate-type bodyguards hanging around. Eventually he'd appear at the top of the stairs and say, "Hi, guys!" He'd sit there with a twelve-string and we'd sing all kinds of songs. This went on for weeks.' Finally, Spector decided on a song by a young Brooklyn-born songwriter called Harry Nilsson, who worked nights in the computer processing department of a bank in the Valley and hawked his songs around the Hollywood publishing companies by day. Recorded at Gold Star in October, 'This Could Be the Night' was pure wall-of-sound Beach Boys, light years from the sound Terry Melcher was getting with the Byrds.

The event which more than any other seemed to tip Phil over the edge was the lawsuit brought against him by the Righteous Brothers during the winter of 1965–6. By January, Bill Medley and Bobby Hatfield had extricated themselves from Philles' licensing deal with Moonglow Records and signed to Verve. The bitterest blow was yet to come: in March, the Brothers were at No. 1 for three weeks with a Mann/Weil-composed simulation of the Wall of Sound called '(You're My) Soul and Inspiration'. Spector almost lost his mind.

The halcyon days of the Wrecking Crew were now well and truly over. 'The enthusiasm was gone,' recalled Jack Nitzsche. 'We'd done it so many times, and now the musicians were changing. They didn't wanna work overtime for a deal.' Nor was it just the musicians who'd changed. Radio was a completely new ballgame since the Bill Drake revolution at KHJ, and Spector could often be heard fulminating against the new breed of DJ. He was also stewing in resentments against his peers. As late as 1969, in an interview with *Rolling Stone*, he was telling Jan Wenner that 'I have a style – as opposed to Lou Adler or any of the other record producers who follow the artist's style.' As if living out his very own version of Billy Wilder's *Sunset Boulevard*, Phil was really doing a turn as Norma Desmond: 'It was the *pictures* that got small!'

As with Norma Desmond, there was one last heroic performance Spector had to give, and it was a performance almost doomed to fail. Determined to top 'You've Lost that Lovin' Feelin''', he forgot all about the Modern Folk Quartet and instead began pursuing Tina Turner, whose raw, gasping voice he loved. After seeing the Ike and Tina Turner Revue at the Galaxy on Sunset, he booked them for a *TAMI Show*-style TV special called *The Big TNT Show*, filmed at the Moulin Rouge theatre in November 1965. In December, he called the newly divorced Jeff Barry and Ellie Greenwich in New York and begged them to overlook their differences long enough to write him an epic pop-soul anthem.

The next step was to offer Bob Krasnow of Warners subsidiary Loma $25,000 for Ike and Tina Turner, on the condition that Ike, already a scary motherfucker with a fondness for drugs and guns, stayed away from the sessions. Ike was far from happy about this, but he was in no position to protest: the Turners hadn't had a hit record to speak of in nearly four years. With that proviso granted, Spector had the song and the voice. Now it was simply a question of assembling 'the old team'. Jack Nitzsche agreed to write the ultimate Wall of Sound arrangement, and out of the woodwork came the familiar faces of Barney Kessel, Jimmy Bond, Ray Pohlman, Harold Battiste, Larry Knechtel, Plas Johnson and Earl Palmer, along with no fewer than twenty backing singers.

Tina, who'd already been coached through the titanic 'River Deep, Mountain High' for two hours a day over a period of two weeks, was thoroughly bewildered when she entered Gold Star studios on the evening of 7 March 1966. By the end of the night, all but drowned by the operatic fury of the instrumentation, she was standing at her mike in a bra, dripping with sweat and screaming the Barry/Greenwich lines about puppies and rag dolls till she could scarcely breathe. 'Even when she was putting on a scratch vocal,' recalled Jack Nitzsche, 'she was so into it she was holding her crotch on the high notes.' Rodney Bingenheimer, who brought Brian Wilson along to the session, says Nitzsche and Spector were 'like co-pilots of the Concorde' as they guided Tina through her vocal. 'They were wearing dark glasses and puff-sleeve shirts, and Phil was screaming like a madman the whole time.'

For Bob Krasnow, it was 'like the whole room exploded' that night. And surely, for anyone who plays the record today, it's still as if the whole room is exploding. Never has such a volcanic din been harnessed in the cause of pop, and never will it be so harnessed again. A stampeding monster of *liebestod* which manages to be at once fantastically overblown and irresistibly funky, 'River Deep' is the sound of a small, asthmatic tyrant overreaching himself to the point of insanity. If it isn't the greatest pop record of all time, I don't know what the hell is.

The failure of 'River Deep, Mountain High', which only reached No. 88 on the American singles chart, remains a tragedy: as a moment of hubris, it is almost unparalleled in pop history. (In England, 'River Deep' climbed all the way to No. 3, with no little thanks to the efforts of Decca promo man Tony Hall. 'We can only assume that England is more appreciative of talent and exciting music than the US,' Spector told one interviewer.) Jerry Wexler, in his memoir, *Rhythm and the Blues*, construes it as '*the* overrated trauma of Western pop', but then Wexler was just one of the many record industry people who had it in for Spector — and who felt he *had it coming to him*. Not least among this group were several important DJs whom Spector had snubbed over the preceding year, and who took particular pleasure in dismissing the record as a kind of unfathomable din.

This view had its adherents even *within* the Spector camp. For Jeff Barry, for example, the record summed up the auteurist conceit behind most of Spector's work. 'To me, what he is saying is: "It's not the *song* . . . just listen to those *strings* . . . it's *me* . . . listen to that *bass* sound!" ' Barry felt that Spector and Nitzsche had effectively buried the song with their arrangement and production. My own feeling is that Spector knew he was going too far with 'River Deep', that he knew the record *exceeded the bounds of sonic acceptability*. He knew it was the last heroic gasp of his Wall of Sound, and that its failure would condemn him to eternal ignominy. No matter that it was too black for pop radio, or too white for the new soul stations; it was *too much*, period. And now, with an irony Spector will probably never appreciate, its commercial failure is part of its enduring legend.

A month after the 'River Deep' session, Spector went into United Studios to record the long-suffering Ronnie — still not his wife, despite being a virtual prisoner in the house on La Collina Drive — on a bleak, cavernous-sounding song called 'I Wish I Never Saw the Sunshine'. Although it only saw the light of day on the *Back to Mono* box set, this Barry/Greenwich song — a dark counterpoint to the ecstatic 'River Deep' — seemed to speak for the *ennui* Spector now felt in LA. 'The one thing I never understood about Phil,' Ronnie Spector once said, 'is how a man who loved California as much as he did could be so afraid of the sun.' Following the failure of 'River Deep, Mountain High', Spector's personal Xanadu became a sunless, sepulchral place — a refuge from the glare of the pop world which had so cruelly betrayed him. Late in 1967, Elliot Ingber saw Spector sitting alone in Canter's Deli. 'It was like he was in a past life,' Ingber recalled twenty years later, 'but it was like no life.'

The Beach Boys at Pacific Ocean Park in 1965. Brian (left) was now fighting a rearguard action against the other members.

VII

'Like me,' Brian Wilson noted in *Wouldn't It Be Nice*, 'the moment Phil Spector was no longer capable [of making the world bend to him], he bowed out of the music scene.' The saga of 'River Deep, Mountain High' must have produced mixed feelings in Wilson: on the one hand, Spector was a hero, but on the other he was a rival. More to the point, both men were responding to the shock of the Beatles and the British Invasion, trying to figure out which way to go next.

1964 was a curious year for Wilson. Although the Beach Boys had four Top 10 hits – with 'Fun, Fun, Fun', the No. 1 'I Get Around', 'Dance, Dance, Dance' and 'When I Grow Up (To Be a Man)' – it must have concerned Brian that 'Don't Worry, Baby', his one real stylistic advance and a taster for the exquisite ballads of *Pet Sounds*, peaked at No. 24. By the fall of that year, he knew he was fighting a kind of rearguard action against everything the Beach Boys stood for: the *All Summer Long* side of life embodied by devil-may-care Dennis. When the group toured Europe, Brian holed up in hotel rooms with food and booze while Dennis and Mike Love sought out the local brothels. In December, with dread in his heart and 'You've Lost that Lovin' Feelin'' in his head, he suffered a nervous breakdown on a flight to Houston and flew back to LA.

Wilson's retreat from the world really began at that point, as did his obsession with bettering the Beatles. For Brian, the rise of the Liverpudlians was experienced as 'an eclipse', especially since the two groups recorded for the same label. 'I must create something to bring me up on top,' he told Earl Leaf. An important presence in his life at this time was that of William Morris agent Loren Schwartz, who was busy discovering psychedelics and related artefacts in his apartment on Harper Avenue, not far from Brian's new duplex on Gardner Street. Without further ado, Brian tuned in and turned on – the dropping out came later. Through Schwartz he not only met such Sunset Strip luminaries as the Byrds and Van Dyke Parks but was introduced to the sacred texts of Hollywood hippiedom: Kahlil Gibran, Hesse, Saint-Exupéry.

'Pot made music grow in my head,' Brian claimed later, and the evidence can be heard in the comparatively complex productions of tracks such as 'Please Let Me Wonder', 'In the Back of My Mind', and 'She Knows Me Too Well'. When the other Beach Boys returned from their winter tour, Mike Love declared that these new songs 'fucked with the formula' – an early indication of the trouble which lay ahead. Love was happier with 'California Girls', despite the fact that it was written while Brian was coming down from his first acid trip. The song was actually pretty ordinary, but it was shot through with the kind of harmonies and production flourishes which would grace *Pet Sounds*. Recorded in April 1965 with the old Wrecking Crew team of Blaine, Pohlman, Campbell, Kaye and Russell, it was also the first session to feature Bruce Johnston, the boyish-looking Beverly Hills brat who had run around with Kim Fowley in high school and then teamed up with Terry Melcher to make surfing records.

'California Girls' encapsulated the Californian summer of '65, yet even as he was producing it Brian was dreaming of music that was altogether less crass – the Beatle-esque 'Girl, Don't Tell Me', for instance, or the nod to Burt Bacharach that was 'Let Him Run Wild', both featuring on the June album release *Summer Days (and Summer Nights!!)*. The 'Fun, Fun, Fun' side of the Beach Boys might temporarily have won out with the dreadful soda-pop-flavoured follow-up *Beach Boys' Party!*, but the real Brian Wilson was contained in the grooves of that beguiling flop single 'The Little Girl I Once Knew'.

Another Beach Boys tour at the end of 1965 left Brian free to dream up his most ambitious music yet. Ensconced in a cork-lined 'piano laboratory' in his new Beverly Hills house on Laurel Way – all shag-pile, wind chimes and lava lights – his head was full of acid flashbacks and the Beatles' new *Rubber Soul* album. Out of this introspection came the stray fragments of melody he called 'feels', germs of songs such as 'You Still Believe in Me' and 'I Just Wasn't Made for These Times', as well as of those marvellous muzak-style instrumentals 'Pet Sounds' and 'Let's Go Away for Awhile'. Brian had already envisaged 'a grand, Spector-like production' for these songs while he was tripping. He wanted to create a new 'spiritual music' which would transcend the limitations of Top 40 pop and be filled with 'the presence of God'.

Brian's only problem in realizing his dreams was his lack of lyrics. With Mike Love away on tour, the brooding, Beethoven-like genius (he was deaf in one ear) needed someone to verbalize the strange new feelings latent in his melodies. Through Loren Schwartz he met a jingle writer named Tony Asher, who was unimpressed by what he called 'Brian's marshmallow mysticism' but entranced by the beauty of the compositions. Together, the two men wrote virtually the whole *Pet Sounds* album through the late winter and early spring of 1966: breathtaking masterpieces such as 'God Only Knows', 'Caroline, No', and 'Don't Talk (Put Your Head on My Shoulder)'.

Asher found Wilson impossible, a man who lay in bed till noon and was prone to violent mood swings, but the end result more than justified all the torment. By the time Brian was directing the sessions at Western Recorders, *Pet Sounds* was a solo album in all but name. None of the other Beach Boys played so much as a note on the record, and in some cases had their harmonies wiped and replaced by Brian, which led Mike Love to castigate the songs as 'ego music'. Only Dennis and Bruce Johnston supported Brian's innovations, responding to the magical sonic world he was creating with the old Wrecking Crew team. They alone understood that he was taking pop into uncharted territory, not merely expanding its language but giving it an entirely new range of textures.

As it turned out, Capitol Records were as worried as Mike Love that Brian was 'fucking with the formula'. When 'Caroline, No' appeared as a Brian Wilson solo single in March and – to Love's secret delight – flopped, their response was to rush-release the dire 'Sloop John B', which leaped to No. 3 before its incongruous inclusion on *Pet Sounds*. In exactly the same way, they panicked over *Pet Sounds* itself and almost killed the album by issuing the greatest hits collection *The Best of the Beach Boys*. *Pet Sounds*, it must be said, was hardly a disaster on the scale of 'River Deep, Mountain High'. With two hit singles in 'Sloop John B' and 'Wouldn't It be Nice', the album did reach No. 10, staying in the Top 40 for twenty-one weeks. In any case, Brian's pop martyrdom was to some extent alleviated by the efforts of Bruce Johnston, who suggested hiring Derek Taylor to do the publicity for *Pet Sounds*. Cyril Maitland, an English photographer who worked for Taylor in LA, remembers sitting with him in the Gaiety Delicatessen across the street from 9000 Sunset when the famous 'Brian Wilson is a Genius' campaign was concocted. Within a matter of weeks – helped along by Kim Fowley, who was in London at the time – *Pet Sounds* had become a *cause célèbre* in Britain, inspiring the Beatles to write 'Here, There, and Everywhere' and alerting numerous other songwriters to the fact that pop had taken another giant step forward.

VIII

There was dark irony in the fact that the Beach Boys' 'California Girls' – an implicitly Aryan anthem described by Brian Wilson himself as 'a song of joy, exultation in nature and sunshine ... a hymn of youth' – was crackling from transistor radios just as a long 'winter of discontent' in South Central Los Angeles was reaching its violent climax.

'I didn't know where Watts was and none of my friends ever went there,' wrote Ian Whitcomb years later. 'Nor did I associate its black residents with the ebony heroes who sang R&B.' Whitcomb's disarming honesty said everything about the gulf between black and white LA in 1965, and more pointedly about the gulf between black and white music in the city. For the riots, which lasted six days from 11 to 16 August and involved at least 75,000 people, appeared to white Angelenos to be taking place in another country, not simply a different neighbourhood. 'Watts just declared war on the city of Los Angeles,' the jazz pianist Hampton Hawes told his wife when he came home on Wednesday 11th. Yet the city of Los Angeles barely registered the impact. With the National Guard swarming in to contain the spontaneous eruption of rage and keep it inside the ghetto, the closest whites came to the looting and pillaging around 103rd Street or Imperial Highway was seeing it on their TV screens.

Still, there were some white Angelenos who couldn't wilfully blind themselves to the meaning of 'the rebellion', as blacks preferred to call it. For Randy Newman, still a comparatively lowly hack at Metric Music, the events of August 1965 were 'the biggest thing that happened, the biggest shock to me and the biggest inequity in this country ... I always felt that the race situation was worse here than anywhere'. Perhaps the most astute white response to the Watts events came nearly a year later in an article by novelist Thomas Pynchon, who understood not only that Watts was 'a country which lies, psychologically, uncounted miles further than most whites seem at present willing to travel', but that the whole LA 'scene' was 'basically a white scene ... from the giant aerospace firms that flourish or retrench at the whims of Robert McNamara to the "action" everybody mills along the Strip on weekends looking for, unaware that they and their search, which usually ends unfulfilled, are the only action in town'. Pynchon, like Newman, perceived that Watts was 'a pocket of bitter reality' within the white fantasia of pop Los Angeles. Other white commentators, predictably, saw the rebellion as the fulfilment of Nathanael West's prophetic 'burning city' image in *The Day of the Locust*. 'For days, one could drive the Harbor Freeway and see the city on fire,' noted Joan Didion, 'just as we had always known it would be in the end.'

'Burn, baby, burn!' hollered KGFJ jockey the Magnificent Montague during that hot August week. 'Burn, Hollywood, burn!' hollered the

A rare sighting of black Angelenos on the Strip, in town for a Trip showcase by Billy Preston.

prescient Public Enemy not long before the 'riots' of 1992. Little had changed in the sociography of Los Angeles in the twenty-seven years which separated the two events. If the violence of 1992 came a little closer to white suburbia, South Central LA was still 'a different country', one in which African-Americans – watched by whites on TV – were still being contained by a militarized police force. But then Los Angeles was never designed to include people who didn't fit the Anglo-Saxon vision of its founding fathers, and in the 'Fortress LA' of the nineties the possibility of that inclusion seems ever more remote. Only the building of the city's Metro rail system seems to offer hope of connecting up the different worlds, provided that the Haves can occasionally be persuaded to leave the hermetic security of their automobiles and join the Have-Nots on the trains.

'A lot of black people have come out of LA and done very well for themselves, including me,' says crime novelist Walter Mosley. 'Yet that wall of racism has gotten more and more oppressive, and there are people I grew up with in Watts whose lives have really been decimated.'

So much for the bright, jingle-jangle morning of California pop.

The Sunset Strip, seen in the distance from Beverly Boulevard.

4 *Maybe the People Would Be the Times, or Between Doheny and La Cienega*

This town makes no demands on you, and offers you everything good. It's all here – the best facilities and the best climate.

Derek Taylor, 1967

The vibe was beautiful. The music was fantastic. To me, that was the purest, most beautiful moment of the whole sixties trip. It seemed like everything had come to that moment. And if that could have continued, it really would have been Camelot.

Dennis Hopper on the Monterey Pop Festival

I

One of the few Los Angeles bands to express any sort of disgust over the city's treatment of blacks were the Mothers of Invention, the freaky pranksters led by Frank Zappa. Their unprecedented clarion call of a double-album debut *Freak Out!* (1966) featured a track called 'Trouble Every Day', which had been regularly performed at the Whisky and the Action as 'The Watts Riot Song'. In his sleevenotes to the record, Zappa wrote that the song reflected 'how I feel about social unrest in general and the Watts situation in particular', adding that he'd 'shopped it briefly all over Hollywood but no one would touch it...'

At a time when the likes of Sonny and Cher were supposedly the very essence of Strip hip, Zappa's Mothers were so far out that people virtually dismissed them as a joke. The band didn't key in to the world of cool youth, nor apparently did they aspire to any form of pop success. 'The Mothers were considered weird,' recalls Danny Hutton, briefly an MGM labelmate of the band's. 'They were almost like *pachuco* guys, a low-rider greaser band, rather than Sunset Strip types.' To Denny Bruce, who played drums in the band's very first lineup, they were refreshing 'for the very reason that they didn't want to be the Beatles or the Stones or the Yardbirds'. Certainly there was little chance anyone would mistake the band for prospective objects of teen lust: if they weren't the first *positively ugly* group in pop, they were definitely – in Zappa's dry phrase – 'not as glandular as most of the rock'n'roll bands'.

The young Frank Zappa drums with his 'desert R&B band' the Blackouts. Left to right: *Dwight Bement, Ernie Thomas, Terry Wimberly, John Franklin, Zappa, Wayne Lyles* (foreground).

In fact, it was almost as a kind of 'low-rider greaser band' that the Mothers had started life. Playing a Pomona bar called the Broadside in the summer of 1964, the then Soul Giants replaced their guitarist with Zappa, only to find the goatee-bearded geek taking them off on an avant-garde tangent that promptly had sax player Davey Coronado jumping ship. Zappa could already boast a minor track record in the pop netherworld of southern California, having freelance-produced surf and neo-doowop sides for Del-Fi and Original Sound in his own tiny studio in Cucamonga. But his ambitions now stretched a good deal further than that. As deeply immersed in the work of composer Edgar Varèse as in the recordings of, say, the Penguins or Johnny 'Guitar' Watson, Zappa saw the Soul Giants, a.k.a. Captain Glasspack & His Magic Mufflers, a.k.a. the Mothers (comprising veteran bar-band singer Ray Collins, 'asthmatic Pachuco' bassist Roy Estrada and Texan Cherokee drummer Jimmy Carl Black), as his ideal vehicle for a new synthesis of satire, theatre and musical experiment.

By the summer of 1965, Zappa was living in a dingy two-room apartment in Echo Park, working part-time at Wallichs' Music City record store and writing more than a few of the songs that would surface on *Freak Out!*: 'Hungry Freaks, Daddy', 'Who Are the Brain Police?', and of course 'The Watts Riot Song'. 'About 50 per cent of the songs were concerned with the events of 1965,' he later said. 'In Los Angeles at that time, in the kiddie community I was hanging out in, they were all getting into acid very heavily, and you had people seeing God and flaking out all over the place. You had plenty of that, yet meanwhile there was all that racial tension building up in Watts.'

No longer employable on the 'Louie Louie' circuit, the Mothers, reinforced by guitarist Elliot Ingber, began making a pitch instead for the freakster crowd in mondo Hollywood. This instantly brought them into contact with all manner of dropouts and deviants, from Lenny Bruce and the Vito crowd to 'Crazy' Jerry (who dug electric shocks) and 'Wild Man' Larry Fischer (who was said to enjoy sex with prosthetic-fitted mannequins). 'Lenny Bruce was quite normal compared to Jerry and Larry,' recalled Zappa, who recorded the bizarre life stories of these creatures; 'it was sort of colourful in southern California in those days.' Instrumental in building the necessary Sunset Strip buzz around the group were Vito's lieutenant Carl Franzoni, to whom 'Hungry Freaks, Daddy' was dedicated, and Pamela Zarubica, a.k.a. Suzy Creamcheese, in whose Laurel Canyon pad on Kirkwood Drive Zappa promptly installed himself.

The group's situation improved marginally when Herb Cohen, who ran the Unicorn folk club, agreed to co-manage them with artist Mark Cheka. After playing the Action, the Mothers briefly took over from Johnny Rivers as the leading attraction at the Whisky a Go Go. Here Vito's saturnalian revellers gathered nightly to take part in the band's neo-Dadaist shows, invariably joining the Mothers onstage for a Love-In-style finale. 'They were this bohemian bizarro group, and every night they'd go out dancing,' Zappa told *Q*'s Andy Gill in 1989. 'As soon as they arrived they would make things happen, because they were dancing in a way nobody had seen before, screaming and yelling out on the floor and doing all kinds of weird things. They were dressed in a way nobody could believe, and they gave life to everything that was going on.'

It was around this time that a young man from Boyle Heights called David Anderle persuaded MGM Records to make him their West Coast 'house hippie'. Anderle had worked with Jim Dickson during the early days of the Byrds and spent much of his time on or around the Strip. 'LA in those days was about hanging,' he remembers. 'It was about checking out the clubs and ending up at Canter's. There was a lot of scening, a lot of stuff going on in the back booths at the Whisky. I'd seen the Mothers at the Action, and I wrote MGM a letter saying that all the other companies were getting in on the scene here. But I couldn't officially get the Mothers signed, because they scared everyone in New York so much.

The Mothers of Invention in LA, 1966. Left to right: Roy Estrada, Frank Zappa, Ray Collins, Jimmy Carl Black, Elliot Ingber.

Nobody could figure out what the hell this music was about or what Frank was about.'

Fortunately for the band, MGM/Verve producer Tom Wilson came to town that fall to work with the Animals. 'Herb Cohen dragged Tom away from a girl he had sitting on his lap at a club down the street from the Whisky,' recalled Zappa. 'We have to be appreciative of Tom. He's passed away now, but he was visionary.' A black Harvard graduate who'd quit Columbia after producing Bob Dylan's *Bringing It All Back Home* (and who went on to oversee the first two Velvet Underground albums), Wilson was hip enough to understand what Zappa was doing – and wily enough to sell the group to MGM's New York honchos as a 'blues' band. When he returned to LA in November, the first Mothers sessions commenced at the TTG studios on Sunset at Highland, complete with an MGM accountant vainly attempting to keep costs down. Nine months and nearly $25,000 later – an unheard-of sum for the time – *Freak Out!* was unleashed on the streets of Los Angeles. The group, re-christened 'out of necessity' (or at the behest of MGM), was now known as the Mothers of Invention.

Much of the satire on *Freak Out!* sounds tame and even a little smug today, but it's still extraordinary to think that music this wild and iconoclastic was being recorded in 1965. From the opening sub-'Satisfaction' riff of 'Hungry Freaks' through the affectionate doo-wop pastiche of 'Go Cry on Somebody Else's Shoulder' to the twelve-and-a-half-minute acid jam that was 'The Return of the Son of Monster Magnet' (featuring everyone from Vito to Kim Fowley), *Freak Out!* blew a lot of minds in the summer of '66.

From the off, Zappa was lampooning his own fellow freaks, finger-pointing the phonies and bandwagon-jumpers and refusing to peddle peace'n'luv clichés. From the off, too, he was pushing the music to new levels of symphonic complexity, using members of the LA Philharmonic to augment the rock instruments. Critics compared the band to New York's Fugs, but the Fugs were satirists first and musicians second, which was never the case with the Mothers. 'The Mothers tended to draw people who were pretty serious about wanting to hear something avant-garde and experimental,' recalls Barry Hansen. 'There were people who painted their bodies, but I wasn't that interested in Vito and his dancers. My friends and I certainly received *Freak Out!* with awe. Only then did we realize the scope of what they could do. I immediately thought, forget the Beatles!'

With hindsight, Zappa's preoccupation with musical discipline could be said to have contained the seeds of his later pomposity. Anxious to avoid the pitfalls of the dropout mentality, he was already exhibiting strong autocratic tendencies. If he was a freak, he was a control freak: the fact that he eschewed the use of drugs was widely remarked upon. It was all very well for Zappa to say that people had been 'fed garbage' like the

Beach Boys' 'Be True to Your School' for too long, but Leslie Fiedler had a point when he wrote in *Freaks* that there was 'something grimly missionary' about Zappa and his manifestos for American youth – 'as if he thought of himself as a kind of Peter the Hermit about to launch a second Children's Crusade'.

To Denny Bruce, however, Zappa was really a beatnik: 'I always thought he was a lot older than people like me. It was sorta hard to tell his age, in any case. But I think he wanted to prove a point, which was that you could be a freak but be disciplined.' For Derek Taylor, Frank was 'quite freaky enough without taking LSD or wearing bells', while Pamela Des Barres saw interesting parallels between Frank and Vito. 'Vito was just like Frank, he never got high either,' she says. 'They were both ringmasters who always wanted to be in control.'

After headlining at such seminal summer events as the Great Underground Arts Masked Ball and Orgy (GUAMBO) in July and the Exposition Hall 'Freak Out' in August, the Mothers returned to TTG studios to record *Absolutely Free*. The album was an even more caustic jab at American *mores* than *Freak Out!*, sending up musical genres along the way and spoofing the denizens of the Sunset Strip in the process. Tracks such as 'Brown Shoes Don't Make It' and 'America Drinks and Goes Home' made it even clearer that Zappa was trying to connect with a substratum of misfits, bypassing touristic hippies to get to what he called 'the cream of the weirdos of each town'. Nor was the music any less ambitious: there were references to Charles Ives on 'Call Any Vegetable' (a gentle poke at the newly Flower Powered Brian Wilson), and to Stravinsky throughout the album.*

'Frank had a vision, and the vision never wavered,' says David Anderle. 'It was as important to him sociologically as it was musically, and yet he was a totally consumed musician. I always felt there was something a little totalitarian about Frank, in the sense that he wanted to create a universe – the universe of Suzy Creamcheese. I was awed by the clarity of the vision and his ability to make it happen, but that was also the thing that made me turn away from it, because it was without warmth.'

II

If *Freak Out!* was a four-sided manifesto of the new music, LA pop was freaking out generally as 1965 turned into 1966. Lysergic acid seemed to be having the same effect on pop as it was having on the state of people's minds, loosening up its structures in the same way that it loosened up the

* Perhaps it was 'Call Any Vegetable' that prompted Tom Nolan in a 1967 issue of the pop magazine *Cheetah* to ask: 'Will the revolution of Brian Wilson have to compete with the revolution of Frank Zappa? Will Los Angeles become the starting place and chief battleground of a confrontation between two lifestyles?'

component parts of identity. 'If in your own mind everything is swimming around, then that's how your music is going to sound,' says Greg Shaw, who coined the phrase 'the revolt against structure' to describe this period. 'That's a large part of why it happened, and why eventually it became so excessive and led back to structure again.'* Late in 1965, four months after they'd dropped acid for the first time (in the company of the Beatles), the Byrds began experimenting with new influences which had been opened up to them by the drug subculture: the free jazz of John Coltrane, for example, and the music of Indian sitarist Ravi Shankar. Jim (now Roger) McGuinn, in particular, was smitten with the new possibilities of rock guitar, emulating the free-form tenor runs of Coltrane's *A Love Supreme* on his famous twelve-string Rickenbacker. The result of this was the first version of 'Eight Miles High' – cut at RCA studios with Dave Hassinger but unreleased for years because of a union infringement – followed by the electrifying shows the Byrds played at the Trip in January 1966.

When the band's *Fifth Dimension* album was released in July – lone wolf Gene Clark having quit the band because of his terror of flying – the band's 'folk rock' survived only in the form of token 'traditional' songs 'Wild Mountain Thyme' and 'John Riley'. McGuinn talked instead of a new 'jet sound' and provided such potent examples of it as a re-recorded 'Eight Miles High', '2–4–2 Fox Trot (The Lear Jet Song)', '5D' (featuring Van Dyke Parks on organ) and the thrillingly trippy 'I See You'. The fact that *Fifth Dimension* seemed to be pulling simultaneously in several other directions – the garage-punk of 'Hey Joe', the instrumental R&B of 'Captain Soul', the protest-rock of Crosby's asinine 'What's Happening?!?' – didn't detract from the fact that the Byrds were taking the cerebral sound of 'Mr Tambourine Man' into a new era.

The Byrds were just one of several groups who covered 'Hey Joe', the song which more than any other summed up the fuzztoned, proto-punk sound of 'garage' rock in 1966. Garage rock was an important strain in the LA pop of this period, especially when bands began fusing the punky energy of the Stones and the Yardbirds with the freaked-out trippiness of the beads'n'bells brigade. The roots of the sound were really in local and national hits by Eastside Chicano bands such as the Premiers, Thee Midniters, and Cannibal and the Headhunters: the Premiers' wild 1964 hit 'Farmer John', for instance, and Thee Midniters' frenzied instrumental 'Whittier Boulevard'. 'Like the surf bands, they all wore white suits and played Fenders,' noted Lester Bangs, who grew up hearing these bands on the radio in a sleepy town outside San Diego. 'But their attitude was *bad*.' The excitement these groups generated when they played East LA's

The Premiers, East LA Chicanos who hit with 'Farmer John' in 1964.

* Lying behind the brave new world of tripping was the quest for the 'unstructured personal consciousness' of Aldous Huxley, who'd first experimented with mescalin in LA back in 1953. It was from his key hallucinogenic text *The Doors of Perception* that an acid-gobbling garage band called Rick and the Ravens took their new name late in 1965.

Golden Gate Theater or Montebello Ballroom translated across the racial divides of the city and fed into the stream of white pop. The impact of 'Farmer John', for example, could be felt as late as 1991, in a savage version by Neil Young and Crazy Horse.

In Hollywood, it must be said, the 'garage' sound of groups such as the Seeds or the Standells was as opportunistic as it was exciting. 'There were great punk records made in LA,' says Greg Shaw, 'but the bands were never able to free themselves from the presence of the industry. There was always one eye on the possibility of making money from this. In Nebraska, the Bleach Boys knew they were never going to be discovered, whereas here you could be the stupidest band in the world playing Bido Lito's and next day you might be touring with the Rolling Stones.'

Undoubtedly the best example of this 'manufactured' punk style were the Standells, whom producer Ed Cobb rescued from the doldrums of cover-band land on the Strip (and occasional appearances on *The Munsters*) and turned into sneering longhair bad boys. With their sub-Stones riffs and bubblegum-punk posturing, the Standells climbed all the way to No. 11 in June 1966 with the classic 'Dirty Water', following it up with the self-explanatory if much less successful 'Sometimes the Good Guys Don't Wear White'. Other notable Standells songs were the cheaply provocative 'Try It' and the neo-folk-rocking 'Have You Ever Spent the Night in Jail?'.

The fact that most of these 'punk' anthems were penned by the straighter-than-straight Ed Cobb, sometime bass singer with the white-buck-shoe Four Preps, didn't seem to bother anybody. 'The group fought me all the way down the line, actually,' says Cobb today. 'I had to record "Dirty Water" three times, because the first couple of times it was absolute dogmeat.' The Standells were really a curious inversion of Paul Revere and the Raiders, who started out in a genuinely punkish vein only to be tamed by Dick Clark. Cobb had a far less contrived act on his hands when he agreed to produce another Capitol signing, San Francisco's extremely Stonesy Chocolate Watch Band. 'The Watch Band was a rough group, a druggy group,' he says. 'I didn't have to write much material for them, I just tried to capture what they were about – which was the most diverse, far-out act I've ever recorded in my life.' A measure of the band's stylistic schizophrenia was that their debut album *No Way Out* (1967) contained R&B and soul covers alongside such spacey psych offerings as 'Gossamer Wings' and 'Dark Side of the Mushroom'.

Almost as exciting as the Chocolate Watch Band – while being almost as ludicrous as the Standells – were the Seeds, a group fronted by the unhinged Richie Marsh, a.k.a. Sky Saxon. Born a Mormon in Salt Lake City, (Little) Richie had tried to make it in the Teen Idol era with sides on tinpot indie labels such as 'Goodbye' and 'They Say' (not to mention 'Do the Swim'), but had reinvented himself as Sky and teamed up with guitarist Jan Savage, keyboard player Daryl Hooper, and drummer Rick Andridge

The Standells: processed bad boys and makers of the mighty 'Dirty Water'.

The Seeds, led by the unhinged Sky Saxon (left).

to form the Seeds. Signed to Gene Norman's GNP-Crescendo label, the band debuted with 'Can't Seem to Make You Mine' but did rather better with the timeless 'Pushin' Too Hard', a Top 40 hit in early 1967. 'Everyone in town had turned down the Seeds, but I liked them,' says the tall, snowy-bearded Gene Norman in his Sunset Boulevard office. 'It wasn't my preferred music, but I could feel the intensity of it. Sky was a mercurial character with a sliver of talent that caught on, and the world seemed to be ready for what he had to say.'

If there was always something of Dick Shawn's Hitler in *The Producers* about Sky, he was none the less possessed of a thrilling Johnny Rotten-esque voice and a nutty kind of conviction. 'Pushin' Too Hard' remains the ultimate leave-us-kids-alone garage anthem. 'He was a nice, stupid guy – what you'd get if Mick Jagger had sex with a donkey,' says Kim Fowley, who produced one of the group's last sessions for Gene Norman. 'He took too many drugs and wandered around with a picture of Jesus Christ as ID.' The legend of Saxon as LA's numero uno acid casualty is certainly one of the reasons why the Seeds have more currency than most of the garage bands from that period. Greg Shaw, however, paints a more complex picture of the guy: 'Sky was always out there, very schizoid, but at the same time he could be quite savvy and calculating. Even now, he'll go on and on about vibrations from Mars melting marshmallows in government vaults, but then suddenly switch into a fairly together business mode. People who've known him since the early days say he's always been like that, that it wasn't drugs.'

With songs such as 'Evil Hoodoo', 'Pictures and Designs', and the fourteen-minute 'Up in Her Room', the Seeds created a mesmerizing and slightly sinister Hollywood version of the mid-sixties 'punk' sound. 'There was real smog in Daryl Hooper's organ melodica,' wrote Lester Bangs, for whom the Seeds 'best epitomized the allure LA had then'. Certainly Hooper's psych-Gothic electric piano sound was to become one of the Doors' trademarks (and one of the Stranglers' in the following decade). Nor did the influence of English manager Lord Tim Hudson, who came on board at the time of the third album, *Future*, and encouraged the band to write such hilarious songs as 'March of the Flower Children', make a lot of difference. Hudson might have claimed that 'Seed music is the original Flower Power music', but the Seeds of *Raw and Alive* (1968) sounded exactly like the same garage-psych outfit they'd been three years before.

LA's garage-punk scene produced several other 1966 one-hit wonders, all bearing traces of British influence. The Leaves' 'Hey Joe' reached No. 31 in June, the only hit version of the song to date. On Art Laboe's Original Sound label, the Music Machine made the Top 20 in December with the terrific 'Talk Talk' (complete with its irresistible line 'My social life's a dud/My name is really mud'!). In January, the Knickerbockers, who were the house band at the Red Velvet, rose to No. 20 with their Who-esque Challenge side 'Lies'. Add to these groups such turtlenecked staples of *Pebbles*-style compilations as the Satans ('Makin' Deals'), the Preachers (the umpteenth version of Bo Diddley's 'Who Do You Love?'), and the Sons of Adam (with the fabulously far-out Arthur Lee song 'Feathered Fish'), and you can understand why sixties punk still attracts such hardcore devotees. 'True punk genius,' wrote Shelly Ganz of painstakingly retro eighties garagists the Unclaimed, 'was overlooked and cast aside as childish rubbish, just because the bands weren't pretentious hippie fucks with a message ...' Even A&M, bastion of easy-listening pop with We Five and the Sandpipers, had a stab at the psychedelic garage sound with the Magic Mushrooms' 'It's-a-Happening', the final track on Lenny Kaye's landmark 1972 compilation *Nuggets*. More important, A&M had the sheer *nous* to sign Captain Beefheart and His Magic Band, whose garage-band mutation of Chicago blues first found its way on to vinyl in 1965.*

Born Don Van Vliet in Glendale, Captain Beefheart had discovered the visceral magic of the blues with teenage crony Frank Zappa in the desert town of Lancaster, subsequently honing his inimitably Howlin' Wolfian voice with an Antelope Valley R&B outfit called the Omens. When Zappa took over Studio Z in Cucamonga in 1963, he and Van Vliet not only talked about forming a band but planned to make a film called *Captain Beefheart meets the Grunt People* – hence Don's new alias. Nothing materialized from this besides some tracks for a 'teenage opera' entitled *I*

Herb Alpert, whose Tijuana Brass outsold the Beatles by two to one in America in 1966.

---

* In 1966 – when 'It's-a-Happening' ascended to the dizzy heights of No. 93 on the pop chart – A&M chief Herb Alpert and his tacky Tijuana Brass outsold the Beatles by two to one, grossing a staggering $32m for the label. 'It's not a protest and it's not a putdown,' said Herb of the Tijuana Brass. 'I think people were bugged with hearing music which had an undercurrent of unhappiness and anger, even sadism.'

Captain Beefheart and his Magic Band in 1965. **Clockwise from top:** *Paul Blakely, Alex St Claire, Jerry Handley, Don Van Vliet, Doug Moon.*

Was a Teenage Maltshop. In due course, Zappa split for LA and Van Vliet returned to Lancaster.

1964 finally saw the debut appearance by Captain Beefheart and His Magic Band, tastefully attired in black leather coats and high-heeled boots. 'When I first saw Beefheart, he was playing R&B, but it was a surreal kind of R&B,' says Pamela Des Barres. 'He was so different, and so scary, like a dangerous, shaggy freak.' After a somewhat jarring appearance at Hollywood's Fourth Annual Teenage Fair in the spring of 1965, word got around about the group and A&M offered Beefheart a two-single deal. The result was a thunderingly fuzztoned version of Bo Diddley's 'Diddy Wah Diddy', produced by the unlikely figure of David Gates and utilizing to full effect the mighty Beefheart larynx. Although it failed even to dent the Top 100, mild reverberations were felt along the Strip, where the Mothers were already favourites with the in-crowd.

A&M's Jerry Moss may have done Beefheart a favour when he declined to take up the label's option on the band, saying he found the original *Safe as Milk* tapes 'too negative'. For when Don and the band came to re-record the material with producers Richard Perry and Bob Krasnow, they delivered themselves of a classic album. If the polo-necked, Brooklyn-born Perry was as improbable a choice of producer as David Gates had been, he caught the mutant Howlin' Wolf flavour of Beefheart's Dadaist blues brilliantly, and did equal justice to songs as diverse as token 'protest' track 'Plastic Factory', Robert Pete Williams' tormented 'Grown So Ugly', and the delectable Impressions pastiche 'I'm Glad'.

Perry's real master-stroke was the hiring of Ash Grove *wunderkind* and Rising Son Ry Cooder, whose bottleneck-guitar playing was the perfect foil to Beefheart's unholy voice. 'In the Rising Sons camp, we thought of Beefheart as the enemy,' says Barry Hansen. 'The other guys in the band were pretty unhappy that Don was trying to hire Ry away from the band. But eventually we became fans, and everyone really liked that first album.' From the opening 'Sure 'Nuff 'n Yes I Do', the trademark Telecaster inter-play of later Magic Band lineups could be heard as Cooder sparred with Alex St Clair and his own brother-in-law Russ Titelman. Unquestionably the album's most exciting track was the deranged 'Electricity', with its stomping bass line, scything slide guitars, and use of that bizarre electronic instrument the theremin: this was about as far out as pop got in 1966.

It wasn't long after the eventual release of *Safe as Milk* in 1967 that Ry Cooder left the group and Beefheart gave the other Magic Band members 'stage names' as eccentric as his own: Alex St Clair became 'Snouffer', for instance, and drummer John French 'Drumbo'. During this period, too, the music began to take on a distinctly polyrhythmic character, blending the old blues influences with those of such Free Jazz innovators as Ornette Coleman and Cecil Taylor. By the time Don's old Lancastrian pal Frank Zappa signed him to the Straight label in 1969, the Magic Band made *Safe as Milk* sound positively conventional.

III

On a warm evening in the summer of 1993, Arthur Lee sits cradling a Bloody Mary in a restaurant on Van Nuys Boulevard. Although he speaks softly, there's more than a hint that he's already fairly soused. 'I went on a big campaign for a year, telling everyone not to drink,' he smiles. 'But, well, you know ...' He's still lean and handsome in his black Levi's and Cuban heels, though as partial as ever to cheap wigs.

'You think I'm gonna talk to you like all the other people have?' he asks. 'Heh heh heh ...'

This is rather what I'd feared. I'm sitting opposite a man I regard as some kind of genius, knowing I've already lost him but still hoping I might get the odd morsel of sense from his notoriously frazzled mind. Two days have passed since I saw him play run-down C&W stronghold the Palomino with his umpteenth edition of Love – a bunch of kids whose enthusiasm just about made up for their insensitivity to such classic ballads as 'Signed DC' and 'Orange Skies'. Although Arthur had received rave reviews for a rare London performance a year before, this here was business as usual: a washed-up cult hero doing a kind of p.a. in a living-room full of fans brandishing album sleeves for autographs. 'I'm so nervous I don't know what to do with myself,' Arthur said at one point. The week after my interview with him, 'Love' were scheduled to support the Doors tribute band Wild Child at the Whisky a Go Go. How the mighty are fallen.

It's difficult now to convey just what a dash Arthur Lee must have cut when he first broke through on the Strip in 1966. On one level, Love were just one of several garage-style bands playing 'Hey Joe' on the scene that year. But on another they were a unique phenomenon: an interracial, 'two-tone' group playing an extraordinary hybrid of R&B, folk-rock and psychedelic pop. And Arthur was at the centre of it all, a black freak on the white scene, a ghetto punk in beads and pebble glasses. 'Arthur was the first guy who really had that LA look, with the fringe jacket and Levi's and little glasses,' says David Anderle, who was in the process of leaving MGM for Elektra Records.

Lee had come to LA from Memphis as 'an only lonely child' in the late forties. 'When I was a boy growing up in Watts, I would listen to Nat 'King' Cole and I'd look at that purple Capitol logo,' he says in a rare moment of lucidity. 'I wanted to be on Capitol, that was my goal, and later on I'd walk from Dorsey High School all the way up to Hollywood just to look at the Capitol building.' Remarkably, he realized this ambition when his instrumental soul combo the LAGs recorded the expendable 'The Ninth Wave'/'Rumble-Still-Skins' for Capitol in 1963.

With LAGs guitarist Johnny Echols, Lee formed the American Four, cutting a single ('Lucy Baines'/'Soul Food') for Bob Keane's Selma label.

'Two-tone psychedelic pop': Love in 1966. Clockwise from top: Arthur Lee, Mike Stuart, Kenny Forssi, Bryan Maclean, John Echols.

A sparsely clad Arthur Lee, up in the canyons with (left to right) John Echols, Bryan Maclean, Ken Forssi and Michael Stuart.

He also produced several sessions for Keane, including 'I've Been Trying', the flipside of chicano heartthrob Li'l Ray's 'I (Who Have Nothing)', and a soul side – Rosa Lee Brooks' 'My Diary' – which he claims to have been the recording debut of one James Marshall Hendrix. But it was only after seeing the Byrds at Ciro's in the spring of 1965 that Lee knew what he wanted to do – a gut feeling confirmed by some Rising Sons gigs and by the spectacle of Mick Jagger singing 'Time is on My Side' on *The Red Skelton Show*. 'When I saw the Byrds, it all just clicked in terms of my own creativity,' he says. 'Up until then, everything was rhythm and blues, but they were doing their own material and it sounded like the music I was writing on *my* own. When the Rising Sons arrived, that's when I really knew something was happening.'

Debuting in April 1965 at the Brave New World on Melrose, the band called themselves the Grass Roots until the Dunhill act of the same name happened along and they became Love instead. Rhythm guitarist and occasional vocalist Bryan Maclean had roadied for the Byrds before meeting Arthur in the parking-lot at Ben Frank's, but gave up the 'day job' after winning out over future Manson acolyte Bobby Beausoleil in the auditions. Maclean's blond, Michael Clarke-ish looks contrasted so strongly with Lee and Johnny Echols that David Anderle wondered if the juxtaposition was intentional. 'There was a twisted, almost homoerotic relationship between Arthur and Bryan,' says Anderle. 'Bryan was very quiet, and Arthur was so dominant that he seemed to make Bryan's life miserable. I don't want to say that Arthur was demonic, but he was very manipulative and destructive. See, Arthur was not really a hippie, he was more of a punk than a hippie. There was almost a gangster thing going on here, rule by intimidation. But at the same time he could be so sweet, it was totally schizoid. And maybe that did have something to do with being black in a white world.'

The sinister side of Arthur Lee's genius was sensed by Elektra's Jac Holzman when he caught the band at Bido Lito's at the tail end of 1965. For that matter, the whole band came across as a bunch of hoods: writer Jerry Hopkins, who briefly managed them at this time, thought they should have called themselves Fist, a sentiment later echoed by Pete Albin of Big Brother and the Holding Company, who felt Hate would have been a more apt name for the group. But if Love were hoods, they were psychedelicized hoods, and the tension within the band between punk and flower power was part of what made their songs so compelling.

'Thirty seconds into "Hey Joe", I knew this was the rock group I was looking for,' Jac Holzman claimed later. If that sounds a mite fanciful, it was certainly true that Holzman was searching for a West Coast act. A key figure on the East Coast folk scene, his New York-based Elektra label had been active since the early fifties, with a roster boasting everyone from Josh White to Judy Collins. More recently, Holzman had made inroads into the white electric blues field with the signing of Paul Butterfield's band. Like Ahmet Ertegun, however, he could see how important LA was becoming as a music town, and he wanted to get in on the act. 'To some extent we were an east-coast label coming west and trying to establish a two-coast presence,' he says. 'I guess we were carpetbaggers in a way.' Ironically, Holzman came to LA to sign Buffalo Springfield, but Ahmet Ertegun beat him to the punch.

Love's debut single was a brilliantly charged version of 'My Little Red Book', the Bacharach and David song from *What's New Pussycat?* subsequently covered by Manfred Mann. Kicked off by the rattlesnake hiss of a tambourine, it was garage-punk at its best, with Arthur snarling through Hal David's lyric like a black Mick Jagger – or at least, in Denny Bruce's words, like 'a black American imitating a white Englishman imitating a black American'. Released in April 1966, 'Little Red Book' stalled just outside the Top 50 but whetted appetites for the album that followed a month later. *Love* wasn't a great record, wearing its Byrds and Stones influences rather too obviously on its sleeve, but it did contain the seeds of *Da Capo* and *Forever Changes* – in the bossa nova-style arrangement of Bryan Maclean's 'Softly to Me', in ballads such as the stark 'Signed DC', which Arthur had written about the group's junkie drummer Don Conka. And the version of 'Hey Joe', sung by Maclean, must count as one of the most exciting ever recorded.

Coinciding with *Love*'s release was a sellout stint at the Hullabaloo Club that saw the band crowned as the pop kings of Hollywood. 'We were the biggest group in LA at that time,' says Arthur. 'We had people lined up around Wallichs' Music City, all the way to Sunset. We sort of inherited the Byrds' audience, the people Bryan knew. And we started the whole hippie thing with Vito and Sue and Carl – Bryan put ribbons in his hair and people would go to Ben Frank's after our shows and hang out with us.'

The 'whole hippie thing' failed to temper the group's intimidating aura. When *KRLA Beat* magazine dispatched the hapless Rochelle Reed to interview them in June, they were living communally in a so-called 'castle' on Commonwealth Road near Griffith Park and putting on displays of monosyllabic moodiness which almost had the girl walking out on them. 'Only when a group really reaches the top can their careers withstand what they may suffer from being continually rude and uncaring to fans and reporters alike,' Reed concluded. 'In my opinion, Love will soon be on many blacklists in the music industry, rather than in the "little red book" where they want so badly to belong.'

Any fears that Love's arrogance was premature were swiftly allayed by the magnificent first side of *Da Capo* (released in January 1967), which saw the birth of a baroque West Coast pop style as melodically luscious as it was lyrically creepy. If there was still garage-punk angst in 'Stephanie Knows Who' and 'Seven and Seven Is', songs such as 'Que Vida', 'She Comes in Colors', and Maclean's 'Orange Skies' employed Latin rhythms and cool jazz shadings to fashion a kind of spaced-out MOR. 'Que Vida', for instance, quoted Bacharach and David's 'A Lifetime of Loneliness' – Jackie DeShannon's follow-up to her 1965 smash 'What the World Needs Now' – while the presence of Tjay Cantrelli's flute gave the song a deceptively breezy flavour. Deceptive because Lee's lyric – like the lyric to the frenzied 'Seven and Seven Is' – suggested major bad-trip paranoia. Arthur's songs never made a lot of sense, often resorting to specious word-play, but his images were demented enough to carry considerable force. 'If I don't start crying, it's because I have got no eyes/My father's in the fireplace and my dog lies hypnotized,' he sang on 'Seven and Seven Is', which as a single made it all the way to No. 33 in September 1966. Strange things were going on at the castle that summer.

The distinctively candy-coated psychedelia of *Da Capo* – discounting 'Revelation', a redundant nineteen-minute blues jam which took up the whole of the album's second side – was partly the result of a kind of stylistic schizophrenia within the band. Here was a guy who on paper should have been leading a soul band but who instead sang his psyched-out lyrics with the precise, plangent intonation of a supper-club entertainer. 'Love started out with a kind of garagey folk-rock, but once they got into their own style it wasn't like anybody else,' says Greg Shaw. 'It had a kind of orchestral sense to it which wasn't influenced by the Left Banke and didn't sound like Tim Buckley but which was really unique. Arthur could put together elements that you'd never think of putting together, and it would work.'

It's interesting how neatly Love's music fits into the tradition of orchestral LA pop, from Spector through *Pet Sounds* to Jimmy Webb. In spite of their heavy use of halucinogenics, they sounded nothing like the San Francisco bands who were beginning to emerge at this time. And when they recorded *Forever Changes* at the new Sunset Sound studio in early 1967, they took the ornate style to its logical conclusion: acid punk with strings. In the words of Sandy Pearlman, '*Forever Changes* finished what *Da Capo* began – Arthur Lee's insane mutation of Mick Jagger into ... Johnny Mathis!'

Here it all is on one album: the sound of Los Angeles undergoing its metamorphosis from jingle-jangle innocence into strange-days weirdness, a band celebrating 'the scene' while hinting strongly that all was not as groovy as it seemed. With a musical backdrop consisting of equal parts mariachi brass, Los Angeles Philharmonic strings, Bacharach-style chord changes and acid-rock guitars, Lee (and Maclean with two songs) captured the surreal flavour of 'the times' in a way that was unrivalled by any other Los Angeles bands. If 'Between Clark and Hilldale' was a gorgeous anthem of Sunset Strip nightlife and Maclean's 'Old Man' was as kitsch as a Montmartre clown, 'The Red Telephone' was as disturbing as *One Flew Over the Cuckoo's Nest*, and 'Live and Let Live' wasn't far behind. By turns hauntingly beautiful and menacingly exciting, these songs were even more unsettling than the self-explanatory 'Like a Rolling Stone' pastiche 'Bummer in the Summer', full of the latent weirdness at large in hippie Hollywood. 'Sometimes my life is so eerie,' sang Arthur on 'The Red Telephone', 'and if you think I'm happy, paint me white ...'

'Arthur had this house right up on top of Mulholland Drive,' recalled Love bassist Ken Forssi, 'and we'd look down over the city from there. Arthur would sit up there staring out and wondering about all the ambulance noise and everything. That's how "The Red Telephone" got written: "Sitting on the hillside watching all the people die/I think it's much better on the other side."' Lee himself has said that he 'had a thing about dying' when he was 26 and that *Forever Changes* was intended to be 'my last words to this life ... it's like death is in there'.

Listening to the album today, it's hard not to think of what was coming over the horizon: the hippie nemesis of Charlie Manson. By the summer of 1968, after recording the extremely spooky single 'Laughing Stock'/'Your Mind and We Belong Together', Love themselves summed up the failure of the hippie dream. Strung out on acid and heroin, they were pulling apart in every direction, with Echols and Forssi keen to go the Cream/Hendrix power-trio route, Maclean tending towards a more commercial Bee Gees style, and Arthur too fucked up to care either way. After the band had finally called it a day, Arthur overdosed in his Mulholland Drive house. 'Some friends of mine found me dead,' he recalled later. 'Luckily, they were paramedic types who knew what to do to save my life. I mean, I was lying in the bathtub, blue.' Less lucky was

Love's road manager Neil Gannon, who died from an overdose and was later mourned in the song 'Your Friend and Mine'.

Quite why Love failed to make it to the bigtime – why *Forever Changes* only just scraped into the Top 100 – isn't entirely clear. Much of the failure has to do with Arthur's baffling personality, which tried the patience of everyone around him. 'Arthur is not of this world,' opined Jac Holzman, who often referred to Lee as 'a genius'. 'He lives in a world of his own creation.' Especially baffling to onlookers was Arthur's apparent lack of ambition, above all when it came to touring. 'I don't think they were willing to travel and go through all the games and numbers that you have to,' said Jim Morrison, who may have felt a little guilty that the Doors, signed to Elektra on Lee's recommendation, did so much better than Love.

'Arthur was always afraid of something, and I could never quite figure out what it was,' says David Anderle. 'When I came to Elektra, it was Love-land, but very quickly it became Doors-land. That had nothing to do with the Doors being all-white, as some people have suggested, it was just that the Doors thing happened so fast. Believe me, Holzman *loved* Arthur. But something happened to Arthur, and I don't know if it was drugs, alcohol or something biochemical. He was *such* an enigma. He was never a real hang at the scene, you wouldn't see him in the clubs. He was more like a Brian Wilson or a Beefheart than a David Crosby.'

Arthur, finishing off another Bloody Mary, tells me he really did want Love to happen. 'I really wanted a Love band, a Love thing,' he says. 'I wanted to be the Beatles, the Stones, a real unit. But everybody had different behaviour patterns. One guy was this way, another guy was that way, and I'm not Atlas, man, I can't hold up the world.' But he also tells me that when he moved to Mulholland Drive, he 'didn't wanna hang out with *anybody*': 'Jim Morrison used to sit outside my door when I lived in Laurel Canyon, wanting to hang out with me. I just let him sit there.'

I ask him how acid affected his life.

'I don't know anything about acid at all,' he says. 'I'm not a Timothy Leary follower, and I have nothing good to say about any drugs or alcohol for young people. I'm not going to elaborate on anything that would put a dent in a young person's mind. I've been out there, man. Now I just live in an apartment, don't worry about the butcher...'

As the speech becomes more slurred, I make out something about Brian Wilson being 'born a with bad body', and then some stuff about Christian Science and 'astroflashes'. I figure that's my lot for the evening.

IV

If Love travelled a long way in the eighteen months which separated 'My Little Red Book' from *Forever Changes*, the more mainstream exponents of

LA pop were hardly standing still. Some of the best LA records in the golden 1966–7 period were made by people who were only tangentially connected to the Byrds/Love in-crowd but who none the less flirted with psychedelia and flower power. The Association, for example, were a bunch of dorkish-looking folkies signed in early 1966 to the local Valiant label, which had hit big three years earlier with the Cascades' 'Rhythm of the Rain'. Assigned producer Curt Boettcher and engineer Gary Paxton, the group recorded 'Along Comes Mary', a Top 10 MOR-pop classic with implicitly druggy overtones then followed it up with the No. 1 hit 'Cherish' and the hilarious pop-psych abomination 'Pandora's Golden Heebie Jeebies'.

Neither the Association nor Boettcher stopped there, however. The group proceeded to juggle Bones Howe-produced hits on Warner Brothers with such lofty, musically ambitious pronouncements as 'The Time It Is Today' and the hysterical 'Requiem for the Masses'. Boettcher, meanwhile, went on to produce an album by Sunset Strip scenester Bobby Jameson and to work with Gary Usher on Sagittarius's brilliant *Present Tense* (1967), a psych-pop masterpiece featuring such mainstays of the Hollywood scene as Terry Melcher, Bruce Johnston and Glen Campbell. Densely orchestrated, this baroque work took as its departure point the *Pet Sounds* spirit of Usher's old collaborator Brian Wilson, and wasn't so far removed from the weirdness afoot on Love's *Forever Changes*. 'We were really getting spaced,' Boettcher later admitted to *Zigzag*. 'We sang about LA falling into the ocean, we were down . . .'

There were numerous other psychedelic cash-ins during that heady summer of flower power. Gary Usher himself produced the Peanut Butter Conspiracy, in Gene Sculatti's words 'a sort of Sunset Stripped-down Airplane making passable, fuzz-tinged folk-rock', signed by Columbia on the urging of Billy James. The West Coast Pop Art Experimental Band were a trio of stoned ex-surfers who recorded three albums for Reprise featuring songs by Frank Zappa ('Help, I'm a Rock') and Van Dyke Parks ('High Coin') alongside such self-penned classics as 'Smell of Incense' and 'Suppose They Give a War and Nobody Comes'. The Electric Prunes were RCA engineer Dave Hassinger's crafty transformation of a bunch of prairie oiks into a Seeds-ish acid-garage combo.

Along with these bands came the Bees, with their bad-trip song 'Voices Green and Purple'; the Gentle Soul, whose Columbia singles were produced by Terry Melcher and arranged by Jack Nitzsche; Gene Clark with his Leon Russell-arranged MOR-psych masterpiece 'Echoes'; the mood-altered Cascades with their double-album rock opera *William Burroughs and Tijuana*; the mind-blasted Leaves with 'Lemon Princess'/'Twilight Sanctuary' on Capitol; the J.J. Cale-fronted Leather-Coated Minds with 'Trip Down Sunset Strip' on Viva; and the United States of America with such psych epics as 'The Garden Of Earthly Delights' and 'Love Song for the Dead Che'. The UNI label had countless

Small ads from World Countdown News, *late 1967.*

Brian Wilson at the time of 'Good Vibrations'.

The erudition and eccentricity of Van Dyke Parks proved a potent spur to the genius of Brian Wilson.

pop-psych bands on their roster, including the Daily Flash, the Factory (featuring a young Lowell George) and Merrell Fankhauser's Fapardokly, not forgetting the Strawberry Alarm Clock, who had a No. 1 hit in October 1967 with 'Incense and Peppermints'. With a few exceptions – notably the United States of America, a highly ambitious electronic outfit formed at the University of California at Los Angeles – these acts were really the psychedelic equivalent of Barry McGuire in the protest genre, or perhaps just the musical equivalent of Sunset Strip hippie shops such as Ye Olde Psychedelic Shoppe and Brian Wilson's Radiant Radish health-food store.

Of course, the ultimate psychedelic pop record to come out of Los Angeles in this heady period was Brian's endearingly ingenuous but fantastically elaborate 'Good Vibrations', a kind of flower-power 'symphony for the kids' which came complete with theremin, cellos, and complex time-changes. This was Brian having his cake and eating it: taking pop to the outer limits of production while keeping it within the bounds of Top 40 catchiness. Originally intended for *Pet Sounds* but then put on hold while Brian turned his attention to 'God Only Knows', 'Good Vibrations' eventually took seventeen sessions to nail down, consuming over $50,000 in the process. Tapes of Brian directing some of these sessions – featuring the inevitable 'Wrecking Crew' stalwarts in their sport shirts and slacks – show just how complex the song's evolution was, with the finished product assembled from fragments recorded in different studios over a period of three months. If engineer Chuck Britz was right when he said that 'that song was his whole life's performance in one track', it was lucky that the record fared rather better than Spector's equivalent masterwork, 'River Deep, Mountain High'.

By the time 'Good Vibrations' had hit No. 1 at the end of 1966, Brian was firmly committed to extending pop's boundaries as far as he could. Gathering around him a coterie of brilliant, precocious scene-makers – Van Dyke Parks, Loren Schwartz, Danny Hutton, David Anderle, writers Jules Siegel and Paul Jay Robbins – he dug in deep and all but kissed goodbye to the Beach Boys of old. Most important among these men was Parks, the diminutive, bespectacled keyboard player whom he'd first met at Terry Melcher's house on Cielo Drive in February 1966.

Parks had first come to Hollywood as a child actor and was already renowned as an eccentric on the LA scene. He lived in a tiny room above a garage on Melrose Avenue, where (in Brian's words) he would hold court in 'funny, poetic, often beguiling torrents' invariably fuelled by amphetamines. For Brian, Van Dyke's 'intellectual passion and esoteric way with words seemed to mesh with the way I was feeling', and he invited him to come up to the house on Laurel Way to write.

'I knew that I could write lyrics and that he was looking for a lyricist,' Parks tells me. 'What I had to offer was the diligence I associated with the crafting of lyrics from what I thought were the halcyon days of the pop song in America ... the days of Cole Porter and great musical theatre. I was interested in the thoughtfulness of cadence that had preceded rock'n'roll. Even if I couldn't pose as a rustic, I thought I might be able to walk away from this thing with the pride in accomplishment that I associated with Hoagy Carmichael.'

Listening to a Van Dyke Parks monologue, delivered in a wonderfully camp, Southern-inflected voice, is a joyous experience. When you do get in the odd question, the reply lasts half an hour and takes in all manner of asides and digressions. Parks is a man who seems to have grasped the essence of Los Angeles as a music town without ever having been tainted by what he calls its 'innate criminality'. It's not hard to understand just how refreshing he must have been to Brian Wilson after five years of Mike Love.

'Brian was in the middle of "Sloop John B" when I first went up to see him,' Parks continues. 'He told me about his hearing loss, and said he was very interested in stereo even though he could only hear monophonically. I'd go to the "Good Vibrations" sessions and play piano or marimba. I enjoyed his daring in the studio, his fantastic enthusiasm. Nobody was doing anything like that anywhere. You can imagine how Brian's recording procedure threatened the record company bureaucrats, but through the force of his personality he changed the equation and got the financiers to accommodate his experimentation.'

After the completion of 'Good Vibrations', Wilson and Parks began working in earnest on a number of new songs intended to form part of a bold new work called *Dumb Angel*. 'I imagined to myself a whole new form of music – religious, white, spiritual music,' Brian later recalled, and he told Van Dyke the album would be 'a teenage symphony to God'. Aided by copious amounts of speed and black Aghani hash, the two men worked through the late summer and fall, writing the epic 'Heroes and Villains' and some of the songs which subsequently wound up on *Smiley Smile* and *20/20*.

Dumb Angel, of course, became known as *Smile*, the title given to the most famous unreleased album of all time and the great rallying-call for Brian Wilson fanatics the world over. Although we'll almost certainly never have the *Smile* that Wilson intended to release, the songs which he and Van Dyke Parks wrote through those months into early 1967 comprise some of the most intoxicatingly beautiful, dementedly ambitious pop music ever committed to tape. This was *Pet Sounds* on twenty tabs of acid, with unabashedly literary lyrics about the Old West, or even stranger ones about vegetables and balding women; it was Brian's very own *Fantasia*. '*Smile* was going to be a monument,' said David Anderle. 'That's the way we talked about it, as a monument.'*

Unfortunately, by the time Brian was recording these songs his mind

* As of early 1996, there is still widespread talk of Capitol issuing a *Smile* box set comprising every *Smile*-related track still in existence.

had really been fried by acid. The domestic situation on Laurel Way was strange enough, what with the business meetings being held in the swimming pool and the construction of a sandpit around Brian's piano, but the *Smile* recording sessions were thoroughly unhinged. If Van Dyke Parks was right that after *Pet Sounds* 'the studio experience itself became more emphatically, demonstrably, and persuasively *dominant* over the way a performance took place in a proscenium', that hardly accounted for Brian freaking out and aborting the orchestral 'Fire' suite because he thought he was causing real fires in Los Angeles. Even more worrying was the psychotic episode that occurred when he went to see John Frankenheimer's film *Seconds* and came out convinced the director had conspired with none other than Phil Spector to 'mess with my head'.

Perhaps the shadow of Spector's failure with 'River Deep' hung over Brian in the first half of 1967, because he seemed to be doing everything he could to sabotage *Smile*. Even Van Dyke Parks found it hard to handle the excess and insanity around Brian, though he remained sufficiently awestruck by the man's genius to continue work on such masterpieces as 'Surf's Up'. For David Anderle, who'd been appointed head of Brian's new Brother label, it was inevitable that two such remarkable men would at some point be unable to work together. 'Van Dyke blew Brian's mind, and I hadn't seen anyone else do that,' Anderle told Paul Williams, but he felt that at most they had 'a great moment of creativity' and thought that 'Surf's Up' was the only 'perfect blending' they achieved. 'Their parting was kind of tragic, in the fact that they were two people who absolutely did not want to separate, but who had to separate.' Ironically, despite its title, 'Surf's Up' did not concern the waves which had inspired Brian's early songs, though its 'surf' did imply the mystical sense of a wave as 'the eternal now'. Performed by Brian alone at the piano during a Leonard Bernstein CBS-TV special on pop music, it was later revisited by the Beach Boys *sans* Brian – and more than creditably – on the title track of their 1971 album.

It didn't help matters that the other Beach Boys were openly hostile to Parks, with Mike Love dismissing his lyrics as mere 'acid alliteration' and the rest of them quick to express their suspicion of the whole clique around Brian. David Anderle urged Brian to make *Smile* a solo project, but the eldest Wilson brother lacked the strength to stand up to the band. 'Brian would go through tremendous paranoia before he'd get into the studio, knowing he was going to have to face an argument,' Anderle remembered. For his part, Van Dyke claims he 'walked away from the situation as soon as I realized it was causing friction between Brian and the group': his final *Smile* session took place on 14 April.

Parks believes that the 'huge mutual lawsuit' which destroyed the dream of *Smile* could only be comprehended by someone who'd read Dickens' *Bleak House*. 'It can consume a life and still the most expressive creative spirit,' he says. 'So that's what happened to our effort, and that's why I am now back at the age of 50 trying to bring meaning to this tremendous and unlimited respect I have for Brian Wilson.' By way of concluding my interview with him, he proceeds to play me two songs ('Hold Back Time' and 'Orange Crate Art') from a new solo-album-in-the-making, both of them featuring Wilson on vocals. They're not quite 'Surf's Up' or 'Cabinessence', but the multi-tracked Brian Wilson harmonies on 'Orange Crate Art' are about as close to the glories of *Smile* as either of the two men has come since they last worked together.

When Brian met Paul McCartney at Derek Taylor's Laurel Canyon house in April 1967, it was already clear that *Smile* might never see the light of day. Instead, Brian cobbled together the *Smiley Smile* album from the debris, including new versions of such *Smile* songs as 'Vegetables', 'Wonderful', and 'Wind Chimes'. After *Pet Sounds* – and despite the inclusion of 'Good Vibrations' and 'Heroes and Villains' – the album sounded extremely spare and pared-down, with low-key instrumentation and only the odd woodblock where there was any percussion at all. It also sounded very stoned and pretty silly, easy to dismiss. But there were beautiful moments and motifs embedded in the curious half-sketches for songs: exquisite, evanescent melodies, honeyed close-harmony singing as lovely as anything the Beach Boys ever did. And there was something to be said for the sheer acid-casualty spookiness of 'Vegetables' and 'Wind Chimes' – the sound of the once squeaky-clean surfer buddies tripping out of the Southern California dream state – especially when one considers Dennis Wilson's association with Charles Manson.

Most of *Smiley Smile* was recorded in Brian's new Bel Air mansion on Bellagio Road, acquired after Capitol's official cancellation of *Smile* at the end of April 1967. This was where the genius would enact, as Phil Spector was doing, his very own version of Norma Desmond's self-incarceration in *Sunset Boulevard* – especially after the epic 'Heroes and Villains' stalled at No. 12 and *Smiley Smile* failed even to penetrate the Top 40. The release of *Sgt Pepper*, meanwhile, was for Brian the equivalent of Amundsen beating Scott to the South Pole. And when the Beach Boys pulled out of the Monterey Pop Festival that summer, afraid to line up alongside the Byrds and Buffalo Springfield, their day was all but done.

        V

Over the course of six years, Brian Wilson had seen Los Angeles pop become the dominant commercial force in the music industry. In 1966, LA had No. 1s not only with 'Good Vibrations', but with Nancy Sinatra's 'These Boots Were Made for Walkin'', her father's 'Strangers in the Night', and with records by the Association, the Mamas and the Papas, the Monkees and Johnny Rivers. For all the flower power in the air, 1967

'A shy kid from Oklahoma': Jimmy Webb in 1967.

was no different: the Turtles topped the charts with 'Happy Together', while Frank and daughter were back at No. 1 with 'Somethin' Stupid'. Both the Monkees and the Association hit the top in '67, as did the Doors and the Strawberry Alarm Clock. LA pop seemed unstoppable, with sales climbing each year.

Perhaps the archetypal pop prodigy on the Hollywood scene in 1967 was Jimmy Webb, who seemed to pick up where Phil Spector and Brian Wilson left off, establishing a kind of MOR 'superpop' sound with his songs and arrangements for the likes of the Fifth Dimension and Glen Campbell. Webb had grown up in rural Oklahoma but moved to San Bernardino to go to college in 1963. 'It was like a microcosm of American culture,' he remembers. 'Cars, Beach Boys on the radio, the second-ever McDonald – it was like "I Get Around" come to life.' By 1965, Webb was placing songs with Tamla Motown's Jobete publishing arm but tiring of the frequent drives between LA and 'San Berdoo'. Moving to Hollywood, he was hired by the Audio Arts studio as an all-purpose copyist and demo-session pianist.

It was only when Webb took the bull by the horns and walked into the Sunset Boulevard offices of a new publishing company set up by Johnny Rivers that he 'started connecting with real movers and shakers'. Rivers loved the lanky farmboy's complex, haunting chords and offered him a publishing deal. The upshot was that Webb wound up working with a black vocal group called the Versatiles, whom Rivers had recently signed to his own Soul City label. 'One day I was dinking around on the piano and I happened to play an old song I'd written called "Up, Up, and Away",' he recalls. 'They went crazy and said they wanted to do it. Then Rivers went crazy, and the next thing you know, the Versatiles are the Fifth Dimension and "Up, Up" is in the Top 10.'

Engineered by Bones Howe, with Wrecking Crew players in the band and strings and horns arranged by jazz maestro Marty Paich, 'Up, Up and Away' defined the breezy, cocktail-pop sound of Southern California, establishing the Fifth Dimension as the so-called 'black Mamas and Papas'.* TWA used the song in a commercial and the 21-year-old Webb won himself the first of eight Grammys, signalling the start of a meteoric rise which climaxed in the bombastic, pseudo-classical *kitsch* of Richard Harris' 'MacArthur Park'. 'Everybody wanted a piece of Jimmy Webb,' noted Hal Blaine, whose inimitable drum rolls were just one of the many Spectoresque ingredients in Webb's sound. Before the boy could even take stock of his success, Sinatra and Streisand were covering his songs and he was being offered $40,000 a week to perform at Caesar's Palace.

---

* The Fifth Dimension resented being called 'the black Mamas and Papas', but their blanched Vegas harmonies were far removed from the gospel roots of soul. Hear the Ashford/Simpson song 'California Soul' on *Stoned Soul Picnic* for an amusing attempt to reconcile the notion of 'soul' with the Aryan fantasy of Southern California.

'The success didn't register immediately, because I was just so extremely busy working. A few years later, I probably started reading a little too much of my own publicity.'

Other practitioners of LA pop found it harder to survive in the new psychedelic climate. Webb's mentor Johnny Rivers, for instance, managed two more Top 10 hits with typically insipid Motown covers, but then failed to score again until 1972. As for Sonny and Cher, the dream was virtually over by the summer of 1966, when their second album *The Wondrous World of Sonny & Cher* climbed no higher than No. 34. Sonny Bono made a belated stab at

'California soul': the Fifth Dimension.

hipness with his *Inner Views* solo album – featuring the ludicrous 'Pammy's on a Bummer' – but never even reached the Top 40. Cher did better on the solo front with 'Bang Bang', a piece of junk which came to Sonny as he motored down Sunset Boulevard in his Aston Martin, but the duo sealed their fate with a disastrous film called *Good Times*.

An act which enjoyed a rather happier interaction with celluloid Hollywood was of course the Monkees, the end-result of a TV company auditioning 437 young male hopefuls and turning four of them into a make-believe pop group. Inspired by Richard Lester's Beatles films, producer Burt Schneider and director Bob Rafelson sat through auditions by everyone from Stephen Stills and Danny Hutton to Van Dyke Parks and Mickey Rooney Jr, settling by the summer of 1966 on draft-dodging folkie Peter Tork, diminutive English cutie Davy Jones, lugubrious Texan Mike Nesmith, and former child star Mickey Dolenz. An outrageous Hollywood attempt to beat pop at its own game, it made such teen-idol-makers as Dick Clark look innocent. It also happened, by sheer good fortune, to be very good: post-moptop surrealism for pre-teens, with great songs thrown in as part of the package.

The quartet's recordings were supervised by none other than Don Kirshner, Brill Building puppetmaster extraordinaire, who brought in Screen Gems writers Tommy Boyce and Bobby Hart to pen their material. It was Boyce and Hart who wrote not only the famous 'Monkees' Theme' but the group's No. 1 debut single 'Last Train to Clarksville', released shortly after the first episode was aired in September 1966. 'The whole creation of the Monkees was fun to see,' says music publisher Dan Bourgoise, who'd come out to LA from Detroit as Del Shannon's road

The lucky four: (left to right) Davy Jones, Peter Tork, Mike Nesmith, Mickey Dolenz.

manager. 'Bobby Hart had a little band that played out on Pico, and that's where all those Monkees songs got their first airings. He and Tommy were putting these songs together for Screen Gems, and I remember thinking, "Who's gonna buy *that?*" But we all went up to see the *Monkees* pilot in Kirshner's Beverly Hills mansion, and the minute it came on I thought, "Oh my God, this is *perfect!*" '

For Bourgoise, the Monkees story summed up the Hollywood pop scene in the sixties. 'Because this is a showbiz town,' he says, 'you could put together a band with a look, a feel, a sound, and the entertainment value was just taken as commonplace. In New York, it was all more faceless and studio-oriented, but here the artist had to have a look. It was much more visceral. A lot of the kids who grew up here saw a new look being put together every six months as each new teen movie came out.' So wide-open was the scene in 1966, moreover, that Bourgoise and a photographer pal were able to shoehorn themselves into doing all the photo marketing for the Monkees. 'Nobody had thought of it, simply because *The Monkees* had come from the film company. I didn't know the first thing about photo marketing, but Hollywood was the kind of place where you could literally sit around and piece together a little hustle. I was suddenly The Guy With the Monkees Pictures! It was typical of the way things were created in LA.'

But if *The Monkees* miraculously turned the Monkees into a *bona fide* pop act, the four actors who comprised the group quickly tired of being puppets for Screen Gems. 'The whole thing was utterly bizarre,' Mike Nesmith recalled. 'Suddenly, Don Kirshner got it in his head that he'd created a pop group.' After Nesmith forced a showdown with Kirshner, the Monkees admitted publicly that they hadn't played on their own records and brought in producer Chip Douglas to help them with their third album, *Headquarters*. So it was goodbye to the Boyce and Hart formula – although the group hit big in 1967 with Goffin and King's 'Pleasant Valley Sunday' and John Stewart's 'Daydream Believer' – and hello to the songs about sex and drugs which surfaced on *Pisces, Aquarius, Capricorn, and Jones Ltd.*

The logical culmination to the *volte face* away from their teen celebrity was *Head*, the wacked-out psychedelic film which was already in production when *The Monkees* was cancelled in the summer of 1968. Directed by Bob Rafelson and written by Jack Nicholson – one of a new breed of rebel Thespians who'd been hanging around the *Monkees* set – *Head* was a far cry from the high spirits of the TV series. 'Hey hey we're the Monkees, a manufactured image,' they sang before proceeding to intercut musical numbers with war footage and images of girls ripping clothes off mannequins. Featuring Annette Funicello, Sonny Liston and Victor Mature in cameo roles, along with Frank Zappa as the critic who tells Davy Jones that 'the youth of America depends on you to show them the way', the film was nothing short of a druggy deconstruction of the group's whole telemyth.*

Another film part-written by Jack Nicholson was *The Trip*, a wonderfully distorted B-movie take on psychedelia directed in 1967 by exploitation king Roger Corman. Bringing together Peter Fonda and Dennis Hopper, who would go on to make their own glorified counterculture B-movie *Easy Rider*, *The Trip* concerned the hallucinatory adventures of a TV commercials director (Fonda) as he mulled over the implications of his impending divorce. The script was a rambling affair – Fonda later complained that if Corman had stuck with Nicholson's original screenplay the film 'could have been the greatest thing in my career, which it was not' – but the visual effects by Peter Gardiner made the film a favourite of apprentice acidheads the world over.

Post-moptop surrealism for pre-teen America: the Monkees, in the episode 'Dance, Monkees, Dance'.

The Trip was just the latest example of Hollywood cashing in on pop, with the difference that its stars were hanging out with Sunset Strip bands in exactly the same way that today's movie brat-packers consort with rock's 'bad boys'. Peter Fonda, who owned a silver station-wagon in which he beetled around town smoking pot with David Crosby, was constantly seen in clubs and studios, and even recorded a single ('November Nights') written by his as-yet-unknown friend Gram Parsons. Hopper, a self-appointed renegade still trading on his appearance in *Rebel Without a Cause*, was almost as ubiquitous, as were Dean Stockwell, Michael J. Pollard, Harry Dean Stanton and ex-child star Brandon de Wilde. Jack Nicholson himself was everywhere.†

* After being ousted by his own creation, Don Kirshner had the inspired brainwave of putting together a recording entity called the Archies. Based on a cartoon strip first syndicated back in 1942, this group never got ideas above their station, because they didn't exist. Released on the Calendar label in 1969, Jeff Barry's song 'Sugar, Sugar' sold three million copies in America alone. 'Let the Archies make it, let the Monkees make it,' whined Phil Spector. 'So they're a lot of shit, so what?'

† Other drecky exploitation movies from this period included Herschell Gordon Lewis's *Blast Off Girls*, David Butler's *C'Mon, Let's Live a Little* (starring Bobby Vee and Jackie DeShannon), Maury Dexter's *Maryjane* (starring Fabian, with a Mike Curb soundtrack), Robert Carl Cohen's risible documentary *Mondo Hollywood* and Barry Shear's *Wild in the Streets*, in which a rock superstar and drug pusher run for president.

VI

The Sunset Strip 'scene' to which these thesps attached themselves was in full swing through the summer and fall of 1966. There were week-long stints at the Trip and the Whisky by Love, the Byrds and the Lovin' Spoonful, and by such Motown stars as Marvin Gaye. Ciro's became It's Boss, and a proto-metal outfit called Iron Butterfly became the house band at the Galaxy. Between Clark and Hilldale, the Eatin' Affair and Hamburger Hamlet were almost as busy as the Whisky itself.

Meanwhile, the scene's stars moved up into the hills of Laurel Canyon, often dropping in on each other to make music and share chemicals. Cass Elliott bought Natalie Wood's house off Mulholland Drive, while Denny Doherty held court in Mary Astor's old place on Appian Way. Peter Tork lived in Studio City, and Peter Fonda had a pad in Hidden Valley. David Crosby set himself up in a little cabin in Beverly Glen Canyon, while the less extrovert Chris Hillman lived high in the hills surrounded by wild flowers and eucalyptus trees.

A pioneer Laurel Canyon settler was scenemaker Billy James, who told Jerry Hopkins of the new in-crowd paper *World Countdown News* that only Arthur Lee was living there before him. 'It's all happened in the last year or so,' James said. 'If creative artists need to live apart from the community at large, they also have a desire to live among their own kind, and so an artistic community develops.' The nerve centre of this growing community was the Laurel Canyon Country Store, where on an average day you might have spotted members of Love, the Turtles or the Monkees, along with Elektra producers Paul Rothchild and Barry Friedman. 'If there were more mobility in this town,' said Billy James, who lived just up the road on Ridpath Avenue, 'the Canyon Store would look like MacDougal Street on a Saturday night.'

Back down on the Strip, one of the best LA bands to emerge in 1966 were the eclectic Kaleidoscope, who mixed up acid-rock and jug-band blues with Turkish influences that came from the bizarre Solomon Feldthouse – a man proficient not only on the guitar but on such exotic instruments as the oud, the caz and the bouzouki. With their roots in the early-sixties folk scene, they sounded at one moment like early Jethro Tull ('Oh Death', 'Keep Your Mind Open'), the next like the average psychedelicized folk-rock band. The critical success of their first album, *Side Trips*, made Kaleidoscope a popular live draw on the Californian circuit, their shows often featuring flamenco and belly dancers. 'Some of the audience would love the middle eastern stuff but hate the blues,' recalled guitarist/fiddler Chris Darrow. 'Some would love the blues but hate the country cajun stuff, and those who loved the cajun music would hate the psychedelic stuff!' After the release of *Beacon from Mars*, Kaleidoscope's second album, Darrow quit to join the Nitty Gritty

Kaleidoscope in 1966. Left to right: Chris Darrow, Fenrus Epp, John Vidican, Solomon Feldthouse, David Lindley.

Dirt Band, and later became a member of Linda Ronstadt's backing group, the Corvettes. Kaleidoscope's putative leader, the great guitarist/fiddler/dobroist David Lindley, went on to become a mainstay of the LA scene, most notably as a member of Jackson Browne's band. Exactly what happened to Charles Chester Crill (a.k.a. Fenrus Epp, a.k.a. Maxwell Buda, a.k.a. Templeton Parceley, etc.) is less well documented.

Less eclectic but far more influential than Kaleidoscope were Buffalo Springfield, who assumed the folk-rock/psychedelic mantle of the Byrds when that group began falling apart in the spring of 1966. With hindsight, there was neat symmetry in the fact that Canadians Neil Young and Bruce Palmer ran into their old folkie pals Stephen Stills and Richie Furay in a Sunset Boulevard traffic jam just as Gene Clark was detaching himself from the Byrds to embark on a rocky solo career.

Steve Stills had grown up in Texas and Florida before moving to New York to be part of the Village folk scene in 1964. It was there that he met fellow folkie Richie Furay, who followed him out to California in the wake of Beatlemania. Once in Los Angeles, Stills attempted to form a band with Van Dyke Parks, and was one of the many struggling musicians to audition for *The Monkees*. Neil Young, meanwhile, had been playing in a Toronto band called the Mynah Birds – with the future Rick James as his frontman – until he too decided to set out for the promised land. With bass player Bruce Palmer, the lanky, intense Ontarian loaded his gear into a 1953 Pontiac hearse and pitched up in Hollywood looking – in his fringe jacket and sideburns – as if he'd been there all the time.

Buffalo Springfield formed almost immediately after the fateful encounter on Sunset, Young recruiting seasoned country drummer Dewey Martin to complete the lineup. The early days of the band's life were difficult –

Buffalo Springfield. Left to right: Dewey Martin, Stephen Stills, Neil Young, Bruce Palmer, Richie Furay.

Bruce Palmer was deported, and Stills and Young were immediately at loggerheads – but with the help of Chris Hillman, who secured them their first gigs, and the clout of Sonny and Cher's managers Charlie Greene and Brian Stone behind them, they were soon causing a major stir on the scene. Like the Byrds themselves, the Springfield were a pivotal group, a link between coffeehouse folk and electric rock'n'roll. 'The point about the Byrds and the Springfield is that we weren't garage rock bands,' said Chris Hillman later. 'We came out of folk music, so the major focus was on the song – if you were gonna get up in front of an audience with just an acoustic guitar, the material had better be good.'

Signed to Atlantic by Ahmet Ertegun, with whom Greene and Stone had an enviably close relationship, Springfield released Young's abstruse if pretty 'Nowadays Clancy Can't Even Sing' as their first single. Unfortunately, it failed to penetrate even the local Top 20, a situation quickly remedied when Stills' instant protest song 'For What It's Worth' shot all the way to No. 7 on the national chart in February 1967.

The success notwithstanding, Buffalo Springfield was made up of too diverse elements to last indefinitely. Like the Byrds, the band found it hard to marshal the different styles of its writers: Stills' fuzzy folk-rock, Furay's country soul, and Young's complex, introspective balladry. Onstage, the ego battle between Stills and Young was only too apparent in what one observer called their 'spiteful guitar duelling'. Their second album, *Buffalo Springfield Again*, has been deemed a classic, but it's as mixed a bag as the Byrds' *Fifth Dimension* and doesn't play comfortably to contemporary ears. If it isn't bad enough that Stills' songs ('Bluebird', 'Rock and Roll Woman') now sound bereft of true inspiration, there is so little in common between, say, Furay's countrified 'Child's Claim to Fame' and Young's epic, Jack Nitzsche-arranged 'Expecting to Fly' that they could be by different bands.

Young, always destined to be a misfit in any music scene, found it especially hard coping with Hollywood. 'There were a lot of problems with the Springfield,' he told Nick Kent. 'Groupies, drugs, shit. I'd never seen people like that before. They were always around, giving you grass, trying to sell you hippie clothes ... I remember being haunted suddenly by this whole obsession with "How do I fit in here? Do I like this?" And then came the managers, Greene and Stone, who were real wheeler-dealers, and suddenly it's all a business and you don't know if you're doing the right thing or not.' It was with a fine irony that Young's churning, Stonesy 'Mr Soul' was 'respectfully dedicated to the ladies of the Whisky a Go Go and the women of Hollywood'.*

Significantly, Young was attracted to Jack Nitzsche, a similarly obsessive maverick who managed to turn 'Expecting to Fly' (and 'Broken Arrow', come to that) into something that sounded like Phil Spector on acid. 'Jack was still living off the tail end of the Spector legend,' says Denny Bruce, who introduced Nitzsche to Young. 'But that era was coming to a close with all the new self-contained groups, and Jack had been checking them out like he'd checked out the Stones.'

By the time the Springfield were lining up to play the Monterey Pop Festival in the summer of 1967, Young had had enough of contending with Stills' ego, however much he respected his musicianship. 'I just couldn't handle it toward the end,' he said in 1975. 'My nerves couldn't handle the trip, it wasn't me scheming on a solo career.' Due to appear on Johnny Carson's *Tonight* show, the band had to cancel when Young flounced off in a huff. 'We fell prey to the whole entourage system,' said Stills. 'Everybody had to have his own entourage, and it got stupid. We forgot the initial brotherhood.'

The same might have been said about the Byrds, who (in Gene Clark's phrase) had been 'kings of Hollywood for a while' but were floundering as 1967 dawned. 'When they first broke, they were the only game in town,' lamented Jim Dickson. 'By 1967, they couldn't draw flies.' Amidst rumours that Clark's departure spelled the end of the band, they came back with the cynical riposte that was 'So You Wanna Be a Rock'n'Roll Star'. An implicit critique of the Monkees phenomenon, the single – which barely edged into the Top 30 – said a lot about how jaded the starry-eyed young

---

* The 'wheeler-dealing' of Greene and Stone later had severe repercussions for Dr John, who played on Sonny and Cher and Buffalo Springfield sessions as a keyboard player. 'Greene and Stone were typical of the Hollywood phenomenon whereby producers and entrepreneurs begin to act like they're artists,' says Dan Bourgoise. 'They started out as publicists, but they wanted to be Phil Spector and Andrew Loog Oldham, with all the airs and the limos. They got a bad reputation, and I think that hurt a lot of things. A lot of bands were overlooked because the people they'd entrusted their careers to were too busy promoting *themselves*.'

things of 'Mr Tambourine Man' had become. Nor was the flipside, Crosby's spooked 'Everybody's Been Burned', much less pessimistic.

As with *Fifth Dimension*, the *Younger than Yesterday* album released that spring had an unsatisfying pick'n'mix quality about it, cobbling together the cod-psychedelic posturings of Crosby's 'Mind Gardens' with the avant-garde experimentation of 'CTA–102', the country flavour of Hillman's 'Time Between' with the fey, fallback Dylanizing of 'My Back Pages'. Meanwhile, rumours abounded that Crosby had become a royal pain in the sphincter, spending most of his time doing drugs and zipping up to San Francisco to hang with the new Haight-Ashbury bands. As with the Springfield, finally, it was the Monterey Festival which signalled the true split within the band.

The song which briefly propelled Buffalo Springfield into the pop limelight, 'For What It's Worth (Stop, Hey What's That Sound)', was Stephen Stills' anthemic response to the riots which occurred on the Sunset Strip in the fall of 1966. With its lines about paranoia striking deep and The Man coming to 'take you away', it struck a more authentic note of political menace than, say, 'Eve of Destruction' – which, given the apathy of the flower children towards the Watts riots the year before, was perhaps more than the riots themselves merited.

The issue at stake on the Strip that summer of '66 was the threat to the thriving youth nightlife posed by a consortium of businessmen who wanted to turn the area into a high-rise business district. When plans were announced to demolish Pandora's Box to make way for a wider road and a three-way-turn signal, a demonstration led to the mass arrest of three hundred people. This in turn prompted the formation by Jim Dickson and Derek Taylor of CAFF (Community Action for Facts and Freedom), which was supported by Woolworth's heir Lance Reventlow, Sonny and Cher, Elmer Valentine, underground DJ Elliott Mintz and *Gilligan's Island* star Bob Denver. Out of the woodwork came all the usual suspects – Sal Mineo, Peter Fonda and Dennis Hopper – and in November there was a huge march down Sunset. 'I watched as Gorgeous Hollywood Boys overturned a bus, and cheered on the offenders from my warm spot on the Sunset Boulevard blacktop,' gushed Pamela Des Barres in *I'm With the Band*. 'I gazed at Sonny and Cher, arms wrapped round each other, wearing matching polka-dot bellbottoms and fake-fur vests, and realized we were all one big huge beating heart.'

In the end, Sheriff Peter Pitchess called off his dogs and the Strip remained an unofficial youth zone, but licences were withdrawn and some clubs forced to close. The ultimate exploitation B-movie, *Riot on Sunset Strip*, followed in due course – a typically covert piece of propaganda starring Aldo Ray as a cop cleaning up the Strip and Mimsy Farmer as the daughter who is drugged and raped at a party. Featuring the Standells and the Chocolate Watch Band on Mike Curb's soundtrack, it made for a perfect piece of pop *schlock*.

The CAFF demonstration was the last time white 'street life' dared to assert itself in the city where jaywalking was deemed to be a more heinous activity than jumping red lights. Rebellion and resistance were the exception rather than the norm in Southern California, where – despite the presence of Professor Herbert Marcuse, the so-called 'Pied Piper of Insurgent Youth' (*Time*) – there was far less agitprop activity or political consciousness than in the north. 'Protest songs are dead,' Roger McGuinn was able to say in November 1966. 'I don't see that anything is to be gained by marching around with a sign or anything.' That month, Ronald Reagan was elected governor of California.

Demonstrators protest against plans to demolish Pandora's Box, at the intersection of Sunset and Crescent Heights, in the summer of 1966.

VII

The lack of real political engagement in Los Angeles was one of the many things which distinguished it from its sister city in northern California. As early as 1965, San Francisco hippies were routinely dismissing LA as a plastic dystopia, the polar opposite of everything Haight-Ashbury stood for. Frisco was the city of Beats, Pranksters and Diggers, of subversive street theatre: Los Angeles was a Mammon of hype and freeways. 'San Francisco is the only city in the US which can support a scene,' the Family Dog's Luria Castel told Ralph J. Gleason that fall. 'New York is too large and confused, and LA is super-uptight plastic America.' A member of Country Joe and the Fish described LA as 'a short-sleeved velour pussycat with a plastic hard-on ... Disneyland all over'.

This Haight-Ashbury disdain had much to do with LA's more studio-oriented music scene. A member of the Jefferson Airplane, signed to RCA in LA, remarked that what Brian Wilson was doing was fine, 'but in person there's no balls'. 'Everything is prefabricated, like the rest of that town,' he continued. 'Bring them to the Fillmore and it just wouldn't work.' The dawning of a San Francisco 'rock' as opposed to a Los Angeles 'pop' sensibility was in great part the result of Bay Area bands providing soundtracks for ritualistic, communal mind expansion. These bands also eschewed the airs and graces of stardom which characterized LA groups. However disingenuous, there was less of a distinction between, say, the Dead or the Airplane and their fans than one found – perhaps inevitably – in Hollywood.

The San Francisco attitude towards the LA scene – relying on the usual plastic/phony/Disneyland tropes – naturally provoked resentment and counter-attack among Angelenos. Whether it was Sunset Strip Valley Girl Pamela Des Barres expressing her distaste at the 'stringy hair' and 'sacky peasant dresses' of hippie chicks on the Haight, or her boss Frank Zappa arguing that LA's 'freaks' were actually far wilder than Frisco's 'hippies', there was widespread repudiation of the Bay Area's snooty self-righteousness – repudiation that, Reyner Banham-style, generally turned LA's supposed defects into assets. 'Whereas in LA you had people freaking out, being as weird as they wanted to be in public,' said Zappa, 'I got to San Francisco and found everybody dressed up in 1890s garb, all pretty specific codified dress. In San Francisco, they had a "more-rustic-than-thou" approach. It was cute, but it wasn't as evolved as what was going on in LA.'

The Hollywood scene found some unlikely allies in this cultural feud when Andy Warhol and the Velvet Underground came to California in the summer of 1966. 'LA I liked because the degenerates there all stay in their separate suburban houses,' said Warhol's director Paul Morrissey. 'That's wonderful because it's so much more modern – people isolated

Freakdom the Hollywood way: Kim Fowley at the 'Love-In' in Elysian Park, 1967.

from each other. I don't know where the hippies are getting these ideas to "retribalize" in the middle of the twentieth century.'* Up in San Francisco, the Velvets clashed with Fillmore proprietor Bill Graham, who called them 'disgusting germs from New York' – this from a man whose ruthless business style came straight off the streets of the Bronx! 'If you didn't smile a lot in San Francisco,' noted Paul Morrissey, 'they got very hostile towards you.' Warhol himself claimed that 'vacant, vacuous Hollywood was everything I ever wanted to mould my life into,' while Lou Reed and Sterling Morrison were effusive in their admiration for the Byrds. (Interestingly, one of the greatest hymns to the troubled genius of Brian Wilson was 'Mr Wilson', from John Cale's 1975 album *Slow Dazzle*.)

Yet despite the protestations of Zappa and others, the fact remains that LA secretly recognized the grassroots authenticity of the Fillmore and Avalon Ballroom scene. At a time when go-go girls still danced in cages at the Whisky, the bacchanalian spectacles which were occurring in San Francisco made the Sunset Strip look prehistoric. LA had its own hippie enclave down in Venice – had the same squats and sandals and cockroaches – but as an underground scene it was a good deal more fragmented than the one in San Francisco. 'Travelling up the Coast from the ruins of the Sunset Strip to the Haight is a Dante-esque ascent,' New Yorker Richard Goldstein could write in 1967. 'Those 400 miles mark the difference between a neon wasteland and the most important underground in the nation.'

'You would have to say that San Francisco had the jump on LA in terms of drugs and psychedelia,' says writer Carl Gottlieb, who saw both scenes at close range as a member of satirical troupe The Committee. 'Up in San Francisco, we felt quite superior because we were actually living it. In LA, then as now, people dressed up and acted it out. In San Francisco, if you have a Harley you're dealing with Angels. In LA, you're dealing with Mickey Rourke or Billy Idol.' But Gottlieb goes on to point out that there was more cross-pollination between the two cities than some would care to admit.

A key commuter between LA and SF was the man whose autobiography Carl Gottlieb would co-write many years later: David Crosby. Of all the LA stars, 'the Cros' was the one who responded the quickest to what was happening in Frisco. Despite being a classic showbiz brat – his cinematographer father had even worked on a number of AIP beach-

---

* Much of the ongoing yin/yang dynamic between LA and SF has to do with the notion that San Francisco is a community-oriented, 'old-world' city and Los Angeles a futuristic and nightmarish autotopia. William Gibson captures this well in his novel *Virtual Light*, when he notes that San Francisco gives Berry Rydell a sense of '*being* somewhere'. 'Maybe it just felt so much the opposite of LA,' Rydell ponders, 'and that feeling like you were cut loose in a grid of light that just spilled out to the edge of everything.' It was significant that in 1967 British director John Boorman rejected San Francisco for his thriller *Point Blank* because it was 'too pretty'. In the film, he presented a sixties LA stripped of glamour, a sort of inverted *noir* hell in which there was no escaping the omnipresent sun.

David Crosby (left), a key commuter between LA and San Francisco, with the Jefferson Airplane's Paul Kantner at Monterey.

party movies – he was a born rebel who refused to play the Hollywood showbiz game. As early as 1962 he was a dope-smoking folkie living communally in Venice with such future mainstays of the San Francisco scene as Paul Kantner and David Freiberg. Four years later, when Kantner's Jefferson Airplane were in town to record for RCA, Crosby brought them along to meet the other Byrds at the 9000 Sunset building. Crosby loved the anti-pop/anti-muso mentality of the San Francisco bands and the long, acid-enhanced jams they were playing in the city's psychedelic ballrooms.

'Someone like Crosby understood that San Francisco had a much more cohesive scene than LA,' says West Coast expert John Platt. 'It was significant that LA never had a Fillmore or an Avalon or a poster artist like Rick Griffin* – although the clichés about LA studio bands and San Francisco live bands obscure the truth that there *were* great live bands from LA. There was also an equivalent to the San Francisco hippie in LA, but it's hard to pin down what he or she was because LA had no Haight-Ashbury. And there was always that affluent aspect to LA, with boutiques on the Strip selling $500 hippie outfits. To San Franciscans, LA was still a place full of on-the-make directors and starlets.'

It was down to people such as Crosby that the LA and San Francisco scenes were able to overlook their differences for long enough even to contemplate the idea of a musical gathering which would bring together the best bands from both cities. As a result, the Monterey Pop Festival, held between 16 and 18 June 1967 in the Monterey Fairgrounds a hundred miles south of San Francisco, turned out to be perhaps the key sixties event in California's pop history.

The idea for the festival had its inception with Alan Pariser, a paper fortune heir and Sunset Strip scenester who'd staged a fundraiser for the CAFF committee in late 1966 starring the Byrds and Buffalo Springfield. Entering into a partnership with another Strip veteran, booking agent Benny Shapiro, Pariser raised $50,000 and hired Derek Taylor to be the festival's publicist. It was through Taylor that Pariser first approached John Phillips to suggest the Mamas and the Papas be one of the headline acts at the festival.

Since reaching No. 1 with 'Monday, Monday' in the spring of 1966, the Mamas had had two more Top 5 hits ('I Saw Her Again' and 'Words of Love') and were currently riding high with their version of the Shirelles hit 'Dedicated to the One I Love'. Michelle Phillips had briefly been ousted from the lineup because of her affair with Gene Clark, but by September 1966 she was back with John, living in Jeanette MacDonald's old mock-tudor pile on Bel Air Road. Early 1967 saw the group established as official rock royalty, driving Jaguars and touring with Lear jets. The Bel

---

* As it happens, Rick Griffin was originally from Southern California, where he'd begun as a cartoonist on John Severson's *Surfer* magazine. After taking part in the Watts Acid Test in early 1966, he headed up to San Francisco. See Paul D. Grushkin, *The Art of Rock.*

Air mansion was stuffed with Tiffany lamps and Lalique crystal, classic appurtenances of *parvenu* Hollywood. Lou Adler bought the Phillipses a pair of peacocks and introduced them to Jack Nicholson and Warren Beatty. 'John and Lou and I were teaching ourselves everything there was to know about snobbery,' Michelle confessed years later.

Phillips was sufficiently intrigued by the idea of the festival to mention it to Adler, who in any case had done business with Benny Shapiro for some years. What then transpired was close to being a palace coup, with Adler and Phillips wresting control of the festival from Alan Pariser and buying out Benny Shapiro for the laughable sum of $8,000. One of the ways they managed to do this was by making the festival a charity fundraiser and persuading the acts to play for free. Such was the clout Adler and Phillips had that they were able not only to put together a star-studded committee – Mick Jagger, Paul McCartney and Brian Wilson among them – but to secure commitments to perform from the Byrds, the Beach Boys, and Simon and Garfunkel. They also discussed the idea of filming the festival with *Monkees* director Bob Rafelson, who later dropped out to make way for D.A. Pennebaker.

But the key to the whole event lay with the San Francisco fraternity, who instinctively regarded Adler and Phillips with deep suspicion. 'The San Francisco groups had a very bad taste in their mouths about LA commercialism,' says Adler. 'And it's true that we were a business-minded industry. It wasn't a hobby. They called it slick, and I'd have to agree with them. We couldn't find the link. Every time John and I went up there, it was a fight – almost a physical fight on occasions. And that was right up to the opening day of the festival, with the Dead – the Ungrateful Dead, as we called them – threatening to do an alternative festival.'

With Bill Graham and Ralph J. Gleason acting as placating inter-mediaries, communications were established and several Bay Area bands were proposed as representatives of the San Francisco scene: the Dead, the Steve Miller Blues Band, the Quicksilver Messenger Service, Country Joe and the Fish, Big Brother and the Holding Company, Moby Grape and Jefferson Airplane. These bands couldn't have provided more of a contrast to the Los Angeles contingent, which included the Mamas and the Papas, Johnny Rivers, the Association and Lou Rawls. 'You could look back and ask what Lou Rawls or the Association were doing there,' admits Lou Adler, 'but we were trying to get across a true cross-section of everything that was happening in pop. The Association was an important part of the LA scene, even though I didn't particularly like their records.'

'I don't think guys like Adler drew a line in their minds between Johnny Rivers and the Grateful Dead,' says Bomp Records impresario Greg Shaw. 'This was the revolutionary new generation of music, and it included *everything* they happened to have a quarter of the publishing on!' To the Haight-Ashburyites, what summed up the Adler camp better than anything

The crowd at the Monterey Fairgrounds, 17 June 1967.

was the release of Scott Mackenzie's cringemaking 'San Francisco (Be Sure to Wear Flowers in Your Hair)' on Lou's new Ode label. Intended by John Phillips to be a kind of theme song for the festival, the record sounded more like an instruction booklet for tourists – or for what Adler himself termed 'uptown hippies'. Compounding the irritation of Country Joe McDonald and others, 'San Francisco' rose all the way to No. 4 on the charts.

In addition to the Californian acts, the Monterey Pop Festival featured a wide range of groups and solo artists from the East Coast and from Britain. Albert Grossman delivered a package that included the Paul Butterfield Blues Band, the Electric Flag, Al Kooper and the Blues Project, while Andrew Loog Oldham talked Otis Redding's manager Phil Walden into letting the Big O play to an audience of white hippies. All the way from Swinging London, bringing rather different vibes, came the Who and the wild young 'psychedelic spade' Jimi Hendrix.

As fans filled the fairgrounds on the night of Friday, 16 June, a strain of acid christened 'Monterey Purple' began circulating, necessitating the opening of a 'Bummer Tent' which had filled up by the next morning. But the Friday night bill was hardly conducive to tripping, featuring as it did the singularly square-looking Association and continuing with Lou Rawls, Johnny Rivers and Simon and Garfunkel. Eric Burdon and his revamped Animals revved things up with their new MGM single 'San

Franciscan Nights', but Rawls' H. B. Barnum-conducted set would have been better suited to Las Vegas, and Simon and Garfunkel sounded like a throwback to the days of the New Christy Minstrels.

Saturday afternoon was all about blue-eyed blues, opening with LA purists Canned Heat and closing with Mike Bloomfield's Electric Flag. The show was stolen outright by the extraordinary sound and spectacle of Janis Joplin wailing her way through Big Mama Thornton's 'Ball and Chain'. While these bands played, the stoned Brian Jones paraded around the festival in silks and brocades like some hippie princeling. Mickey Dolenz sported an Indian headdress, and Dennis Hopper photographed the sea of beads and patches and caftans. Terry Melcher's girlfriend Candice Bergen put a flower in her mouth, and Derek Taylor dropped Owsley-manufactured acid with Harry Dean Stanton, writing afterwards that 'so many of us were able so substantially to shed our egos and float downstream on people, music, love and flowers'.

The evening show commenced with Moby Grape, one of the best new San Francisco bands, and featured the Byrds, Laura Nyro, Jefferson Airplane and Otis Redding. The Byrds' appearance confirmed that all was not well with the band. Crosby, as it happened, had spent the preceding two weeks rehearsing with Buffalo Springfield, keen to replace the errant Neil Young in the group. Onstage at Monterey, he made various attempts to politicize the occasion – introducing 'He Was a Friend of Mine', for instance, with a little *spiel* about the Warren Report on the Kennedy assassination – none of which went down too well with Roger McGuinn. 'David hated being a Byrd,' recalled road manager Jim Seiter. 'He didn't consider it hip, for some reason, and he wanted to be a Buffalo Springfield or a Jefferson Airplane. David's a groupie, always was and always will be.'

After the disaster that was the unknown Laura Nyro's short set, Jefferson Airplane took the stage and played much of the material from their spanking-new *Surrealistic Pillow* album. Like the other San Francisco bands, they were unhappy at having their set limited to a mere forty-five minutes – it took the Grateful Dead that long just to warm up – but their performance was sufficiently commanding for Phil Walden to wonder how Otis Redding could follow it. As anyone who has seen D. A. Pennebaker's marvellous *Monterey Pop* will know, of course, Redding went down a storm as the Saturday night headliner, connecting almost immediately with what he called 'the love crowd'.

Sunday afternoon had the same crowd entranced by Ravi Shankar's three-hours-plus set. Big Brother and the Holding Company took the stage around teatime and repeated the highlights of their Saturday set in order for D. A. Pennebaker to capture them on film. Hal Blaine sat in with ex-Modern Folk Quartet singer Cyrus Farrar as 'The Group With No Name', while David Crosby added insult to the injury he'd dealt Roger McGuinn, joining Buffalo Springfield for almost the whole of their set. No one was quite prepared for the Who, least of all Lou Adler, who

The tense relationship between Crosby and McGuinn was reflected in their Monterey performance.

rushed frantically on to the stage as the sometime mods began laying waste to their equipment.

By the time the Grateful Dead came on, providing a kind of cushion between the Who and Jimi Hendrix, it must have been obvious to the Haight-Ashbury contingent that the festival had provided them with priceless exposure. Country Joe might have trashed Monterey as 'a total ethical sellout of everything we'd dreamed of', but he later conceded that the 'sellout' was 'something we desperately needed, because we were totally isolated'. In the words of Jann Wenner, who was about to co-found *Rolling Stone* with Ralph Gleason, 'Monterey was the nexus – it sprang from what the Beatles began, and from it sprang what followed.'

Most people associate the Monterey festival with an indelible image of Jimi Hendrix setting fire to his guitar during a crazed rendition of the Troggs' 'Wild Thing'. As an almost apocalyptic climax to three days of 'peace'n'love', it seemed to signal the beginning of a new era in rock'n'roll. When the Mamas and the Papas came on to conclude the evening, the feeling of anti-climax was palpable. They may have been Hollywood royalty, but their performance was one of the last gasps of sixties pop. It was also riddled with contradictions: Michelle claimed that John Phillips 'forbade us to wear makeup or mess with our hair, because it would be bad for our contemporary hippie image', but that didn't stop Mia Farrow packing them off to Profile De Monde in Beverly Hills for their flamboyant silk robes.

What Monterey really represented was the transition from Pop to Rock – from toe-tapping teen discotheque music to FM Art for young adults. Back in February, Paul McCartney had told Cass Elliott that it was time for pop to be recognized as 'an art form'; now the just-released *Sgt Pepper's Lonely Hearts Club Band* was the unofficial soundtrack to the whole festival, redefining the possibilities of pop and turning the Beatles into high priests of the Global Village. Nor was the record industry exactly slow to recognize the changes in the wind. Gene Sculatti may have overstated things when he wrote that Monterey was simply 'a combination trade show and shopping spree' for the major labels, but it was all very neatly done. Lou Adler, whose Ode label was being distributed by Columbia, urged Clive Davis to make the trip from New York, while other honchos in the audience included Mo Ostin of Warners, Jerry Moss of A&M, and Jerry Wexler of Atlantic.

Ostin and Joe Smith at Warner-Reprise were already one step ahead of the game, having signed Hendrix and the Grateful Dead, but Clive Davis managed to nab the rest of the field – Big Brother, the Electric Flag, even Laura Nyro – while Capitol snapped up Steve Miller and the Quicksilver Messenger Service. In addition, all the majors began hiring in-house hippies or 'company freaks' with fingers on the pulse of the times: Andy Wickham at Reprise, Derek Taylor at A&M, David Anderle at Elektra. Even as unadventurous a label as Liberty admitted that 'we can't be complacent and just sit and watch the San Francisco scene'. Only RCA, who'd been so fast off the mark in signing Jefferson Airplane in 1966, failed to get in on the act.

After Monterey, Warners even opened an A&R office in San Francisco, installing Lovin' Spoonful producer Eric Jacobsen in the Columbus Towers and bankrolling him to the tune of $250,000. His only signing, however, was Norman Greenbaum. Liberty, meanwhile, signed the Nitty Gritty Dirt Band and Hour Glass, both of whom fell foul of the company's conveyor-belt packaging of bands. 'Liberty was that kind of a company,' recalls Dan Bourgoise, who joined United Artists as an A&R man after it had bought Liberty in 1968. 'Everything was marketing and merchandising. Jan and Dean was about as creative as the label got, though when they bought Imperial they inherited a few interesting things, including Kim Fowley. After Monterey, suddenly everyone in the company was wearing Nehru jackets and goatee beards. It was instant psychedelia. Monterey Pop was the death of pop. When the executives started looking like the bands, we were in trouble.'

Prior to Monterey, 'company freaks' had fought in vain to get new bands signed. At Columbia, for example, Billy James had been unable to drum up any enthusiasm for a new band called the Doors, while David Rubinson beat his head against brick walls to get Moby Grape signed. 'Their A&R department didn't want to know about hippies and long hair,' Rubinson recalled. 'Paul Revere and the Raiders was a heavy duty rock band for them.' Post-Monterey, record company bigwigs fell over each other to sign *anyone* with long hair. 'I had to be very careful not to disenfranchise our substantial roster of MOR, country, jazz and other artists,' Clive Davis wrote of his task at Columbia, which he described as the 'General Motors' of the record industry. That he managed to raise Columbia's share of the market from 6 per cent in 1965 to 17 per cent in 1968 showed he was right to take rock so seriously. In swift succession, the label would sign Santana, Sly and the Family Stone, Blood, Sweat and Tears, Chicago, It's a Beautiful Day, and finally – in what at the time was the biggest record deal ever made – Johnny Winter. 'Executives grew sideburns,' noted Clive Davis. 'Some even wore stack-heel boots and bellbottoms...'

Roll over Tony Bennett, and tell Andy Williams the news.

A gilded palace of sin: the Chateau Marmont, Sunset Boulevard.

5 *Strange Daze, Weird Sins*

I

Nothing was the same after Monterey. That 'international pop festival'
signalled not only the birth of the rock industry as we know it today, but
the onset of the decadence which characterized the music scene in
general — and the Los Angeles scene in particular — through the late sixties
and seventies.

Monterey was the end of the innocence, the High Moment of the
hippie dream which inadvertently opened up pop to every mogul in the
record business. 'Before Monterey, the music business was still making it
up as it went along,' says Denny Bruce. When Clive Davis took over, he —
and the whole New York business mentality — really ruined it.'

Perhaps it was no coincidence that just as the Clive Davises leapt on to
rock'n'roll, so the hippie dream began to turn sour. Even before Monterey,
Haight-Ashbury was being invaded by people to whom flower-power
ideals of peace and love were of scant concern: con-men, mobsters,
dealers, biker gangs. From all over America, they came to take advantage
of the stoned hippies. 'Rape is as common as bullshit on Haight Street,'
wrote Beat veteran Chester Anderson. 'Minds and bodies are being
maimed as we watch, a scale model of Vietnam.'

The Mothers take Manhatton, 1967. Top row, left to right: Billy Mundi, Roy Estrada, Ray Collins, Don Preston; bottom row, left to right: Jimmy Carl Black, Bunk Gardner, Frank Zappa.

When Joan Didion came up from Hollywood Babylon to take a peek in the late spring of 1967, she discovered that more kids were shooting crystal methedrine – an extremely potent and dangerous speed – than were tripping the light fantastic on acid. 'In the beginning, the drugs were being dealt by guys who looked like Jesus Christ, with robes and flowing hair,' says Dan Bourgoise. 'By the end of the sixties, these same guys had filthy beards and they were ripping people off. Everybody got real crazy. You started to see needles and crystal meth and guys who'd just got out of prison.' Nor was it long before heroin followed, as the only drug powerful enough to cushion the comedown from meth. If Joan Didion's conclusion that 'the centre was not holding' (a quote from Yeats' 'The Second Coming') was a mite histrionic at this point, it was certainly borne out by what happened in California over the subsequent decade. And by the fall of that year, Haight-Ashburyites themselves knew the dream was over. On 6 October 1967 they organized a 'Death of Hippie' march to mark the passing of the genuine article.

That month, Frank Zappa and the Mothers of Invention were putting the finishing touches to their satirical masterwork *We're Only In It for the Money*, which targeted 'phony hippies' as mercilessly as it did cops or nine-to-five suburbanites. By the time the album was released the following year, Zappa's sneering at 'Friscoids' seemed to have been vindicated. 'With Zappa, it was like he had X-ray vision and could see into the future,' says Pamela Des Barres, who babysat Zappa's kids. 'He could see where all the hippie bullshit was going, and when everything else got weirder, Frank got *less* weird. He saw the sixties run their course, and he started doing really hardcore music – *music* music. He'd just sit there in his basement and work.'

It wasn't only in San Francisco that the drugs were changing. Down in LA, unbeknownst to many, the likes of David Crosby and Cass Elliott were already starting to dabble with harder drugs, including heroin. 'David Crosby, Keith Richards and me turned half of Hollywood on to heroin,' CSNY drummer Dallas Taylor told *Spin* in 1990. Cass Elliott, when she wasn't stuffing her face with Twinkies, was particularly partial to such pharmaceutical opiates as Dilaudid and Demerol, often shooting opiate/methedrine speedballs with the Cros. More generally in LA, a methedrine/downers combo served as a kind of interim stage between pot/psychedelics and cocaine. By 1969, coke would be the preferred rock'n'roll mood-alterer.

The new decadence reflected the disarray of the LA music scene after Monterey: something was rotten in the state of Tinseltown. Michael Vosse, who'd worked for the Monterey Festival committee and later became 'house hippie' at A&M, felt the earth in LA was in need of immediate medical attention. 'The business is sick,' he told *World Countdown News*, 'and we have to keep attacking and working to make it well.' For the Mamas and the Papas, Monterey proved to be the climax of their career. While the perpetually fried Denny Doherty sped around the canyons Crosby-style on his Triumph, Cass Elliott surrounded herself with what John Phillips called 'a band of stoned hippie worshippers – poets, struggling musicians, would-be actors, sun-fried beach bums, debauched playboys, drug sponges, and bikers': pretty much your usual Hollywood detritus, in other words. The group's late-summer hit 'Twelve Thirty (Young Girls are Coming to the Canyon)' seemed to sum up where their heads were at.

On their way down: Mama Cass Elliot and Papa Denny Doherty.

John and Michelle Phillips, meanwhile, lived the Bel Air high life, mingling with their new movie-star pals at a Rodeo Drive celeb hangout called the Daisy. Their social career was to reach its zenith at the 1967 New Year's party they gave on Bel Air Road, with its guest list organized by archetypal Hollywood hanger-on Steve Brandt. Brandt's particular talent lay in bringing together people from the twin spheres of music and movies, and the New Year's party rounded up 900 of them. Eighteen months later, he killed himself with an overdose. So how *did* it feel to be one of the beautiful people?

After a Hollywood Bowl show in late August 1967, when Steve McQueen and Warren Beatty turned up to rub shoulders with the likes of Keith Richards and Anita Pallenberg, recording sessions for the Mamas' fourth album ground to a halt and John Phillips announced at a press conference that the group was taking a break. 'We're just grinding the songs out,' he said. 'We're not in any kind of groove. We're beginning to feel phony as artists.' By 1968, their fortunes were on the slide, with Cass Elliott thinking about a solo career on RCA and the Phillipses conducting a messy open marriage after the birth of their daughter Chynna.

The Papas and the Mamas, which failed even to make the Top 10 that summer, was in great part about the group's experience of fame, drugs and insulation. Songs such as 'Mansions' and the haunting 'Safe in My Garden' said everything about how far the quartet had come since their arrival three years before. 'The last album was torture to make, just torture,' recalled John Phillips. 'It contains some of the best songs, but we couldn't do them properly, everything was flat. We didn't really have the interest. I was glad to see the Mamas and Papas go. I didn't want to be the Brothers Four working off a hit for the next ten years.'

'By then, we were all burned out completely,' admits Lou Alder, who was now contemplating the formation of a partnership (MAP) with John Phillips and Terry Melcher. 'We were on such a high for those three or four years, everything we touched turned to gold, and the lifestyle was incredible. We were so high, there was no place left to go. And for some reason, everyone felt okay about quitting. The Mamas were at the very top and decided that was it.'

After 'Dream a Little Dream of Me' was released by Dunhill as a Cass Elliot solo single – making No. 12 in July 1968 – the big mama signed up for a $40,000-a-week stint at Caesar's Palace, a world away from her druggy inner echelon on Woodrow Wilson Drive. Following a disastrous opening night, John and Michelle Phillips flew out to give her moral support. In the backstage dressing-room they ran into some of the Hollywood hangers-on they'd met at Elliott's house: the celebrity hairdresser Jay Sebring, for example, and a dissolute pal of Roman Polanski's called Wojtek Frykowski.

Cass's next single was called 'California Earthquake'.

II

Few of the other big LA bands were in better shape than the Mamas. After the débâcle of *Smile*, the Beach Boys – in Carl Wilson's words – 'cooled out' with a fresh-faced, unfussily recorded album of California pop called *Wild Honey*. It was subsequently described by Bruce Johnston as 'probably the funkiest Beach Boys album', a fair summary if one can conceive of the group as being in any sense 'funky'. By the time of its release in late 1967, the band had followed the Beatles' suit and embraced the teachings of the Maharishi, which didn't stop the incorrigible Dennis Wilson holing up with his pal Gregg Jakobson in Benedict Canyon and bombing around on his bike stoned on nitrous oxide. Nor did Transcendental Meditation seem to interfere with his and Jakobson's formation with Terry Melcher of the self-explanatorily named 'Golden Penetrators', a triumvirate whose exploits occasionally saw them enjoying carnal knowledge of the hippie chicks who ran around with Dennis's new pal Charlie Manson. (The fact that Dennis claimed he felt the same 'weirdness and presence' on meeting the Maharishi that he'd felt when he first met Manson says a great deal about the thin sixties line between hippie spirituality and cultist brainwashing.)

The Maharishi's TM programme did inform the recording of *Friends*, however – to the extent that hardcore Beach Boys fans still refer to it as *The TM Album*. Despite the fact that it featured only two real Brian Wilson compositions, 'Busy Doin' Nothin'' and the sub-*Smile* instrumental 'Passing By', he subsequently called *Friends* his favourite Beach Boys album. 'Busy Doin' Nothin'', as it happened, was an accurate description of the bloated genius's zen torpor at the time, as well as being a veiled set of instructions on how to reach the Bellagio Road house where the album was recorded. The more encouraging signs on *Friends* were two gems penned by Dennis, 'Little Bird' and 'Be Still' – signs of a latent and overlooked talent which would only reach its fruition in his *Pacific Ocean Blue* album a decade later. Brian himself found no great solace in TM, for all the purported pleasure he took in *The TM Album*: by the end of 1968, he was close to suicidal. One chilly December night at the Whisky a Go Go, someone introduced him to cocaine – a constant companion for the next five years.

Love were even more obviously rent apart by drugs, for all of Arthur Lee's peevish claims that the other band members 'couldn't cut it'. According to Bruce Botnick, co-producer with Arthur of *Forever Changes*, the Love frontman was tripping virtually twenty-four hours a day, which can hardly have enhanced the band's chances of survival. Two final recordings – the spooky, self-referential 'Laughing Stock' and the equally psyched-out 'Your Mind and We Belong Together' – appeared on the 1968 Elektra sampler *Begin Here*, but sessions for the projected fourth album *Gethsemane* were aborted by Arthur, who retreated into the Hollywood hills and only re-emerged when Bob Krasnow signed a new and markedly inferior version of Love to his Blue Thumb label. Bryan Maclean, meanwhile, was lined up to record a solo album for Elektra, but also disappeared from the scene, later becoming a born-again Christian.

The Byrds got themselves back on course with the release of a Top 10 *Greatest Hits* album in August 1967, but it wasn't enough to prevent the inevitable ousting of David Crosby. 'McGuinn and Hillman came zooming up my driveway in their Porsches and said I was impossible to work with,' the Cros recalled, though he later claimed it was the Byrds' new manager Larry Spector who'd set the pair against him. Spector, no relation to Phil, had been introduced to the band by some of his other clients (including Peter Fonda and Dennis Hopper), and the introduction had prompted the unceremonious firing of Jim Dickson and Eddie Tickner. The new manager's first task had been to bring Gene Clark back into the fold, but the return was disastrous: Clark lasted a mere three weeks.

By January 1968, when *The Notorious Byrd Brothers* was released, Michael Clarke had also quit the band, replaced by former Rising Sons drummer Kevin Kelley. Produced by Gary Usher and featuring sessionmen such as drummer Jim Gordon and steel player Red Rhodes, *Notorious* was another mixed Byrds bag but a more cohesive album than *Younger than Yesterday*. Opening with the brass-bolstered 'Artificial Energy', a suitably edgy tribute to amphetamine, it moved through such spacey new songs as 'Draft Morning' and 'Tribal Gathering' and two numbers by Usher's old Brill Building pals Gerry Goffin and Carole King. Goffin and King had managed to keep their feet in pop's door via acts like the Animals, Paul Revere and the Raiders, and the Monkees, and now saw the Byrds not only covering their 'Goin' Back' – a Dylanesque elegy for the betrayed ideals of the folk-rock era – but turning 'Wasn't Born to Follow' into a piece of neo-psychedelic country rock.

The shakeups and personnel changes within Love, the Byrds and other bands were symptomatic of the gradual disintegration of the Sunset Strip scene. Smaller clubs such as the Trip had closed, and now the live circuit was made up of larger-capacity, Frisco-style ballrooms more suited to the post-Monterey status of bands such as Cream or Jefferson Airplane. The Kaleidoscope had a capacity of almost 1,500, while the Cheetah on Santa Monica Pier could accommodate well over 2,000. Originally built in the thirties and featuring an eighty-foot revolving stage, the Kaleidoscope was one of the most spectacular psychedelic ballrooms in America. Even bigger shows took place at the Shrine Exposition Hall or at the Santa Monica and Pasadena Civic Auditoriums. The whole scale of live rock entertainment had changed, and – despite the survival of the Whisky and Gazzari's – the small in-crowd club was the first casualty. 'The industry is generating product at an incredible pace, and new groups and record companies are appearing hourly,' said John Hartmann, co-owner of the Kaleidoscope. 'Now stand back and watch out!'

One could say that the end of a golden era was marked by the party Derek Taylor gave at Ciro's in March 1968 to say goodbye to LA. With the return to London of this much-loved Brit hipster, the Strip would never be quite the same place again. That summer the Byrds, who'd provided the music for Taylor's party, played in blazing 102° sunshine at an Orange County pop festival near Newport Beach. 'There wasn't the same spirit of camaraderie,' noted McGuinn. 'It was just an imitation of Monterey, like a huge beach with umbrellas.' In the same interview, McGuinn opined that there was 'no close-knit musical community in LA', as compared to the Greenwich Village he nostalgically remembered. 'There's always a competitive thing going on,' he said. 'Who's bigger than whom this year, you know?' Perhaps it wasn't entirely coincidental that the Byrds weren't very big that year.

III

One band, of course, had emerged from the Sunset Strip scene to drag the LA scene into a new era. Of all the LA groups, the Doors were the only one to register the profound psychic change in post-flower-power America, taking as their cue the sinisterly ambivalent songs of Love and the *Aftermath*-period Rolling Stones. Like their labelmates Love, they were the true sound of 'the bummer in the summer', when beautiful people started to look strange. 'The Stones were dirty, but the Doors were *dread*,' wrote Lester Bangs. '[And] dread is the great fact of our time.'

The early Doors were essentially a collision between garage punk and Beat poetics. When their ground-breaking first album was released at the beginning of 1967, it sounded like an art-rock version of all those Californian garage bands. There was no jingle-jangle folk-rock in the sound and no fey, wispy folk-rock in Jim Morrison's wholly original rock voice. 'There's an early Doors demo called "Go Insane", which is a total garage song,' says Greg Shaw. 'They only ever did it live, never recorded it properly, but it's a real three-chord Farfisa punk song, and of course they did "Gloria" and "Louie Louie" like every other band did.'

What people often fail to realize about the Doors is just how unhip they were initially considered to be on the Sunset Strip. The very fact that they were from boho mecca Venice counted strongly against them, while Morrison's poetic pretensions were antithetical to the pop cool of the Trip and Whisky in-crowd. 'Nobody ever wanted to jam with the Doors,' says writer Eve Babitz, who as an apprentice groupie none the less made it her business to bed the young Jim Morrison. 'They never fit in, because they weren't Dewey Martin sort of people.'

At the UCLA Film School in the spring of 1965, Jim Morrison had been a dorkish Nietzsche junkie, a wannabe martyr-to-art searching for a Parisian garret in Lotusland. But something happened while Jimbo was living on Venice Beach that summer, reading Rimbaud and

'They never fit in, because they weren't Dewey Martin sort of people': the early Doors on the Strip. Left to right: Robbie Krieger, John Densmore, Jim Morrison, Ray Manzarek.

scarfing tabs of acid like there was no tomorrow: he got skinny. And one night, the Doors were born when Morrison recited the first verse of his poem 'Moonlight Drive' to fellow UCLA student Ray Manzarek on a moonlight beach: 'Let's swim to the moon, let's climb through the tide,' went the lines, 'penetrate the evening that the city sleeps to hide.'

The song was like a *noir* inversion of the Californian surfing dream, a dark ode to the Pacific which turned Los Angeles back into a city of night and encapsulated the menace which would become the group's stock-in-trade. Manzarek, four years Jim's senior, was sufficiently impressed to dragoon him into his little Santa Monica bar-band Rick and the Ravens. By September, the Ravens had evolved into an early version of the Doors and were recording demos at the World Pacific studio, home only a year before to the Byrds.

Few were impressed by the resulting demo-tape. Lou Adler muttered that 'there's nothing I can use here' and Liberty virtually threw the band out of his office. The only person to show the slightest interest in the Doors was Columbia's Billy James, who not only offered them a six-month contract but arranged for the purchase of the Vox organ that would give their sound its pronounced psych-punk flavour. When Manzarek met guitarist Robbie Krieger in a meditation class and asked him to join, the lineup was complete. Several bar mitzvah jobs later, the Doors were more than proficient at hammering out versions of 'Gloria', 'Money', and 'Louie Louie'.

Despite the fact that Terry Melcher had expressed some interest in producing them, Billy James couldn't persuade the bigwigs at Columbia to commit themselves to the Doors: by the late spring, he'd reluctantly let them go. All the band had going for them now was a residency at terminally unfashionable dive the London Fog, a little way along from the Whisky on the Strip. Haunted by hookers, drunks and down-at-heel lounge lizards – not forgetting the requisite go-go blonde in a cage – it was the perfect place for Morrison to hone his stage act. Already in the band's repertoire were 'The End' and the Brecht–Weill 'Alabama Song', though the former at this stage was merely about the termination of some wan romance and lacked its shocking Oedipal climax.

Someone who happened to catch the Doors at the Fog was Ronnie Haran, who booked bands for Elmer Valentine at the Whisky. Smitten with Morrison's moody looks and the band's distinctive sound, she persuaded an unenthusiastic Valentine to give the group a shot as the Whisky's house band. Over the course of three months the Doors got to support Them, the Seeds, the Mothers, the Animals, Buffalo Springfield and Captain Beefheart. The UCLA's *Daily Bruin* labelled them 'Artaud Rock' and hailed Morrison as 'a gaunt, hollow Ariel from hell'.

With Jim installed in Ronnie Haran's little apartment behind the Whisky, the Doors continued to meet a barrage of indifference. Only Haran's efforts in persuading teenage girls to call into the Whisky to ask about Jim made Elmer Valentine persevere with them. Even Jac Holzman of Elektra was unimpressed: had it not been for Arthur Lee urging him to see the band a second time, Holzman might never have signed them. 'Bruce Botnick would tell Jac the Doors were the American Stones, but Jac wasn't having any of it,' recalls Denny Bruce. 'The beatnik poetry shit and the fake Jagger pose were as much of a turnoff for him as they were for everyone else.'*

Once signed – to a mere one-album deal – the Doors went into Sunset Sound with producer Paul Rothchild, who'd just emerged from eight months inside on a hash-smuggling charge. The son of an opera singer and a British businessman, he'd grown up in Greenwich Village and engineered Bob Dylan's infamous electric set at the 1965 Newport Folk Festival. At the behest of Holzman, he'd moved to the Coast to be part of Elektra's attempt to stamp its presence on the LA scene. Along with Bruce Botnick, who engineered the sessions, Rothchild had a lot to do with the way *The Doors* turned out in the fall of 1966.

Certainly it needed someone with Rothchild's authority to keep Jim

---

* In later years, of course, Holzman downplayed his early reservations, claiming that in the Doors 'I recognized our ticket to the big time' and that 'I pursued them vigorously'. Among the other West Coast acts Elektra signed during the second half of the sixties were tousle-headed troubadour Tim Buckley; Clear Light, featuring Dallas Taylor and Danny Kortchmar; Rhinoceros, a would-be 'supergroup' featuring fomer Mothers drummer Billy Mundi and two ex-members of the dreadful Iron Butterfly; the intriguing singer-songwriter David Ackles; Michael Fennelly's Crabby Appleton; and Bread, the soft-rock brainchild of Oklahoman songwriter/producer David Gates. Elektra were also quick to home in on the emerging late-sixties sound of Detroit, signing both the Stooges and the MC5.

Morrison in check, since the singer was already demonstrating some of the traits which in time would nearly destroy the band. During the recording of the newly extended 'The End', for example, Morrison hurled a TV set through the control-room window, then hosed down the studio with a fire extinguisher. Rothchild thought Morrison was 'a true chemical schizophrenic', someone who underwent a Jekyll and Hyde transformation on acid, but other people suspected the whole thing was as much a sham as 'The End' itself, exposing the adolescent exhibitionism at the heart of the Doors' 'theatre'.

'We felt that if Elektra could make us as big as Love, that would be fine,' recalled drummer John Densmore in his book *Riders on the Storm*. Little did he know how much more Jac Holzman would be prepared to do to make the Doors happen. Most famously, of course, *The Doors* was the beneficiary of the very first advertising billboard for an album to appear on the Sunset Strip. 'The Doors Break On Through With An Electrifying Album', read the sign, and the band – still rather collegiate in appearance – posed beneath it for photographs.

Lizard man cometh: Morrison and the Doors in late 1967.

Despite the ferocious excitement of the first single, 'Break On Through (to the Other Side)', it wasn't until the release of the edited 'Light My Fire' that the album began taking off in the early summer of 1967. Shortly after the Monterey festival, for which they were overlooked until it was too late to add them to the bill, 'Light My Fire' made it to No. 1 and the little girls definitely understood the sex appeal in the beguiling croon of this 'psychedelic Sinatra'. 'The End', meanwhile, caught the ominous underside of the Summer of Love, in which all the stoned children were actually deranged, 'lost in the Roman wilderness' of free love and chemical experimentation. Morrison celebrated the success of both the single and the album by investing in a custom-made black leather suit: the Lizard King was born.*

That summer, Morrison was ensconced with the feisty Pamela Courson

* For the post-punk generation, 'The End' is inextricably wedded to the stunning opening sequence of Coppola's *Apocalypse Now*, a film which deploys Vietnam as a *locus* to which America has removed its worst sixties nightmares. But it may be more appropriate to think of the song in terms of the dysfunctional bourgeois psychopathology Frank Zappa confronted on *We're Only In It for the Money*: middle-class hippie kids from the same repressive background as Morrison himself, initially liberated by sex and drugs and rock'n'roll but now simply disoriented, frightened and potentially dangerous.

in an apartment fifty yards from the Laurel Canyon Country Store – 'the store where the creatures meet' in 'Love Street'. Most nights they lived it up together on the Strip, Pamela already flirting with the heroin that would later kill her. By day, Jim was back at Sunset Sound, cutting the Doors' second album with Rothchild and Botnick. Briefly in attendance was Joan Didion, who included her account of the Doors at the end of *Slouching Towards Bethlehem*.

Strange Days, released shortly after Love's equally creepy *Forever Changes*, was an even more compelling statement about fear and alienation than *The Doors*: even Morrison's dreamy 'girl' songs ('You're Lost, Little Girl', 'Unhappy Girl', 'I Can't See Your Face in My Mind') sounded sinister. From the hypnotic organ riffs of the title track to the Dionysiac blowout of the epic 'When the Music's Over', via the Top 20 single 'People are Strange' and the surreal Beat nightmare of 'Horse Latitudes', the album suggested the lurking malevolence which had begun to encroach on LA's good vibrations. 'This city is looking for a ritual to join its fragments,' Morrison told *Time*. 'The Doors are looking for such a ritual, too – a sort of electric wedding.' For Greg Shaw, the best music by the Doors, like that of Love and the Rolling Stones, was 'a kind of invocation'.

Of course Morrison was pretentious, parlaying his high-school take on existentialism into black-leather rock mystique. Of course he knew how to play the media, 'turning keys' – in his own words – when it suited him. 'He was pure Hollywood,' says Eve Babitz. 'It was showbiz meets Aleister Crowley.' (This was why Morrison was made to be reinvented as a demonic rock god by his disciple Danny Sugerman and *The Doors* director Oliver Stone: he'd already done their work for them.) In his book *West Coast Story*, Rob Burt argues that most of Morrison's songs were pulp – 'in the sense that a song like "End of the Night" bears about as much relation to Louis-Ferdinand Celine as Mickey Spillane does to Ernest Hemingway'. But if they were pulp, says Burt, they were pulp with 'a certain sleazy grandeur'.

The trouble was, no sooner had the Doors defined their time with the first two albums than they lost their own plot. 'I mean, what else can you *say* after you've said "This is the end"?!' laughs Eve Babitz. Lester Bangs felt that even by *Strange Days* 'it was becoming apparent that the group was limited ... and that Morrison's "Lizard King" vision was usually morbid in the most obvious possible way.' By the time they released *Waiting for the Sun* in 1968, their street credibility had gone down the toilet. The album was at No. 1 for four weeks, spawning the sub-bubblegum No. 1 single 'Hello, I Love You', but the darkness of the earlier music had given way to the staggering pretension of 'Not to Touch the Earth', 'Yes, the River Knows', and the anti-Vietnam song 'The Unknown Soldier', all horribly over-arranged and inauthentic attempts at art-rock. Worst of all was 'Five to One', a facile attempt to cash in on the violence and insurrection of 1968.

As the critical acclaim faded, so Morrison increasingly resorted to the kind of 'theatrical' outrage which saw him arrested for exposing himself onstage in March 1969. Offstage, he'd become a slobbering alcoholic, provoking people to beat him up and generally exhausting the patience of the other Doors and anyone associated with the group. 'I saw him go from being that amazing Lizard King creature to being someone you'd just walk past lying in the gutter in front of the Whisky,' says Pamela Des Barres.

The Soft Parade went even further than *Waiting for the Sun* in the pretension stakes. Recorded for $86,000 in the late spring of 1969, the album had more in common with the orchestral superpop of Brian Wilson and Jimmy Webb than with the garage punk of the early Doors. Paul Rothchild hired Paul Harris to arrange horns and strings – an ensemble dubbed 'the La Cienega Symphony' by one Doors acolyte – while Ray Manzarek brought in West Coast Jazz veterans Curtis Amy (tenor sax) and George Bohanan (trombone) to play on the Top 5 hit 'Touch Me'. There was still cod-revolutionary stuff on 'Do It', but it sounded hollower than ever.

IV

By *The Soft Parade*, the Doors were *passé*. In LA, new bands were emerging – or evolving out of old bands – and establishing fresh styles and movements. The nascent heavy metal of Steppenwolf and Iron Butterfly mirrored the 'heavy' English blues-rock of Cream and Led Zeppelin and the sound of American power trios such as Blue Cheer. Electric blues was itself back on the map courtesy of ex-Rising Son Taj Mahal, signed as a solo artist to Columbia, and Canned Heat, who enjoyed Top 20 hits with 'On the Road Again' and 'Going Up the Country' after wowing the crowd at Monterey. For Heat guitarist and sometime Mother Henry Vestine, white blues was part of a 'general trend' towards non-harmonic music. 'White America is

Refried boogiemen Canned Heat. Left to right: Larry Taylor, Henry Vestine, Bob 'the Bear' Hite, Al Wilson, Fito de la Parra.

in for the drone,' he proclaimed, and the sludgy 41-minute 'Refried Hockey Boogie' on Canned Heat's 1968 double-album *Living the Blues* seemed to bear out his prophecy.

Spirit, whom Lou Adler signed to his Ode label in late 1967, were part of the same Ash Grove/ Topanga Canyon scene – bassist Mark Andes had even played in Canned Heat's second lineup. The group was a decidedly het-erogeneous outfit: drummer Ed Cassidy was a 36-year-old jazz veteran who'd played with Art

Spirit in Topanga Canyon, 1969.
Left to right: Randy California, Ed
Cassidy, Mark Andes, John Locke,
Jay Ferguson.

Pepper and Gerry Mulligan long before winding up in the Rising Sons, and Randy California was a wild lead guitarist in the Hendrix mould. After playing briefly as the Red Roosters, under which name they became the house band at It's Boss in late 1965, they broke up, re-forming in April 1967 as Spirits Rebellious. When Lou Adler saw Spirit at the Whisky that fall – California, Cassidy, Andes, jazz-rooted pianist John Locke and singer Jay Ferguson – their jazz/blues/hard-rock fusion seemed to point the way forward from folk-rock. 'The combination of Cass and California was very unique,' Adler recalls. 'If Hendrix hadn't existed, Randy would have been him. And Cass had every possible style: big-band jazz and everything else.'

Barry 'Dr Demento' Hansen, who lived in Spirit's Topanga Canyon house on Cuesta Cala Road through this period, says that it was to Adler's credit that he 'would only go so far in making them commercial', even though the second album's 'I Got a Line on You' turned out to be a surprise Top 30 hit in March 1969. (1969 was also the year of Jacques Demy's film *The Model Shop*, in which Anouk Aimée drifted aimlessly around Los Angeles with a morose young architect and Spirit appeared in an embarrassing rehearsal scene.) Hansen remembers the band's Topanga neighbours: Neil Young grumbling about Buffalo Springfield's managers Greene and Stone, Charlie Manson wandering up the driveway one afternoon to ask if he could listen to Spirit jam. In point of fact, Spirit only really came good when Lou Adler entrusted them to Neil Young's producer David Briggs and they recorded the late psychedelic masterpiece *12 Dreams of Dr Sardonicus* (1970) – by which point the original lineup was on the verge of splitting up.

The recycled blues of bands such as Canned Heat reflected a general swing away from the experimentation of acid rock and a return to the 'roots' of rock'n'roll. This was particularly evident in the country rock sound which began to spread through the LA scene in 1967–8. Country, as it happens, had always been big in Southern California. Bands such as the Beverly Hillbillies, no less, had based themselves in Hollywood in the twenties, while countless singing cowboys flocked to the city through the 1930s. The roots of Californian country lay in the migrations of the Depression era, when dustbowl refugees came in their thousands to find jobs in the oil fields and fruit farms. With the influx of Okies came hillbilly laments and the protest songs of Woody Guthrie, who broadcast from KFVD Los Angeles in the mid thirties. Ironically, LA's first major radio 'barn dance', 'Town Hall Party', was broadcast in the late forties from Compton, later the seedbed of gangsta rap. This was where *Hee Haw* star Buck Owens got his first break before becoming one of the stars of the country scene in Bakersfield, a hot, dry little city a hundred miles north of LA in the San Joaquin Valley.*

Artists such as Owens, Rose Maddox, Wanda Jackson and Merle Haggard put Bakersfield country on the map after signing to Capitol in the late fifties and early sixties. Using some of the transplanted southerners who were playing on the big LA pop hits – guitarists such as Glen Campbell and James Burton – these acts enjoyed big country hits in a western honky-tonk style very different from the polished 'countrypolitan' records coming out of Nashville. Ex-con Haggard, for example, established himself as a kind of lone-wolf blue-collar hero, hitting with records such as 'Branded Man', 'Lonesome Fugitive', 'Workin' Man Blues', and the notoriously reactionary but only half-serious 'Okie from Muskogee'. Capitol's country roster probably explains why the label had a pronounced southern flavour in the late sixties, what with hit singles by Glen Campbell, Joe South, Bobbie Gentry and others.

In February 1966, no less a figure than Rick Nelson, reeling from the body-blow that was the British Invasion, turned his wayward talents to country music. Alongside songs by the likes of Willie Nelson, *Bright Lights and Country Music* featured the self-penned 'You Just Can't Quit', a fitting title for the man stranded by the outgoing tide of his teen-idol fame.

* Country music even had its very own *Hollywood Babylon*-style scandals, as Nick Tosches was only too delighted to point out in his scabrous *Country: The Biggest Music in America*. One of the most popular Western Swing bands in the LA barn-dance circuit in the late forties and fifties was that led by Spade Cooley, who – sixteen years after being arrested for rape in 1945 – murdered his wife because she'd once slept with his old pal Roy Rogers. No wonder James Ellroy gave ol' Spade a cameo appearance in the grisly *LA Confidential*.

Playing on a country bill at the Shrine Auditorium that June, he was backed not only by his trusty Imperial-era sidemen James Burton and Glen D. Hardin, but by Clarence White, the brilliant young bluegrass guitarist whom Chris Hillman brought in to grace the two country songs on the Byrds' *Younger than Yesterday*.

Along with Gene Clark, whose early-1967 album with bluegrass duo the Gosdin brothers can lay claim to the title 'First Country Rock Album', it was Chris Hillman who was primarily responsible for the growth of country rock in LA. A veteran of the LA bluegrass scene of the early sixties and still a formidable mandolin player when the occasion demanded, Hillman had always pushed the Byrds to include country material on their albums. Other LA country acts – John Hartford, Stone Country, Nashville West, Hearts and Flowers and the evergreen Dillards – only made Hillman the keener to steer Roger McGuinn away from the spacey 'jet sound' of *The Notorious Byrd Brothers*. When Byrds manager Larry Spector introduced Hillman to a lanky, trust-funded southerner called Gram Parsons, Chris figured he'd found the vital ingredient to help the Byrds change course.

Gram Parsons had first come out to LA in the early spring of 1967, at the suggestion of Brandon de Wilde. This fast-living thespian, a crony of Peter Fonda's and Dennis Hopper's, had met Parsons and his International Submarine Band in New York and set about pushing them to Peter Fonda and Roger Corman as a group they might be able to use in *The Trip*. Although the ISB did appear as the featured band in the film's nightclub scene, Corman felt that Gram's song 'Lazy Days' wasn't 'freaky' enough and replaced it on the soundtrack with music by the Electric Flag.

Corman's reaction to 'Lazy Days' was hardly surprising, since Parsons and lead guitarist John Neuse were edging towards the country rock which would dominate the Submarine Band album *Safe at Home*. Parsons was a middle-class folkie who'd majored in theology at Harvard after disbanding his group the Shilohs in 1965. 'He was an outcast southerner,' wrote Long Ryder Sid Griffin. 'He'd lost his accent and felt guilty about it.' John Neuse claimed that it was *his* influence in the ISB that turned Gram back on to country from folk-rock: if that was the case, it still wasn't enough to convince drummer Mickey Gauvin and bassist Ian Dunlop, who split to form a loose, embryonic version of the Flying Burrito Brothers.

With drummer Jon Corneal and bassist Chris Ethridge, a new ISB was signed to Lee Hazelwood's fledgling LHI label in the summer of 1967, after auditioning for Hazelwood's girlfriend Suzi Jane Holkom. The resulting *Safe at Home*, 'produced' by Holkom (with Hazelwood looking over her shoulder) but only released after Parsons' departure the following spring, was another claimant to the title 'First Country Rock Album', featuring not only Gram originals but versions of songs by Johnny Cash and Merle Haggard. While it wasn't *GP* or *The Gilded Palace of Sin*, the seeds of both those albums were in the grooves of 'Blue Eyes' and 'Do You Know How it Feels to be Lonesome?', which Parsons revisited on

Gram Parsons joins the Byrds in February 1968. Left to right: Parsons, Kevin Kelley, Chris Hillman, Roger McGuinn.

The Gilded Palace. John Neuse recalled the sessions taking place during 'a heavy, emotional period for Gram', when the singer was involved with a highly strung beauty named Nancy Lee Ross, then pregnant with his child. The strange, fatalistic pain of Parsons' voice certainly transformed the cover versions on *Safe at Home* – including Porter Wagoner's 'A Satisfied Mind', which Chris Hillman had sung on *Turn! Turn! Turn!* – from respectful interpretations into genuinely heartfelt performances.

Unimpressed by either Holkom or LHI Records, Parsons was ripe for the poaching when he bumped into Chris Hillman in a Beverly Hills bank one February afternoon. Roger McGuinn later claimed he'd thought they were 'just hiring a piano player' when they invited Gram to join the Byrds that month; he'd had no idea the guy was 'a monster in sheep's clothing . . . George Jones in a sequin suit'. McGuinn, in any case, was less keen on taking a country deviation than Hillman. For him, *Sweetheart of the Rodeo*, part-recorded in Nashville with Gary Usher still at the helm, was merely 'a feature on country music, a close-up, a special issue' – at most, just part of an ambitious 'five-stage chronology of twentieth-century music' he wanted the Byrds to record. None the less, it was enough to see the band making a somewhat tense appearance on that bastion of the country establishment, the Grand Ole Opry. The new lineup made its LA debut shortly afterwards, providing the live entertainment at Derek Taylor's farewell party.

There were those, including Gary Usher, who suggested that McGuinn was more than a little threatened by the way Parsons seemed to be taking over the Byrds; and that his paranoia was such that he replaced most of Parsons' vocals on *Sweetheart* with his own. Both McGuinn and Hillman deny this, attributing the removal of Gram's vocals to a threatened lawsuit by Lee Hazelwood. But it was certainly true that McGuinn felt he'd been outvoted by the triumvirate of Hillman, Parsons and Gary Usher, who – in his own words – 'didn't want to go along with the electronic music idea'.

All this might lead the unacquainted listener to suppose that *Sweetheart of the Rodeo* was a hotchpotch of an album, yet Gary Usher managed not only to pull the sessions together but to produce a coherent country-rock statement a full year before Dylan's *Nashville Skyline*. 'The Byrds have approached country music as an entity in itself and have aimed for a greater degree of fidelity to the rules of the style,' wrote Jon Landau in *Rolling Stone*, comparing the band to the more dilettante-ish Buffalo Springfield. 'In doing country as country, [they] show just how powerful and relevant unadorned country music is to the music of today. And they leave just enough rock in the drums to let you know they can still play rock'n'roll.' The boldness of the album, with its songs about liquor, murder and Christianity, was reflected in its minimal sales: released in that summer of violent protest and equally violent repression, *Sweetheart* sounded almost quaint. 'It wasn't the hippest music, but that was maybe why we wanted to do it,' McGuinn later said. 'Maybe it was a little too country, but it did kinda start things off.'

'Start things off' is an understatement. Within a year of *Sweetheart*'s release, Parsons and Hillman had quit the Byrds to form the official Flying Burrito Brothers, Richie Furay and Jim Messina had left Buffalo Springfield to form Poco, Gene Clark and Doug Dillard had cut the classic *Fantastic Expedition of Dillard and Clark*, and Rick Nelson had played six nights at the Troubadour with his new Stone Canyon Band. The marriage of redneck roots and longhair modernism was finally being consummated. As the decade drew to a close and the hippie ideals of 1967 looked increasingly bankrupt, rock'n'roll retreated to the safe harbour of tradition. LA may have been a long way from the Appalachian mountains, but the canyons and deserts provided perfect backdrops for the Cosmic Cowboy imagery which began to proliferate at this time.

Although he was never to receive due recognition in his lifetime, Gram Parsons continued to pave the way forward for the 'country rock' genre. Quitting the Byrds on the eve of their notorious and disastrous South African tour in the summer of 1968, he hung out with the Rolling Stones and exerted a considerable influence over Keith Richards.* On his return to California, he holed up in Topanga Canyon with Chris Hillman, smoking large quantities of reefer and writing some of the songs which would end up on *The Gilded Palace of Sin*: 'Juanita', about a screwed-up girl Gram had met at the Troubadour; 'Christine's Tune', about super-groupie Miss Christine; and 'Sin City', about the venal goings-on of the LA music

---

* *Let It Bleed*'s 'Country Honk' was essentially Gram's version of 'Honky Tonk Women', while 'Wild Horses' – recorded by the Burritos before even the Stones had cut it – had Parsons stamped all over it. For an interesting pseudo-fictional depiction of the relationship between Parsons and Richards, see 'Rosewood Casket' in Eve Babitz's *Eve's Hollywood*.

industry – specifically those of their former manager Larry Spector. Hillman admired the fact that Parsons had no time for contemporary rock, listening only to George Jones and Hank Williams on the one hand, or James Carr and Bobby 'Blue' Bland on the other.

Mo Ostin got wind of the nascent Burritos and expressed an interest in signing them to Warner Brothers. But then out of the blue swooped A&M, perhaps the least hip label in LA. With the nucleus of the band consisting of Parsons, Hillman, pedal-steel maestro Sneaky Pete Kleinow and ex-ISB bassist Chris Ethridge, the band recorded *The Gilded Palace of Sin*, an inspired blend of soulful ballads ('Do Right Woman', 'Hot Burrito No. 1') and up-tempo country numbers ('Christine's Tune', 'My Uncle') which went some considerable way towards realizing Gram's dream of a new 'Cosmic American Music'. David Crosby sang harmony on 'Do Right Woman', and Miss Christine's fellow GTOs (Girls Together Outrageously) Mercy and Pamela sang along on the chorus of the gospel sermonette 'Hippie Boy'.

With *The Gilded Palace*, Gram established himself as the rock'n'roll Hank Williams he'd always wanted to be. Barry Feinstein's album cover shot showed the Burritos in the suits they'd ordered from Nudie's of North Hollywood, Gram's adorned not with the standard roses and cacti but with pills, naked women and marijuana plants. 'He was true glitter-

Nudie's, 'rodeo tailors' to the space cowboys of country rock.

glamour rock,' wrote Miss Mercy: a space cowboy with babyfaced sex appeal and a recondite vision of freaks and rednecks in harmony.

Parsons should have been a huge star, but the Burritos fell into a kind of fault line: too country for the rock audience, too rock for the country audience. *The Gilded Palace* flopped miserably. 'Nobody gave a shit about Gram, he never sold any records,' says Pamela Des Barres. 'No one took him seriously except people like Don Henley. Henley was definitely watching him, and of course Bernie Leadon brought a whole lot of Gram's influence from the Burritos to the Eagles.' Paying their dues in the numerous country & western dives which littered North Hollywood and the San Fernando Valley – places like the Prelude, the Palomino, the Plantation and Snoopy's Opera House – the Burritos honed their Cosmic American Music in front of ornery Waylon Jennings fanatics. Chris Hillman remembered people yelling 'Goddam queers!' at the band, but Parsons' wavering, tears-in-beer twang usually won them over. 'The best performances he'd do were at the Palomino on Talent Night, where he'd come out and just do a song or two,' recalled Jim Seiter, who co-managed the band with a grizzled ex-con named Phil Kaufman.

By the end of 1969, after the Burritos had played Altamont and begun work on their second album, *Burrito Deluxe*, the group's lack of success had started to tell on Parsons, who in any case was less of a team player than had once been supposed. Despite the fact that he was living with Chris Hillman and new drummer Michael Clarke in the so-called 'Burrito Manor' off Beverly Glen Canyon, Gram was frustrated by the group's shortcomings as country musicians. 'I always thought the Burritos had a drummer problem,' he said later, adding that 'Sneaky wasn't the right steel player for the group'. Nor was he thrilled at the choice of former Byrds mentor Jim Dickson as the producer for the less countrified *Burrito Deluxe*. After taking a bad spill riding his motorcycle with his friend John Phillips, he quit the Burritos, moved in with Terry Melcher, and spent much of the ensuing two years as a glorified Stones groupie.

None of this changed the fact that Parsons had done more than anyone to – in John Rockwell's words – 'disseminate country music' through 'a tightly knit circle of associates', making country rock the predominant sound of Los Angeles as the new decade dawned. By 1970, this 'tightly knit circle' was so interconnected and incestuous that it was hard to keep track of the constant personnel changes. (It

The Burritos were regulars at C&W dives like the Palomino.

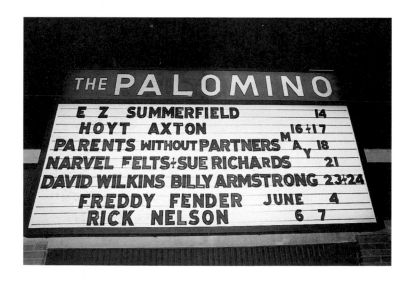

took an obsessive Englishman named Pete Frame to map out the scene's genealogy in his famous 'Family Trees' for *Zigzag* magazine.) It said everything about the LA scene that even Michael Nesmith, the success of whose band the Monkees had partly given rise to the country-rock backlash against prefab pop, was re-emerging from the haze of the sixties as a country- rock singer-songwriter – an outstanding one at that, as his 1970 RCA debut *Magnetic South* showed. Other LA acts picking up where Parsons had temporarily left off included Linda Ronstadt, whose Stone Poneys had made the Top 20 with Nesmith's song 'Different Drum' at the tail end of 1967; Richie Furay's Poco, who made an auspicious debut at the Troubadour in November 1968 but then produced a series of rather bland albums for Epic; Rick Nelson and the Stone Canyon Band, whose 1969 *In Concert* album garnered a great *Rolling Stone* review from Lester Bangs of all people; the ex-Kingston Trio folkie John Stewart, with his fine, Nashville-recorded *California Bloodlines* album; and the Troubadour-formed duo Longbranch Pennywhistle, comprising J. D. Souther and future Eagles frontman Glenn Frey. Country also tinged the music of Crosby, Stills, Nash (and Neil Young), though you could never have described them as 'country rock'. Up in San Francisco, meanwhile, the Grateful Dead betrayed distinct country leanings on *Workingman's Dead* and *American Beauty*, then gave birth to the spinoff country-rock band New Riders of the Purple Sage.

V

Country rock was symptomatic of the general swing back to rootsy music in Los Angeles – a swing exemplified by the loose coalition of singers and musicians that had formed earlier in the decade around 'the Oklahoma Mafia' of Leon Russell, David Gates, Jimmy Markham, Jesse 'Ed' Davis, Carl Radle and others. Out of this funky Valley scene, affiliated to the original Flying Burrito Brothers, came Delaney and Bonnie, Leon Russell's Asylum Choir, Mad Dogs and Englishmen, and the motley entourage who backed Mac Rebennack in his new incarnation as voodoo shaman Dr John Creaux, the Night Tripper – aggregations made up substantially of transplanted southerners who'd been playing sessions for the likes of Phil Spector, Lou Adler, Snuff Garrett and Jimmy Bowen. The result was what David Anderle (who signed Delaney and Bonnie to Elektra) calls 'American white roots blues', a kind of sanctified hippie-soul music which was perfectly in synch with the Stones of *Let It Bleed*, The Band of *Music from Big Pink*, and the Van Morrison of *Moondance*. 'It was Delaney and Bonnie who got me locked into England, as well as into Leon Russell and that whole crowd,' says Anderle. 'It was blues and it was Stax, but it was very LA, too. Glyn Johns told me the Stones loved the Delaney and Bonnie album, and as a result he brought them over to LA to finish *Let*

Mac Rebennack, who'd come to LA from New Orleans as a sessionman before reinventing himself as 'Dr John the Night Tripper'.

It Bleed at the Elektra studio.' (Featured on *Let It Bleed* were such LA linchpins as Leon Russell, Ry Cooder, Bobby Keys and the group's long-time man-in-LA Jack Nitzsche.)

The avant-garde alternative to this retrogressive, post-psychedelic music was the genuine freakdom of the artists Frank Zappa was signing to his new Bizarre production company. Zappa himself had spent most of 1967 in New York, returning to LA in the spring of 1968 and moving with his wife Gail and seven-month-old daughter Moon Unit into an old Laurel Canyon 'cabin' which had belonged to the twenties western star Tom Mix. After the New York sessions for the wildly experimental, pre-dominantly non-vocal double album *Uncle Meat* (and for *Cruising with Ruben & the Jets*, his affectionately skewed tribute to the LA doo-wop sound of his youth), Zappa spent the spring securing the rights to material by those pioneering LA freaks Lenny Bruce and Lord Buckley and recording the demented Larry Fischer, a Sunset Strip vagrant who, for a dime or two, would produce 'songs' out of thin air. The latter's *An Evening with Wild Man Fischer* was part of a 'social documentary' series Zappa intended to issue on Bizarre.

Alongside Bizarre, Zappa and Herbie Cohen formed the sister label Straight, to which they promptly signed the GTOs, a troupe of wild creatures who'd danced with Vito and become Hollywood super-groupies. Comprising the Zappas' babysitter Miss Christine, along with the Misses Pamela, Mercy, Sandra and Cynderella, the GTOs couldn't play any instruments but they did embody the dissolute spirit of the LA rock scene that Zappa liked to observe from a distance. When Zappa put on a big Christmas show at the Shrine in December 1968, the GTOs cavorted onstage with the Mothers while Larry Fischer lapped the auditorium between verses of 'The Circle'. Also on the bill was Vince Damon Furnier, a.k.a. Alice Cooper, a renegade Arizonan whom Christine had introduced to Zappa at LA's new groupie HQ the Landmark Motel and who would shortly be added to the Straight roster.*

But the most auspicious signing to the Bizarre/Straight empire was unquestionably Zappa's old boyhood pal Don Van Vliet, who by the late summer of 1968 had parted company with the Magic Band and returned to Lancaster. Beefheart had had a torrid time of things since *Safe as Milk*, what with Ry Cooder quitting the band on the eve of their Monterey Festival appearance and Bob Krasnow releasing the electronically 'psyche-delicized' *Strictly Personal* on Blue Thumb without Beefheart's approval. Zappa knew this and offered Beefheart the opportunity to record for Straight. By the end of the year, the Captain had put together a new edition

---

* Frank Zappa later fell out with Herb Cohen, claiming his partner/manager ripped him off to the tune of several million dollars. They were in litigation for ten years. 'People like Herb Cohen ruined the business,' says Pamela Des Barres. 'He never gave a shit about the music, unlike Joe Smith or Jerry Wexler or people like that. He wasn't the slightest bit eccentric, he just stood around scowling.'

of the Magic Band and installed them in a run-down ranch way out in the Valley near Topanga Canyon.

For a long time, the story was that Beefheart wrote all the songs on *Trout Mask Replica* in eight and a half hours, then spent months teaching them to the Magic Band note-by-note. Now it seems more likely that the band – with fellow desert drongoes Rockette Morton (Mark Boston) and Zoot Horn Rollo (Bill Harkleroad) drafted in alongside Antennae Jimmy Semens (Jeff Cotton) and Drumbo (John French) – had a major hand in such extraordinary songs as 'Dachau

Captain Beefheart with the Trout Mask Replica *lineup of the Magic Band.* Left to right: Zoot Horn Rollo, Beefheart, the Mascara Snake, Antennae Jimmy Semens, Rockette Morton.

Blues', 'Moonlight on Vermont', and 'When Big Joan Sets Up'. Whatever the truth, the fact remains that when Beefheart was finally ready to record *Trout Mask Replica*, the Magic Band knew the arrangements to all twenty-eight songs backwards. And what arrangements they were: never had rock come so close to the discordant, near-chaotic improvisation of avant-garde jazz, or broken so radically with orthodox language forms. 'Rock'n'roll is a fixation on that bom-bom-bom mother heartbeat,' Beefheart said years later. 'I don't want to hypnotize, I'm doing a non-hypnotic music to break up the catatonic state.' The shock of the frenetic, chopped-up sound, 'produced' by Frank Zappa in the spring of 1969, was enough to make people dismiss the double album as a mere exercise in absurdity.

Burrow beneath the puns, playfully hybridized words and hilarious spoken interludes and you can't miss the Captain's more serious concerns: who, indeed, could dismiss the harrowing, black-humoured 'Dachau Blues' and 'Veterans' Day Poppy' as the work of a prankster? Listen to 'Wild Life' or 'Ant Man Bee' for the protestations of a true primitivist, angry at the destruction of the ecology; listen to 'When Big Joan Sets Up' for the other side of the Beach Boys' 'California Girls' fantasy, rooted in Van Vliet's own painful memories of visits to the beach. 'Dali's Car' saluted the inspirational Spanish surrealist, 'Pachuco Cadaver' drew on Beefheart's love of Mexican style, and 'Fallin' Ditch' was a meditation on death that now sounds like a premonition of Tom Waits' *Swordfishtrombones*.

Despite all this, Beefheart felt that Zappa was parading him as a 'freak' on a par with the GTOs and Wild Man Fischer. An old love/hate friction between the two men had already been rekindled by Don's suspicion that Frank was doing *Trout Mask* on the cheap, commencing the sessions with a mobile unit at the Canoga Park ranch. 'I wanted to do the album as if it was an anthropological field recording,' Zappa claimed later, but Beefheart took exception to being viewed as a 'field study' or 'social document' and forced him to shift the sessions to a proper studio in Glendale. Moreover, Beefheart has maintained that Zappa was 'asleep at the switches' throughout the *Trout Mask* sessions. Given the tetchiness and need-to-control of both men, it is fair to assume that the truth lies somewhere in between their respective accounts.

After the release of *Trout Mask Replica*, Beefheart and band recorded the equally audacious *Lick My Decals Off, Baby* for Straight, although the departure of Jeff Cotton robbed the sound of its predecessor's mesmerizing guitar interplay. In amongst the mordant, grown-so-ugly blues of 'Doctor Dark' and 'Woe-Is-Uh-Me-Bop' could be found the ecological themes of 'Petrified Forest' and 'The Smithsonian Institute Blues', but the sporadic humour of *Trout Mask* had gone. Certainly it was an altogether more brooding affair than the GTOs' *Permanent Damage*, a 'social document' of the Hollywood rock scene overseen by Zappa but part-produced by apprentice Mother of Invention Lowell George.

The GTOs celebrated everything about life on – or on the margins of – the Sunset Strip. Whether they were poking sly fun at arch-scenester Rodney Bingenheimer ('Oh Rodney, if you introduce me to Mick Jagger/I'll let you meet my little sister/And she's only twelve years old!'), warbling about a purported *ménage à trois* involving Miss Mercy, Brian Jones and a certain Bernardo, or 'discussing the manner in which local Hollywood soul brothers made sexual advances in front of the Whisky a Go Go', these she-creatures of the Hollywood Hills sounded like they were having the most debauched fun in town. In the words of Alice Cooper, who began squiring Miss Christine after meeting her at the Landmark, 'there wasn't a zanier entourage in existence'.

'Mercy, Cynderella and Lucy were the only GTOs never entrusted with the job of babysitting Frank's children, because they were all completely out there,' says the comparatively undebauched Miss Pamela (Des Barres). 'But it was Frank who insisted that Mercy and Cynderella join the band, because he said they gave it a really important twisted element. It was a little too cutesy till they came along.' A co-conspirator of the band's was Cynthia Plaster-Caster, whose infamous plaster casts of rock stars' erect penises summed up the phallocentric times. The fact that more than a few of these super-groupies did indeed wind up suffering permanent damage – Christine died of an overdose in 1972, Lucy of AIDS in 1992 – should not detract altogether from the memory of the good times the GTOs had in those heady days.

Alice Cooper was a Zappa natural: a geeky, beer-guzzling preacher's son who wore a feather boa and amputated dolls onstage. With a band made up of 'upper-middle-class suburban brats' from Phoenix, he'd realized in a blinding flash that he detested peace and love, something which was bound to endear him to the head Mother. If their first Straight album *Pretties for You* showed them to be, in Charles Shaar Murray's words,

The GTOs, or Girls Together Outrageously. Left to right: Christine, Cynderella, Sparky, Mercy, Pamela.

'a vastly pretentious and laughably inept psychedelic-punk garage band', it set them on course for the campy, schlock-horror success they subsequently enjoyed with Canadian producer Bob Ezrin. 'Basically, what they're doing is a cosmeticized version of the same thing we were doing in 1967,' said Zappa in 1973, after Cooper had quit Straight and was cleaning up with the platinum *Billion Dollar Babies* album. 'He's taken the obvious showmanship aspects without doing the difficult musical things.'

'The difficult musical things' were what Zappa himself continued to pursue as the sixties came to their messy end. Tired of 'grinding it out on the road' and playing for 'people who clap for all the wrong reasons', he disbanded the existing Mothers shortly after completing the solo album *Hot Rats*. Thenceforth, from the glorious mutant muzak of 'Peaches En Regalia' onwards, his music veered between japery and virtuosity. Where his satire had once stung, now his tirades against ignorance and hypocrisy reeked of superciliousness. 'I think a lot of Frank's standoffishness came from the fact that people were afraid to be themselves around him,' says Mark Volman, the ex-Turtles frontman who reinvented himself as 'Flo' in the revamped 1971 edition of the Mothers. 'I think that happens to a lot of guys who are in that situation where their theatre takes over their personality.' Thanks in part to Volman and his old Turtles partner Howard 'Eddie' Kayan, the Dada spirit of *Freak Out!* gave way to the puerile, groupie-obsessed bawdiness of *Chunga's Revenge* (1970) and *Live at the Fillmore East* (1971).

Even Zappa seemed to have realized that his story became less interesting after 1969. In *The Real Frank Zappa Book* (1989), he recounted events chronologically up to 1970 but thereafter resorted to a series of mini-rants on subjects like smoking, televangelists and Tipper Gore's Parents' Music Resource Center, a campaign against which took up much of his time in the eighties. At the time of his death from cancer in early 1994 he was the same workaholic disciplinarian he'd always been, and was still hard at work in his basement composing non-glandular music for non-idiots.

VI

In 1969, the year of *Trout Mask Replica* and *The Gilded Palace of Sin*, Exploitation Hollywood finally produced a film that made some kind of rock'n'roll sense. Roger Corman had followed up *The Trip* with *Psych-Out* (1968), a distorted LA take on Haight-Ashbury starring Jack Nicholson as gallery owner 'Stoney'. Now Nicholson and two other Corman acolytes, Peter Fonda and Dennis Hopper, were scheming to make a film about a couple of bikers who decide to get out of LA and ride across America.

'The era when cheap and sleazy films sold well with kids is over,' wrote critic Richard Staehling that year, and he was right. Which was why *Easy Rider*, directed by Hopper and co-scripted by Nicholson and novelist Terry Southern, transcended cheap sleaze and felt like a statement made from inside the counterculture. Granted, Hopper and Fonda were a pair of shameless rock'n'roll groupies, but – sitting astride their motorbikes as they cruised out across the California desert – they could almost have been David Crosby and Gram Parsons. Fonda was a little too scrubbed and handsome, maybe, but there was something authentically nervy and stoned about Hopper, who came across like the missing link between *Rebel Without a Cause* and Charles Manson. The film caught the edgy paranoia of the times, the weirdness of the desert. The brilliant soundtrack, including the Byrds' 'Wasn't Born to Follow', Steppenwolf's proto-metal 'Born to be Wild', and Jimi Hendrix's 'If Six Was Nine', helped to set the film in a kind of outlaw-rock'n'roll context.

There was an inspired touch, meanwhile, in the casting of the one and only Phil Spector as the cocaine dealer of the film's pre-credits sequence – particularly since it was the post-Monterey rock counterculture celebrated by *Easy Rider* that had confirmed the death of the tiny tyrant's pop dreams. True, Spector was back on the LA pop map in 1969 with the Top 20 hit

Uneasy riders: Peter Fonda, Dennis Hopper and Jack Nicholson discover America.

'Black Pearl' by 'soul' band the Checkmates Ltd, and with a new A&M deal for 'Phil Spector Productions', but he remained bitter – as he told Jann Wenner that year – about the way the manipulable 'group on the corner' had been usurped by the self-sufficient 'white psychedelic or guitar group'. To Nik Cohn, who visited him that summer with a view to writing his biography, Spector seemed 'blank, catatonic' unless he was talking about the past. 'Only the trappings were left,' remarked Cohn. It was significant that Spector was disparaging about the Stones' brilliant *Beggars Banquet*, doubtless because it obviated the need for an auteurist producer of the Spector/Nitzsche/Loog Oldham variety. Even more significantly, Spector's assistant Danny Davis told Richard Williams that casting Phil as 'The Connection' was Hopper's way of 'shutting [Phil] up'.

Playing George Hanson, the alcoholic lawyer Hopper and Fonda pick up in the south, Jack Nicholson in *Easy Rider* was like a study for the misfits of *Five Easy Pieces* and *One Flew Over the Cuckoo's Nest*, a psychonerdish cross between Jerry Lewis and the Paul Newman of *Hud*. 'What you represent to them is freedom,' Nicholson's George Hanson tells his new buddies after they've endured taunts from 'weirdo hicks' in a southern town. The film's denouement, after the obligatory acid sequence, seemed to put paid to Gram Parsons' fanciful notion that one could somehow unite hicks and hippies through a new 'Cosmic American Music'.

If *Easy Rider* suggested that storm clouds were gathering ahead, the real-life events of the summer of '69 annihilated the hippie dream of 'peace and love' once and for all. Talk to almost any musician who was in LA that summer and she or he will tell you there was a palpable sense of evil in the air, a menacing instability that had more than a little to do with the ever-increasing decadence of the music scene. In *The White Album*, Joan Didion wrote that 'a mystical flirtation with the idea of "sin" – this sense that it was possible to go "too far" and that many people were doing it – was very much with us in Los Angeles in 1968 and 1969'. A 'demented and vortical tension', she added, was 'building in the community'.

There was a distant portent of the darkness in store when Brian Jones drowned in his Sussex swimming pool in July. The first major rock death, it made a martyr of a fuckup for whom no one any longer had any time, but it also showed that things had indeed gone 'too far'. The fact that the Stones of *Beggars Banquet* – with its opening track 'Sympathy for the Devil' – embodied the 'mystical flirtation with the idea of "sin"' made it all the more significant that they maintained a strong connection with Los Angeles during this period.

A key artefact of the time was the film *Performance*, shot by Nic Roeg and Donald Cammell in 1968 but shelved by Warner Brothers for two years. Starring James Fox as a cockney hoodlum who swims innocently into the Notting Hill ken of the reclusive rock legend Turner (Mick Jagger), it brilliantly portrayed the strange and jaded hedonism which had replaced the breathless euphoria and experimentation of the mid sixties. 'With the really intelligent people, it's almost of matter of inbreeding at this point,' said John Phillips, whose would-be-aristocratic airs defined the mood of the times. 'You estrange yourself from the world, you create your own society, and that's what *Performance* is about.' The film also featured a mesmerizingly sinister soundtrack by Jack Nitzsche, written in a witch's cottage off Laurel Canyon and recorded with Ry Cooder, Randy Newman, Lowell George and Russ Titelman, almost a nucleus of the group of musicians who would help to make Warner Brothers the quintessential Los Angeles record label of the early seventies. William Friedkin proclaimed *Performance* 'the best integration of music and moving images ever' and later hired Nitzsche to score *The Exorcist.**

It was said that James Fox became so enmeshed in the amoral milieu of the Rolling Stones that he suffered a drug-related breakdown after

Phil Spector samples a little snow in Easy Rider.

---

* Following up *Performance* and *Easy Rider*, Michelangelo Antonioni's *Zabriskie Point* (1970) – in which a student radical steals a plane and ends up in the Mansonesque desert of Death Valley – also caught the sense of unrest and disorientation at large in late-sixties America. The film's explosive climax, set to the sound of Pink Floyd's 'Careful With That Axe, Eugene', provided a suitably apocalyptic finale to the decade.

Performance. The Stones' own 'flirtation' with evil continued when Mick Jagger, Keith Richards and Marianne Faithfull became involved in Kenneth Anger's infamous *Lucifer Rising*, eventually released with a prison-recorded soundtrack by Manson acolyte Bobby Beausoleil. Jagger was supposed to play Lucifer to Richards' Beelzebub but – in Anger's words – 'backed away from being identified with him'. 'Kenneth had a huge and very conscious influence on the Stones,' Marianne Faithfull told Mick Brown. 'I think he thought Mick and the rest of the group could embody his vision.'

Charles Milles Manson: 'A lot of pretty well-known musicians around LA knew him, but they'd probably deny it now.'

Although *Lucifer Rising* wasn't seen until 1977, its making coincided with the increasingly weird scenes transpiring in the rock'n'roll goldmine of southern California. The 'tension' Joan Didion felt in her Hollywood neighbourhood through 1968 and 1969 may have seemed more 'demented and vortical' with hindsight, but it wasn't really so remote from everyday life. The essence of the LA music community at this time was its manifold interconnections – and the fact that the boundaries between sanity and madness, pleasure and self-destruction, good and evil had become hopelessly blurred. How else could a group such as the Beach Boys, who only five years before had epitomized everything that was healthy and clean-cut about Californian youth, be mingling so perilously with the band of psychopathic hippie criminals who rampaged through California under the name 'The Family'?

Charles Milles Manson had first ventured out to the promised land in the summer of 1955, driving from Ohio in a stolen car with his pregnant teenage bride. Four years later, emerging from the aptly named Terminal Island, he formed a Hollywood-based 'agency' which was nothing more than a front for a prostitution ring. For much of the sixties he was banged up in Washington state, where he began studying magic, the occult and the guitar.

By the time he was released in the spring of 1967, Manson was priming himself for success as a hippie troubadour, with a twisted head full of Robert Heinlein and L. Ron Hubbard. Busy collecting a retinue of damaged hippie chicks, he briefly checked out the Haight-Ashbury scene, but by November he was in Hollywood, chasing up a contact at Universal Studios. Thanks to producer Gary Stromberg, Manson even got to record a three-hour session for the movie studio's short-lived label Universal Records.

After a good deal of peripatetic wandering around the deserts of California, Nevada, Arizona and New Mexico, Manson and his growing 'family' – just another bunch of itinerant desert hippies of the kind portrayed in *Easy Rider* – decided to settle in Topanga Canyon, home to a number of marginal and not-so-marginal LA musicians. (Among them was one Bobby Beausoleil, fresh from working on the original *Lucifer Rising*.) Topanga was where you lived if you wanted to get *really* rural, which was how come the scene-o-phobic likes of Neil Young were starting to pitch up there. 'A lot of pretty-well-known musicians around LA knew Manson, though they'd probably deny it now,' Young later remembered. 'The girls were always around, too. They'd be right there on the couch with me, singing a song.* And Charlie'd talk to me all the while about how he'd been in jail so much there was no longer any difference between being "in" or "out" of jail ...' Unlike the majority of musicians who crossed Manson's path and now dismiss his songs, Young claims he was impressed enough to suggest that Mo Ostin sign him to Warner Brothers. 'I mean, if he'd had a band like Dylan had on "Subterranean Homesick Blues", then ... but he was never gonna get that band, because there was just something about him that stopped *anybody* from being around him for long.'

Young, who later based 'Revolution Blues' and 'Mansion on the Hill' on the Manson killings, first met the creepy, devil-dabbling figure at the Rustic Canyon house belonging to Dennis Wilson. Dennis was one of the people who subsequently did his best to deny any involvement with Manson after it all came down – 'as long as I live, I'll never talk about that,' he told *Rolling Stone* – but the truth was that the middle Wilson brother, more than any other LA musician, was Manson's ticket to the heart of the rock community. Not only did Charlie meet Neil Young in Rustic Canyon, he also met the other members of the 'Golden Penetrators', Gregg Jakobson and Terry Melcher, both of whom were as happy as Dennis to penetrate the gonorrhoea-ridden girls who made up the Manson family. 'Terry Melcher and Dennis Wilson used to call me all the time and say come on over,' remembered John Phillips. 'I'd just shudder every time and say no, I think I'll pass. I just wouldn't get into it.'

Manson quickly homed in on Melcher, whose stepfather Marty had recently died, leaving the financial affairs of Terry's mother Doris Day in total disarray. Learning that he'd produced the Byrds and Paul Revere and the Raiders, Manson decided that Terry could make him a star. Gregg Jakobson recalled Dennis Wilson driving Melcher back to the imitation chateau on Cielo Drive where the producer was living, with Manson sitting in the back of the Rolls strumming a guitar. (On another occasion, Jakobson and Wilson took Charlie to the Whisky a Go Go, where his frenzied dancing managed to empty the dancefloor.) Listening to the demos Manson recorded at the instigation of Gregg Jakobson in August 1968 – songs which are almost famous now, such as 'Cease to Exist', 'Sick City', 'Look at Your Game, Girl', and 'Home is Where You're Happy' – it's not hard to see why Melcher was intrigued enough to make encouraging noises. Charlie the singer was certainly no worse than many of the other

---

* Young told an interviewer at the time that there were 'about eight girls' in Topanga Canyon who 'go around keeping house, cooking food, and making love to everyone'. Among them, most likely, were the killers Linda Kasabian and Patricia Krenwinkel. As Phil Kaufman put it in his memoir, *Road Mangler Deluxe*, 'I realised I'd had sex with every one of those murderesses.'

spaced-out troubadours swarming around California that summer. As is well known now, 'Cease to Exist' was included on the Beach Boys' 1969 album *20/20* as 'Never Learn Not to Love', alongside the magical *Smile* tracks 'Our Prayer' and 'Cabinessence'. Manson claims he gave the song to the group in order to soothe their differences, which only made their reworking of his lyric all the more infuriating.

The soothing music notwithstanding, Charles Manson embodied a frighteningly schizoid mix of hippie values, satanism, pornography and apocalyptic prophecy. As the bad vibes of 1968 began to pierce the thin membrane of peace and love, so evil took root within the Family, which henceforth adopted every conceivable kind of brainwashable lowlife and sociopath. By the time Manson shifted base from Rustic Canyon to an old ranch in Chatsworth, he'd begun formulating the notion that he and his followers had to prepare themselves for a race war with black America.* Things were certainly creepy enough for Dennis Wilson to start edging away from the Family, especially after Manson pulled a knife on Brian Wilson's engineer Stephen Despar. Touring England with the Beach Boys in the early summer of 1969, Dennis mentioned 'The Wizard' to a reporter from *Rave* magazine. 'Fear is nothing but awareness,' he said. 'Sometimes The Wizard frightens me. The Wizard is Charlie Manson, who is a friend of mine who thinks he is God and the devil. He sings, plays, and writes poetry, and he may be another artist for Brother Records.'

By the end of 1968, Manson was convinced he'd found confirmation of his neo-Nazi race-war theories in five songs on the Beatles' newly released 'white album'. 'Helter Skelter', in particular, became the theme song of the Family's preparations for the impending apocalypse. Holed up in the rambling, tumbledown Spahn ranch, surrounded by rusting cars and dilapidated farm machinery, Manson began gathering the chosen ones who would accompany him into the desert. In addition to making frequent *Mad Max II*-style reconnaissance trips to Death Valley in the souped-up dune buggies they'd constructed out of stolen cars, the Family was busy collecting guns, walkie-talkies and other supplies. Convinced there was an underground people living in the desert, Manson spent weeks searching for holes that would lead to them.†

* Manson's racism was shared not only by Bobby Beausoleil, who was to lead a chapter of the notorious Aryan Brotherhood in a California prison, but also by Dennis Wilson, albeit in more covert form. In the seventies, Dennis had a bizarre recurring nightmare/fantasy that he'd been raped by a black man, perhaps influenced by Bobby Beausoleil's remarks to Truman Capote that blacks in prison 'really go for the young white kids ... they love to shove those big black dicks up those tight white asses'.
† Los Angeles has always been haunted by the desert that surrounds it – by its emptiness, its inhospitability to life and the way it provides a refuge for freaks, cultists and killers. As everyone from Aldous Huxley to Jim Morrison to Gram Parsons has understood, the desert lends itself to apocalyptic fantasy. 'Let it come and clear the rot and the stench and the stink,' says Marion Faye as she looks eastwards towards the desert in Norman Mailer's Hollywood novel *The Deer Park*. 'Let it come for all of everywhere, just so it comes and the world stands clear in the white dead dawn.'

10050 Cielo Drive, Benedict Canyon.

Early in 1969, Terry Melcher moved out of 10050 Cielo Drive and Roman Polanski moved in. With the Polish film director, whose satanist movie *Rosemary's Baby* had been a smash hit the previous summer, was his actress wife Sharon Tate, a Californian blonde who'd somehow got caught up in his exotically dark world. For a little over a month they lived the hedonistic high life in Benedict Canyon, entertaining the hip elite of the movie and rock communities: Warren Beatty, Roger Vadim and Jane Fonda; hairdresser-and-dealer-to-the-stars Jay Sebring; John Phillips and Brit-in-LA director Mike Sarne; and Mama Cass and her crew.

When Polanski went to London in late March to work on *The Day of the Dolphin*, an old Polish chum named Wotjek Frykowski agreed to house-sit the Cielo Drive house with coffee heiress Abigail Folger, a volunteer social worker in the ghettos of south-central LA. Manson and the Family, meanwhile, were gearing up for the ritual slaughter of the 'piggies', their

Beatles-derived term for the rich and hedonistic of Hollywood Babylon. At least some of Manson's growing hatred of this crowd stemmed from the lack of commitment to his musical career shown by Terry Melcher. Although Melcher came up to the Spahn ranch to see Manson several times during the spring and early summer, he still made no firm undertaking to sign him. The Family tried other ways to get their music recorded: Bobby Beausoleil approached Frank Zappa, and former prodigy 'Gypsy' Share played a tape for Doors producer Paul Rothchild. (Ironically, Bobby Beausoleil had made a brief appearance in the 1966 documentary *Mondo Hollywood*, a section of which was devoted to the salon of Jay Sebring.) It is said that Manson and his girls would occasionally drop in on Cass Elliott and play her their songs. None of this hustling resulted in anything.*

The rumours in July that some of the Manson crew had shot a black dope dealer named Bernard Crowe may have been enough for Terry Melcher to decide he wanted nothing more to do with Manson. Little did Melcher know that the Crowe shooting was merely the tip of the terrifying iceberg. No one knows exactly how many people the Family tortured and/or killed that summer, but there were several gruesome deaths in and around the areas where they lived, and they certainly offed an old Topanga acquaintance named Gary Hinman. Manson also initiated the practice of 'creepy-crawling' the houses of people on their hit list, breaking in and silently rearranging their furniture and possessions.

By the beginning of August, Manson was almost certainly contemplating the idea of killing Terry Melcher. At the same time, strange scenes were unfolding at the house on Cielo Drive, to which the heavily pregnant Sharon Tate had recently returned. Jay Sebring and Wotjek Frykowski had apparently been burned in a cocaine deal by Mama Cass's dealer Billy Doyle, and decided to exact their revenge by flogging him in front of an invited audience at the house – an event which may have coincided with a party thrown there for Roger Vadim. Bobby Beausoleil contended that 'Sharon Tate and that gang ... picked up kids on the Strip and took them home and whipped them', while Dennis Hopper claimed that they'd 'fallen into sadism and masochism and bestiality'. In the authorized biography of his mother, Terry Melcher told A. E. Hotchner that he'd 'presumed the murders had something to do with the weird film Polanski had made, and the equally weird people who were hanging around that house' – people who'd been 'making a lot of homemade sadomasochistic-porno movies with quite a few recognizable Hollywood faces in them'.

On the evening of Friday 8 August, Manson commanded Linda Kasabian, Charles 'Tex' Watson, Susan 'Sadie Glutz' Atkins and Patricia

* In Thomas Pynchon's *Vineland*, record producer Mucho Maas, a.k.a. 'Count Drugula', is 'one of the very few to audition, but not, he was later to add hastily, to call back, fledgling musician Charles Manson'.

'Katie' Krenwinkel to drive to 10050 Cielo Drive and kill the occupants of the house. Shortly after midnight, they shot dead Steven Parent, a friend of guest-cottage caretaker Bill Garretson, then entered the house. While Garretson sat in the cottage fifty yards away listening (with a certain grim appropriateness) to a Doors album, Watson, Atkins and Krenwinkel butchered Jay Sebring, Wotjek Frykowski, Abigail Folger and Sharon Tate. One hundred and two stab wounds later, the three killers rejoined Linda Kasabian and returned to the Spahn ranch.

By the following afternoon, the Olympian denizens of LA's canyons were in a terrified panic. Word of the murders had spread like fire in a Santa Ana wind, and a Beverly Hills gun store sold 200 shotguns in two days. 'There was this instant flash that maybe Phil Spector had been right all along,' says Carl Gottlieb, whose pal David Crosby had been to the Cielo Drive house many times. 'Suddenly it made sense to be living behind gates with dogs and guns.' For Joan Didion, with the music of the Doors still resounding in her hypochondriacal head, 'the tension broke that day, the paranoia was fulfilled.' The swirling hallucination of the sixties had climaxed in the ultimate 'summer bummer', and it all made a grotesquely twisted sense.

The very same night, a repeat performance took place at the Silverlake residence of Leno and Rosemary LaBianca. As orchestrated by Manson, the middle-aged couple were murdered by Tex Watson, Katie Krenwinkel and Leslie Van Houten, who then daubed the words 'RISE', 'DEATH TO PIGS' and 'HEALTER SKELTER' [sic] in blood on the walls. (Supposedly, the intention was to convince the police that the murders had been committed by black revolutionaries, and so trigger a race war. Similar graffiti was found at the home of Gary Hinman, for whose killing the racist Bobby Beausoleil had been arrested shortly before the Cielo Drive killings.) A few days after the double-murders spree, Manson appeared on Dennis Wilson's doorstep claiming that he'd 'been to the moon'.

When the Family were finally connected to the murders in November, the paranoia really *was* fulfilled. This was LA *noir* on a grand scale, a watershed event which brought together the music and movie industries in a horrific, beyond-*Hollywood Babylon* orgy of evil. For Manson was that unforeseen monster the Nightmare Hippie, a blue-collar psycho who'd fucked up the bourgeois dropout dream. 'Manson raked beneath the skin of white middle-class California,' wrote David Toop, 'and revealed through himself its incipient violence, misogyny, anti-semitism and hatred of blacks.' Manson himself, in language worthy of James Ellroy, claimed he was 'what you have made of me, and the mad dog devil killer fiend leper is a reflection of your society ... in my mind's eye my thoughts light fires in your cities.'

'The Manson killings just destroyed us,' says Lou Adler. 'I mean, everyone was looking at everyone else, not quite sure who was in that house and who knew about it. It was a very paranoid time, and the easiest

HCP081106-8/11/69-LOS ANGELES:A police officer blocks the driveway while other officers
search in front of the house where a middle-aged couple was stabbed to death late 8/10.
There were striking similarities between the double murder of Leon La Bianca,44, and his
wife Rosemary,38, and the mass murders of actress Sharon Tate and four other persons the
day before. UPI TELEPHOTO clm/bf

*The La Bianco residence on Waverly
Drive, Silverlake.*

thing to do was to get out of it. Everybody went behind closed doors,
and the scene went really quiet.' While Terry Melcher and others lived in
fear of their lives, the Sunset Strip became a virtual ghost town. Elmer
Valentine tried to keep the Whisky a Go Go alive and Marshall Brevitz
opened a new place called Thee Experience, but most nights that winter
the clubs were empty. Eric Burdon, living his own dissolute life in Boris
Karloff's old Laurel Canyon mansion, recalled a coked-out wig-store
owner called 'The Princess' dancing alone on the Whisky floor.

For Eve Babitz, the dream was finally over: 'Everything had been so
loose, and now it could never be loose again. Two years earlier, a guy with
long hair was a brother – now you just didn't know.' Others were more
sanguine. Kim Fowley, who had recently been banned from the Whisky a
Go Go for staging a wild show involving bikers and onstage sex, says
'street Hollywood' was hardly shocked by the killings. 'People in mansions
were nervous, but I was living over a garage opposite Gazzari's. 'No
hippies were gonna murder *me* in my sleep.'

'*LA noir on a grand scale*': the arrest of Charles Manson.

But whichever way you looked at it, Manson had left an indelible mark – on the rock subculture of California in particular and on America in general. Ever since the killings, Charlie has functioned as an anti-hero for all kinds of deviants, Nazis and *noir* poseurs. Psychic TV sported Manson T-shirts and splattered walls with Family slogans like 'Getting the Fear'. Sonic Youth, New Yorkers fascinated by sleazoid California, recorded the brutal 'Death Valley '69' with Lydia Lunch. The Lemonheads covered 'Home is Where You're Happy' on *Creator*, with Evan Dando stating that 'Charlie was just a good symbol of the beginning of my life in America, of how messed up things were getting.' Axl Rose appeared onstage in a Manson T-shirt and tucked a not-so-discreet version of 'Look at Your Game, Girl' on the end of Guns N'Roses' *The Spaghetti Incident?* album. 'The song talks about how the girl is insane and playing a mind game,' Rose said in a statement defending the decision to record the song. 'I felt it was ironic that such a song was recorded by someone who should know the inner intricacies of madness.' Topping all of these was Nine Inch Nails' Trent Reznor, who actually moved into 10050 Cielo Drive and recorded his 1994 album *The Downward Spiral* there. 'Everybody's looking for a hero,' said Reznor, 'and there's your ultimate taboo icon.'

As the taboo icon puts it himself, 'the myth of Charles Manson has twisted more minds than I was ever accused of touching.'

VII

Not even the Woodstock festival, staged in upstate New York a week after the killings, could restore the good vibes of hippie America pre-Manson: the murders managed to undo the whole notion that rock music was a positive force for change. And by the time the Rolling Stones' 1969 tour of America reached California in December, the dream which had begun with Monterey was dead on its legs. Two years of evil seemed to climax at a free festival at a speedway track on the outskirts of San Francisco, when Hell's Angels hired as security for the show began beating members of the audience and ended up stabbing a man to death.

A traumatized Terry Melcher at the Manson trial in December 1969.

'I would never have been at Altamont, either as a performer or as a spectator,' claimed John Phillips. 'I would *know* not to do that. God has been losing his percentage, and the Devil has been picking up a lot of that percentage.' It was all very well for Phillips to say this after the fact, but he himself seemed unable to make the connection between the events at Altamont and the demonic rock aristocracy of which he was such a proud member. Nor was it exactly fair of David Crosby to castigate the Stones for turning 'a party' into 'a grotesque, negative, ego star trip' – especially since it had been the California bands who'd recommended hiring the Angels in the first place. The fact was that all these bands were playing with fire in 1969: one viewing of the Maysles brothers' riveting film *Gimme Shelter* is enough to show that it wasn't just their satanic majesties the Stones who were out of their depth. If anyone still had sympathy for the devil prior to 6 December, they knew better than to invoke him thereafter.

One person who seemed to understand the sheer *dread* in the air of Los Angeles as the decade reached its near-apocalyptic finale was the drunken, derided frontman of the Doors. Perhaps there was even a mild sense of vindication for the would-be shaman, whose best songs had presaged the horror which had unfolded over the preceding two years: the assassinations of Bobby Kennedy and Martin Luther King, the escalation of American involvement in Vietnam, the brutal oppression at the Democratic Convention in Chicago, the violence on the streets of Europe in May 1968, the increasing tension between blacks and whites in America, the growing use of mind-contracting drugs – and now the Californian double whammy of Manson and Altamont. Indeed, Morrison's own arrest in Miami in March 1969 had been almost as pivotal a pop event as Altamont.

A year after the death of Meredith Hunter at the Altamont speedway, Jim Morrison began a collaboration with Fred Myrow, a former assistant to Leonard Bernstein, on 'a show about Los Angeles'. 'What we wanted to crystallize or capture,' Myrow told Jerry Hopkins, 'was that moment of transition we all felt so strongly in Los Angeles in the late sixties … what'd Huxley say? "Between the evergreens and the garages, something was lurking"? It was a weird environment. Los Angeles … whatever the fuck that means … that's what we were gonna explore on the show.' The plans for this Los Angeles 'show' were symptomatic of Morrison's growing need to prove himself as something more than a rock'n'roll star. By the spring of 1969, he'd already had two collections of rather jejune poetry published and made the short films *Feast of Friends* and *Hiway*, the latter featuring Morrison wandering out of the mountains near Palm Springs and murdering the driver who offers him a ride to LA.

Given Morrison's artistic pretensions – the undoing of both *Waiting for the Sun* and *Soft Parade* – it was remarkable that the Doors managed to get themselves back on track as a musical outfit capable of making exciting rock'n'roll. Although the singer and Paul Rothchild were coked out of their skulls during the recording of *Morrison Hotel* (1970), the album was a return to the garage-rock energy of 'Break On Through' and 'Back Door Man' and restored at least some of the credibility they'd forfeited after *Strange Days*. On the song 'Waiting for the Sun', moreover, they caught the eerie feel of southern California in the wake of Manson and Altamont – 'the strangest life I've ever known', as Morrison crooned. The sun they were awaiting was no longer the sun of the early Beach Boys records, it was a scorching god, an apocalyptic destroyer. On the funked-up 'Peace Frog', a catalogue of the violence of 1968–9, Morrison sang of 'blood in my love in the terrible summer/Bloody red sun of Phantastic LA'.

LA Woman, recorded at the end of 1970 after the increasingly incapacitated Morrison had installed himself in a cottage at the Chateau

The Doors in 1970, under the boardwalk. Left to right: Ray Manzarek, John Densmore, Robby Kreiger, Jim Morrison.

Marmont, was an even more cogent statement about Los Angeles as a 'city of night'. (Morrison even told critic Dave Marsh that the album was his vision of LA as 'a microcosm of America'.) Produced by Bruce Botnick in a makeshift studio beneath the Doors' office at 8512 Santa Monica Boulevard, the album's raw spirit was reflected in the collective songwriting credits. With its tough, bluesy sound bolstered by bassist Jerry Scheff and rhythm guitarist Marc Benno, it produced Top 20 singles in 'Love Her Madly' (a reprise of all those 'Love Her Two Times'/'Hello I Love You'-style songs) and the shimmering cocktail-croon epic 'Riders on the Storm'. But its greatest track was the near-eight-minute 'LA Woman' itself, rendered in Morrison's jowelliest growl of a voice. In this brilliant swansong, not only to his pop career but to the whole era of the great Sunset Strip bands, Jim Morrison sang of a washed-up groupie in the city of night, and of the 'motel money murder madness' of Manson's Hollywood.*

By the time the album was released in the spring of 1971, Morrison knew the Doors were over. When he dropped in at a party celebrating the opening of Elektra's new LA office at 962 North La Cienega, he'd already made up his mind to take his bohemian American-in-Paris fantasies to their logical conclusion and actually move there. During his last drunken days that summer, he managed to transport his sleazy Santa Monica Boulevard world all the way to the Left Bank. Some time after midnight on 3 July he died in the bath of his Paris apartment, though only Pamela Courson ever saw the body.

Morrison's death was the guarantor of his rock'n'roll martyrdom, enabling the likes of Ray Manzarek and Danny Sugerman to turn a bloated alcoholic into the Lizard King deity of Oliver Stone's *The Doors*. 'My personal belief is that Jim Morrison was a god,' states Sugerman, a man who has virtually built a career on the fact that he ran a few errands for the Doors in the final two years of their existence. 'With Sugerman as the religious zealot and Manzarek as St Paul,' wrote John Densmore, 'the crusading has worked.' It certainly brings in a pretty penny or two for all concerned.

Morrison's death was also the final bowing-out in that unholy trinity of rock deaths which inaugurated the seventies. First Hendrix in London; then Janis Joplin in LA's now-infamous Landmark Hotel; and now, in Paris, Mr Mojo Risin' himself. If people hadn't got the message with Manson and Altamont, they were certainly getting it now. The party was over, and it was time to go home.

* The sense that *LA Woman* was a swansong was compounded for drummer John Densmore by its Sunset Boulevard billboard, featuring a woman crucified on a telephone pole. 'Our first album billboard had faced east,' he wrote in *Riders on the Storm*, 'towards the rising sun, the occidental, a land we conquered. The *LA Woman* billboard, our last record, faced west, towards the setting sun, the end of western civilization, and the end of our public life as a group.'

6 Ladies and Gentlemen of the Canyon

The public relates very strongly to the music and to the lifestyle –
it's all one thing ... there's an aristocracy of lifestyle. It's a
popstar's life that counts, that's what involves you, not his
performance.

John Phillips, 1970

I'm getting a little tired of hearing about, you know, everybody's
emotional problems ... they're not writing songs anymore, they're
only writing ideas.

Phil Spector, 1969

I

Such was the ugliness and confusion of the LA music scene in 1969 that
it was hardly surprising when people decided to up and leave the place.
'Working in and around Hollywood sometimes obscures memories of the
healthy heartland of America,' remarked the duo Brewer and Shipley, who
went home to Missouri. 'Nice to know it's still there.'

Brewer and Shipley were in a tiny minority, however. Most people –
many of them also non-natives – weathered the collective Freakout of the
times, opting to retreat instead into the hills and canyons encircling
Hollywood. By the beginning of 1970, Laurel Canyon in particular had
become a kind of Olympus for the rock community, a place where the
survivors of the Sunset Strip's halcyon days could chill out in rambling
split-level cabins with their cats and marijuana and write soul-searchingly
introspective songs about the affairs they were having with each other.

Laurel Canyon was already established as a kind of rock sanctuary by
the summer of 1968 – to the extent that Jackie DeShannon could actually
name an album after it. Assisted by Mac (Dr John) Rebennack and Liberty
'office rat' Russ Titelman, DeShannon used *Laurel Canyon* to celebrate
what Reyner Banham memorably called 'the fat life of the delectable
mountains'. DeShannon even included a rhapsodic ode to LA itself on
the album, showing just how the sprawling city had managed to outgrow
the stigma of its 'plasticity'. 'I belong to LA/Can't go wrong in LA/Gonna

'The fat life of the delectable canyons...' (Reyner Banham).

stay in LA,' she sang with a kind of defiance which would have been unheard of even a year earlier.

Eric Burdon, busy enjoying 'two years of lunacy' after reinventing himself as an acid-rocker at Monterey, perhaps came closer to the truth when he wrote that 'living up in the canyon, you had the feeling you were out of reach, and what went on in the world below just didn't bother you.' But DeShannon's nostalgia is shared by many other rock veterans: for John Densmore, the entrance to Laurel Canyon was a 'shrine', while Pamela Des Barres called the canyon 'God's golden backyard'. Billy James's wife Judy felt that 'it was as if the canyon at the time was everybody's house, there wasn't any front door . . . you drove around and you walked around and you knew everybody.'

Who could blame the rich and hip for staying in their eyries, gazing down over the endless grid-spread of steel and stucco that stretched thirty miles south to San Pedro – or alternatively, over the Valley flatlands on the other side? As John Rockwell has pointed out, it was the very 'endlessness' of the LA basin which meant that 'socializing tended to be cliquish, with like-minded souls seeking one another out and guarding what they share against the environment'. The fact that the ecology of canyon life was, in Reyner Banham's words, one 'imperilled by its own desirability' in the form of mud-slides, brush fires and 'hill cropping' didn't seem to detract from the general post-hippie *pastorale*.

Of course, there were those who chose to remove themselves still further from the plastic freeway madness of LA: in Laurel Canyon you rode motorcycles, but in Topanga Canyon you rode horses. Twenty miles west of Hollywood, Topanga became home not only to lone-wolf Neil Young, who met his first wife Susan at the Topanga Canyon Café, but to Steve Stills, Chris Hillman, Barry McGuire and Linda Ronstadt and her fellow Stone Poney Bob Kimmel. 'One of the reasons people slipped out to Topanga was that you could pretend you were in Kentucky or Tennessee or wherever you wanted to be,' says music publisher Dan Bourgoise. 'People like Young and Ronstadt left the Hollywood Sunset Strip scene – where the bands were getting heavier and heavier – and became kinda folksy. The music was sort of Creedence and The Band and even Merle Haggard, and everything was getting more woodsy and rustic.' Neil Young recalled that he 'just needed to get out to the sticks for a while and relax', claiming later that his third album *After the Goldrush* (inspired by a screenplay written by his Topanga neighbour Dean Stockwell) embodied 'the spirit of Topanga Canyon'.

Not that Topanga's rustics were any less partial to mood-altering substances than their Laurel Canyon counterparts: a 1968 bust at a ranch belonging to producer David Briggs rounded up not only Neil Young and Jim Messina of the decomposing Buffalo Springfield but a visiting Eric Clapton into the bargain. Much of the dealing – and general carousing – took place in the Topanga Corral at 2034 Topanga Canyon Road, where everyone from Spirit and Taj Mahal to Canned Heat and Gram Parsons played. The Corral is gone now, but other hippie landmarks – the Topanga Country Store, the Inn of the Seventh Ray restaurant – remain. 'Topanga Canyon is probably the last refuge of hippie culture in southern California,' wrote Stephen Brook in his Clive James-ish *LA Lore* (1992). 'The unregenerate long-haired, flower-power, keep-a-few-chickens, prefer-the-children-naked, bake-it-myself, jingle-jangle-mobile-making, pass-me-a-joint kind of hippie ... is still here with his girlfriend, ekeing out a living with carpentry, odd jobs, construction work.'

Jackie DeShannon's *Laurel Canyon* not only celebrated rock's new haven-in-the-hills, it also marked the coming-of-age of a new breed of 'singer-songwriter'. With his/her antecedents in the folk singers of the early sixties – Dylan, Tim Hardin et al. – the LA singer-songwriter emerged from two parallel backgrounds: first, from bands who were splitting up as the decade came to an end; and second, from the 'song factories' of publishing companies such as Metric Music, whose hack tunesmiths could now poke their heads out of the backroom and be taken seriously as artists.

'The canyon aristocracy of solo performers really began with Gene Clark quitting the Byrds,' says Eve Babitz. 'That kicked off the tradition of leaving a band and setting up on your own.' By 1969, going solo was almost *de rigueur*. 'I just ain't into this old group thing anymore,' said Gram Parsons, though it didn't stop him cronying with the Rolling Stones. 'I think a lot of other musicians feel the same way these days – they don't want to be tied into an organization. It's like being in a penitentiary.' If at least part of the reason for this was simply that all the original mid-sixties bands were finding it hard to stay together through the inevitable bickering and resentment, another part of it was that the magic and power of *a rock'n'roll band* had somehow begun to wane. As Jim Morrison remarked presciently after being busted in Miami, 'the initial flash is over – the thing they call rock, what used to be called rock'n'roll, has gotten decadent.'

Certainly it was hard to make a case any longer for the importance of, say, the Byrds. With the departure of Chris Hillman, Roger McGuinn was the sole original Byrd left in the group, and not even the excellent new guitarist Clarence White could do much to arrest their slow artistic decline. The mordant 'Bad Night at the Whisky', from *Dr Byrds & Mr Hyde*, said everything about McGuinn's mindset in early 1969, and the album itself attracted hostile criticism from both Hillman and Parsons, who questioned the very use of the Byrds' name.

The Byrds in 1970. Left to right: Skip Battin, Roger McGuinn, Gene Parsons, Clarence White.

That summer, McGuinn and Clarence White drove out to Doris Day's Malibu beach house to ask Terry Melcher if he would produce the next Byrds album. They were still in the studio with him at the time of the Manson murders, which may have had something to do with the awfulness of *The Ballad of Easy Rider*. Another factor was the old Phil Spector complex which still bedevilled LA record producers: Melcher couldn't leave the title track alone, for example choosing to smother it with strings in an effort to turn it into a 'Gentle On My Mind' or an 'Everybody's Talkin''.

Melcher made amends, however, by helping the Byrds to record their last halfway-decent album. Featuring new bassist Skip Battin, a smattering of good songs and a rousing live disc overseen by the group's original mentor Jim Dickson, *(Untitled)* did almost enough to put the Byrds back up there with the West Coast greats. But then Melcher went and blew it again with *Byrdmaniax*, to which he added strings while the band was on the road, bringing the cost of the record up to a staggering $100,000. Drummer Gene Parsons called the album 'Melcher's Folly'.

It didn't help the Byrds' or Melcher's causes that more than a few of the songs on *Byrdmaniax* had been conjured up rather hastily by Battin, with the aid of pop veteran Kim Fowley. 'Kim wrote things like "Citizen Kane" incredibly quickly,' Skip recalled. 'It was novelty in one sense, but it was also true. Kim had lived that Hollywood life and he saw a lot of that stuff as a kid.' *Farther Along* (1971), the Byrds' final album for Columbia, showed that McGuinn had all but given up on the group. For Johnny Rogan, author of the Byrds biography *Timeless Flight*, the Battin/Fowley folly 'America's Great National Pastime' represented 'the severest loss of musical identity the band suffered', though 'Precious Kate' (with its typically Fowley-esque reference to the earthquake which hit LA in February 1971) was marginally better.

It is hard to overestimate the effect which the breakup of the original Byrds and Buffalo Springfield had on the LA scene. Out of those groups alone came Dillard and Clark, the Flying Burrito Brothers, Poco, Crosby, Stills and Nash (and Young and Crazy Horse), who in turn gave birth to Manassas, Country Gazette, Linda Ronstadt's band, the Eagles, and still more acts who helped to make up what John Rockwell called 'the mythically tangled genealogy' of the Los Angeles scene. 'The Springfield were kind of the catalyst, because people like Crosby wanted to be in that band,' says Denny Bruce. 'So there was a little incestuous feeling starting, and it became totally incestuous when Crosby and Stills got together with Graham Nash.'

David Crosby and Stephen Stills had cemented their association at the time of Monterey, when the Cros had been on the point of replacing Neil Young in Buffalo Springfield. After being booted out of the Byrds, the walrus-moustached singer had spent several months doing little more than hanging out in Laurel Canyon and spending time up in Marin County with the Airplane and the Dead. 'Because he "hangs out" so much, there's a tendency to think he isn't producing much,' wrote Jerry Hopkins in *World Countdown News* in June 1968. 'In a sense this is true. Yet he is an integral part of the LA scene, thanks largely to his track record, but also because he is volatile and opinionated.'*

In actual fact, Crosby's 'volatile and opinionated' personality had given him a bad rep in the Sunset Strip scene: not everyone was as keen as Steve Stills to work with the guy, and Columbia's Clive Davis was only too happy to trade him – along with Graham Nash – for Richie Furay's new band Poco. This inter-company bartering freed up the relevant parties in the late fall of 1968, by which time the almost telepathic harmonic chemistry between Crosby, Stills and Nash was enough to persuade Atlantic's Ahmet Ertegun to part with some development money for the trio dubbed 'The Frozen Noses' by DJ B. Mitchell Reed.

The sound that Crosby, Stills and Nash had hit on was really a Hollywood hippie version of the very folk-pop trios in which Crosby and Stills had learned their harmonic craft. Added to that were what Crosby called the 'nonparallel' influences of jazz, Latin and classical music, which had a lot to do with Steve 'Captain Manyhands' Stills' versatility and desire to experiment in the studio. When the trio went into Wally Heider's Studio No. 3, they established a new and hermetic LA approach to 'holing up in the studio' that spelled the end of the regimented studio discipline of old.

With Phil Spector in tow, Ahmet Ertegun came by the Heider studio the night Stills had finished work on 'Suite: Judy Blue Eyes', the ambitious opening track on *Crosby, Stills & Nash*. Blown away by the guitar/bass/organ combination and the post-Byrds/Springfield style of vocal interplay, Ertegun decided to put all Atlantic's guns behind the trio. Encouraging him to do this was the ferociously ambitious young agent they'd employed to administer their business dealings – a New Yorker named David Geffen, whose later claim that Atlantic at this early stage had no real interest in the trio may have been a way of maximizing his own contribution to the group's success. And success it was: when the album was released in June 1969, it rapidly climbed into the Top 10, remaining in the Top 40 for a total of forty weeks.

Astutely balanced between the breezy balladry of 'Helplessly Hoping' and the brooding rock of 'Long Time Gone', *Crosby, Stills & Nash* was *the* FM album of the summer. Most of it was crap, of course: who can honestly listen to the fey hogwash of 'Guinnevere' or 'Lady of the Island' with a straight face today? It also articulated the escapist elitism of the new Laurel Canyon aristocracy, with the 'silver people on the shoreline' of

---

* Of all the principal LA rock figures, Crosby was the one who most fervently embraced the San Francisco ethos: he even bought property in Marin County, inspiring other LA stars to do likewise. Tellingly, however, Jefferson Airplane's Grace Slick remembered the priapic ex-Byrd as 'kind of like a little sultan', adding that 'it was a sort of Hollywood hippie thing, having these long-blond-haired lovely young human beings running around, sometimes with no clothes'.

Crosby's 'Wooden Ships' almost bringing to mind the Aryan super-beings of Ray Bradbury's 'Dark They Were and Golden-Eyed'. When Jackson Browne later wrote 'For Everyman' as a kind of response to 'Wooden Ships', he asked: 'What about all the people who can't afford a yacht?'

II

Perhaps the real point about CS&N – about their very name, in fact – was that they weren't a group at all. They were three singer-songwriters who'd left bands and formed a loose triad in which each of them could get his own material recorded. 'It's important that you don't talk about us as a group,' Graham Nash said in September 1969, 'because we're three individuals.' As such, they fitted in perfectly with the countless solo performers who began popping up in LA between the Monterey and Altamont festivals.* Indeed, it was Crosby who took under his wing a young Canadian folk singer he'd befriended in Florida, helping to make Joni Mitchell the outstanding female singer-songwriter of her generation.

The figure of the self-accompanied folk singer had never really gone away: he or she had merely been overshadowed by the bands who'd formed in the wake of the British invasion. It was significant, for example, that young folkies like Tim Buckley and Jackson Browne had had to reverse an earlier trend and go to New York to achieve any kind of recognition in 1966–7. Buckley had been playing around his native Anaheim and writing songs with poet Larry Beckett since leaving high school, but it was only when Mothers of Invention manager Herb Cohen took the tousle-headed troubadour to Greenwich Village that Jac Holzman signed him to Elektra.

Buckley's first album for Elektra boasted Jack Nitzsche and Van Dyke Parks among its credits, but the gauche songs – 'Valentine Melody', 'Strange Street Affair Under Blue' – later made their own author cringe. *Goodbye and Hello*, recorded in LA in June 1967, abandoned what his guitarist Lee Underwood called 'the Bambi-eyed littleboy poet prattling about paper hearts and Valentines' and moved closer to the strange-days spirit of Buckley's labelmates the Doors. Despite the dated pseuderies of the lyrics – Beckett's and Buckley's own – songs such as 'Hallucinations' and 'Pleasant Street' were all about coming down from the giddy euphoria of psychedelia. On the six-minute 'I Never Asked to be Your Mountain',

'A Bambi-eyed littleboy poet': Tim Buckley with percussionist Carter C. Collins.

* A film which reflected this shift from band culture to singer-songwriter culture was Bill L. Norton's *Cisco Pike* (1972), which starred Kris Kristofferson as a washed-up rock star whose band had played the Shrine Auditorium in 1967. In addition to Kristofferson's hippie troubadour, there were hilarious cameos from Doug Sahm, who told Cisco that 'that California shit ain't happening no more', and from Harry Dean Stanton as Cisco's speed-addled ex-bandmate Jesse. There was also Viva as the stoned, ostrich-feathered swinger who takes Cisco and Jesse to the Troubadour to reminisce about the good old days of Fred C. Dobbs.

moreover, Buckley's pure counter-tenor gave way to the cracked and ranting 'jazz' voice which would blossom on *Happy/Sad* (1969) and dominate the bravely experimental albums he subsequently recorded for Frank Zappa's Straight label. By the release of *Starsailor* (1971), Buckley had moved so far beyond the limpid melancholy of his folk-rock period it was hard to think of him any longer as a 'singer-songwriter'.

When Jackson Browne – who'd also grown up in Orange County – drove across America in January 1967, he arrived in New York to find that Buckley was supporting Nico at the Dom. He himself subsequently became Nico's lover and musical arranger, working on her *Chelsea Girl* album before returning to LA in the early summer. Not that his work with the Velvet Underground *chanteuse* made much difference to his prospects in Hollywood. Despite *Cheetah* magazine lauding him alongside Buckley and Steve Noonan as one of 'The Orange County Three', the freshfaced surfer boy couldn't seem to get signed for love nor money.

Only the belief of the perennial Billy James, in the laundry room of whose Laurel Canyon house he lived for the best part of a year, kept Jackson Browne from starving. A modest publishing advance from Elektra, for whom James was now working, resulted in Browne's songs being recorded by everyone from Linda Ronstadt to the Byrds – Terry Melcher drowned 'Jamaica, Say You Will' beneath a forty-piece orchestra on *Byrdmaniax* – but the kid still couldn't secure his own record deal. 'I guess he didn't seem particularly special to a lot of people,' James was to reflect. 'He seemed like another young folksinger to them. Also, there was the problem of his voice – people felt he couldn't sing, that he wasn't a singer, so it was extremely difficult for me to stir up any interest in him among people at record companies.'

Browne epitomized the kind of aspiring singer-songwriter – folk-rooted but country-tinged – who hung around Doug Weston's Troubadour club. 'The Troub was the only place where you could go and showcase for record companies,' he remembers. 'You went there on Mondays just to try and get a job. You signed on to this list at 4 p.m. and if you were lucky you might get to sing three or four songs that night. Monday nights also happened to be industry nights at the bar, so you had a lot of actors and agents and record executives and beautiful women around. It was a teeming scene, and people like Crosby were always flying in and out with girls.'*

'Just another young folk singer': Jackson Browne.

---

* Browne's fellow Troubadour aspirants included Ned Doheny and Jack Wike, with whom he took part in the ill-fated 'Elektra Music Ranch' near the remote California town of Paxton. Green-lighted by Jac Holzman and staff producer Barry Friedman in the late summer of 1968, the ranch sessions began with a view to forming an entity known as 'The Los Angeles Fantasy Orchestra'. Six months and $75,000 later, with little to show for the experiment, Jac Holzman closed the place down. Another singer-songwriter signed to Elektra at this time was David Ackles, who recorded two albums between 1968 and 1970 before releasing the cult favourite *American Gothic* (1972), a panoramic if patronizing sweep of smalltown Americana which sounded like John Cale meeting Tim Buckley over arrangements written by Jimmy Webb.

'Our local club': the Troubadour on Santa Monica Boulevard.

By the time Browne had landed a support slot during a Troubadour residency by Linda Ronstadt, the 'singer-songwriter' had become a ubiquitous figure on the LA scene. 'You started to get songs that only the songwriter could have sung – that were part of the writer's personality,' says Browne. 'You didn't think in terms of "confession", just in terms of intimacy, description, story-telling. Suddenly there was a whole universe of ideas out there, and you could discuss *anything* in a song. There were no more rules as such.' For Browne, the singer-songwriter 'school' was inaugurated by two key records: Joni Mitchell's *Song to a Seagull* and the solo debut by Neil Young.

Born in Alberta, Canada, Joni Mitchell had wound up singing in the folk clubs of Greenwich Village, booking her own little gigs outside New York. One night in 1967, Buffy Sainte-Marie brought a junior agent from Chatkoff-Winkler down to see her at the Café a Go Go, and the guy flipped. 'I told her I'd kill for her,' says the Bronx-born Elliot Roberts, who promptly jacked in his job and accompanied her on a jaunt to Florida. 'Everything about her was unique and original, but we couldn't get a deal. The folk period had died, so she was totally against the grain.' On the advice of David Crosby, with whom Mitchell had a brief affair while playing the Florida folk circuit, Roberts and his charge packed their belongings, left the enchanted Village world of 'Chelsea Morning', and split for Los Angeles.

Sitting in the Santa Monica office of the former Elliot Rabinowitz –
lean and tanned, with sun-bleached hair and biker's boots – Roberts could
almost be Woody Allen on steroids. LA is full of New Yorkers come
good in paradise, guys who should have been schlepping into midtown
Manhattan from Forest Hills every morning but instead took a rock'n'roll
detour and lucked out beneath the palm trees. When Roberts thinks back
to the halcyon days of California in the sixties, the Bronx seems a lifetime
away.

Crosby advised Roberts to go to the Warners-affiliated Reprise
label and talk to Andy Wickham, the Englishman who'd served his
apprenticeship working for Lou Adler at Dunhill. 'Andy was a folkie at
heart,' says Roberts. 'His best friend during this whole period was Phil
Ochs, with whom he roomed and who was undervalued as an influence
on the whole singer-songwriter sound.' (For Roberts, Ochs' 1968 album
Tape from California did a great deal to shape the emerging aesthetic of the
Warners-Reprise roster.) With Wickham as Mitchell's first real champion,
Reprise boss Mo Ostin agreed to pay for a David Crosby-produced demo,
and the demo duly turned into *Song to a Seagull*.

The album, recorded at Sunset Sound with Buffalo Springfield across
the hall in Studio B, wasn't quite a classic debut – the title track itself was
typical of the winsome sub-Richard Bach mysticism of the time – but the
fact that Crosby had produced it, and was touting her around as a genius
to all his friends, counted for a great deal. 'David was very enthusiastic
about the music,' says Mitchell. 'He was *twinkly* about it! And his instincts
were correct: he was going to protect the music and pretend to produce.
Without that protection the record company might have set some
producer on it who'd have tried to turn an apple into an orange.'

'Crosby was the main cultural luminary to me,' says Jackson Browne.
'He was a fascinating character, because he consciously went about
mythmaking. He had this legendary VW bus with a Porsche engine in it,
and that summed him up – a hippie with power!' For Elliot Roberts,
'everything centred around Crosby' in 1968, and many were the fellow
musicians to whom the Cros showed off the young Canadian that summer.
Such was the word-of-mouth he built up with aid of B. Mitchell Reed that
Joni's first stint at the Troubadour was a four-night sellout. Coupled with
this acclaim were the covers of songs such as 'Michael from the Mountains'
(Judy Collins) and 'The Circle Game' (Tom Rush and Buffy Sainte-Marie).
Having only just arrived in LA, she was already at the heart of the Laurel
Canyon scene.

By early 1969, Mitchell was ensconced with Graham Nash in a little
house at the foot of Lookout Mountain Avenue, polishing the songs
which would appear on her marginally more assured second album. A
decade later she would tell Cameron Crowe that *Clouds* was an 'irritating'
emulation of Crosby, Stills and Nash, but the album contained 'Both Sides
Now', 'Chelsea Morning', and 'I Don't Know Where I Stand', all covered

*Stranger in a strange land: Joni
Mitchell arrives in LA, 1968.*

in due course by major pop artists. Already a perfectionist, she was determined not to be dismissed as a poor woman's Baez or Collins.

Joni finally fulfilled her promise with *Ladies of the Canyon* (1970), whose title betrayed its preoccupation with the scene that had midwifed it. On this third record she was less of a hippie/folk maiden, more of a pop/rock musician: gone was the acoustic-troubadour style of 'I Think I Understand' or 'Song to Ageing Children Come', in their place arrangements featuring piano and percussion. 'My music is becoming more rhythmic,' she told an interviewer. 'It's because I'm in LA and my friends are mostly rock'n'roll people ...' The swooping, vibrato-heavy soprano was still piercingly pretty, but there was a new maturity to both the sound and the conception of the record. While the title track wryly encapsulated the cosy life of Lookout Mountain, moreover, 'Woodstock' and 'For Free' confronted the death of the rock dream born at Monterey. Heard after the horror of Altamont, 'Woodstock' was an almost chillingly beautiful song about the final gathering of the sixties tribes: 'We've got to get ourselves back to the garden,' she sang, making clear the impossibility of regaining pop's innocence. 'For Free', meanwhile, was the song of a superstar who has forfeited the integrity of the busker. 'I was the queen of the hippies in a way,' says Mitchell, 'but in a way I wasn't a hippie at all. I was always looking at it for its upsides and its downsides, balancing it and thinking, "Here's the beauty of it and here's the exploitative quality of it and here's the silliness of it."'

By the time *Ladies of the Canyon* was in the Top 30 in the spring of 1970, the implications of 'For Free' seemed to have caught up with Mitchell, who'd spent much of the previous year on tour and rather over-exposed herself into the bargain. Feeling like the proverbial 'bird in a gilded cage', she decided to take time off and travel around Europe, hooking up with some diehard hippies on the island of Crete. But her place in the Canyon firmament was now as assured as that of her fellow Canadian Neil Young, whose *After the Goldrush* was an even bigger seller that year than *Ladies*.

Young had been on the point of quitting Buffalo Springfield when he ran into his compatriot at Sunset Sound. The two singers knew each other from their folkie days in Toronto's Yorkville scene, and were glad to share their feelings of disorientation in Hollywood. If Mitchell was almost a gamine in this new milieu of drugs and groupies, Young was shellshocked by it. He'd discovered he was epileptic only weeks after arriving in the city, and was now obliged to take drugs that made him grouchy and withdrawn. In addition, he'd been through a harrowing acid phase, inspiring the Springfield songs 'Burned' and 'Flying on the Ground is Wrong'.

When Young finally severed his connection with the band in the late spring of 1968, it was Mitchell's manager who helped him get back on his feet. 'Joni introduced me to Neil at Sunset Sound, and we hit it off,' Elliot Roberts remembers. 'The Springfield had started to dissolve, and Neil and

Troubled troubadour: Neil Young quits Buffalo Springfield, 1968.

Steve were never in the studio at the same time during those last sessions. I tried to save the band, who'd just sacked their original managers Charlie Greene and Brian Stone, but Neil simply walked out of the meeting I called. Two weeks later, he shows up at my door and tells me he wants me to manage him solo.' As he had with Joni Mitchell, Roberts approached Andy Wickham and Mo Ostin and secured a deal with Reprise.

Neil Young, released in January 1969 after the singer's post-Springfield Topanga chillout, was effectively the consummation of the orchestral, overdub-heavy style he'd created with the help of Jack Nitzsche on 'Broken Arrow' and 'Expecting to Fly'. Nitzsche continued his involvement with Young on the record, writing arrangements for several songs and even contributing the instrumental piece 'String Quartet from Whiskey Boot Hill'. Also involved with *Neil Young* were David Briggs, the Topanga neighbour who oversaw most of its production, and Ry Cooder, who co-produced three tracks with Young and Nitzsche. 'The album itself was great,' Young would tell Nick Kent years later. 'But then they put this new process on the original mixes called the haeco-csg system and it just fuckin' killed it ... literally squashed the sound so the music sounded the same in mono and stereo.'

Actually, songs such as 'I've Loved Her So Long' and 'The Old Laughing Lady' – with their sweeping strings and black female soul choruses – would have sounded over-ambitious even if Reprise had never decided to try out the system on them. But it was typical of Neil Young as we now know him to react violently against the elaborate arrangements of his debut by pairing up with a grungey rock'n'roll bar band called the Rockets, whose 1968 album on White Whale had sounded to him like 'the American Rolling Stones'.

Evolving out of loose jam sessions that Young held with the Rockets in the spring of 1969, *Everybody Knows This is Nowhere* was raw and gritty, sparer than anything else coming out of Los Angeles that year: next to *Crosby, Stills & Nash*, 'Cinnamon Girl' sounded like punk rock, while 'Cowgirl in the Sand' and 'Down by the River' established the slow, churning groove the band – rechristened Crazy Horse – would make their own. Young loved the 'feeling of togetherness' on tracks such as 'River', 'Cowgirl', and 'Everybody Knows This is Nowhere': the deep throb of Billy Talbot's bass, the interplay between his own squalling guitar style and the simpler rhythmic counterpoint of Danny Whitten. Even on the acoustic 'Round and Round' and the countrified, Burritos-esque 'The Losing End', Crazy Horse stamped Young's songs with their band identity.

Everybody Knows was already a hit album by the time Stephen Stills asked Young if he was interested in joining Crosby, Stills and Nash as a kind of floating fourth member. Insiders were surprised that the lanky Canadian even considered the idea of working with his old bandmate, but Young claimed that 'playing with Stills was special'. He also liked the notion of being able to 'lay back' within the group while pursuing his own solo career, and was on board by the time the group played their second-ever show – the Woodstock Festival.

But it was Young's solo career which held up the process of recording the follow-up to *Crosby, Stills & Nash*, since he was already committed to recording his next album for Reprise. 'I'd usually go in and record with Crazy Horse at Sunset Sound every morning, then go to a CSNY rehearsal in the afternoon through to the evening,' he told Nick Kent. 'Then I'd go home, crash out, get up the next morning and do the same routine all over again. That's when "I Believe In You", "O Lonesome Me" and a couple of others on *After the Goldrush* were conceived.'

Recorded in Wally Heider's new studio up in San Francisco, where Crosby, Stills and Nash were busily reinventing themselves as northern Californians, *Déjà Vu* was a miserable experience for all concerned. Cocaine was everywhere, and engineer Bill Halverson was drunk from start to finish. People dropped in and out at all hours, yet the four men were almost never in the studio at the same time. Worse still, hanging like a pall over the sessions was the death in a head-on car crash only weeks before of David Crosby's beautiful girlfriend Christine Hinton.

Even Hinton's death could not excuse Crosby's lamentable 'Almost Cut My Hair', as phony a statement of radical politics as a rock musician has ever written. Neil Young must have blanched at the song's banality, especially after the Kent State massacre had inspired the instant agitprop of his own 'Ohio' – a last gasp of rock'n'roll rage before (in the words of Bruce Pollock) 'events conspired to sweep the sixties actions and philosophies under the rug of memory'. God knows what Neil made of 'Our House', Graham Nash's trite ditty about his Laurel Canyon love-nest: the journey from 'Ohio' back to 'Our House' seemed to sum up a general failure of nerve in the LA music scene. Perhaps the best song on *Déjà Vu*, besides Joni Mitchell's 'Woodstock', was Young's 'Country Girl', a sumptuously Nitzschean piece of orchestral rock that recalled 'Broken Arrow' and came complete with Spectoresque timpani.

By the release of *Déjà Vu*, which occupied the No. 1 spot in April 1970, Young was already finding the mega-success of CSNY hard to handle. He was altogether happier getting back to Topanga and rehearsing with the homegrown, hype-free Crazy Horse. 'Crazy Horse is funkier, simpler, more down-to-the-roots,' he said. Augmenting the band with the piano-playing of Jack Nitzsche, he set off on a tour which packed all the punch of 'Cinnamon Girl' and more. The only drawback to the experience was the heroin addiction of Danny Whitten, which ultimately forced Young temporarily to jettison Crazy Horse. Late in 1970, the band recorded their own, eponymously titled album for Reprise, co-produced by Bruce Botnick and Jack Nitzsche and featuring Whitten's famous song 'I Don't Want to Talk About It'.

That spring Young recorded *After the Goldrush*, a predominantly acoustic album which none the less made room for such electric tracks as the crunching 'When You Dance I Can Really Love' and the epic 'Southern Man', a savage indictment of Bible-belt racism. Songs such as 'Birds', 'Tell My Why' and 'I Believe in You' were high-water marks of quasi-autobiographical singer-songwriting, with Young's wavering falsetto creating a simultaneously intense and fragile persona that epitomized post-hippie masculinity.

Just as Young had held up the *Déjà Vu* sessions, so the sessions for *After the Goldrush* held up the CSNY *Déjà Vu* tour in the summer of 1970. Young enjoyed the tour as little as he'd enjoyed making *Déjà Vu*, though his performances were easily the most affecting things on the resulting live album, *Four Way Street* (1971). If Neil did his share of coke, he was dismayed by the fact that everyone on the tour seemed permanently wired, with more than a few of them using heroin to cushion the continual comedowns. When he came off the road in the late summer of 1970, he holed up in a new ranch in the Santa Cruz mountains south of San Francisco. (It was while lifting some heavy wooden slabs in the ranch that he put his back out of traction, landing him in hospital for much of 1971.) At the end of the year he would record the album which defined the LA singer-songwriter genre better than any other.

III

When Joni Mitchell and Neil Young signed to Reprise in 1968, they were pinning their colours to the mast of what would become *the* LA record company of the early seventies: Warner Brothers, of which Frank Sinatra's Reprise label had been a part since September 1963. Ironically, of course, Sinatra detested pop music, but even he had to sit up and take notice when his own daughter reached No. 1 in 1966 with her Reprise hit 'These Boots Were Made For Walkin''. (The whole Reprise story came full circle when Ol' Blue Eyes recorded Joni Mitchell's 'Both Sides Now'.)

'By the time *I'd* arrived at Warners, it was a pretty solid operation,' says former promo man Russ Regan, who found 'That's Life' for Sinatra. 'They'd done very well with Peter, Paul and Mary, and with comedy acts like Allan Sherman, and now they had Bill Cosby too. Plus they'd moved very quickly into the pop field, and were doing well in it. Mo Ostin was a wonderful man and a great leader – very warm, very bright – and all his executives were very musical and artist-oriented.'

Just before Regan left to become head of promotion at Uni Records in January 1967, Mo Ostin called him into his office and played him 'Purple Haze' by the Jimi Hendrix Experience. It said everything about Ostin that, despite starting out as Sinatra's administrative V-P at Reprise, he could see that the future of pop lay with this psychedelic black dandy, rather than with the Rat Packers – Sinatra, Dean Martin, Sammy Davis Jr – whose Reprise hits had been masterminded by producer Jimmy

Warners head Joe Smith in the late 1960s.

Bowen. By September 1967, following his historic appearance at Monterey, Hendrix's Reprise debut *Are You Experienced?* was at No. 5 in the American charts.

If Warner-Reprise's commercial base was still MOR/pop – acts such as Kenny Rogers and the First Edition – Mo Ostin and Warners head Joe Smith (who'd signed the Grateful Dead) were gradually transforming the company into a rock label. With the help of executives Joel Friedman and Stan Cornyn, and an A&R staff that included Andy Wickham and Lenny Waronker – son of Liberty founder Si Waronker – Ostin and Joe Smith created an empire which was soon home to the best the West Coast had to offer. 'Warners was a big standard-bearer for the hip Hollywood fraternity,' says the company's current publicity director, Bob Merlis. 'It said that you didn't have to be in the Village to be hip, and I think that was one of the reasons a person like Joni Mitchell was prepared to risk leaving New York for Hollywood Babylon.'

Part of the genius of Warner Brothers-Reprise was that it was able to project a 'small company' image, even after it had merged with the Seven-Arts film distribution company, acquired Atlantic Records, and been sold in turn to Steve Ross's Kinney Corporation in New York.* The combination of the company's pseudo-rustic headquarters on Burbank's Warner Boulevard and the droll, self-deprecating ad campaigns dreamt up by Stan Cornyn ('Pigpen Lookalike' and 'Win a Fugs Dream Date' contests; the offer of a free bag of Topanga Canyon dirt to anyone who bought the first Neil Young album) gave it a friendly character that its principal rivals – the faceless and monolithic Columbia label – never had. 'The really important factor was that we were a younger company than, say, Columbia,' recalls Stan Cornyn, who'd joined Warners in 1959. 'We weren't structured so tightly that we couldn't *bend*.' (The furore that greeted the resignation of Mo Ostin in late 1994 – a resignation prompted by attempts at Time-Warner in New York to curtail his authority – was testament to the profound affection in which he was held by almost all his artists.)

Warner-Reprise were particularly alert to the new breed of singer-songwriters who emerged in late 1967–8. 'When the Laurel Canyon scene

* The merger with Seven-Arts came about because of the poor performance of the Warners movie studio since the late fifties, but was generally felt within the company to have been a rash decision on the part of the ageing Jack Warner, especially since Seven-Arts was an insignificant company with alleged mob connections. The Kinney Corporation was similarly tainted by mob links in New York, but Steve Ross had already transformed it, and would go on to create the corporate climate in which both the movie and music divisions of Warners thrived throughout the seventies and eighties. It was Ross, for example, who fought to persuade Ahmet Ertegun to stay with Atlantic; Ross who fired Warners president Mike Maitland when he failed to reward Mo Ostin and Joe Smith; and Ross who engineered the acquisition of Elektra in 1970. 'Steve didn't try to GI his division heads,' recalled former Warners executive David Horowitz. 'The record people had their own styles and logos. They presented a picture to the world they wanted.'

'A wonderful man and a great leader': Mo Ostin of Warner-Reprise.

started,' says Cornyn, 'we were just awash in it.' In addition to Mitchell and Young, the labels between them signed Van Morrison, Arlo Guthrie, Ramblin' Jack Elliott and even the zany Tiny Tim. But the two 'singer-songwriters' who best summed up what the company was all about were Randy Newman and Van Dyke Parks, bespectacled backroom boys suddenly given a shot in the limelight. Both men had had a hand in pop hits from the Warner-Reprise stable in 1967. Newman had helped to arrange Harpers Bizarre's version of Paul Simon's '59th Street Bridge Song (Feelin' Groovy)', while Parks – recovering from the nightmare of *Smile* – had produced both the group's follow-up 'Come to the Sunshine' and the Mojo Men's hit version of Stephen Stills' song 'Sit Down, I Think I Love You'.

When former Metric Music songplugger Lenny Waronker signed his boyhood chum Randy Newman to Warner Brothers in August 1967, the singer wasn't even a particularly successful writer. Sure, he'd had a fair number of songs covered – most recently, Judy Collins had done 'I Think It's Going to Rain Today' and Alan Price had recorded 'Simon Smith and His Amazing Dancing Bear' – but none of them had set the pop world on fire. Nor was he exactly gung-ho to make it as a recording artist in his own right. 'I don't think I was ever hungry for success, because I was never really poor,' he confessed, adding that LA itself had 'probably

Randy Newman, least confessional of singer-songwriters.

affected my work habits in an adverse way, in that it's a difficult town to bear down in'. Waronker, whose father had played viola in the Fox studio orchestra when Randy's uncle Alfred was under contract as a composer there, was unimpressed by his friend's indifference to fame. He thought so highly of Randy's songs, moreover, that he was prepared to exploit their childhood connection in order to fend off the $10,000 advance being offered to Newman by A&M.

As it happened, Newman was an entirely atypical example of the LA singer-songwriter. For starters, he had no interest in singing about himself, claiming it was 'hard to write for yourself, to think about yourself as an artist'. For seconds, his songs came out of a Tin Pan Alley pop tradition which had nothing to do with folk or rock or country music – or anything else his Laurel Canyon peers were doing in 1968. Which may have been why his Warners debut fared so poorly on its release. Co-produced by Waronker and Van Dyke Parks, *Randy Newman* was sumptuously orchestrated, betraying not only the avowed influence on Newman of his uncle's movie scores but the four years he himself had spent studying music at UCLA.

True, offsetting these was Newman's profound love for the easy-rolling rhythm and blues of New Orleans, where he'd briefly lived as a child. But the album's sound was weighted much more heavily towards the vaudeville eccentricity and deranged Broadway schmaltz of Van Dyke Parks than towards, say, Huey 'Piano' Smith. 'I took an aggressive part in championing the excellence of Randy's material,' says Parks. 'For "Linda", for example, I suggested borrowing an idea from his uncle Alfred's score for *Carousel*. It was a wonderful time to experiment with pop music, you see.' Everything that is great about Randy Newman was there on that first album: the benign condescension towards Middle America ('The Beehive State'), the effortlessly modulated melancholy ('Living Without You', 'I Think It's Going to Rain Today'), the penchant for grotesquerie ('Laughing Boy', 'Davy the Fat Boy'). It was just that *Randy Newman* went so far beyond the concerns of his rock peers it simply passed over everyone's heads.

Equally ambitious was *Song Cycle* (1968), the debut album by Van Dyke Parks himself. 'Lenny Waronker was a filthy-rich kid who drove a Lamborghini but stayed off his dad's yacht because he was interested in music and wanted to stay involved,' says Parks. 'He invited me over to Warners, not for who I was but for what I'd learned from Brian Wilson. He's never admitted that to me, but it's no offence to him to say that. If it wasn't his ulterior motive it should have been, because I'd learned a lot from Brian – among other things, a balance between rationality and instinct and play.' Parks jokes that he dismissed Waronker's 'sincerity of purpose' until he lent him one of his 'fine Italian cars', but the real proof was in the pudding of the recording contract Waronker offered him – and in the bankrolling of the fabulously complex *Song Cycle*.

When Parks went out to Palm Desert to prepare *Song Cycle* – 'just me and a piano in a house on the edge of a tract development' – he knew that he wanted to create a concept album about Hollywood and southern California. Parts of the album had been written as early as 1964, when Parks' fascination with Los Angeles began. For all its Debussy and Charles Ives quotes, the album essentially concerned the story of the diminutive southerner's journey to California – above all, his first visit to Hollywood as a child actor in the mid fifties. (Little Van Dyke had appeared in Charles Vidor's *The Swan*, the last film Grace Kelly made before settling down to her royal duties in Monaco.) 'I wanted to capture the sense of California as a Garden of Eden and land of opportunity,' he says. 'It was a very big deal to me: What *was* this place? What has it become? What *will* it become? And what does it mean to be here?'

From the wistfully whimsical opening track 'Vine Street', specially written by Randy Newman, *Song Cycle* was as baroque and kaleidoscopic as 'pop music' got in the sixties. 'Not since Gershwin has someone so completely involved in the pop holocaust emerged with such a transcendent concept of what American music really means,' wrote Richard Goldstein. With its playful orchestration and dense, cryptic word-play, the album took the experimentation of *Smile* into a completely new sphere of intellectual brilliance: Sandy Pearlman called it 'a true idealization of the Muzak idea', while Richard Meltzer deemed it to be 'the most formidable Muzak doing of all time'.

'I didn't think it would make anybody mad if I free-related, using a Joycean stream-of-consciousness approach to the lyrics,' says Parks. 'I got into a lot of trouble for the album, but secretly I think I fascinated the musicians by revealing to them some of the possible approaches to this new 8-track recording equipment.' Actually, the highbrow complexity of *Song Cycle* was deceptive, because perseverance revealed countless beautiful details, moments of moving insight. 'A novelist would have gotten away with it, but in music if something doesn't satisfy the libido it's taboo,' sighs Parks. 'So the record was condemned to the safety of some white southern nursery. You listen to it and you think, "Isn't this effete?" or "Nice parlour music", but there's nothing but sorrow attached to it – sorrow born of a traumatic personal experience.'

Song Cycle also functioned as a documentary of its time, superimposing (in 'Palm Desert' and 'Laurel Canyon Boulevard') an older Hollywood on the pop LA of the sixties. Parks says he wanted *Song Cycle* to be 'relevant to its time and part of the free press of its time, as a watchword to the errant youth that was showing up here in droves', but one suspects that he rather overestimated the intellectual capacities of the youth in question. He admits this was 'rather confirmed' by the album's pronounced failure, though he did not appreciate one of Stan Cornyn's most (in)famous ad campaigns – one designed to drum up fresh interest in *Song Cycle*. 'HOW WE LOST $35,509.50 ON THE ALBUM OF THE YEAR (DAMN

IT)', read the ads which appeared in *Rolling Stone* and the underground press.

Perhaps it should have been no surprise after the failure of both *Randy Newman* and *Song Cycle* that Lenny Waronker not only elected to produce Newman's *12 Songs* without Parks' help but gave the album a markedly more contemporary production. Opening with the horn-driven rhythm and blues of 'Have You Seen My Baby?', subsequently covered by the Flamin' Groovies, *12 Songs* was a decidedly more rootsy affair than Newman's string-engulfed debut. Also featured were 'Mama Told Me Not to Come', a No. 1 hit for Danny Hutton's Three Dog Night in June 1970, and the usual assortment of deadpan, killingly ambiguous middle- and-southern Americana. Still, *12 Songs* hardly played it safe: 'Suzanne' was the creepily beautiful first-person song of a rapist stalking his victim, while the cover of the 1934 Cotton Club anthem 'Underneath the Harlem Moon' confronted racism by talking happily of 'darkies'. 'The scariness of the songs was not smug on Newman's part, but simply presented as what he did for a living,' wrote Greil Marcus. 'Here he was [on 'Harlem Moon'], a struggling singer whose only possible audience would be urbane, liberal rock'n'roll fans, and he was unveiling ... the charms of racism.'

This willingness to burst through the presumed liberalism of rock fans was part and parcel of Newman's distance from the singer-songwriter community in LA. Working almost deliberately against the grain of confessional writing – the folk music of the new 'Me Generation' – Newman had limited appeal for people who liked to *take their stars literally*, as heroes rather than as artists. 'You see, *I* don't interest me,' said the man Lenny Waronker described as 'the king of the suburban blues singers'. Significantly, he also told an interviewer that he wasn't 'exactly socially oriented'. 'Laurel Canyon has got an awful lot of musicians living in it,' he said, 'but I really don't know anybody. And if [the music community] is there, I don't know about it, and don't care too much.'

A curator of American musical tradition: Ry Cooder in 1970.

Notwithstanding the black humour of his writing, Newman was actually just as angst-ridden about the craft of his songs as any of his more navel-gazing Laurel Canyon peers. 'You bust your ass with a crazed kind of worrying about every little thing,' he said, 'and then you wind up seeing all these bad things about it two weeks later. It's a psychosis.' For Van Dyke Parks, who claims that after the failure of *Song Cycle* he was happy to 'subsume my own lofty artistic goals to the interests of other artists like Randy', Newman 'had seen the dark side of the moon ... for some reason I couldn't figure out' and would get 'real sick' on the mornings of recording sessions.

Another of the Warners artists to whose interests Parks was happy to subsume his own aims was Ry Cooder, whose debut album fell into the same rootsy-Americana bag as his slide-guitar playing on Randy Newman's 'Let's Burn Down the Cornfield'. 'When Ry wanted the opportunity to pursue his sense of geography, there was no question at Warners but that he should have it,' says Parks, who co-produced *Ry Cooder* (1970). 'We didn't know whom we were selling Ry or Randy to, it was strictly on a wing and a prayer, but we did our darnedest to sell them anyway.' Signed as a solo artist by Lenny Waronker after his work on the *Performance* soundtrack, the ex-Rising Son/Magic Band guitarist wasn't a singer-songwriter, but his music defined the spirit in which LA musicians were rediscovering tradition in blues, gospel and hillbilly music. 'Warners sort of indulged me in making that kind of music,' Cooder said in 1972. 'That first album was very experimental and kinda shaky. I'd never done anything like it and I didn't really have a direction in mind. It was chaotic at times, but there was some good stuff on there.'

The difference between Cooder and the Leon Russell/Delaney and Bonnie 'sanctified hippie' mob lay in Cooder's scholarly approach to musical tradition. If *Ry Cooder* drew from the same well as the classic second album by The Band, there was a dryness and a precision about Cooder's treatment of mountain fiddler Blind Alfred Reed's 'How Can a Poor Man Stand Such Times and Live?' which distinguished it from the earthy, rollicking – and self-written – songs of *The Band*. The scholarliness was symptomatic, too, of an aloofness that made the virtuoso guitarist even more distant from the LA/Laurel Canyon scene than Randy Newman. The idea of Cooder replacing Brian Jones in the Rolling Stones – mooted at the time of *Let It Bleed*, on which he played – now seems positively laughable.

Parks, Newman and Cooder defined the sensibility of Lenny Waronker, who became head of A&R in June 1971, but they didn't exactly swell the Warner-Reprise coffers. While these 'prestige artists' made their wonderful and enduring records, Mo Ostin and Joe Smith kept busy signing the acts that enabled Warners to close the gap on industry leaders Columbia between 1970 and 1973. 'Eventually, Warners was forced to broaden its approach,' wrote Clive Davis in his autobiography; 'even its artists started complaining.' The signings included such British hard-rock bands as Black Sabbath and Jethro Tull – who complemented Atlantic's signing of Led Zeppelin and audacious deal with the Rolling Stones – but they also included James Taylor, America, Alice Cooper, Gordon Lightfoot and the Doobie Brothers.

James Taylor was a troubled junkie from a well-heeled Boston family who'd fled to London in 1968 after playing with guitarist Danny Kortchmar in a New York band called the Flying Machine. While living in a basement flat in Chelsea, he'd recorded a demo tape which found its way into the hands of retired teen idol Peter (and Gordon) Asher. Asher had just been made head of A&R at the Beatles' new Apple label, and liked Taylor's songs enough to sign him and produce the gaunt bard's eponymously titled debut album. Frustratingly, *James Taylor* got lost in all the shenanigans going on at Apple, and Taylor ended up back in the States – as did Peter Asher, himself weary of the chaos at Apple. Coming out to LA in

'A mellow kind of a James Taylor kind of thing': Mr Introspection in 1970.

December 1969, the carrot-haired Englishman had breakfast with Joe Smith at the Continental Hyatt on Sunset and made a deal for James Taylor. 'I brought James over here because I really thought his songs were important,' he says. 'They were just so incredibly well-crafted and musical, and the lyrics were so fascinating. I thought, I've got to make people listen to them, there was a genuine proselytizing aspect to it all.'

The resulting *Sweet Baby James* (1970), produced by Asher, was in the Top 40 album chart for a stupendous fifty-four weeks, spawning a Top 5 single in 'Fire and Rain'. With it, Asher put himself on the map as an LA player and Taylor put his seal on the genre of anguished, introspective singer-songwriting. 'My style at that time was very intimate,' he later said. 'To criticize it, I think it was very self-centred, very autobiographical, and you could call it narcissistic. But the upside of that was that it was very accessible, and I think people liked that. It was just guitar and voice with some embellishments, and it was miked very close. It was a mellow kind of a James Taylor kind of a thing.'

Ah, that word 'mellow' – a key California term in the early-to-mid seventies. It seems paradoxical now that such 'mellow' music could have come out of such torment, but the combination of bland tunefulness and harrowing introspection definitely struck chords with American twentysomethings recovering from their dazed hippie youth. Post-Woodstock, as Janet Maslin noted, 'the time was ripe for reactionary expressions of frustration, confusion, irony, quiet little confidences, and personal declarations of independence.' Somehow it was appropriate that Los Angeles, never exactly a locus of sixties togetherness, should produce the first flag-bearers of the 'Me Generation', navel-gazing in their canyon lairs.*

Sitting in his swanky Doheny Drive office, a copy of Mike Davis's *City of Quartz* visible on a shelf behind his desk, Peter Asher disavows the 'mellow California' tag affixed not only to James Taylor but to his protégée Linda Ronstadt. 'The singer-songwriter thing *did* get very identified with LA, and I thought that was rather unfair,' he says. 'We did a show in Japan once – James, Linda and J. D. Souther – and they were going to call it "California Live". We pointed out that not one of those people was actually from California. They went, "Oh, it doesn't matter," but it did matter to us. It's true that Linda and the Eagles and the rest of them all *met* in LA – the Troubadour was the crucible of the whole scene. But James, for example, always hated LA.'

Maybe Taylor did hate Los Angeles, but that didn't stop him taking his place in the singer-songwriter firmament, especially after he began the affair with Joni Mitchell which she part-documented on *Blue* (1971). 'It

---

* For the best statement on the way Taylor and his kind represented the death of everything dionysiac and incendiary in rock, see Lester Bangs' 1971 piece 'James Taylor Marked for Death', reprinted in *Psychotic Reactions And Carburetor Dung* from Greg Shaw's mag *Who Put the Bomp*.

was a wonderful year, performing and recording together,' he remembered. 'I was pretty unconscious around then, but she was writing "A Case of You" and the *Blue* album in a single-storey, rough-cut wooden house up on rock piers in Laurel Canyon.' Just as Joni sang on the title track of his second Warners album, *Mud Slide Slim and the Blue Horizon*, so Taylor played guitar on the title track of the album that was almost the high-water mark of the acoustic, soul-unburdening school. A song cycle about love's joys and miseries. *Blue* was so nakedly personal for Mitchell that she locked everyone except engineer Henry Lewy out of the studio.

'I perceived a lot of hate in my heart ... my inability to love,' Joni later admitted about *Blue*, and the closing 'Last Time I Saw Richard' certainly bore that out. Bitterly reproaching her former husband – who'd mocked her questing romanticism only to plump for a supposedly stable life – 'Richard' sounded angrily defensive, especially when a song such as 'River' dealt with the desire to get away from the LA rock scene. Then again, 'California' was a song written in Europe that expressed her 'longing for that kind of creative climate where we did drop around with our songs to play'.

Both Taylor and Mitchell wrestled with the competing claims of solitude and community – a 'community' of solo artists who found it hard to operate within fixed musical units. After *Mud Slide* and *Blue*, Taylor sank deeper into drugs, then married Elektra star Carly Simon, while Mitchell retreated into 'melancholy exile' in the forests of northern British Columbia, where she wrote the songs that made up the even more inward-looking *For the Roses* (1972). The same year also saw the release of Neil Young's *Harvest*, another definitive singer-songwriter document. 'Somehow, I just wanted to get really laid-back,' Young recalled. '*Harvest* was me saying, "Okay folks, I can do all those other things, play out on the edge, go nuts and do 'Ohio' and 'Southern Man' ... but later for that." I was saying, "Okay, let's just get really, really mellow and peaceful ... make music that's just as intense as the electric stuff but which comes from a completely different place, a more loving place." ' It wasn't as if, in any case, Young was fit to play raging electric rock'n'roll: having been laid up in hospital for months, he was still in a brace when he went into the studio.

Recorded with a band that included steel guitarist Ben Keith and Nashville sessionmen Kenny Buttrey (drums) and Tim Drummond (bass), *Harvest* boasted a sleepy, easy-rocking country groove that answered perfectly to the name Young gave them: the Stray Gators. For the most part the songs were about getting out of the city, searching for a rural peace of mind; one of them ('Heart of Gold') was the cutest, catchiest thing the man had ever written. Standing out like sore thumbs, however, were two songs orchestrated by Jack Nitzsche, whose piano-playing had earned him a place as the fifth Stray Gator: sweeping, grandiloquent and ever-so-slightly kitsch, 'There's a World' and 'A Man Needs a Maid' took their place in the series of near-MOR-ish deviations Young has continued to take over the years.* Not that either of them was enough to stop *Harvest* reaching No. 1 on the *Billboard* album chart in March 1972, with 'Heart of Gold' already having topped the singles chart.

The influence of Neil Young (and CSNY) was all over the album that nudged it from the top of the chart at the end of March. *America* was the self-titled Warner Brothers debut by a trio of army brats who'd bonded together in Britain and only relocated to LA after Dewey Bunnell's song 'Horse With No Name' had steamed up the charts towards the No. 1 spot. Bunnell had lived out in the California desert in his early teens, and the haunting 'Horse' – not actually about heroin, for all the rumours – was written and recorded in London as a virtual act of remembrance. A similar inspiration lay behind the wind-in-your-hair classic 'Ventura Highway', in which Bunnell attempted to capture 'the total feeling of California', drawing on deeply rooted images of 'sun, surf, and pop-tops'. America epitomized everything which was sickly and nauseating about Californian soft-rock, but Bunnell's voice and songs – 'Horse', 'Ventura Highway', 'Sandman', 'Tin Man' and others – had a redeeming mysticism that distinguished them from those written by Dan Peek and Gerry Beckley.

An equally suspect Warners act was the Doobie Brothers, a kind of LA version of the Allman Brothers who signed to the label in late 1970. Lead singer Tom Johnston had started out playing in blues and R&B bands in 'every fuckin' bar and Okie stomp club in the Valley', but had moved to San Jose and linked up with drummer John Hartman to form the acoustic-oriented, America-esque lineup of the Doobies' 1971 debut. But it was with the funky-cowboy posturings of *Toulouse Street* (1972), and its Top 20 single 'Listen to the Music', that the Doobies found their feet. Produced by Theodore 'Ted' Templeman, the ex-lead singer of Harper's Bizarre, the album paved the way for a series of platinum albums which made millions for Warners: *The Captain and Me* (1973), *What Were Once Vices are Now Habits* (1974), and six more Top 10 albums between 1975 and 1980.

If America and the Doobie Brothers coined it for Mo Ostin and Joe Smith, the two men were still prepared to take risks with acts whom critics chose to stigmatize as 'prestige artists', all but subsidizing the careers of Van Dyke Parks (with *Discover America*, the follow-up to *Song Cycle*) and Ry Cooder (with *Into the Purple Valley*) and signing not only the washed-up Beach Boys but the certifiably uncommercial Captain Beefheart.

The deal Mo Ostin cut with the Beach Boys and their Brother label in late 1969 had more to do with his own sentimental feelings for the group's

---

* It was entirely fitting that when Young revisited the terrain of *Harvest* with the even more obviously autumnal *Harvest Moon* (1992), he should ask Nitzsche to arrange the string charts on the serene 'Such a Woman'. 'There's a real "In My Room"/"Surfer Girl" feel to it,' he said at the time. 'Jack's one of the modern-day masters. His creations are on a par with Mozart and the composers of the renaissance.'

status as a Californian institution than with any real rekindling of their commercial potential. Nevertheless, the signing seemed to mark a symbolic ascendancy over Capitol, helping to elevate Warner-Reprise to the position of premier Los Angeles label. All the more pity that *Sunflower* (1970) was as lacklustre as its immediate predecessors *Friends* and *20/20*. Recorded while the band was recovering from the Manson killings and Brian Wilson from the blow of his father selling the entire Sea of Tunes publishing catalogue for a risible $700,000, the album featured only minimal contributions from the former head Boy, who was spending much of his time behind the counter of his Radiant Radish

Dennis Wilson and James Taylor roll up in Monte Hellman's Two-Lane Blacktop *(1971).*

store, dressed only in pyjamas. True, Brian's name appeared on the credits of seven songs, and 'This Whole World' was a track he'd written by himself, but it wasn't as though one could really feel his presence on the record – other than in fleeting moments such as the incorporation of the chant from *Smile*'s 'The Elements' in 'Cool, Cool Water'. The rest of the album was a mixed bag of compositions by various combinations of writers: 'Forever' was a pretty thing Dennis had written with Gregg Jakobson, while 'Tears in the Morning' was a solo effort by Bruce Johnston. *Sunflower* never even penetrated the Top 100 in *Billboard*'s album chart.

Yet *Surf's Up* (1971), the next album, was not only close to being a masterpiece but saw the Beach Boys reinventing themselves as a seventies rock band, complete with facial hair and ecology songs. If Brian wasn't in any better shape for the record than he'd been in for *Sunflower*, the last two tracks – ''Til I Die' and 'Surf's Up' itself – were indisputable masterworks anyway. By all accounts, Wilson was horrified that 'Surf's Up' was seeing the light of day after all this time, but the song sounded just as breathtakingly baroque and California-mystical as it had done back in 1966. ''Til I Die', meanwhile, used the Pacific once more to symbolize the vast and empty universe in which Brian felt so alone: Mike Love called it 'a fucking downer', but its sadness was almost ecstatically beautiful. The other Brian song, the hymnal and disarmingly ingenuous 'Day in the Life of a Tree', was also bizarrely affecting – despite being sung by Jack Rieley, the extraordinary manager who'd helped to restore some of the band's credibility by booking them into the Whisky for a four-night stand in November 1970.

What was impressive about *Surf's Up* was its coherence as an album: even the songs by Carl Wilson and Al Jardine were close to being worthy of Brian himself. There were throwbacks, too, to the Los Angeles of the band's youth in Bruce Johnston's song 'Disney Girls (1957)' and in the unlikely adaptation of the Robins' Leiber and Stoller classic 'Riot in Cell Block No. 9', retitled – and this from the Beach Boys! – 'Student Demonstration Time'. All of which helped put the band back on the pop map, and gave *Surf's Up* a respectable chart placing of No. 29 in late 1971.

Still, Mo Ostin must have regretted his sentimental indulgence of the Beach Boys after the Jack Rieley-inspired debacle that was *Holland*. After the dismal *Carl & The Passions/So Tough* (1972), which featured a Brian Wilson song ('Marcella') about a Sunset Strip masseuse, the entire Beach Boys entourage decamped for Europe, setting themselves down in the Low Countries with the intention of making an album. If it wasn't bad enough that Warners had to foot the bill for the shipping-out of an entire studio, Brian proceeded to lock himself away in his hotel room with a small mountain of hash and a copy of Randy Newman's *Sail Away*. It took Van Dyke Parks, by now a director of 'audio-visual services' at Warners, to dig out an old song called 'Sail On, Sailor' in a vain attempt to give Ostin the hit single *Holland* so evidently lacked. All told, the little 'woodshedding' experiment had cost an astronomical $500,000.*

IV

If it seems perverse to classify Captain Beefheart as a 'singer-songwriter', it's difficult to know how else to categorize the man. And the fact is that by the time he signed to Reprise after a 1971 row with Frank Zappa, Don Van Vliet's songs had become a good deal more accessible than those on *Trout Mask Replica* or *Lick My Decals Off, Baby*. With a new Magic Band lineup consisting of Drumbo, Zoot Horn Rollo, Rockette Morton, Art Tripp, a.k.a. Ed Marimba and guitarist Elliott Ingber, a.k.a. Winged Eel Fingerling, he cut *The Spotlight Kid* (1972), a downbeat and rather sombre collection of songs such as the moving 'White Jam', the moaning de-evolution blues of 'Grow Fins', and the train song 'Click Clack'.

But it was the Ted Templeman-produced *Clear Spot* (1973) which gave

* In the same spirit that prompted Mo Ostin to sign the Beach Boys to Reprise, Joe Smith brought none other than Phil Spector to Warners in late 1973, offering the little megalomaniac his own label and the opportunity to record artists such as Dion, Cher and Harry Nilsson singing pointless new versions of, for example, 'Baby, I Love You' and 'A Love Like Yours (Don't Come Knockin' Every Day)'. (As Marc Ribowsky remarked, Spector was 'the prize moose on Smith's office wall'.) For Dion, Spector pulled out all the old stops – Gold Star, Stan Ross, songs by Goffin, Mann, Weil, Barry and company – on the depressing *Born to be With You*, but it was all to no avail. The only great record Spector made at this time was Darlene Love's mighty 'Lord, If You're a Woman', an extraordinary hurricane of sisterly rage that's fit to stand with almost anything he ever produced.

the world a Beefheart who verged on being radio-friendly. Reputedly written on a car journey between Boston and Yale, *Clear Spot* was a thrilling rock'n'roll record made up of equal parts guitar-slashed swamp-funk and baleful moon-howling balladry. With Ed Marimba in the drum seat, the up-tempo tracks packed much more of a rock punch, while 'Too Much Time' was a funky soul number with Memphis-style horns and 'Her Eyes are a Blue Million Miles' were almost heartbreakingly tender. The standout track by a long way was 'Big-Eyed Beans from Venus', one of the most cataclysmically exciting pieces of rock'n'roll ever recorded. It was hardly surprising that this maelstrom of surreal, surging, frenzied noise, dominated by a virtual six-string duel between Zoot Horn Rollo and the newly reinstated Alex St Clair, became the showstopping highlight of many a Beefheart/Magic Band show on the European tour of 1973.

Beefheart was always one of a kind, but *Clear Spot* wasn't a million miles from the sound of a Warners band who had one foot in the Zappa/Beefheart camp and the other in the retro-Americana camp of Ry Cooder and The Band. Formed by native Angeleno and movie-brat Lowell George from the ashes of the Factory, a Sunset Strip band who'd operated in a folk-psychedelic crack somewhere between Kaleidoscope and the Strawberry Alarm Clock, Little Feat were born after George had served a brief apprenticeship as a Standell and then as a Mother of Invention. The swarthy, dungareed guitarist later griped about the lack of accreditation on *Hot Rats*, although his deranged vocals on *Weasels Ripped My Flesh* received their due acknowledgement. He also claimed to have found Zappa as workaholic and unapproachable as most of the other Mothers did, which was why he quit the band in the summer of 1969. 'I don't even know what Lowell was doing in the band, because it wasn't really his sort of music,' says Pamela Des Barres, whom Lowell produced as a GTO. 'I guess he saw it as a stepping-stone, which was what it turned out to be.'

Zappa was keen to sign Little Feat – George, ex-Factory drummer Richie Hayward, ex-Mothers bassist Roy Estrada and would-be-Mother Billy Payne on keyboards – but Warner Brothers snuck in there and bagged them instead. 'Lowell was rehearsing Little Feat and was going to sign with Herbie Cohen or Gabriel Mekler's Lizard label,' recalls Russ Titelman. 'I said, "You don't wanna do that, why don't we go talk to Lenny Waronker?" So I took Lowell and Billy Payne up to Burbank and they sang "Willin'", "Truck Stop Girl" and "Brides of Jesus". And Lenny just said, "Make a record – it's a deal."'

Titelman admits that all he wanted to do with *Little Feat* (1970) was re-create the flavour of the first two Band albums, then exerting a huge influence on the LA scene. 'We didn't manage to do it,' he says, 'probably because Little Feat were much more bluesy than The Band.' None the less, like The Band and Gram Parsons, George was tuning into a new-old spirit of roots Americana, revamping the blues and country music he loved. There was Stonesy sass in 'Hamburger Midnight' and 'Snakes on

Little Feat, Venice, 1970. Left to right: Roy Estrada, Billy Payne, Lowell George, Richie Hayward.

Everything', Burritos-style balladry in 'Brides of Jesus' and 'I've Been the One', and Beefheartian delta dirt in the Howlin' Wolf medley of 'Forty Four'/'How Many More Years'. Part Jagger, part Dr John and part Boz Scaggs, Lowell George came as close to White Negrohood and ersatz Dixie hip as anyone did in 1971. Equally important as time went on was his humming, swarming slide guitar, developed after he'd injured his left hand building a model aeroplane.

Appropriately, Feat's first American tour saw them bottom of the bill on a Beefheart/Ry Cooder Warners package, but the exposure did no more to sell the album than did Ed Ward's rave review in *Rolling Stone*. 'In the early days it was Starvation Central,' George remembered. 'Richie and his wife and kids slept in my living room and Billy slept out in my Volkswagen van.' Only the continuing popularity of 'Willin'' – covered by everyone from the Byrds to Linda Ronstadt – kept George's name alive on the LA scene. By the mid seventies, this ode to 'weeds, whites, and wine' had become the ultimate truckers' anthem.

Even when Warners assigned Ted Templeman to produce *Sailin' Shoes*, something seemed to jinx the band. People have argued that Lowell George wasn't a charismatic enough frontman to carry the band on a visual or performance level, but a more fundamental problem was that he refused to deliver the kind of mainstream Californian rock which

Templeman's other charges the Doobies were purveying. There was always something gritty and knotty about the best Feat songs – invariably those written by George – which ruled out the possibility of real commercial success.

With its unforgettable, Fragonard-derived Neon Park cover – a grotesque cake with eyes and limbs on a swing, observed by a giant snail – *Sailin' Shoes* quickly became something of a cult album. If 'Easy to Slip' wasn't so far from Crosby, Stills and Nash, the caustic raunch of 'Tripe Face Boogie' or 'Teenage Nervous Breakdown' was harder than anything else coming out of California at the time. There was also a new'n'improved 'Willin'' to savour, along with the supremely soulful title track. These songs came closer to the glory of, say, *Exile on Main Street* than any of Feat's mutton-chopped, southern-rocking contemporaries. They were also witty, sexy and surreal at a time when, as Denny Bruce puts it, most Californian songwriting was about 'drinking apple juice and walking down a dusty road with your dogs'.

The expanded Feat lineup. **Left to right:** *Kenny Gradney, Billy Payne, Richie Hayward, Lowell George, Sam Clayton, Paul Barrere.*

Shortly after the album's release in March 1972, Roy Estrada split to join the Magic Band, prompting a hiatus which saw Lowell playing sessions for everyone from Etta James to Carly Simon and hanging out with Jackson Browne. When Little Feat returned to the fray in 1973, it was with an expanded lineup featuring guitarist Paul Barrere, together with ex-Delaney and Bonnie sidemen Kenny Gradney (bass) and Sam Clayton (percussion). The fact that Gradney and Clayton hailed originally from New Orleans suited Lowell George down to the ground. Increasingly smitten with the black music of the magical Crescent City, he wanted to build Feat into a 'sophisti-funk' unit around a potent piano/slide/congas enginehouse. The resulting *Dixie Chicken* (1973) boasted not only the pure second-line propulsion of the title track and 'Fat Man in the Bathtub' but an ultra-soulful rendition of Allen Toussaint's 'On Your Way Down' and a wordless hymn to Louisiana called 'Lafayette Railroad'. The whole album encapsulated LA's tequila-soaked love affair with rootsy, sensual southern rock. With Bonnies Raitt and Bramlett on backing vox, it was funky country chased with bayou soul – what Chris Darrow called 'lizard-skin music'.

For Van Dyke Parks, who produced the wonderful 'Spanish Moon' on the follow-up *Feats Don't Fail Me Now* (1974), George was a close friend and a fascinating phenomenon. 'Lowell taught a lot of people to sing, and you can hear his style in a number of the people he worked with,' he has said. 'It was that melisma of madness I refer to as "white boy got the woo-woos" or "vanilla grits".' The only problem was that Feat's expanded lineup ultimately proved to be Lowell's undoing, since as time 'went on the rootsy, swampy soul of his songs increasingly lost out to the fusionesque noodlings of his band. The indications were already there – in the instrumental break on 'Texas Rose Café', in the synth work on 'Kiss It Off' – but it took *Feats Don't Fail Me Now* for the awful truth to register: that Billy Payne really wanted to be Joe Zawinul, that the others wanted to prove they could cut the mustard with the likes of Steely Dan. It was the old Frank Zappa hangup about being taken seriously as 'players', and Lowell's battle to keep things simple was harder to fight within the band's new democracy. It didn't help, of course, that he was undermining his own authority by indulging in sensual gratification on a heroic scale. 'When you look up the word "hedonism" in the dictionary, there should really be a picture of Lowell there', says Rick Harper, who road-managed George on and off from the earliest days of The Factory to the last days of Little Feat.

The picture could just as easily have been of Gram Parsons, who in the fall of 1972 returned from his trust-funded adventures with the Rolling Stones and moved into – where else – Laurel Canyon. 'The Stones were always wary of strap-hangers, people who didn't pull their own weight,' recalled Phil Kaufman, the road manager who'd done time with Charlie Manson and even bankrolled his early demos. 'But Gram could have the same dirty habits and pay his own way. He could also talk to them on a one-to-one level, which afforded him the opportunity to create with them.' Keith Richards was always supposed to have produced Parsons' solo debut, but not surprisingly he was seldom in a fit state to do so. There were also tapes lying around at A&M of songs Gram had cut with fellow rich-kid Terry Melcher, both men stoned out of their minds. By the end of the year, Gram had signed to Reprise and recruited East Coast folkie Emmylou Harris, whom he'd met through Chris Hillman. His respect for Harris brought out the best in him, and the two of them set to work like a modern-day version of George Jones and Tammy Wynette.

Parsons' first choice as a producer for *G.P.* was none other than Merle Haggard, the Bakersfield superstar whose reactionary 'Okie from Muskogee' Gram liked to think of as the country equivalent of a Randy Newman redneck song. But Haggard's innate distaste for druggy longhairs prevailed over any other considerations: like almost everyone else around Parsons, he was alarmed by the sheer volume of drink and drugs the guy ingested. So instead, while he was holed up at the Chateau Marmont with Phil Kaufman, Kim Fowley and others for company, Gram ran into ex-Blind Faith bassist Rick Grech by the pool and asked him to co-produce the album.

G.P. was a country-rock masterpiece, the consummation of everything

Parsons had been working towards on *Sweetheart of the Rodeo* and *The Gilded Palace of Sin*. Released in March 1973, it featured some of the more established LA country sessionmen, including James Burton and Glen D. Hardin, both of whom were by now playing regularly with Elvis Presley. This was neo-honky-tonk, cry-in-your-beer music for rock'n'rollers, with Gram's own songs standing out alongside covers such as Tompall Glaser's 'Streets of Baltimore': above all, the achingly plaintive ballads 'She' and 'A Song for You', and the briskly up-tempo 'Still Feeling Blue' and 'How Much I've Lied', all of them enhanced by the pellucid harmonizing of Emmylou.

That spring, Parsons and Harris hit the road with a band he dubbed the Fallen Angels. 'I was put on a converted Greyhound bus with "Gram Parsons" emblazoned across the side and surrounded by various musicians and fugitives from love and law and order,' recalled Emmylou. 'We set out to play country music and rock'n'roll in the better hippie honky tonks of the nation. The rooms were small but the energy generated was of a special intensity. We didn't exactly break any box-office records, but there are people who will remember.' The 1982 album *Live 1973*, hailing from a Long Island show recorded after the band's three-night NYC stand at Max's Kansas City, featured half of the *G.P.* songs and a clutch of covers like Merle Haggard's 'California Cottonfields', the tailor-made Everlys classic 'Love Hurts', and truckers' favourite 'Six Days on the Road'.

Parsons began work on the self-produced *Grievous Angel* after the Fallen Angels tour finished in the summer of 1973. If anything it was even better than *G.P.*, again blending Parsons originals with covers. A 'Medley Live from Northern Quebec' – featuring 'background blah-blah' by Phil Kaufman, manager Eddie Tickner, and the ubiquitous Kim Fowley – consisted of 'Cash on the Barrelhead', by Gram's beloved Louvin Brothers, and his own *Sweetheart* evergreen 'Hickory Wind'. The whole album was shot through with glitz and guilt, romance and Vegas tack, everything that made Parsons an icon to stoned slackers in the early nineties.

When the Lemonheads' pinup frontman Evan Dando decided to try his hand at a spot of auto-destruct crack-bingeing in the late summer of 1993, he chose the Chateau Marmont to do it in – that strange Sunset Boulevard hotel which Nik Cohn remembered as 'full of corridors and dark corners ... Filipino bellhops, aged courtesans, ghost-white junkies'. 'Gram was real talented, a real tragic figure,' commented Joe Robb of the Robb Brothers, who produced the Lemonheads' *It's a Shame About Ray* at their Cherokee Studios. 'I think Evan recognized similarities without ever knowing the guy. Although Gram was in the middle of the music business out here, he was completely isolated from it. He was one of those people who went to where the business was – Hollywood – but really had nothing to do with it. And he was a hard liver. He had that dark side to him, the urge to jump off the cliff.'

Early in September 1973, Parsons recorded 'In My Hour of Darkness', a song of mourning for such fellow hard-livers as Brandon De Wilde, who'd exited the world in a car crash in June 1972, and for Clarence White, killed by a drunk driver that very July. The song suggested that once again the LA drug scene was getting out of hand, with the twin devils of heroin and cocaine wreaking havoc in the canyon communities. John Neuse of the old International Submarine Band told Sid Griffin that Gram had 'wanted to cool it with the whole Hollywood scene and get into a more relaxed and easier thing like he'd experienced with the ISB', adding that he was helping Gram to set up a new band to take *Grievous Angel* out on the road.

In his last interview, Gram said he'd spent a lot of time in the desert – often driving out to Joshua Tree National Monument for conventions of UFO freaks – and liked to look down at the San Andreas fault, wishing he was 'a bird drifting up above it'. With *Grievous Angel* completed, he made his customary LA getaway, except that this time there wasn't any convention to keep him from zoning out big time. On 19 September, after ingesting a huge amount of morphine and booze, he turned an ominous shade of blue in Room 10 of the Twentynine Palms Motel. When the motel owner's son wandered over, sensing some 'weird vibes' from the room, he found a stoned, frightened girl called Dale McElroy giving Parsons mouth-to-mouth resuscitation. The singer was rushed to the Hi Desert Memorial Hospital in Yucca Valley but died shortly after arrival.

'Warners was comfortable,' says Russ Titelman. 'It was people who knew about music and had a lot of fun making it. Mo and Joe were responsible for some incredibly hip signings – Jimi, Joni, Van – and Lenny did an amazing job turning Arlo Guthrie into a pop act and making hit records with Gordon Lightfoot. It created a certain vibe and a certain perception about the company. In a way – in a good way – it was all things to all people.' Barry Hansen, who worked at the company in the early-to-mid seventies, remembers a permanent mood of buoyancy around the Burbank offices. 'It was always very business-like, but there were a lot of smiling faces around,' he says. 'On Friday afternoons they'd usually break out the champagne and toast their latest hit record. And they gave people room to grow. I mean, they hired people like Van Dyke just because they liked having him around.'

For someone like Russ Titelman, of course, Warners was about as 'comfortable' as life got. But to outsiders, the company began to exude the smugness of a country club. One Parsons-style maverick who felt the pain of not fitting in was Jack Nitzsche, especially after the solo album he presented to Mo Ostin – an ambitious affair in the *Smile/Song Cycle* mode, with lyrics by his film-director buddy Robert Downey – never saw the light of day. (Meanwhile his 1972 classical opus *St Giles' Cripplegate* sold a less-than-awesome 2,000 copies.) 'You've got to understand that Ry

'Something's got to shake this city loose': the irascible Jack Nitzsche (right) with his friend Denny Bruce.

Cooder, for example, only got his Warners deal because Jack brought him in on the *Performance* soundtrack,' says Nitzsche's friend Denny Bruce. 'Cooder stabbed Jack in the back, told Mo he wasn't together enough to produce him. Jack also did a whole lot to help Neil get his deal, and again there was no production job for him. Remember that Jack's "Lonely Surfer" was one of the very first pop hits on Reprise, when Mo Ostin was still just an accountant.'

After his stint with the Stray Gators, Nitzsche finally quit LA, fulminating against an industry he felt had betrayed him. 'I'll work in a gas station before I go their route,' he told *Crawdaddy!* in 1974. He even took a potshot at Neil Young, claiming he'd only written the string arrangements on *Harvest* so that he could use the London Symphony Orchestra for *St Giles' Cripplegate*, and adding that the Young/Stray Gators tour of 1972–3 was 'torture'. 'Neil's whole lifestyle is that of the millionaire who doesn't give a shit about anybody but himself,' he said. Moving to the redwoods of northern California, the bespectacled Hollywood malcontent set up a mutual admiration society with Bob Downey, another self-proclaimed Misunderstood Genius, fantasizing about a *Day of the Locust*-style 'purification' of the Hollywood scene. 'I really think there should be something happening like a liberation movement in Hollywood,' he railed. 'A drastic one like the Symbionese Liberation Army … something's got to shake this city loose.'

V

The singer-songwriter 'school' which Warner-Reprise did so much to foster impacted not only on the scene which had evolved from the scattered ashes of the Byrds and Buffalo Springfield, but on a wide range of songwriters – from diverse backgrounds – who were able to re-present themselves to the record industry as thoughtful 'voices', alone at a piano or clutching an acoustic guitar. The singer-songwriter vogue particularly helped women break through the stifling norm of male 'gangs': Laura Nyro may have bombed at Monterey, but four years later Joni Mitchell was a superstar. Hell, even John Lennon was a singer-songwriter now, primal-screaming his angst on the Phil Spector-produced *Plastic Ono Band*.

Without any question, the single most remarkable case of 'self-reinvention' was that of Carole King, the Brill Building veteran who'd penned so many pop classics with her husband Gerry Goffin. In 1970, King was almost thirty and all but washed up. In New York, she'd put together the City with guitarist Danny Kortchmar and bassist Charlie Larkey, but their LA-recorded debut album sold poorly. Moving into a house on Wonderland Avenue, she set about writing the bulk of the songs that surfaced on *Writer* and – more importantly – the 1971 album *Tapestry*.

'The timing was perfect because there'd been a transition from cool to mellow...': Carole King and her producer Lou Adler.

'Carole had moved to the Canyon around 1969, when I was doing Spirit and getting ready to produce *Brewster McCloud*,' says Lou Adler, who added King to his Ode roster in early 1970. 'I'd been too busy to do the *Writer* album, but by 1971 I was free to work with her, and out of that came *Tapestry*. The timing was perfect, because there'd been a transition from cool to mellow, with James Taylor as the leader of them all. Everyone was playing on everyone else's records: Carole on James', James on Carole's, Joni on James', James on Joni's.'

Once again, Adler's touch in the studio – 'I was simply trying to re-create her demos,' he says modestly – proved to be a magic one, as *Tapestry* went on to sell an astonishing five million copies, sitting pretty at the top of the album charts for fifteen weeks in the late spring and early summer of 1971. It helped that the LP's release coincided with King commencing a tour as the support act to James Taylor, whose version of her sappy 'You've Got a Friend' climbed to No. 1 in June. But Adler was right: the timing was perfect, and America was ready for the bland, singalong 'mellowness' of 'It's Too Late' and 'I Feel the Earth Move', together with the 'Carole-sings-Carole' versions of old pop hits such as 'Will You Love Me Tomorrow?' and '(You Make Me Feel Like a) Natural Woman'. This was the polar opposite to the bone-shaking, little-girl-blue frenzy of Janis Joplin, tearing the heart out of Big Mama Thornton or Berns and Ragovoy songs. It was the autobiography of a grown woman looking over the 'tapestry' of her life as she sat at the piano in her idyllic Canyon home.

(Another Lou Adler artist making a bid for solo fame as a singer-songwriter was John Phillips, whose *Wolfking Of LA* album was produced by Adler. Heavily influenced by Gram Parsons, on the back of whose motorcycle the ex-Papa had been riding when the ex-Burrito Brother crashed in Bel Air in May 1970, *Wolfking* was overloaded with vignettes of the drug-addled rock/movie 'aristocracy' Papa John was so chuffed to belong to: songs such as 'Malibu People' and 'Topanga Canyon', along with 'Let It Bleed, Genevieve', addressed to the South African-born actress he'd met through reviled Brit-in-LA director Mike Sarne.)

Tapestry was the new sound of Los Angeles: spare and pared-down, tastefully understated. It was living-room soul music. 'The sound of those records had a lot to do with the rhythm sections we used,' says Adler. 'James and Carole brought in the Section guys, Danny Kortchmar and Russ Kunkel and those guys. Funnily enough, Kootch [Kortchmar] wasn't that thrilled by *Tapestry*. He asked me what I thought of the record, and I said it was the *Love Story* of the record industry. I knew there was something very special about it, and I wasn't surprised that it hit a nerve.'*

Robert Christgau called *Tapestry* 'a triumph of mass culture', and it was one which encouraged all manner of hitherto invisible songsmiths to come out from behind the conveyor-belts, usually relocating to LA in the process. Barry Mann, for example, became just one of a hundred MOR-rock 'piano men' floating around Hollywood when he recorded *Lay It All Out* (1972), while Ellie Greenwich chose to call her 1973 Verve album *Let It be Written, Let It be Sung*, a title that could almost have been a mantra for singer-songwriters. Mann bounced back from the conspicuous failure of his solo debut with the more overtly rocking *Survivor* (1975), produced by Bruce Johnston with help from Terry Melcher. Unfortunately, songs such as 'Crazy Ladies' and 'My Rock and My Rollin' Friends' betrayed the same mild desperation that the album's title did. The New York version of Mann and Weil, cooped up in a stuffy Brill Building cubicle, made more sense than the LA version.

Barry Mann was suffering from a fear of becoming obsolete that haunted many behind-the-scenes songwriters in the early seventies. The problem was twofold: successful artists wanted to be seen as capable of creating their own music, while the songwriters themselves wanted the credibility that came with recording their material. 'The truth was that I felt deeply envious of people like Joni and Jackson, because I couldn't find an identity like that for myself,' says Jimmy Webb, whose run of smash hits had climaxed with the simultaneously sublime and ridiculous 'MacArthur Park' (1968). 'I was very uncomfortable with the way I was being perceived, politically and every other way. I didn't feel a part of my own generation, I felt somehow lost in a much older and more conservative group, so I immediately began to plot a way out of this cul-de-sac.'

Jimmy Webb joins the pack, 1972: 'The truth was, I felt deeply envious of Joni and Jackson...'

---

* The very name 'The Section' revealed the degree to which the LA session muso had become fetishized. Even more so than the diffuse 'Wrecking Crew', the Section became the nucleus of a new California studio mafia. Consisting of Kortchmar (guitar), Kunkel (drums), Leland Sklar (bass) and Craig Doerge (keyboards), they even had their own, eponymously titled album on Warners, released in 1972.

Webb recalls the poignant moment when he sat listening to Jackson Browne sing in front of the very fireplace where he'd sung for Johnny Rivers four years earlier. 'Here was Jackson asking me what *he* should do, in the same room where I'd asked *Johnny* what to do. That was such a weird kind of repetition, and it made me feel like an old, old man. I realized how quickly time was passing, and how quickly one had to act in rock'n'roll.'

As it happened, Jimmy Webb did become a singer-songwriter – and a very good one – but he found it just as hard to sell records as Barry Mann did. His first solo album was *Jim Webb Sings Jim Webb*, a collection of 1965–6 demos tarted up without his approval and released in 1968 to capitalize on the huge hits he'd written for other artists. Two years later he became yet another of the solo artists on Reprise, cutting *Words and Music* with the aid of multi-talented sessionman Fred Tackett. In pronounced contrast to the Spectoresque scale and contrapuntal complexity of the Fifth Dimension's 'Carpet Man' or Richard Harris's 'The Yard Went on Forever', the album was an almost DIY affair, sounding as though it had been recorded in a garage. It also – in tracks such as 'Songseller' and 'Dorothy Chandler Blues' – gave vent to a cynicism that might have surprised fans of the Fifth Dimension.

Particularly significant was the song 'P. F. Sloan', a tribute to 'one of the first writers I ever knew who tried to make his own records' and a man Webb thought was being treated very poorly by Dunhill. Sloan had made an early body-swerve away from hack pop/surf writing and jumped on the folk-protest bandwagon with the 1965 Dunhill album *Songs of Our Time*, but his solo career was distinctly petering out when Webb wrote his tribute. 'The last time I saw P. F. Sloan,' Webb sang, 'he was summer-burned, he was winter-blown/Did you hear, he turned the corner all alone?' Webb knew that 'Flip' Sloan had provided a kind of bridge between the Aldon/Brill Building writers and the Laurel Canyon navel-gazers, paving the way for people like himself to attempt the jump into the limelight.

Jimmy Webb cut two further albums for Reprise, filled with such brilliant MOR-pop songs as 'Met Her on a Plane', 'One Lady' and 'When Can Brown Begin', along with a very Tim Buckley-ish treatment of his own 'Galveston'. Both *And So: On* (1971) and *Letters* (1972) showed the influence of Joni Mitchell, with whom Webb had struck up a close friendship. 'I got extremely under her spell as a writer, and I still am,' he told Peter Doggett. 'I used to go to the studio and listen to her records, sitting quietly in the back of the control room. I definitely envied that part of her work – the idea that this was just a conversation you were listening in on. It was still poetry, but it wasn't self-conscious or forced.'

A more successful transition from hack-songwriting to stardom was that made by Harry Nilsson, whom Derek Taylor had met shortly before moving back to London in the spring of 1968. It was Taylor who, by

Harry Nilsson, fresh from the First National Security Bank in Van Nuys…

mailing several copies of Nilsson's debut album *Pandemonium Shadow Show* to the Beatles, ensured that the tall, Brooklyn-born songwriter became virtually a household name. Nilsson was still working at the National First Security Bank in Van Nuys when he signed his deal with RCA, but with the release of the album (which featured an eleven-song Beatles medley), he kissed goodbye to his old night-shift life in the Valley. 'Harry worked in the bank right up to the point where he'd met everyone he needed to meet,' says Derek Taylor. 'He was right there in the interstices of the business.' *Pandemonium* stiffed, but *Aerial Ballet* (1968) included the hit version of Fred Neil's 'Everybody's Talkin'' which was used in the final sequence of *Midnight Cowboy*, as well as the original of Three Dog Night's top five smash 'One'.

By 1970, when he recorded an entire album of Randy Newman songs, the bashful Mr Nilsson was squarely on the LA map, his songs neatly blending the influences of Broadway and Tin Pan Alley with those of Bacharach and the Beatles. 'The records we made were like we hadn't heard rock'n'roll, like the Rolling Stones didn't exist,' recalled Randy Newman, who played piano on *Nilsson Sings Newman*. 'We thought rock would go in a completely different direction, like a branch of *homo sapiens* which didn't become *homo sapiens*.' The following year, *Nilsson Schmilsson* made it all the way to No. 3 after Harry's heartrending version of Badfinger's 'Without You' topped the charts.

The same year, significantly, Nilsson's producer Richard Perry – the very same Richard Perry who'd produced Captain Beefheart – assembled a kind of 'greatest hits' of the new singer-songwriter brigade in the form of Barbra Streisand's *Stoney End*. Desperate to update her MOR/easy-listening image, Streisand put herself in the hands of a man who'd already overseen an album of Beatles songs by Ella Fitzgerald. Any misgivings she might have had were instantly dispelled by Nilsson's 'Maybe', the first song they worked on. The rest of *Stoney End*, a Top 10 album in February 1971, was made up by three Laura Nyros and two Randy Newmans, together with Joni's 'I Don't Know Where I Stand', Gordon Lightfoot's 'If You Could Read My Mind' and a song apiece from Mann/Weil and Goffin/King. With the musicians including most of the Phil Spector/Lou Adler veterans, the whole thing amounted to a kind of LA version of *Dusty in Memphis*. *Rolling Stone* ran a mocking piece about her pop makeover called 'The Jeaning of Barbra Streisand'.

Notwithstanding the apparent hegemony of the singer-songwriter brigade, California pop made an impressive comeback with hit singles by artists as various as Gary Puckett and the Union Gap, Three Dog Night, Cher, Bread, and even the teen bubblegum of that archetypal Valley boy Bobby Sherman. (It's easy to forget that the real pop supergroups of the early seventies were 'family' groups such as the Carpenters, the Osmonds and the Partridge Family.) The Union Gap, for example, were a San Diego band spotted by Columbia producer Jerry Fuller, who'd written songs for

*The A&M lot on La Brea Avenue:
'There should always be some place
you can get your record played.'*

Ricky Nelson and Eddie Cochran back in the fifties: picking up where
Paul Revere's Raiders and Gary Lewis's Playboys left off, they had four
massive hits in 1968, including the enduring 'Young Girl'. Three Dog
Night, meanwhile, evolved from a group Brian Wilson had recorded in
his Bellagio Road studio, led by his pal Danny Hutton. Christened by Van
Dyke Parks and supplied with a constant stream of songs by Harry
Nilsson, Laura Nyro, Randy Newman and Paul Williams, the terminally
unfashionable trio chalked up an astonishing ten Top 10 hits between
1969 and 1974.

In contrast to Warner-Reprise, a company such as A&M felt little need
to project an image of hipness or discrimination to the rest of the record
industry. 'There was a very, very specific philosophy at A&M,' says Bones
Howe. 'It was that there should always be some place else that you can
get your record played. If you can't get it on Top 40 radio, you should be
able to get it on a late-night MOR station.' If Herb Alpert and Jerry Moss
gave David Anderle room to experiment with the likes of Rita Coolidge
and the Ozark Mountain Daredevils, they played things altogether safer
with the Carpenters, a brother-and-sister duo who'd moved to the LA
suburb of Downey from Connecticut in 1963. At a Hollywood Bowl
'Battle of the Bands' concert in 1966, the siblings cleaned up in the awards
and won themselves an RCA contract, but it was only when USC music
major Richard Carpenter began cutting multi-track demos in a garage
belonging to bassist Joe Osborn that the distinctive MOR/pop sound of

the Carpenters was born. Within three years, the duo had notched up six consecutive Top 5 A&M hits, beginning with the Bacharach/David song 'Close to You' and including Paul Williams' 'We've Only Just Begun' and Leon Russell's 'Superstar'. Their crystalline arrangements and superlush harmonies helped to create some of the greatest LA pop records of the seventies.

The Carpenters' third hit was 'For All We Know', which had originally been written by James Griffin and Robb Royer for a group called Pleasure Faire. When all-purpose producer/arranger David Gates was assigned to the task of producing Pleasure Faire's 1968 album on UNI, the sessions led to the formation of Bread, initially intended to be a mere studio vehicle for the songs of the three men. Signed to Elektra in 1969, they released an inauspicious debut album in February 1970 but then had a No. 1 hit with 'Make It With You' that summer. Further hits such as 'If', 'Baby I'm-a-Want You', and 'Everything I Own' showed that Gates was firmly in the melodic soft-rock tradition of the Association and the Mamas and the Papas, his plangent voice lending his songs an ethereal prettiness. Bolstering the sound by late 1971 was Wrecking Crew keyboard maestro Larry Knechtel.

MOR genius: Richard and Karen Carpenter.

VI

By the end of 1971, the LA record industry was a very different beast from the one it had been before the Monterey Pop Festival. Over the course of four and a half years, countless managers, musicians and all-round hustlers had gravitated towards southern California, looking for the gold in them thar Hollywood hills. Meanwhile the industry had consolidated its operations through a series of mergers such as those which brought United Artists together with Liberty in 1968 and Warners and Atlantic together with Elektra in 1970. Profits were increasing annually, and corporate rock capitalism was now the name of the game. 'Things had been much more interbred before Monterey,' says Elliot Roberts. 'It wasn't a money market yet, everyone was just shooting craps. But as the pop festivals started to blossom and the West Coast bands began to proliferate, every talent scout of every record company was signing anyone even *affiliated* with acts on other labels.'

For some veterans of the Sunset Strip halcyon days, this new and ruthless business sense was destroying the spirit of the LA music scene. 'This city *was* the David Hockney LA,' says Denny Bruce, one of many music men to have been shut out of the LA mainstream. 'But Clive Davis scooping up all those bands at Monterey was the kiss of death. Suddenly you had all these horrible New Yorkers coming around – Elliot Roberts, David Geffen, Jeff Wald. Suddenly there was a whole New York Jewish management factor that everybody wanted.' As spoken by the Teutonic-

looking Bruce this sounds worryingly anti-semitic, but it was hardly as if Gentiles alone detested David Geffen: Jerry Wexler, for example, physically threw Geffen out of his office when the young upstart came to ask if Atlantic would release Stephen Stills from his contract. In fact, the two 'horrible New Yorkers' seem to have made enemies almost wherever they went. What really provoked people's hatred (or envy) was simply that they represented almost the entire Laurel Canyon aristocracy.

David Geffen had started out in the now time-honoured fashion of working in the New York mailroom of entertainment super-agency William Morris, where by the winter of 1967 he was head of the TV-packaging department. 'He was already legendary,' says Elliot Roberts, who himself joined the mailroom team just as Geffen left it. By the time Roberts had moved to LA with Joni Mitchell, Geffen was managing Laura Nyro, making a pretty penny from her publishing catalogue in the process. 'Everything was happening so fast in Los Angeles,' says Roberts, 'and the only person I thought could help me was David. He was in TV at Ashley Famous at this point, but he was making a lot of side deals for everyone. See, you could hire David to make deals without having the *involvement* of David. He preferred it that way because it gave him a broad spectrum of people from movie stars to rock stars to producers. Pretty soon Crosby, Stills and Nash had formed, and we worked things out for them. So within five months it had all come together: Crosby, Stills and Nash, Neil Young, and Joni Mitchell.'

Roberts called his management company Lookout Management, after Lookout Mountain Road in Laurel Canyon. One afternoon, when he and Geffen were driving to Carl Gottlieb's house, the workaholic legend turned to him in the car and said: 'Listen, let's just do this.' Lookout Management became Geffen-Roberts, with Geffen looking after the deals and Roberts looking after the artists. Soon it was the most powerful management stable on the West Coast. 'The word got around that there were these music-industry guys who were also human beings,' says Jackson Browne, the only artist to be signed to Geffen-Roberts on the basis of an unsolicited tape. 'Crosby told me that Geffen was really brilliant but that you could also trust him. And you could. David and Elliot would have done *anything* for their artists. In an industry full of cannibals, they were like the infantry coming over the hill.'

Geffen's ulterior motive in forming a partnership with Elliot Roberts was the formation of a record company. Significantly, he called it Asylum, indicating the kind of refuge he was offering the Laurel Canyon elite: Browne, Mitchell, the Eagles and Linda Ronstadt. With a corporate philosophy of 'benevolent protectionism', Geffen and Roberts buffered their artists from the riff-raff of the media and the music industry at large. 'David may have wanted to have a successful business, but he also wanted to be part of a community of friends,' says Jackson Browne, whose first album was released early in 1972.* 'He became our champion, and years later – after a lot of therapy – he finally got over his need to caretake people to the detriment of his own life.'

Geffen even persuaded Atlantic to finance the label – despite his little contretemps with Jerry Wexler – after Ahmet Ertegun, recognizing a fellow shark when he saw one, took a shine to him. 'Someone said Geffen didn't have an ear for music,' recalls writer Eve Babitz; 'Ahmet said, "No, but he has a nose for it."' A gauge of Geffen's colossal ego was the way he stood his ground with the makers of the *Woodstock* documentary. 'I would not allow them to use the footage of Crosby, Stills, Nash and Young in the movie unless they used Joni Mitchell's song with CSNY singing it as the theme of the movie,' he recalled. 'The producers were simply going to give me what I wanted or that was it. And since I represented a lot of important acts on Warners, Atlantic and Elektra, they just weren't going to fuck with me.'

Elliot Roberts says he and Geffen were fortunate that Crosby and Mitchell and Young 'drew great people to them like a magnet', but few could have foreseen just what a formidable power base Asylum would become over the ensuing years. From the tiny, localized scene that was the Troubadour bar, a whole Asylum subculture seemed to grow. In addition to Jackson Browne, there was Linda Ronstadt, J. D. Souther, Ned Doheny and four renegades who banded together in August 1971 as the Eagles. Country rock lived on at the Troub, and these artists were about to turn it into a multi-million-dollar industry.

* *Jackson Browne* was one of the first four Asylum album releases; the others were by David Blue, Judee Sill and Jo Jo Gunne, a Spirit spinoff who instantly hit with 'Run Run Run'.

For Billy James, the signing of Jackson Browne felt like a personal vindication. If the music on *Jackson Browne* was blandly James Taylor-esque, the lyric writing was impressive – introspective but chiselled. 'He worked with such an extraordinary understanding of who he was and what he was doing,' recalled Billy's wife Judy. 'He would not record before he thought he was vocally ready to, and when he did – when he pushed into it – he was ready and he knew about himself.' By the time he'd recorded *For Everyman* (1973), Browne was playing with a band that included ex-Kaleidoscope virtuoso David Lindley. While there was no overt country-rock influence in his songs, both Linda Ronstadt and the Eagles covered them, and he rapidly became identified with their laid-back, patched-denim sound.

When the Eagles' 'Take It Easy' – co-written by Browne – reached No. 12 in June 1972, it seemed to sum up the new spirit of LA as a paradise of freewheeling ease: suntanned longhairs marketing desert imagery for a mass American audience. (The very name, the Eagles, derived at least partly from the rock community's infatuation with Carlos Castaneda.) 'They all looked like Jesus Christ after a month in Palm Springs,' says Eve Babitz, who by her own admission 'practically lived in the corner of the Troubadour bar', and who later wrote a famous *Rolling Stone* article in which she said you could 'smell the sex' from the sidewalk outside. 'David took the *crème de la crème* from that scene and signed them on the basis of their cuteness.'

What the Eagles actually did was take what Gram Parsons had done and give it a radio-friendly pop sheen. (What is 'Lyin' Eyes' but 'Hickory Wind' without any of the real country-soulfulness?) 'The Eagles were different,' admits Elliot Roberts. 'They were *made* to sell a million records. Bernie for the most part put them together, and they wrote to be huge. You could sit in a room with Don Henley, Glenn Frey and J. D. Souther and they'd come up with three songs. With Neil or Joni, you couldn't say on Monday that you needed a song by Wednesday. The way we broke the Eagles was really much more conventional than the way we'd broken Neil or Joni. They were made as a bridge between avant-garde and commercial, between the Dead and Chicago.'

Drummer/singer Henley, who hailed from smalltown Texas, once argued that the famed 'California sound' of the seventies was mostly hype, since most of its practitioners weren't native Californians. It was a disingenuous claim that avoided the paradoxical point that the Californian Dream is a myth constructed – or recycled – by people who come to LA in search of the Californian Dream. The fact that the original lineup of the Eagles was composed of a southerner and three midwesterners only confirmed that Los Angeles was still as much a place of self-reinvention as it had been for a hundred thousand movie starlets. When Glenn Frey and J. D. Souther (another southerner) were living in penury in Echo Park in 1969, they were hard at work turning themselves into Hollywood outlaws. In the words of Eve Babitz, 'J. D. Souther once told me he spent his first years in LA learning how to stand.'*

Elliot Roberts' reference to the 'making' of the Eagles is not some far-fetched piece of Svengali-esque grandiosity: the group really was as manufactured as Crosby, Stills and Nash. In the spring of 1971, Glenn Frey sidled up to Don Henley at the Troub and told him David Geffen was planning to put a band together around Bernie Leadon and himself. By the time Frey and Henley returned from backing Linda Ronstadt on a summer tour, they had it all figured out. 'We'd watched bands like Poco and the Burrito Brothers lose their initial momentum, and we were determined not to make the same mistakes,' recalled Frey. 'Everybody had to look good, sing good, play good, and write good. We wanted it all. Peer respect. AM and FM success. No. 1 singles and albums, great music, and a lot of money.' Added incentive was provided by the potent atmosphere around the Geffen-Roberts stable. 'Being in close proximity to Jackson and Joni and Crosby, Stills and Nash, this unspoken thing was created between Henley and me. It said, "If we wanna be up there with the big boys, we'd better get our game together."'

Teaming up with Leadon and recruiting ex-Poco bassist Randy Meisner from Rick Nelson's Stone Canyon Band, Frey and Henley had themselves the band they wanted. 'They were very good from the very start,' says Jackson Browne. 'The first time I ever heard Henley sing, he was doing "You Don't Know Me", and I knew this was gonna be a giant band.' All that let the group down was their lack of cohesion as a performing unit, a factor which concerned David Geffen enough for him to pack them off to Colorado to hone their live act four times a night in an Aspen bar. With the kinks ironed out, the Eagles flew to London in April 1972 to record their first album, complete with 'Take It Easy', 'Witchy Woman', and a song whose title almost codified the laid-back LA sound: 'Peaceful Easy Feeling'. Produced by Glyn Johns, with a cover shot at dawn in the Joshua Tree desert, *The Eagles* was in the Top 30 by the summer.

Glyn Johns also produced *Desperado* (1973), the follow-up album that summed up the Eagles' extraordinary sleight-of-hand. It was this record more than any other which perpetrated the hoax that there was some kind of analogy to be drawn between rock'n'roll stars and outlaws. With its concept-album storyline taken from the exploits of real-life Oklahoma gunfighter Bill Doolin, *Desperado* presented the Eagles as a renegade gang,

* When Ed Sanders of the Fugs came out to begin research on his Manson book, *The Family*, in 1970, he stayed in Echo Park with Frey and Souther, who would sit up with him all night in case any Family members decided to make an attempt on his life. On another occasion, when Frey and Souther visited him at the Tropicana Motel, a ripple of panic went round the rock hotel's famous pool when its guests assumed they were Mansonites come to be interviewed by the Fug. Sanders subsequently wrote a 900-page biography of the Eagles, which remains unpublished to this day.

Arizona-born Linda Ronstadt in 1974: 'She did of course seem to me the ultimate Californian...'

four cowboys against the world. It also marked the ascendancy of Henley and Frey in particular as songwriters capable of harnessing their outlaw themes to easily digestible hard rock ('Out of Control') and limpid balladry ('Desperado', 'Tequila Sunrise'), all of them songs rendered in clean, sexless Californian voices. The Eagles subsequently condemned Johns' weedy production, but it was on *Desperado* that the group really defined its identity.

The Eagles were at the heart of the Asylum community, writing and/or touring with the likes of Jackson Browne, J. D. Souther and David Blue, as well as maintaining their association with Linda Ronstadt. 'It really was a "little village",' says English rock writer Nick Kent, who first came out to LA in 1973. 'In London it took you a while to see all the famous rock stars, but in Los Angeles you'd see everyone within two weeks. The Eagles were everywhere, and they were always wearing denim.' For the likes of Ronstadt, however, the Canyon scene wasn't an altogether benign one. 'There were too many drugs and the attitude was too judgemental,' she says. 'You didn't dare open your mouth in case you had the wrong opinion. To this day I think that's what's responsible for the very neutral accent that comes out of Southern California – there are a lot of feelings stuffed down.'

Ronstadt was herself in the process of moving over to Asylum, having tired of Capitol's failure to reactivate the career which had begun so promisingly with the Stone Poneys' 1967 hit 'Different Drum'. By now a veteran of what she called 'the freshman class at the Troubadour', the Arizona-born singer recorded the greater part of *Don't Cry Now* with producer J. D. Souther, whose own Asylum album, *John David Souther*, was released that year. She also began an affair with Souther, true to her not-always-felicitous propensity for mixing work and romance; indeed, the affair may have contributed to the fact that the sessions didn't work out, necessitating the hiring of Peter Asher to tidy up the tracks.

Described by Ronstadt as 'the first person willing to work with me as an equal', Peter Asher subsequently went on to produce the No. 1 album *Heart Like a Wheel*, her last for Capitol, as well as several more platinum sellers for Asylum. Such was the success she enjoyed with him that many critics charged him with being her Svengali. 'She of course did seem to me the ultimate Californian,' he says, 'but anyone who's met Linda for ten seconds will know I couldn't have been her Svengali. She's an extremely determined woman, in every area. To me, she was everything that feminism's about, at a time when men still told women what to sing and what to wear.' If Asher exerted any influence on Ronstadt, it was simply to encourage her to cover old songs such as the Everlys' 'When Will I Be Loved' and Buddy Holly's 'It Doesn't Matter Anymore' alongside the songs of her Laurel Canyon peers (J. D. Souther's 'Faithless Love', Lowell George's 'Willin'', James Taylor's beautiful 'You Can Close Your Eyes'). Benefiting from the Englishman's crisp, radio-friendly production,

'When Will I Be Loved' followed 'You're No Good' into the Top 5 in the spring of 1975.

It was apt somehow that when a reunion of the original Byrds took place in 1972, it was Asylum who released the sorry effort resulting from it. Marred by what Roger McGuinn called 'a definite ego vendetta' on the part of David Crosby, *Byrds* was the same old 'mixed bag' story, throwing in covers of Neil Young and Joni Mitchell songs alongside originals that veered from the near-sublime to the absolutely ridiculous. Crosby's production had much to answer for: Chris Hillman told Elliot Roberts he thought the sound needed 'filling out', but he was overruled. Slaughtered by reviewers, *Byrds* kicked off what was probably the worst year in the band's life.

VII

If one takes stock of the music scene in Los Angeles circa 1973, one finds once again that the sound of the city was predominantly a white one, anchored in white musical tradition. Randy Newman might have incorporated the feel of New Orleans rhythm and blues into his arch vignettes (and confronted race issues head on in songs such as 'Sail Away'), but his records were produced by white producers, played by white sessionmen and bought almost exclusively by white people. By the same principle, the Laurel Canyon rockocracy might have rallied round the Lou Adler-organized LA Forum benefit for the 1972 McGovern campaign, but its stars were just as removed as they'd ever been from the reality of black life a few miles east of the Forum along Manchester Boulevard.

'You could go down to the Parisian Room on La Brea and Washington, and you could even go down to Dolphin's of Hollywood to buy records,' says photo-archivist Michael Ochs, who first came out to LA from New York in 1968 to manage his brother Phil. 'But geographically it was almost impossible to have black friends, because LA is far more ghettoized than New York. I was never afraid to hang out in black areas, but I could never develop any black friendships. LA is a very sick place, frankly – sicker than I realized until recently. It's so unreal and isolating. There is no natural mingling of people, you're always in your own car by yourself. You're never aware of other people's problems. But then that's what drags people out here in the first place, especially obsessive music-business types. The essence of this place is that you can work your ass off here and not be disturbed by reality.'

Writer Carl Gottlieb also recalls shows at the Parisian Room: 'You could venture that far and see someone like Aretha Franklin, but otherwise the clubs outside the ghetto didn't feature black music. South Central was and is truly isolated from the white West Side, and it's very efficiently done. The A&R people didn't go down there. If you were a black act, you stood a better chance of being heard in Memphis or Muscle Shoals than in LA.'

Simply on a musical level, it was remarkable that Los Angeles had failed to produce a recognizable soul scene. With no power base to speak of, the LA soul/R&B community was fragmented and scattered, lacking a true voice. Since the death of Sam Cooke, black artists had cut hits in LA, but it was hardly as though they were integrated into the Hollywood music industry. Nor was there any LA equivalent of a Motown or a Stax or a Philadelphia International. Modern's Kent subsidiary was home to singers such as Z. Z. Hill, but the glory days of Aladdin and Specialty were long gone.

'People *tried* to create indigenous Motowns here,' says Barry Hansen, whom Art Rupe employed as a liner-note writer for Specialty's reissue series in 1968. 'Even Rupe tried, hiring Mike Akapoff away from Modern because he'd produced Ernie Freeman and Lowell Fulson. But he never gave it a chance. Modern kept trying, but if I associate LA soul in the sixties with anything, it's with half-decent singers and woefully out-of-tune bands. The fact was, Art Rupe had had a house band of dependable musicians who'd drifted to the winds by the late sixties.'

One exception to Hansen's rule was the Watts 103rd Street Band, led by doo-wop veteran Charles Wright and featuring the formidable rhythm section of Melvin Dunlap (bass) and James Gadson (drums). Thanks in part to the patronage of comedian Bill Cosby, the Street Band switched from Fred Smith's Keymen label to mighty Warner Brothers, climbing all the way to No. 11 in March 1969 with 'Do Your Thing'. It was the Street Band, too, who played on the gritty funk hits – 'We Got More Soul', 'Let a Woman Be a Woman – Let a Man Be a Man' – by Dyke and the Blazers, a Phoenix-based outfit whom Art Laboe had signed to his Original Sound label.

There were also fine soul sides on Liberty's R&B arm Minit by Bobby Womack, who'd sung with Sam Cooke's protégés the Valentinos, and by Jimmy Holiday, who co-wrote the smash hit 'Put a Little Love in Your Heart' with fellow Liberty artist Jackie DeShannon – a rare Californian example of a black/white songwriting partnership. Womack cut most of his Minit material in Memphis, but his 1968 album *The Womack Live* was recorded at the California Club in Hollywood and included a sublime medley of Sam Cooke's 'Laughing and Clowning' and Percy Mayfield's 'To Live the Past'. Minit boss Ed Wright called the label's sound 'bright and happy, which means it can go pop', a philosophy reflected by Womack's peculiar choice of covers: the Beatles' 'Something', Fred Neil's 'Everybody's Talkin'', and the Mamas and Papas' 'California Dreamin''. For Wright's Liberty bosses, however, Minit's releases didn't go pop enough. They pulled the plug on the label in 1970.

The pressure on LA soul acts to 'go pop' – and quickly – explains not only why Bobby Womack could cover 'California Dreamin'' but why Hollywood was the capital of what one might term *trans-soul* – as in the music of acts as different as Lou Rawls and Brenton Wood, the Fifth Dimension and the Friends of Distinction. Throughout the sixties, Hollywood had taken black R&B and turned it into MOR-flavoured 'champagne soul': not much had changed since the days of Sam Cooke at RCA. Significantly, there was a dearth of black producers fit to rank alongside the great pop *auteurs*. One of the precious few to make any kind of mark in Hollywood was Barry White.

Barry White accepts a gold record from UNI's Russ Regan, 1973.

'Barry's big claim to fame was that he'd stolen three TV sets during the Watts riots,' says Bob Keane, who hired White as an all-purpose A&R man/producer for his Mustang and Bronco labels in 1966. 'He was as poor as a church mouse, so we gave him a couple of heaters and some blankets for his kids. He lived, ate and slept Tamla Motown, and he wrote great little story songs.' White engineered Mustang sessions by the Bobby Fuller Four – at least until the Texan singer's mysterious 'suicide' in July 1966* – but it was his production on soul sides such as Viola Wills' cataclysmic 'Lost Without the Love of My Guy' and Felice Taylor's 'It May Be Winter Outside' (a Top 50 R&B hit in January 1967) which got him noticed.

In 1971, White turned a female trio from San Pedro into Love Unlimited, a master of whose brilliant 'Walkin' in the Rain with the One I Love' was enough for UNI's Russ Regan to sign them on the spot. When the record became a Top 20 pop hit in March 1972, Regan signed the producer himself to UNI's new 20th Century label. White's sequence of crossover mega-hits began with the insidiously funky 'I'm Gonna Love You Just a Little Bit More, Baby' in April 1973, but his quasi-Spectoresque tendencies as a producer were more evident in the way he turned his version of the Four Tops' 'Standing in the Shadows of Love' – on his first album *I've Got So Much to Give* – into a full-blown California soul

---

* The death of Bobby ('I Fought the Law') Fuller remains one of the dark mysteries of LA rock history. Found outside the Hollywood apartment he shared with his mother, he was ruled to have killed himself by inhaling petrol, a police verdict no one has ever believed. Rumours of loan sharks and mob interest have never been substantiated, though Bob Keane may know more about Fuller's death than he's ever let on.

Motown on the Coast: Berry Gordy (left) with Ewart Abner (centre) and Jay Lasker.

symphony. (His co-arranger on most of his hits was Gene Page, who'd written the charts for the Righteous Brothers' 'You've Lost That Lovin' Feelin''.) White's soft-porn, aural-chocolate sound was not to everyone's taste, but at least it was a black sound – which was more than could be said for, say, O. C. Smith's Jerry-Fuller-produced pop/country hits on Columbia.

One wonders what Barry White made of the decision by his beloved Tamla Motown to move their operations from Detroit to Los Angeles in 1971. Certainly the uprooting was not without its casualties: in swift succession, Berry Gordy lost Gladys Knight and the Pips, the Four Tops, Ashford and Simpson, Mary Wells, Martha Reeves, the Spinners, the Isley Brothers, Jimmy Ruffin and the vital songwriting/production team of Holland, Dozier and Holland. Gordy may have been more concerned with breaking into Hollywood (via *Lady Sings the Blues*), but he can hardly have viewed these defections with equanimity. The signings of such MOR stalwarts as Sammy Davis Jr and Diahann Carroll looked even more ominous, as did the launch of the Mowest label, with a roster that included Thelma Houston and Frankie Valli and the Four Seasons.

Three things saved Motown's credibility in the pop marketplace: the ongoing success of the Jackson Five, complete with their own cartoon show on TV; the sound commercial touch of 'psychedelic soul' magician Norman Whitfield; and the emergence of Marvin Gaye and Stevie Wonder as artists on a par with the singer-songwriters now dominating the white rock scene. With *What's Goin' On* (1971) and *Music of My Mind* (1972), Gaye and Wonder boldly went where no soul artists had gone before, writing and producing their own brilliantly experimental music. Wonder's use of the latest synthesizer technology in particular broke new ground for seventies soul. (Gaye even moved into a wooden cabin in Topanga Canyon, spending several mellow months there smoking dope and reading Carlos Castaneda.)*

What's love got to do with it?: Ike and Tina Turner in LA, 1973.

None the less, despite the success of newer Motown artists (Syreeta, the Commodores, the solo Eddie Kendricks), the move to California did irreparable long-term damage to the company's identity. 'The moment Motown moved to LA, it was a dead issue,' says R&B scholar Jim Dawson — a harsh judgement when one considers the company grossed $40 million in 1973, but not so severe when one jumps forward a decade and considers what had become of, say, head Commodore Lionel Richie, transformed from a funk supremo to the fireside MOR balladeer of 'Hello'. True, Stevie Wonder continued to make astonishing records throughout the decade, and the ever-loyal Smokey Robinson could still knock out the odd classic song. But Berry Gordy's priorities now lay elsewhere, with his Hollywood megalomania reflected by the firing of Tony Richardson from *Mahogany* (1975) and the decision to direct the film himself.

The effect Los Angeles had on Tamla Motown was nothing compared to the effect it had on such prime movers in black music as Ike Turner and Sly Stone. Ike's association with the LA scene dated back to the fifties R&B sides he'd recorded in Memphis for the Bihari brothers, but he'd been based in the swanky black neighbourhood of View Park Hills since the mid sixties. For several years the Ike and Tina Turner Revue toured constantly around California, the early run of hits having dried up.

For Tina, the lack of commercial success was compounded by what she remembered as the 'horror movie' of life with her cheating, coke-psychotic husband. One night in 1967, before a show at the new Apartment club on Crenshaw Boulevard, she tried to top herself by downing fifty valium, only to wake up in hospital to the sound of Ike shouting at her. Two years later, by which time the Revue had managed to get on to the Vegas circuit, Bob Krasnow signed Ike and Tina to his

---

* A more orthodox kind of 'singer-songwriter' was Bill Withers, who moved to LA in 1967 and demo'd his own songs while working in an aerospace factory. Early in 1970, Sussex Records paired him with Booker T. Jones, who produced *Just as I Am* using musicians such as Stephen Stills. The album included the No. 3 hit 'Ain't No Sunshine', paving the way for the hugely successful *Still Bill* (1972) and further Top 5 singles in 'Lean On Me' and 'Use Me'. Withers' gravelly folk-soul style was as close as any black artist came to Laurel Canyon singer-songwriterdom.

'There were guns, rifles, machine guns and big dogs': Sly and the Family Stone in Hollywood Babylon.

new Blue Thumb label, resulting in the minor hit version of Otis Redding's 'I've Been Loving You Too Long'. As an ironic comment on the manner in which R&B had been appropriated by 'blue-eyed soul' revues such as that led by Delaney Bramlett and his ex-Ikette wife Bonnie, Krasnow suggested Ike and Tina make up in whiteface for the cover of the *Outta Season* album. Said Krasnow later, 'I thought, hey, that's the only way a black act can do the blues now!'

It was only when Tina began belting out Beatles and Creedence songs, reinventing herself as the rock goddess we know today, that the Turners got themselves back on track. As one of the last acts signed to Minit they cut 'Come Together', then switched over to parent label Liberty for 'Proud Mary' (1971), the biggest hit of their career. As the money started to come in, Ike not only turned the View Park Hills house into a pimp's palace but built his own Bolic Sound studio down the road on La Brea, complete with a superkitsch orgy pad. (*What's Love Got to Do With It*, the acclaimed 1993 biopic of Tina Turner, actually used the View Park Hills house as a location.) Not that a lot of work was accomplished at Bolic Sound, since guns and cocaine paranoia were more the order of the day. When Delaney and Bonnie booked into the studio in 1972 to cut an album for Atlantic, the sessions disintegrated into coke marathons. After one last sizeable hit in 1973 – Tina's semi-autobiographical 'Nutbush City Limits' – bands stopped using Bolic Sound because of the drug craziness. Even Tina found the courage to leave her ogre of a husband.

Guns and drugs, mink and pantyhose: Ike Turner certainly had a lot in common with Sly Stone. Hollywood Babylon seemed to bring out the worst in its exogenous black stars, and it certainly brought out the demons in the former Sylvester Stewart, who'd been a key figure as a DJ and producer on the San Francisco scene before the success of Sly and the Family Stone turned him into an LA kingpin at the tail end of the sixties. More so than Arthur Lee or even Hendrix, Sly was the 'psychedelic spade' to end them all, a flower-power James Brown leading a motley, multi-racial band of Bay Area freaks into the new hippie dawn. (What Hendrix began at Monterey, Sly finished at Woodstock.) But Babylon beckoned, and by the spring of 1970 he'd moved into a house in Coldwater Canyon and opened an office on Vine Street for his Stone Flower production company.

Cue the cocaine, exit the everyday people. 1970 was the beginning of the madness, as Sly became a frozen-nosed, no-show potentate hob-nobbing with the Hollywood rockocracy. Twenty-six out of eighty gigs that year were cancelled, and he was invariably late for the performances he did make. More worrying for his label, Epic, Sly wasn't delivering any product. 'I heard stories that he was laying down hundreds of instrumental tracks in southern California studios,' recalled Columbia/Epic chief Clive Davis. 'There was strong speculation that he would never sing again.' The only new recording to see the light of day in 1970 was 'Thank You (Falettinme Be Mice Elf Again)', a No. 1 single for two weeks in October. A brilliantly nervy vignette of Sly's teenage years up in Vallejo, 'Thank You' could just as easily have been about the hair-raising netherworld of Hollywood drug deals.

Early in 1971, Terry Melcher took Sly up to John Phillips' mock-Tudor mansion in Bel Air to discuss buying the property. Instead of buying, Stone began renting 783 Bel Air Road for $12,000 a month, installing most of his 'family' there in the process. 'His goons were sullen, unfriendly and armed,' recalled Phillips, who quickly regretted renting out the property. 'These people were *rough*. They laughed at me. There were lots of guns, rifles, machine guns and big dogs.' In the end, Phillips resorted to bringing a small army of machete-wielding Mexican gardeners to the house to encourage 'the family' to honour the original terms of the agreement or leave.

By the summer, Epic were withholding advances and freezing royalties in an effort to encourage Sly to finish the group's next album. Living for the most part in an enormous motorhome which he parked outside recording studios, he worked on the tracks which made up the extraordinary *There's a Riot Goin' On*. 'We used to ride around in his motorhome, getting high and writin' songs and makin' music,' says Bobby Womack, who'd been adopted as an honorary member of 'the family' and was pictured on the sleeve of *Riot*. 'We'd ride up in the Hollywood hills and he would never stand still. He'd say, "Keep *drivin'*!" Only thing was, I was already spaced out because I was losin' my wife, but at least he kept me so busy I didn't have a chance to think about it.'

Womack, whose own 1971 album *Communication* was dripping with Sly's influence, remembers the sessions for *Riot* as 'very spacey': 'I was sittin' there in the dark, coked to the brain, tryin' to sing, staying up four, five, six days. That's just the way he was. You're lookin' at this guy and thinkin', where in the fuck he come from? He's dressed all in red leather, handin' out the orders, like, "Tiffany, baby, I want you to take Bobby to your room, fix him up." So I'm fuckin' some chick, and then I'm right back into the music again, and it was gettin' to a point where I forgot where my wife was, where my son was ... I was just *spaced*. I became paranoid at *everything*, I was always thinkin' I was gonna get killed and that the Feds was gonna bust in on Sly. Everybody had pistols. It got to the point where I said, I gotta get away from here. Sly be talkin' to you, but he ain't *there*.'

One can hear all this in the stoned, dragging music of *Riot* – the muted funk grooves, Sly's wasted croak of a voice. Whether he was singing about the 'Family Affair' or the 'Spaced Cowboy', about Africa or the hippie comedown of 'Luv 'n' Haight', the freaky superpimp sounded like he was living in his own solipsistic universe. Timothy White went into rock-crit overdrive when he called the album 'a brooding, militant, savage indictment of all the decayed determinism of the sixties': Sly was too wasted to indict anybody other than his dealers. Delivered two weeks after Stone rolled up at the Beverly Hills Hotel in a red satin jumpsuit to beg Clive Davis for money, *Riot* was a No. 1 album by November, with the magnificent 'Family Affair' sitting simultaneously at the top of the singles chart.

From thereon in it was downhill most of the way. In July 1972, police stopped the motorhome on Santa Monica Boulevard and found a humungous stash of coke on board. Regular raids on the Bel Air house followed. Manager David Kapralik, who'd signed the group to Epic in the first place, sued Sly for $250,000 in loans and back commissions. All this while, Sly was contending with pressure from black nationalist groups who wanted him to take more of a role in the struggle for black pride and didn't approve of the racial mix within the Family Stone.

Another two years went by before *Fresh* saw the light of day, by which time Clive Davis was so exasperated he went to the lengths of temporarily suspending Sly's contract. 'There's a mickey in the tasting of disaster,' went the opening line of the nervy, supertight 'In Time', and it summed up just how perilously close to the edge of dementia Sly was dancing. He was still capable of Stevie-style catchiness ('If You Want Me to Stay'), but the wired, sexless funk of 'Frisky' was almost sinister, and delivered in a voice which sounded hollowed out by cocaine. Meanwhile, the stoned gospel treatment of 'Que Sera Sera' took on an extra layer of irony when one learned that Sly was not only running around with Doris Day's son Terry Melcher but was rumoured to be stepping out with Day herself.

Small Talk (1974) signalled that the game was up. The title track had the same spacey feel as 'In Time', and 'Say You Will' suggested a polyrhythmic Al Green, but 'Loose Booty' was a lame disco song by any standards. By now, Sly's whole 'family'/'Babies Makin' Babies' trip seemed a hollow sham, despite his onstage wedding at Madison Square Garden. By the end of the decade, he was a spent force, a freebasing wreck of a man who'd been dropped by Columbia, only to subject his new label, Warner Brothers, to the same nerve-wracking treatment.

As Greil Marcus showed in *Mystery Train*, Sly was at the heart of the black *zeitgeist* in 1972, the year of *Superfly* and 'Back Stabbers' and 'Papa was a Rolling Stone'. How ironic that at the very point at which the white LA music scene opted to kick back and 'take it easy' in a mellow denim heaven, Hollywood chose to depict the black ghetto as a place of unremitting greed and violence. Blaxploitation movies – *Shaft*, *Superfly*, *Trouble Man*, *Across 110th Street* (with soundtracks by Isaac Hayes, Curtis Mayfield, Marvin Gaye and Bobby Womack) – simultaneously demonized and cartoonized black America, titillating whites with images that kept the problems of black/white relations firmly at one remove. Curtis Mayfield was not alone in protesting that *Superfly* (entirely financed by blacks, as it happens) looked more like 'an advertisement for cocaine' than a condemnation of trigger-happy drug dealers: the film was picketed by an organization called BANG (Blacks Against Narcotic Genocide).

Two of the best black records of 1972 were 'Slippin' into Darkness' and 'The World is a Ghetto', by the LA band War. War's roots were in the Long Beach area, where most of them had performed as the Creators in the mid sixties, releasing the obscure single 'Burn, Baby, Burn' shortly before the Watts riots. Regrouping at the end of the decade as Nite Shift, the band were heard one night at a Valley dive called the Rag Doll by none other than Eric Burdon, along with his harmonica-playing pal Lee Oskar and a semi-retired New York pop producer called Jerry Goldstein. The upshot of this fateful encounter was that a rechristened Nite Shift became the ex-Animal's backing band.

Burdon had been profoundly affected by Jimi Hendrix, who was managed and produced by ex-Animal Chas Chandler. When he heard Nite Shift at the Rag Doll, he zeroed in on the chance to put together a kind of revolutionary funk band. Managed by Jerry Goldstein and his tenacious partner Steve Gold, Burdon and War were off and running,

*The world is a ghetto: War in 1973.
Clockwise from top left: Howard
Scott, B.B. Dickerson, Papa Dee
Allen, Harold Brown, Lonnie Jordan,
Charles Miller, Lee Oskar.*

hitting almost immediately with the Top 5 'Spill the Wine' in July 1970. The only problem was that War simply wanted to play funk, and were unimpressed by the Geordie acid-casualty's honky-Panther rhetoric. (With exquisite bad taste, the second album by Burdon and War was entitled *Black Man's Burdon*!) 'The American black group I was looking for was not War,' Burdon huffed after an acrimonious European tour in 1971.

Mercifully free of Burdon, War matured into one of the best black acts of the seventies, releasing a steady stream of classic soul/funk singles which included 'The Cisco Kid', 'Why Can't We Be Friends?' and the staple Chicano favourite 'Low Rider'. But it was the brooding 'Slippin' into Darkness' and 'The World is a Ghetto' (from the No. 1 album of the same name) which most astutely addressed the racial segregation of Los Angeles, portraying the city, in Dave Marsh's words, 'not as an enlarged anonymous suburb ... but as the home of millions of black, brown and white people, stuck together in a cauldron where they cannot melt'. The influence of War on the LA rap scene twenty years later was encapsulated in the compilation *Rap Declares War*, featuring War-sampled tracks by the likes of Ice-T and Latin Alliance.

Like the Watts 103rd Street Band, War were an exception to the rule, an isolated instance of LA ghetto funk. The real lack of a black soul scene in the city was summed up by the fact that when a huge concert was held in August 1972 to commemorate the Watts uprising of 1965, the entire bill (from the Staple Singers to Isaac Hayes) was supplied by Stax artists from Memphis.

The Rainbow, hard-rock watering hole par excellence.

7 Crawling Down Cahuenga on a Broken Pair of Legs, or What Were Once Vices are Now Habits

When I get mellow, I ripen and rot.

Alvy in *Annie Hall* (1977)

I am beginning to think everyone in California is here by mistake.

Julia Phillips, *You'll Never Eat Lunch in This Town Again* (1991)

I

'If you want to talk about what happened to the LA scene in the first half of the seventies,' says David Anderle, head of A&R at A&M Records, 'you can sum it up with one name. David Geffen happened. All the major companies were consolidating, but the really big deal was the merger between Elektra and Asylum. A bunch of hippies had become major players and were now calling the shots.'

When David Geffen sold Asylum to Warner Brothers for $7 million in 1973 – effecting a merger with Jac Holzman's Elektra label – he helped to forge what Art Fein has described as 'a latterday folk-rock axis that took hold of America'. As the new head of this 'axis', Geffen immediately set to work with his scalpel, purging Elektra of all but thirteen acts. When he left the company in 1975, it had the highest net profit of any record company in the world. The man whom Jerry Wexler castigated as someone who'd 'dive into a pool of pus to come up with a nickel between [his] teeth' had turned rock'n'roll Babylon on its head.

'The thing about David was that this was his entire life': David Geffen (right) with Lou Adler and Britt Ekland.

'The thing about David was that this was his entire life,' says Ron Stone, who worked as Elliot Roberts' right-hand man at Geffen-Roberts. 'I'd get to the office early in the morning and he would already have been there for a while. I'd leave in the evening to have dinner with my family and he'd still be there. His business relationships *were* his relationships, whereas I didn't invest quite as much emotion in them. See, once you have young kids you realize there's a great similarity between your three-year-old and your clients.' Retrospectively, Stone feels that he and Elliot Roberts were in the music business, whereas Geffen was in 'the finance business'. 'Elliot in some strange way was the vehicle for David to be so

'They were different – they were made to sell a million records': the Eagles with new guitarist Don Felder (far right).

successful, because it was really his musical taste which defined all of this. He had this amazing sensitivity to the music and made some incredibly insightful choices. I forgive him all his other foibles, because there was a touch of genius there.'*

Following the merger between Elektra and Asylum, the Geffen-Roberts stable went from strength to strength. The Eagles, for example, dispensed with producer Glyn Johns and became the AM/FM-crossover monster they were always destined to be. Johns' replacement Bill Szymczyk had already produced the Asylum debut by Jo Jo Gunne, and his pop-rock touch was just what the Eagles needed to push them into the big league, especially after the last-minute addition to the *On the Border* lineup of lead guitarist Don Felder. By early 1975 the band was at No. 1 with the syrupy 'Best of My Love', co-written by Don Henley, Glenn Frey and J. D. Souther. It was the start of a phenomenal run of six consecutive Top 5 singles, including four No. Ones, over a two-year period. Throughout that period, moreover, the Eagles were at the heart of the Laurel Canyon sound, appearing not only on Linda Ronstadt's *Heart Like a Wheel* and Jackson Browne's *Late for the Sky*, but on Randy Newman's brilliant Dixie opus *Good Old Boys* – all three released in 1974.

The only twist in the tale was that the Eagles, despite remaining on Asylum, were no longer handled by Geffen-Roberts. Indeed, many people would have attributed the group's changes in fortune to Irving Azoff, the

* The amiable Ron Stone manages to function in today's corporate rock universe while keeping one laid-back foot in the Laurel Canyon cosiness of yesteryear. Despite the fact that the roster of his Gold Mountain management company included (until Kurt Cobain's suicide) Nirvana, he still lives in the quaint house which inspired Graham Nash's 'Our House'. The day after I interviewed him in the company's North Hollywood offices, I saw him screaming down Lookout Mountain Road in – what else? – a red Ferrari.

so-called 'Poison Dwarf' who'd joined the Geffen-Roberts team only to walk off with Messrs Frey, Henley, Leadon and Meisner early in 1974. 'Azoff was ultra-ambitious from the off,' says Denny Bruce. 'He was Sammy Glick in a Nehru jacket.' Hailing from Champaign, Illinois, 'Irv' had pitched up in LA with ex-James Gang guitarist Joe Walsh, as well as his own pet singer-songwriter Dan Fogelberg, whom he promptly signed to Epic. Quickly acquiring a rapacious, terrier-like reputation around Hollywood, he was thrown in at the deep end when Elliot Roberts fell sick and asked him to take over Neil Young's turbulent 1973 tour of America and Europe.

It was during this tour that Azoff cemented his relationship with support act the Eagles, instinctively sensing that they could be his one-way ticket to the big time. Responding to the group's dissatisfaction with *Desperado*, he pointed them in the direction of Bill Szymczyk (who'd just produced Joe Walsh's smash hit 'Rocky Mountain Way'), then made his move. 'I don't think David or Elliot realized quite *how* big the Eagles would be, especially since *Desperado* wasn't doing too well,' says Ron Stone. 'Otherwise they'd have been more upset when Azoff walked off with them.' Geffen, smarting from the unfamiliar sensation of being out-sharked, subsequently claimed he'd given Azoff the Eagles 'to start him off on his own', but Azoff maintained the band were profoundly unhappy with Geffen-Roberts. The feud which then escalated between the two powermongers has never been resolved: years later, Geffen's popularity in Hollywood briefly soared after he punched Azoff in the face.

Elliot Roberts may have lost the Eagles, but he continued his association with Joni Mitchell and Neil Young, both of whom were writing songs which reflected their changing relationship with the LA scene. When Mitchell returned from the introspective wilderness of *For the Roses*, it was with *Court and Spark* (1974), in part an admission that she 'couldn't let go of LA/City of the fallen angels' – or of 'the work I've taken on/Stoking the star-making machinery/Behind the popular song'. Musically, the album was a giant leap forward, employing Tom Scott's LA Express band to fashion a chic jazz-tinged sound which perfectly suited the social milieu she was exploring in songs such as 'People's Parties'. This was a soundtrack for the new seventies rock elite – the old canyon crowd who'd now moved out to Malibu to join their movie-star cronies on the beach – but it was also persuasively beautiful. To her own surprise as much as anyone's, *Court and Spark* climbed all the way to No. 2 on the album chart, as did *Miles of Aisles*, the live double-album recorded with the LA Express.

Mitchell's need to slough off the trappings of her folkie past – and simultaneously to distance herself from contemporary rock'n'roll – led her to attempt something even bolder on *The Hissing of Summer Lawns* (1975). Here she used not only jazz inflections but African polyrhythms, incurring the wrath of critics who thought she was being too clever for her own good. As far as she was concerned, what they couldn't handle was the fact that their Joni was no longer giving them the 'personal confessions' they'd come to expect, instead using the album to paint a panoramic portrait of sunny suburban America and its dark underside. 'I can't speak for how you're perceived,' says Mitchell now. 'I can only say that you write about that which you have access to. It's not a Zelig thing: life is short and you have an opportunity to explore as much of it as time and fortune allow.'

Doubtless it was her feeling of hurt at this resentment which caused Mitchell to assume a somewhat haughty air towards the rock community in general. 'I had no choice but to go with jazz musicians,' she said, oblivious to the arrogance in her tone. 'I tried to play with all the rock bands, but they couldn't play my music because it's too eccentric.' This high-handedness put more than a few backs up in the mid seventies, and even prompted Neil Young to deride her on *Zuma*'s 'Stupid Girl'. 'She was unbelievably snobbish,' remembers English rock scribe Nick Kent, who saw the Asylum in-crowd at close quarters during this period. 'She'd walk into a room, and if she needed something she'd get some other rock

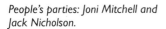

People's parties: Joni Mitchell and Jack Nicholson.

star to ask some mere mortal to get her a drink. She was like Bianca Jagger or someone – she couldn't talk to anyone who wasn't famous because it would fuck with her aura so badly she wouldn't be able to have these superior thoughts.'

The Hissing, a Top 5 album in December 1975 despite the misgivings of her critics, set Mitchell on a path which led firmly away from the rock mainstream. Over the course of three albums – *Hejira* (1976), *Don Juan's Reckless Daughter* (1978), and *Mingus* (1979) – she explored the ever more abstruse terrain between rock and jazz, weary of the self-imposed limitations of her contemporaries. For her pains she was neglected by her old fans and scorned by jazz purists as a pop carpetbagger: *Mingus* was the first Mitchell album not to go gold since *Songs for a Seagull*. Not that she cared any more what 'rock' critics thought of her music. It meant a great deal more that a jazz hero such as Charles Mingus wanted to work with her than that her albums went platinum.

Neil Young had none of these problems to contend with when he recorded *On the Beach* (1974), a rather different take on the Malibu blues. Not for Neil the ice-cool nuances of *Court and Spark*; instead, an album characterized by glazed *ennui*, reflected in the cover shot of Young – his back to the camera – staring out across a misty Pacific. Furthermore, where everyone else had tried to bury their memories of the Manson killings, Young typically chose to dredge them up on 'Revolution Blues', with its line about killing the stars of Laurel Canyon in their cars. ' "Heart of Gold" put me in the middle of the road,' he wrote in the liner-note to *Decade* (1978). 'Travelling there soon became a bore, so I headed for the ditch. A rougher ride, but I saw some more interesting people there.'*

Young's 'rougher ride' was in great part his ambivalent response to the toll drugs were taking on the LA rock'n'roll scene. The seventies had started with the drug-related deaths of Jimi and Janis, followed by those of Jim Morrison, Canned Heat's Al Wilson (found dead in a sleeping bag in Topanga Canyon in September 1970) and the Association's Brian Cole, who overdosed on heroin in the summer of 1972. Closer to home for Young were the deaths of Crazy Horse guitarist Danny Whitten and CSNY roadie Bruce Berry, epitomizing 'the needle and the damage done' in those scarily hedonistic times.

Danny Whitten briefly joined up with the *Time Fades Away* tour in late 1972, but was in such a hopeless state that Young felt obliged to send him back to LA. The night of his return he overdosed and died, prompting Young to hook up with the remaining members of Crazy Horse for the tour which gave birth to the stoned wake of *Tonight's the Night*. The death

---

* Playing on 'Revolution Blues' were Levon Helm and Rick Danko of The Band, a group that relocated from Woodstock to LA not long after the Dylan/Band tour of early 1974. The change of environment had the same hazardous effect on the group that it had had on so many musicians. See Part Four, Chapter One, of this author's *Across the Great Divide: The Band and America* for further elucidation.

of Bruce Berry, brother of Jan of Jan and Dean, only compounded the sense of despair that informed both the tour and the album, especially with Young himself indulging almost as heavily in coke and booze as Whitten had indulged in smack. 'Neil was dribbling from the side of his mouth on that tour,' remembers Elliot Roberts. 'I mean, he was getting booed off the stage every night, the mood was so down. He wasn't playing one of his hits, one song from *Goldrush* or *Harvest* that you came to lay down your good poundage for.' Young himself recalled wanting the tour to be 'as sleazy as possible … basically saying, "This is total bullshit, you might as well be gambling and eating while you're listening to this music."'

As an *in memoriam* to Whitten and Berry, *Tonight's the Night* was admirably free of maudlin grief. Alongside the soused romp of 'Come On Baby, Let's Go Downtown' and the deceptively mellow-sounding 'Borrowed Tune' – borrowed from the Rolling Stones' 'Lady Jane' because Young was 'too wasted to write my own' – the album boasted the chilling 'Tired Eyes', which, over a sepulchral country groove, starkly recounted the deaths of four men during a backfired cocaine deal. Recorded more or less live at SIR rehearsal studios, the album wasn't released until 1975 but continues to stand alongside such artefacts as Robert Frank's Stones movie *Cocksucker Blues* as a definitive early-seventies document of life on rock's wild side.

By the time he came to record *On the Beach*, Young knew he had to remove himself once again from the madness of the road and the madness of LA: 'I need a crowd of people/But I can't face them day to day', he sang on the title track. The downbeat mood of the album also owed something to his imminent breakup with actress Carrie Snodgress, then living apart from Young with their son Zeke on the ranch up in San Mateo. Yet scarcely had he committed this mordant masterpiece to tape than he effected another *volte face* and once more became the Y of CSNY.

The Crosby, Stills, Nash and Young 'reunion' tour of 1974 was all the evidence anyone could have required that rock was now a multi-million-dollar circus. Following on from the Dylan/Band tour at the beginning of the year – a tour which coincided with David Geffen's extraordinary coup in luring Dylan over to Asylum for *Planet Waves* and *Before the Flood* – it was the biggest and most profitable rock'n'roll jaunt that had been mounted to date, complete with all the merchandising we associate with today's stadium superstars. 'The tour was sort of scary, because no one had ever imagined it could get that big,' says Carl Gottlieb, co-author of David Crosby's autobiography *Long Time Gone*. 'Suddenly the money was just *huge*, and life was pretty extraordinary for those at the top of the food chain. Touring became an exercise in indulgence, with thirty-seven people travelling on ahead to set up stages.'

For Neil Young, who travelled in a separate bus from the others, the 34-date tour was less 'an exercise in indulgence' than 'the swansong of Crosby, Stills, Nash and Young'. If the sheer scale of the thing wasn't obscene enough, the vanity and venality of CS&N themselves turned Young's stomach. When he wanted to play 'Revolution Blues', the others told him they didn't want to be onstage during the song. 'I was going, "It's just a fuckin' song, what's the big deal? It's about the culture, it's about what's really happening."' After the tour, having had enough of the drugging and internecine warfare, Young walked out of the Record Plant sessions for one last CSNY album. Later, on an acerbic song called 'Thrasher', he wrote of 'the motel of lost companions' that 'waits with heated pool and air-conditioned bar', lamenting the dead weight of his association with the trio. Even David Geffen, despite profiting enormously from the 1974 tour, could only take so much of the drugs and ego battles, eventually pulling out of his involvement with the group. So driven to distraction was he by David Crosby that he even advised United Artists to cancel a movie deal he'd set up for the singer.

David Crosby epitomized the gross hedonism of Hollywood in the mid seventies, when cocaine ran riot through the entertainment industry. Whether it was Julia Phillips, whose *You'll Never Eat Lunch in This Town Again* stands as a definitive memoir of the deluded megalomania that dances hand in hand with cocaine, or bubblegum tycoon Neil Bogart, whose Casablanca empire was a mini-Babylon built on the artificial bravado of coke euphoria, pop's prime movers were indulging in toot on a scale that would have appalled even Aleister Crowley. 'I never was a fan of drugs myself, although I took them from time to time,' says Linda Ronstadt. 'Cocaine made people deaf, it made people dead and it made people real obnoxious. There was a direction in which friendships could have gone that was enormously complicated by cocaine.'

'For a while, no one could say a bad thing about cocaine,' remembers Elliot Roberts. 'You were literally offered it by everyone, from your accountant to the head of your record company. Everyone was like, "Wanna bump?" No one realized that it was *totally* addictive, that it ate your cells away and made your nose fall off, because no one had taken it for long enough to find that out.' Nor was the impact of cocaine on the LA scene confined simply to nasal cavities: to Joni Mitchell, who came comparatively late to the party, coke 'sealed off the heart', producing a numbness one could hear in the sterile, clinical sound of mid-seventies Californian rock. It remains a paradox of the period that behind so much of this 'mellow' West Coast music lay the most potent stimulant known to man.

The records of those Asylum superstars Jackson Browne and Linda Ronstadt in particular exemplified the sound of LA circa 1974–5: faultlessly crafted, often deeply tedious. For all the difference David Lindley made to Browne's sound, and for all the thoughtfulness of the songs on *Late for the Sky*, there was still something soporific and vacuum-packed about this spiritual godfather to Album-Oriented Rock. As for La Ronstadt, not even the heartfelt pleadings of the gallant John Rockwell to

The canyon aristocracy live onstage: (left to right) Randy Meisner, Glenn Frey, Don Henley, Jackson Browne, Don Felder, Linda Ronstadt, Bernie Leadon.

the effect that she was possessed of 'the strongest, most clearly focused, flexible and simply beautiful voice in popular music' are enough to persuade one that her Peter Asher-produced albums aren't for the most part stupefyingly lifeless. True, the fact that she didn't write her own material made her an easy target for male critics who liked to dismiss her as a doe-eyed sex kitten, but her reduction of everything – country, Motown, Buddy Holly – to a kind of generic Californian pop-rock remains deeply suspect.

By the time Ronstadt was high in the charts with *Prisoner in Disguise* (1975) – featuring Motown chestnuts 'Heat Wave' and 'The Tracks of My Tears' alongside songs by Neil Young, James Taylor, Lowell George and J. D. Souther – the three-year-old Asylum label had turned out to be a nice little earner for the astute David Geffen. That summer, the Eagles chalked up their second No. 1 with the blatantly poppy 'One of These Nights', then sat pretty at the top of the album chart for five consecutive weeks with the LP of the same name. Geffen had even attempted the year before to repeat the prefab success of the Eagles by prodding J. D. Souther, Chris Hillman and Richie Furay into forming the CS&N-style Souther Hillman Furay Band. The fact that the trio's Asylum debut ascended all the way to No. 11 in August 1974 was attributable less to their intrinsic worth than to the hackneyed 'supergroup' factor in their hyping. 'I was working with these guys and they just weren't getting along,' recalled Phil Kaufman, who provided SHF with the same 'Executive Nanny' service he'd given Gram Parsons. 'It was like trying to mix oil and water.'

Despite the mega-success of the Eagles and Linda Ronstadt – or because of it – Asylum briefly lived up to its name by providing sanctuary for a handful of throwbacks to the folkie-singer-songwriter heyday: men such as David Blue, Steve Goodman, Ned Doheny and Tom Waits. In addition, the label signed Andrew Gold, leader of Ronstadt's backing band, and Gene Clark, whose extraordinary, Castaneda-influenced *No Other* was released at the end of 1974. Finally, seeking asylum in the bosom of the Geffen-Roberts stable after being dropped by Reprise, Jimmy Webb made another stab at credibility with *Land's End* (1974), featuring the Spectoresque 'Just This One Time' and the epic, string-swept *tour de force* 'Land's End/Asleep on the Wind'.

None of this was enough, however, to quell the restless spirit of David Geffen, who decided in 1975 that he'd had enough of rock and instead moved on to become vice-president of Warner Brothers Pictures. 'What David really wanted was to take over Warner Communications,' says Elliot Roberts. 'But Steve Ross was too formidable at that time, and David saw that it just wasn't going to happen.' 1975 effectively saw the carving-up of the Geffen-Roberts empire, Irving Azoff having walked off with the Eagles, Roberts keeping Neil Young and Joni Mitchell, and John Hartmann taking Poco and America. 'I think Geffen-Roberts just imploded from its own weight,' says Ron Stone. 'When David went off to conquer the world, Elliot really slowed things down, and I had to find my way on my own.'

Geffen's immediate successor at Elektra-Asylum was none other than Joe Smith, the Burbank veteran who'd done so much to make Warner Brothers a viable pop label in the sixties. Warner-Reprise had itself consolidated its position in the rock marketplace with the continued success of acts such as Alice Cooper, the Doobie Brothers, James Taylor, Gordon Lightfoot and – to a lesser extent – Neil Young, Randy Newman and Van Morrison. (Morrison's career had been a 'personal crusade' for Joe Smith, culminating in a major showdown shortly before Smith went to Elektra-Asylum.) 'In a way, the whole excitement of the period ended after James Taylor made the cover of *Time*,' says Stan Cornyn. 'That was the ultimate mainstream accolade.'

Even Little Feat had started to make money for Warners, though they were hardly selling records in bucketloads: *Feats Don't Fail Me Now*, featuring the astoundingly funky 'Rock and Roll Doctor', barely scraped into the Top 40 at the tail end of 1974. Feat's Lowell George defined the funky-boho house style at Warners, a style characterized perfectly by his labelmate Bonnie Raitt, as music for 'the seventies tequila circuit'. Inevitably, it was Ry Cooder who managed to take the style to its folklorist limit: on *Paradise and Lunch* (1974) and *Chicken Skin Music* (1976) he attempted everything from a reggaefied version of the Valentinos' 'It's All Over Now' to Tex-Mex treatments of Leadbelly's 'Goodnight, Irene' and Jim Reeves' 'He'll Have to Go'. 'I've redone all my tunes to accommodate what became a Tex-Mex/R&B sound,' he told *NME*. 'It works like a

Paul Barrere and Lowell George of Little Feat, live in England in 1977.

charm.' He lamented the fact that 'the kids in the middle of the United States just aren't ready for me', adding that 'the Doobie Brothers are very advanced for them'.

Warners even did something to redress the imbalance between white and black artists on their roster. Russ Titelman signed the Family Stone spinoff Graham Central Station, producing their first Warners album in 1973, and there were somewhat unlikely albums by Arthur Alexander and Lorraine Ellison, the latter produced by Ted Templeman. 'The trouble was, Warners had so little black music that Arthur Alexander rather stuck out,' says the company's current Head of Publicity, Bob Merlis, who came out to LA from New York in 1975. Warners would later be renowned as the company that signed such black superstars as Prince and Ice T, but in 1975 it was still a pretty vanilla operation.

Although Warners hung on to its so-called 'prestige' artists, giving the Ry Cooders and Randy Newmans the room to explore their quirks and idiosyncrasies, an indication of the changes in store came with the 1975 debut album by the new edition of Fleetwood Mac, whose Brits-in-LA nucleus had been bolstered by native Californians Lindsey Buckingham and Stevie Nicks.* Buckingham and Nicks already had an album out as a duo, but were working respectively as a road guitarist for Don Everly and as a Beverly Hills waitress when Mick Fleetwood fortuitously heard a tape of the album in a Valley studio called Sound City.

It was Sound City engineer Keith Olsen, one-time member of the Music Machine, who co-produced the platinum-selling *Fleetwood Mac*, with its hit singles 'Over My Head', 'Rhiannon', and 'Say You Love Me'. Like the Eagles, the new Mac seemed to get the pop/rock balance just right, with the Buckingham–Nicks influence expanding the original blues-based lineup's vocabulary and giving the sound that crucial Californian feel. With her lacy attire, Nicks quickly became a kind of space-cadet sex symbol, while Buckingham's infatuation with Brian Wilson came through in the orchestral intricacy of the album's arrangements.

* When the band had first arrived in Los Angeles, shortly after the Sylmar earthquake of February 1971, guitarist Jeremy Spencer told Mick Fleetwood there was an 'evil' cloaking the city, and that it was out to 'get him'. After they'd checked into their hotel, Spencer went out to buy some magazines and never came back. He subsequently joined a Californian religious cult. A very apt beginning for the LA saga of Fleetwood Mac...

II

Like Peter Frampton, whose 1975 album *Frampton* crept into the Top 40 in May 1975, Mick Fleetwood, John McVie and Christine McVie had managed to reinvent themselves as honorary Angelenos, shaking off the grime of England as their skins tanned in the sun. But the fact that they had joined forces with two real Californians guaranteed for Lindsey Buckingham 'that we would get to know one another as friends only to a certain point'. That was putting it mildly, as subsequent events revealed. But at least Fleetwood Mac sold trillions of records in the process of trying to bridge what Buckingham called their 'cultural differences'.

By 1975, Los Angeles was once again infested with Brits of every description. Joining the entrenched elite of Isherwood and Hockney, Asher and Nash were the likes of David Bowie, Keith Moon and Rod Stewart, who'd signed to Warners, made his *Atlantic Crossing*, and feathered a Beverly Hills love-nest for himself and Britt Ekland. But the archetypal seventies Brit-in-LA was none other than John Lennon, who began a protracted 'lost weekend' in the city not long after finishing the tired *Mind Games* album.

With his assistant/lover May Pang in tow, Lennon arrived in LA in October 1973, having agreed to a trial separation from Yoko Ono. 'It was as if Yoko was saying, "Go to Disneyland, go to Hefner heaven, get your hit of all that stuff and get it out of your system,"' recalls Elliott Mintz, who picked Lennon and Pang up at LAX. For the next eight months, Lennon kissed goodbye to politics, feminism and world peace, living a dissolute bachelor existence in the company of Harry Nilsson and fellow soaks Ringo Starr and Keith Moon. Drunk, violent and suicidal, he rampaged through Hollywood like a one-man hurricane.

It didn't help matters that the ex-Beatle was working with the equally demented Phil Spector, in whose fortress-like mansion he and Yoko had stayed while undergoing Primal Scream treatment early in 1970. Although Spector had salvaged his career through his association with the Beatles, by the end of 1973 he was in almost as crazed and paranoid a state as Lennon. Most crippling to his ego was the fact that Ronnie had finally escaped from the La Collina Road compound and fled back to New York. When she later came to record Billy Joel's 'Say Goodbye to Hollywood', one could almost hear the relief in her voice.

Booking into the A&M studios, Lennon and Spector set to work on an album of R&B/rock'n'roll oldies, symptomatic of the wave of nostalgia which was responsible for films such as *American Graffiti*. Among the tracks they recorded were 'Be My Baby' and 'To Know [Her] is to Love [Her]', featuring Spector's old mainstays Hal Blaine and Larry Knechtel. A decade on from the glory days of Gold Star, Phil was using John Lennon as he'd used, say, the Crystals – as a mere vehicle for his own glory. So drunkenly

A contrite John Lennon takes refuge chez Lou Adler the morning after being ejected from the Troubadour.

chaotic were the sessions, however, that A&M turfed them out of the studio, obliging them to move to Record Plant West. There, things degenerated even further: Lennon physically attacked guitarists Danny Kortchmar and Jesse Ed Davis, and Spector pulled a gun on Stevie Wonder because the Motown star was using an engineer he wanted. Lennon couldn't even get his hands on the tapes once it was all over: Spector had taken the precaution of paying for the sessions, which meant that technically he owned them. It was only many months later that he agreed to sell the tapes to Capitol, leading to the appearance on Lennon's *Rock and Roll* album of the Spector-produced tracks 'Stand By Me', 'Sweet Little Sixteen', 'You Can't Catch Me' and 'Just Because'.

It was while Lennon was recording the thoroughly expendable *Pussy Cats* album with Harry Nilsson (and fellow inebriates Ringo Starr and Keith Moon) that the two men were ejected from the Troubadour one night for heckling satirical comedians the Smothers Brothers. This was the lowest point to which the ex-Beatle had sunk in LA: the next day he seemed to English photographer Cyril Maitland to be in 'a very contrite, humble state ... a sort of rock bottom'. 'He appeared so fragile and small in the pale, grey light,' recalls Maitland, who photographed him by the pool at Lou Adler's Bel Air mansion on the afternoon of 13 March 1974.

'He realized how badly he'd fucked up, and pretty soon after that he went back to Yoko in New York.'*

Lennon's 'lost weekend' was typical of the self-destructive hedonism prevalent in LA between 1973 and 1975. 'By now the innocence had *completely* gone,' says Danny Hutton, whose own 'party house to end all party houses' Lennon and Harry Nilsson often visited. 'You'd notice people you'd never seen before turning up at your house, and they'd be over in the corner selling coke. Things would go missing, and you'd start putting up barbed wire and cameras. Eventually people realized they weren't having fun any more.' It was a paradox of the times that the rest of the world jeered at LA as a pseudo-paradise of laid-back bliss, when the reality of the place was that people were running around with their nerves frayed by cocaine. This was the 'Hefner heaven' of which Elliott Mintz spoke, a tacky playground for fame sluts like Joan Didion and John Gregory Dunne, who appropriately began the seventies with a move to Malibu – in Didion's words, 'that shorthand for the easy life'.† 'Although they both pretend to be disenchanted by the Hollywood scene,' wrote John Lahr of the Didi-Dunnes, 'they are spellbound by celebrity.' The fact that LA symbolized the detritus of Western capitalism for the couple didn't make their jaded Malibu starfucking any more admirable.

Perhaps it was no coincidence that Kenneth Anger's *Hollywood Babylon* was printed in America in unexpurgated form for the first time in 1975. Following the deaths of Danny Whitten and Gram Parsons, further casualties joined the list of rock's deceased. After years of chronic obesity and drug abuse, Cass Elliott's heart finally gave out at the end of a two-week London Palladium stint in July 1974. Two months later, the Average White Band drummer Robbie McIntosh died in a North Hollywood motel after ingesting a fatal combination of powders at a party to which Cher had taken him. The following summer it was the turn of Tim Buckley, who'd emerged from the avant-garde wilderness of *Lorca* and *Starsailor* to reinvent himself as the blue-eyed-funk sex machine of *Greetings from LA* (1972), *Sefronia* (1973) and *Look at the Fool* (1974). Returning from a short

* Paralleling the Troubadour incident, Phil Spector was himself thrown out of the Whisky for shouting through a Dixie Hummingbirds set. He also came to blows with David Geffen when the latter supposedly patronized him during the Warner–Spector session for Cher's 'A Woman's Story'. But the most bizarre Spector incident during this period was an automobile accident which occurred somewhere between LA and Phoenix in February 1974. Although the crash remains shrouded in mystery, Spector was said to have suffered multiple head injuries, necessitating major surgery and an apparent hair transplant. Certainly he was looking fairly strange when he re-emerged to work on further recordings for his Phil Spector International label, with his hair sprayed silver and gold and his neck adorned by a cross to ward off evil spirits.

† The arrival of Hugh Hefner's *Playboy* empire in the early seventies brought together the various strands that made Hollywood what it was: lechery, narcosis and rabid ambition. When Hef's private secretary Bobbie Arnstein killed herself after involving the company in a drugs scandal, her suicide revealed the murky truth behind all that perfect golden flesh.

tour of the southwest at the end of June 1975, Buckley died – so it was said – after mistaking heroin for cocaine and overdosing in his Santa Monica apartment.

Few of the survivors from the sixties were in much better shape. While Capitol cashed in on the nostalgia boom by releasing two extremely lucrative Beach Boys compilations – with the insidious titles *Endless Summer* and *Spirit of America* – the 'boys' themselves were falling apart. Terry Melcher and Bruce Johnston attempted to sign Brian to a production deal with their Equinox label, but when he got into the studio he was too freaked-out to touch anything, and appeared not to recognize the old Wrecking Crew musicians Melcher had hired for the session. Wilson, by now almost as obese as Mama Cass, was another of the regular guests at Danny Hutton's 'party house', occasionally running into Lennon and Nilsson there. Constantly hallucinating as he snorted coke, devoured caramel sundaes and watched endless hours of television, he was finally diagnosed as a schizophrenic. Of primary concern to the other Beach Boys was the suspicion that the likes of Sly Stone were hitting on Brian for drug money. Hence the hiring of Mike Love's 6' 8" brother Stan as a minder, followed by the first fateful approaches to a doctor named Eugene Landy.

After the death of Cass Elliott, John Phillips descended ever deeper into coke – and eventually into heroin – only emerging from his stupor to provide the soundtrack for Nic Roeg's *The Man Who Fell to Earth* (1976). If he and Genevieve Waite could still number Mick Jagger, David Geffen and Jack Nicholson among their friends, it was becoming increasingly hard to ignore Phillips' failure as a solo artist. Not even Waite's interesting album *Romance is on the Rise* (1974) was enough to put Papa John back on the map, especially after they turned down the chance to have it distributed by Warners. Denny Doherty, meanwhile, was virtually destitute in Florida, hitting rock bottom after jumping from a second-storey window and breaking both legs. And what of the lissome Michelle? Why, having an affair with Warren Beatty, of course.

If the official, 'export' version of southern California was embodied by the Beach Boys' *Endless Summer* (1974) – or by the breezy sound of the Eagles – the unofficial version was to be found in films such as Robert Altman's *The Long Goodbye* (1973) and Roman Polanski's *Chinatown* (1974). *Chinatown* in particular, directed by an immigrant who'd experienced the menace of *noir* Los Angeles at first hand, was a brilliant exposé of the evil and corruption at the heart of the Californian dream, starring that iconoclastic anti-star Jack Nicholson as a sub-Philip Marlowe detective investigating the political chicanery behind the piping of water to LA. Where *The Long Goodbye* updated Raymond Chandler's novel to the seventies, *Chinatown* used the forties as a prism for looking at the Los Angeles of the present – in Richard Rayner's words, 'a city of blinding white light by day and velvety purples and blues by night ... corrupt, exotic, dangerous'. Here again was the dark counterpoint to the received picture of LA as a kind of giant beach.

One of the key elements in LA *noir* is that bad things happen behind closed doors (or electronic gates): it is the indoor life of Los Angeles which makes it so bereft of community. When gonzo scribe Richard Meltzer quit New York for 'Dummdumm' LA in 1975, he arrived to find an antiseptic new world of glistening skin, 'autopilot smiles' ... and *no bars*. At first he couldn't figure out how Hollywood had ever come to be called 'Babylon', but then – like Paul Morrissey before him – he realized that all the degeneracy was taking place inside. Linda Ronstadt made roughly the same observation in 1978. While appreciating the 'comfort' of LA in the seventies, she said that it had 'reflected an empty sort of disillusioned hollowness', adding that 'the tendency to make strong friendships' was much more pronounced in New York.

The Los Angeles that Polanski and writer Robert Towne captured in *Chinatown* was one that very few bands or songwriters acknowledged in 1974, mainly because most of them were so steeped in it. If Neon Park's spooky cover painting for Little Feat's *The Last Record Album* (1975) showed that Lowell George at least was aware of LA's precariously apocalyptic character, it took a pair of cynical East Coast smartasses to see rock'n'roll Babylon for what it really was in the mid seventies.

Donald Fagen and Walter Becker were college boys and jazz *cognoscenti* who'd come in at the tail end of the New York pop era, working briefly in the Brill Building before being contracted as 'rewrite men' by a publishing company called the Jay Organization. By Becker's own admission, their earliest songs were 'too far out' to stand any chance of being recorded, but 1971 saw them working with Kenny Vance of the Brooklyn pop group Jay and the Americans on the soundtrack to a movie called *You Gotta Walk It Like You Talk It*.

Through pitching a song for Barbra Streisand to Richard Perry's right-hand man Gary Katz, Becker and Fagen came to be signed as staff writers to ABC-Dunhill. Following Katz out to Los Angeles, they began writing songs for acts like Tommy Roe and the Grass Roots. 'We found places to live in Encino, this oasis of nothing in the desert,' recalled Fagen, 'and every morning we'd hitch a ride to West Hollywood, where we had an office and a piano.' Becker claimed later that he and Fagen 'really had to go out of our way' to write a song ('Tell Me a Lie') for the Grass Roots: 'You could tell we were laughing down our sleeves at the band ... we were the Grateful Dead of Beverly Boulevard.'

Eventually, Becker and Fagen put their own band together around guitarists Denny Dias and Jeff 'Skunk' Baxter, drummer Jimmy Hodder, and one-time Goffin/King protégé David Palmer. Calling themselves Steely Dan after William Burroughs' term for a mechanical dildo, they recorded their ABC debut *Can't Buy a Thrill* in the summer of 1972, with Gary Katz producing. Already they were showing their preference for

'Nobody seemed to understand us in LA': Steely Dan at the time of Countdown to Ecstacy *(1973). Left to right: Jim Hodder, Walter Becker, Denny Dias, Jeff Baxter, Donald Fagen.*

session specialists, drafting in Elliott Randall to play the blistering guitar solos on 'Reelin' in the Years' and the mighty 'Kings'.

Perhaps this was why Skunk Baxter claimed the sessions were stilted, since 'hardly anybody knew anybody'. But then Becker and Fagen preferred it that way, since they had no time for the vestigial 'band' ethos of rock'n'roll. In fact, they had little time for rock'n'roll *per se*, deeming themselves simply to be above it. 'The newly formed amalgam [of Steely Dan] threatens to undermine the foundations of the rock power elite,' wrote Fagen in his 'Tristan Fabriani' guise on the sly sleevenote to *Thrill.* The band, he added, 'cast a long shadow upon the contemporary rock wasteland ... struggling to make sense out of the flotsam and jetsam of its eclectic musical heritage'.

Becker and Fagen were equally scathing of California itself: the album's title derived partly from Becker's contention that 'you can't buy a thrill living in California – it's like living in a morgue'. 'For subject matter, LA was certainly a lotta laughs, as it has been for many a satirist,' says Fagen. 'Neither of us really liked it, because we just weren't LA-type people. We called it Planet Stupid. Nobody seemed to understand us in LA. There were of course a lot of New Yorkers in LA, including some of the people at ABC-Dunhill, and they pretty much got it. But we felt sorta stranded otherwise. Our first manager made me buy a pair of green velour pants, and we didn't understand what that was all about. We just did what they said until we'd figured it all out for ourselves.' Doubtless it was a surprise to many when Steely Dan's very first single, the slinky 'Do It Again', rose all the way to No. 6 at the end of 1972.*

What an astonishing debut it was, crammed with endlessly hummable tunes, irresistible grooves and quirky, cryptic lyrics that set new standards in rock literacy. The album seemed to span the entire spectrum of American pop, from the Latin cha-cha of 'Only a Fool Would Say That' to the muted funk of 'Fire in the Hole'. Like Randy Newman, they wrote in character, putting suspect sentiments into other mouths; like Newman, too, they set sinister notions and events to bewitching melodies. The Dan stance was never confessional, invariably ironical. Their songs were filled with oblique allusions to figures and events from history, literature and mythology: Fagen claimed they were akin to junk sculpture, but taken as a whole the records comprised some of the most withering statements about the alienation of urban America in the seventies.

Of all the bands to emerge in the early seventies, Steely Dan owed possibly the least to the legacy of the sixties. Nor could they be appraised within the standard pop/rock, songwriter/band opposition: in the fissure between edification and entertainment, singer-songwriter authenticity and rock'n'roll decadence, they staked out their own patch and made a home in it. 'I think we used the medium for our own ends, and in that sense there was definitely a detachment,' says Fagen. 'We were just reflecting the *zeitgeist*, essentially. It became obvious later what was going on, and it wasn't like we were *promoting* that attitude or endorsing it. We were simply talking about the way everybody seemed to us.'

Although the band's first American tour was a disaster, it had the effect of bringing the members closer together. For 'Skunk', certainly, the sessions for the second album *Countdown To Ecstacy* were an altogether happier experience, as his splendid soloing on 'My Old School' attests. *Countdown* was easily the equal of its predecessor, boasting certified Dan classics in 'Razor Boy' and 'The Boston Rag'. Nor did Becker and Fagen miss the opportunity to express their moral outrage at the inequalities of life that they perceived in Los Angeles: 'Show Biz Kids' was a stark polemic about the Californian abyss between the Hollywood elite – in their Steely Dan T-shirts! – and the third world poor. 'Show biz kids

---

* Along with Steely Dan, ABC was home to artists such as B. B. King, Jimmy Buffett, Bobby Bland, Freddy Fender and the Amazing Rhythm Aces. After acquiring Dunhill Records in 1969, the label was run by Lou Adler's old partner Jay Lasker, while its staff producers included Steve Barri, who was not only responsible for albums by Cher, Mama Cass and Bobby Bland but also took an active interest in the development of Steely Dan. 'It was a horrible racist place,' says Michael Ochs, who worked in the publicity department at the time Bland recorded the Barri-produced *His California Album* (1973). 'They told me not to work Bobby, and they wouldn't give us Rufus T-shirts. Jay Lasker was this brusque old-school Broadway character who was always yelling at everybody, but the company was even worse after they replaced him with this accountant type called Jerry Rubinstein. They told me not to work Freddy Fender because he was Mexican, over 40, and an ex-convict. But then "Before the Next Teardrop Falls" went to No. 1, so they fired me.'

The Dan in the studio during the Katy Lied sessions. Left to right: Donald Fagen, Walter Becker, Michael McDonald, Denny Dias.

making movies of themselves,' sang Fagen in his inimitably non-rock voice; 'you know they don't give a fuck about anybody else ...' For Greil Marcus, *Countdown* turned the Band's second album inside out, refusing the refuge of the past as it asked questions of bourgeois America that were becoming hard to evade.

In 1974, Steely Dan were back in the Top 10 with 'Rikki Don't Lose that Number', a typically conversational (and typically cryptic) Becker/Fagen song based around an old Horace Silver riff. Jazz permeated *Pretzel Logic*, with the resurrection of their early song 'Parker's Band' and a witty version of Ellington's 'East St Louis Toodle-oo'. Once again the Dan universe was one slightly askew, peopled by marginal, Mamet-esque lowlifes and shot through with a melancholy regret. And once again there was an impressive array of settings for their jewel-like vignettes: the soft acoustic/electric rock of 'Any Major Dude Will Tell You', the cop-show jazz-funk of 'Night By Night', the Bach-like piano motif of 'Charlie Freak', the California boogie of the title track. 'I think one of the best things about rock'n'roll as opposed to jazz is precision and a professional sound,' said Fagen, going against the grain of rock orthodoxy. 'That's what I like about popular music. We strive for that sort of slick sound.'

'Donald and Walter were funny people, eccentric in a very normal way,' recalled Michael McDonald, whom drummer Jeff Porcaro brought along to audition as a backing singer. 'They were temperamental but never malicious. Musicians usually have an overblown opinion of themselves, but these guys weren't like that. They worked me very hard, but they were harder on themselves, and on the road they were reckless.' As it happened, it was the *Pretzel Logic* tour of 1974 which killed off any remaining enthusiasm Becker and Fagen may have had for having a band around them. An ill-tempered experience for all concerned, it confirmed the duo in their resolve to operate as a primarily studio-oriented entity and prompted the mutton-chopped 'Skunk' Baxter to defect to that very different LA band, the Doobie Brothers.

Only Denny Dias remained for *Katy Lied* (1975), which was otherwise performed by the new LA session mafia of Jeff Porcaro, Larry Carlton, Chuck Rainey, David Paich et al. – the pool of musicians who, along with the Crusaders and Tom Scott's LA Express, were helping to fashion a definitive LA sound on albums by Joni Mitchell and Boz Scaggs. The 'slick sound' Fagen loved reached its apogee on this album, which tore into its targets (Wall Street, pornography, the fallout from Vietnam) with a vicious cynicism that went beyond the playful irony of the earlier albums. *The Royal Scam* (1976) was more of the same, its title track picking up where 'Show Biz Kids' left off and its cover painting (of monster-headed skyscrapers bearing down on a sleeping tramp) seemingly summing up the Steely Dan worldview. William Gibson, whose novels are peppered with allusions to the group, laments the fact that 'a lot of kids today think of them as the epitome of boring seventies stuff, never realizing this is probably the most subversive material pop has ever thrown up.'

Even the drug problems hinted at in songs such as 'Doctor Wu' and 'Kid Charlemagne' were treated more as a conceptual game than an overtly hedonistic pastime. 'We had a complex sort of relationship to drugs,' says Fagen. 'The idea of pleasure for pleasure's sake was something we saw as good, but at the same time it was kind of a cliché. Walter got a little too deeply into it, but he eventually pulled himself out of it. I never really had a drug problem as such, though I had plenty of other problems.'

With the sublime *Aja* (1977), Steely Dan took their studio fetishism to its logical conclusion, recording it in five different studios and supposedly remixing it thirteen times in five months. With the aid of such super-sessionmen as Tom Scott, Plas Johnson, Victor Feldman and Steve Gadd, Becker and Fagen created a masterpiece of what they defined – on their contribution to the soundtrack of *FM* (1978) – as 'funked-up muzak'. The painstaking process duly reaped rewards when *Aja* climbed to No. 3 on the *Billboard* album chart, going on to spend an unprecedented fifty-one weeks in the Top 40. Ken Tucker of *Rolling Stone* bemoaned the distance the pair had travelled from 'the quirky, opaque little pop tunes' of 1972–3, but for those prepared to tolerate what he called the session 'tastymeisters' there was infinite richness in *Aja*'s arrangements.

III

Taking a cue from William Gibson, one could argue that Steely Dan were the only credible alternative to the quagmire of seventies rock until punk came along. Even then, of course, the pristine brilliance of *Aja* meant that Becker and Fagen were seen as arch-enemies by punks all over the world. And certainly they stood in clear opposition to a vibrant anti-mainstream scene which developed around Hollywood towards the end of 1972: Glam Rock.

Perhaps it was inevitable that Glam Rock would take root on the Sunset Strip – that a street/club scene would reassert itself as a kind of resistance to the cheesecloth-and-calico hegemony of the Warners/Asylum canyon aristocracy. As Todd Rundgren sang in 1973, 'when the shit hits the fan/I guess I'll have to make my way back to Sunset Boulevard . . .' And perhaps it was inevitable that at the heart of this scene would be those perennial scavengers Rodney Bingenheimer and Kim Fowley, both of them denied access to the higher echelons of power within the LA record industry. 'Everybody got really bored with the canyon sound,' says Greg Shaw, who moved down to LA from San Francisco in 1972. 'Apart from the odd band like Christopher Milk, people were falling asleep in their shoes. I never liked Jackson Browne or Joni Mitchell, and I hated almost everything to do with David Geffen. To me, it was all lifestyle wallpaper music.'

Rodney Bingenheimer, sometime 'Mayor of the Sunset Strip', had briefly interfaced with Canyon Rock when Nik Venet hired him to do some publicity for Linda Ronstadt and the Stone Poneys at Capitol. But by 1971 he was so disenchanted by the LA scene that he split for London to hang out with David Bowie and Rod Stewart. When Glam Rock began to break in Britain with T-Rex, Slade and the Sweet, Bingenheimer knew he'd finally found himself another pop niche. For him, the glam/glitter bands represented a kind of happy, exhibitionistic playfulness in the face of the new singer-songwriter 'maturity'. 'There's no doubt that Bowie made everything a lot more interesting than James Taylor and Jackson Browne,' says Denny Bruce.

It was Bowie who suggested that Rodney start a new club on the Strip. Returning to LA, the pint-sized scenester formed a partnership with producer Tom Ayres and in October 1972 opened the E Club at 8171 Sunset. Among the first guests, inevitably, were Bowie himself – 'as Ziggy', says Bingenheimer – and several of the barely pubescent boys and girls who would go on to become the real star(let)s of the scene when the club was moved eastwards along Sunset to No. 7561 and renamed Rodney Bingenheimer's English Disco. The name spoke for the rampant Anglophilia of the new scene, an Anglophilia that had everything to do with the androgyny and sartorial outrageousness of the English groups. 'Alone

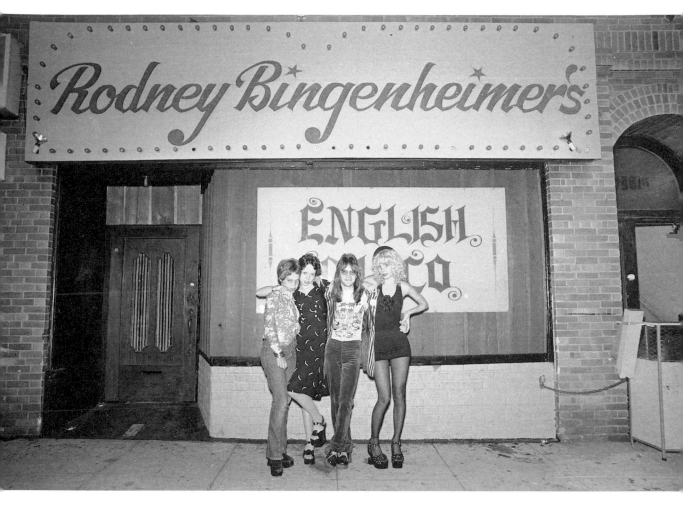

in LA, Rodney seemed like an island of Anglo "nowness",' recalled Bowie. 'He even knew British singles and bands that *I* wasn't aware of. Rodney single-handedly cut a path through the treacle of the sixties, allowing all us "avants" to parade our sounds of tomorrow dressed in our clothes of derision.'

In some senses it was Vito and his freaks all over again, which was probably why that old reprobate Kim Fowley had no problem fitting in. 'I walked into the English Disco in a rabbit coat I'd bought in London, picked up this amazing bitch and took her back to the Marmont,' says Fowley, whose own English sojourn lent him all the cachet he needed to score with the foxy nymphets pitching up at the club; 'if David Bowie was Jesus Christ, then Rodney's was the Sistine Chapel.' Fowley even managed to parlay his 'cachet' into a deal with Capitol which saw the release of his solo albums *I'm Bad* (1972), *International Heroes* (1973) and *Visions of the Future* (1974) – none of which sold more than a few thousand copies but all of which contained some amusingly trashy songs. He was also one of the artists whom Phil Spector signed in a one-off deal to Phil Spector International, recording him on the trash-glam throwaway song

Rodney outside the English Disco with Mackénzie Phillips (second from left) *and Sable Starr* (right).

'Give It to Me' in what Fowley remembered as 'some shitty studio across from the Chinese Theater on Hollywood Boulevard'.

'I'll never forget the image of Rodney and Kim walking around the club,' recalled screenwriter Amy Freeman for *Details* magazine. 'They looked like Lurch and Cousin Itt.'* While Bingenheimer and Fowley held court at the English Disco, all of Hollywood came to gawp at the black-lipsticked, Quaalude-gobbling, platform-booted groupies. 'The groupies were usually girls who did not have fathers, lived in disenfranchised homes and had mothers who worked,' recalled Fowley. 'They came for feminine men who weren't queer. Of course, anyone who had Bowie-esque qualities automatically got lucky.' Two of the more celebrated girls were Sable Starr and Lori Lightning, remembered by aspirant Brit glamster Michael Des Barres as 'the most committed of them all in terms of being able to manifest the ultimate groupie fantasy'; other tank-topped vixenettes included the 13-year-old Joan Jett and Laura (Mackenzie) Phillips, wild-child daughter of John Phillips. There was even a groupie band called Backstage Pass, the missing link between the GTOs and the Runaways.

Not everyone has the rosiest memories of this new breed of groupie. Miss Pamela, for example – shortly to marry the above-mentioned Des Barres – was miffed to find that she was now deemed too old to attend to the sexual needs of visiting Englishmen. 'When Led Zeppelin were due to hit town, the groupie section went into the highest gear imaginable,' she wrote in her bestselling *I'm With the Band*. 'You could hear garter belts sliding up young thighs all over Hollywood. I believed the GTOs had paved the way for these infant upstarts, and I thought they should show me some kind of respect.' To me, over breakfast in a café near her cosy Santa Monica apartment, Des Barres says the Rodney's scene was really a desperate attempt to re-create what had been there on the Strip eight years before. 'And there was such backstabbing in the groupie scene. In the sixties we were all for each other, there was a feeling that was more important than any one *guy*.'

One of the few Englishmen not to plunge into this ocean of muff was Nick Kent, the stick-insect journalist who often came over to report on the scene for *New Musical Express*. Like Pamela Des Barres, he was faintly appalled by what he saw at the English Disco. 'The really famous groupies were extremely tough and unpleasant,' he recalls. 'Jimmy Page told me that one of his Hollywood girlfriends bit into a sandwich that had razorblades in it. I mean, seeing these conniving, loveless little girls really affected my whole concept of femininity for a while. Talk to the bass player from the Sweet and he would probably say those were the best

---

* One of their fellow sexual vampires was bit-part actor Blackie Dammett, father of Red Hot Chili Pepper Anthony Kiedis. 'He was your basic semi-subversive underground hooligan playboy womanizer type of character,' remembered Kiedis, who came to LA to live with pater in 1973 and through him met everyone from Bowie and Keith Moon to Nilsson and Alice Cooper.

Led Zeppelin hold court at the English Disco: Robert Plant with Sable Starr (left); John Bonham with Lori Lightning (right).

months of his life, but to someone with a bit of taste, who wasn't just hopelessly addicted to pussy, it was pretty sordid. It was a period of time when, if you were skinny and English and dressed like some horrible Biba girl, you could have anything you wanted.'

It almost goes without saying that the British contingent in LA produced the most overtly decadent specimens on the Rodney's scene. Whether it was such comparative small-fry as Michael Des Barres and Ian Hunter or major stars like Keith Moon and Jimmy Page, the Brits lived up to their hooligans-in-the-sun reputation by indulging in every conceivable manner of abuse. 'What I remember most is when Led Zeppelin got in there, because they really believed they owned the place,' says Nick Kent. 'I've never seen anyone behave worse in my life than John Bonham and Richard Cole [Zeppelin's road manager]. I once saw them beat a guy senseless for no reason and then drop money on his face. It makes me feel sick when I hear Robert Plant talking about what a great geezer Bonzo was, because the guy was a schizophrenic animal, he was like something out of *Straw Dogs*.'

When Zeppelin occupied the top floor of the Continental Hyatt House, a.k.a. the 'Riot House', or held court at a new Sunset Strip watering-hole called the Rainbow Bar and Grill, they dragged rock'n'roll degeneracy down to new depths. 'Something about Led Zeppelin's energy really altered the *joi de vivre* of the LA rock scene,' says Pamela Des Barres. 'They thought they could get away with anything, and they could, because everybody wanted to get near them. They were very debauched, and the girls got younger and younger and more willing to do anything. It got to be incredibly sick. I mean, it's weird to see Richard Cole today, because I have images of him kicking people's teeth out.'

Although Rodney's was primarily what it said it was – a 'disco' in which the clientele danced to glam-rock records from England – Bingenheimer occasionally staged live performances by acts such as the New York Dolls, whose debut album in August 1973 was one of the only authentic American responses to British Glam Rock. Ironically, given their identification with Manhattan, the Dolls were the perfect Sunset Strip band, and were a major influence on the countless generic spandex bands who dominated the Strip metal scene in the late seventies and eighties. 'I was never quite the same after seeing the Dolls,' says former Cramps guitarist Kid Congo Powers, who was one of the teenage androgynes in attendance at Rodney's. 'They were just the greatest fun you could imagine, loose but never sloppy. I mean, I was just a young suburban bumpkin, but I wasn't gonna be left out of this. It was too exciting.'

Such was the impact of the Dolls, indeed, that Kim Fowley attempted to create an LA version of the band called – what else? – the Hollywood Stars. 'Kim found a kid at the Rainbow with, quote unquote, "Marc Bolan rhythm",' says Denny Bruce, who ended up managing the band with Fowley. 'He then handpicked five Bay City Roller/New York Doll-type guys, composed a handful of songs, and rammed them into a four-track studio. We got them a real good deal on Columbia, and my favourite expression from this time came out of a meeting that Kim and I had with a guy at the label called Ted Fagen, who said to us: "Guys, we're at the point now where we have to have *real* producers." With about a second's pause, Fowley says: "In other words, you're telling us we're too urine-stained to join your country club." *Urine-stained* subsequently became a giant street expression, and was eventually abbreviated to just *urine*.'

Rodney Bingenheimer with Cherry Vanilla and Iggy Pop (right).

Another American act that occasionally played the English Disco was Iggy and the Stooges. The world's forgotten boy had already done the LA sleazoid trip when the original Stooges recorded the proto-punk classic *Fun House* (1970), but now he was back in town with David Bowie's entourage, having just finished the *Raw Power* sessions in London. Although he blew most of his $100,000 advance from Columbia on his bills at the swanky Beverly Hills Hotel, the Ig was in relatively good shape at this point. Seven months later he was back on heroin, furious at Bowie's mix of *Raw Power* and at his continuing neglect by MainMan management.

'Iggy was going out with Sable Starr's sister Coral Shields,' remembers Nick Kent, who served as a kind of Sancho Panza to the silver-haired crazyman. 'He tried to stop using heroin and then got into an even worse state with 'ludes and other tranquillizers. He was very quickly regarded as a loser, mainly because he wasn't English. My most abiding memory is of him standing at the English Disco in his *Raw Power* clothes, stoned, looking at himself in the mirrored walls for hours on end. It was pretty sad.'

Things went from bad to worse when MainMan despatched ex-Warhol acolyte Leee Black Childers to turf Iggy and his pals out of the house he was renting atop Mulholland Drive. MainMan boss Tony DeFries terminated the band's contract, and David Bowie was too busy being broken as a major star in the States to sort it out. Instead, the Stooges – Iggy, guitarist James Williamson, pianist Scott Thurston and the brothers Asheton – came together for one last death-defying crawl through America. This was the period which saw the writing of such nihilistic, death-trip classics as 'Head On', 'Open Up and Bleed', and 'Cock in My Pocket', as performed during an insane five-night stand at the Whisky a Go Go in the fall of 1973. 'There was no pattern to the gigging,' Iggy recalled. 'I'd just do the shows and then stumble back to LA with a coupla hundred bucks and just flop for a week till I could go out again. Whatever I didn't spend on the motels I'd spend on drugs.'

After playing their final, apocalyptic shows on their home turf back in Michigan – the four-track *Metallic K.O.* recordings from those performances being the band's parting shot – Iggy headed back to Hollywood for further mental obliteration. With Danny Sugerman acting as his nanny, he was cajoled into performing as a kind of Jim Morrison surrogate at Ray Manzarek's Whisky show marking the third anniversary of Jimbo's death. 'Jim Morrison died today,' improvised the wasted Iggy over the final bars of 'LA Woman'. 'Jim Morrison was more beautiful than any girl in this town and now he's dead, and now I cry ...' Thankfully nothing came of Sugerman's absurd scheme to put together a 'New Doors' around the Pop.

On 11 August 1974 Iggy appeared at the English Disco improvising a 'play' called 'Murder of the Virgin' – in which he was whipped by a Nazi-uniformed James Williamson – and performing such immortal numbers as 'Wet My Bed', 'Rich Bitch' (about Coral Shields), and the self-explanatory 'She-Creatures of the Hollywood Hills'. 'Just before the show, it had been rumoured that he was planning to kill himself onstage at the end of the act,' recalled Tom Ayres. 'Sure enough, when the set was coming to a close, Iggy got out a butcher's knife and went wild, all across his chest. The security guards had to jump onstage and literally carry him off.' Danny Sugerman, naturally, was on hand to give the press some *spiel*

Iggy after the 'Murder of the Virgin' show, August 1974.

Kim Fowley onstage with friend at the Starwood.

about 'Iggy's most totally committed artistic statement ever!', prior to driving his charge out to Santa Monica and hurling him in the Pacific to heal his wounds.

By the time Iggy starred in Fowley and Bingenheimer's 'Hollywood Street Revival and Trash Dance' show at the Palladium later that year – along with Silverhead, the New York Dolls and the resurrected GTOs – the LA Glam scene was all but over. Fowley even subtitled the show 'The Death of Glitter', as though in homage to the 'Death of Hippie' march organized in Haight-Ashbury at the end of 1967. 'All over Hollywood that night it was glitter,' recalled Chuckie Star, whose legendary fourteen-inch platforms were reputedly the highest in the world. 'Everyone in LA knew it was going to be their last chance to wear platform shoes and eye-shadow. Surfers from Malibu were there in midriff shirts, silver space boots, and blue eye makeup ...' After the show had climaxed with the Dolls' 'Personality Crisis', Chuckie himself was carried onstage in a glitter coffin. As the coffin went past them, people tossed lipsticks and roses on to his chest.*

What Michael Des Barres called 'tainted show biz', and punk scribe Craig Lee remembered later as 'drugged-out ersatz Hollywood glamour', was in hindsight the most vital thing happening in Los Angeles between 1972 and 1974. But in true Hollywood style, the English Disco was corrupted, above all by the English. By the time of the 'Death of Glitter' show, the decadence had become only too real. 'It was exactly the same kind of decadence as you'd had thirty years earlier, and in exactly the same neighbourhood,' says Kim Fowley. 'You had guys saying, "I think this is a good place to get my cock sucked," not realizing that about a thousand cocks had been sucked there thirty years before, and for the same ridiculous reasons.'

'If it wasn't quite *The Beautiful and the Damned*, it was certainly the *pretty and the damned*,' says Nick Kent. 'Everyone was, you know, "going to hell" and nobody cared. It was as if they'd all taken up residence in Leiber and Stoller's "Is That All There Is?" To me, that was *the* song of the seventies, even if it was written in 1966. I mean, quite honestly, Rodney

---

* If Glam died in Hollywood that night, it lived on in the rest of the nation, most obviously in the success of the compulsively awful Kiss. It was curious, however, that San Francisco produced the most hypertrophied version of this Sunset Strip overkill in the shape of Tubes frontman Fee Waybill's giant-stacked stage character Quay Lewd.

himself was one of the most boring and sexless human beings that ever existed – he literally just wanted to spend his time hanging in the shadows of David Bowie talking about Jobriath. Fowley at least had a brain: as Iggy once said to me, "Kim Fowley is bullshit, but it's a better class of bullshit." *

'There was something horrible permeating the air in LA in those days…' David Bowie at the time of Station to Station.

The Englishman who embodied the 'Is That All There Is?' spirit better than anyone was David Bowie himself, then cruising on the Top 10 success of his blue-eyed funk album *Young Americans*. If John Bonham was a schizophrenic animal and Keith Moon a manic-depressive jester, Bowie by the spring of 1975 had become a skeletal vampire, virtually burned out on cocaine. To put his health in perspective, he was in an even worse state than Iggy Pop, who in June committed himself to the Neuropsychiatric Institute at UCLA. 'There was something horrible permeating the air in LA in those days,' Bowie recalled. 'I collected a motley crew of people who would keep turning up at the house – a lot of dealers, real scum.'

Regularly staying up for six or seven days on the trot, the former Ziggy Stardust – the man whose 'Rebel Rebel' had been *the* theme song of the English Disco scene – entered a psychotic, hallucinatory world of occult ritual and totalitarian fantasy, alternately convinced that satanists were out to abduct him and that he was some new fascist dictator. Even after Angie Bowie flew out from London and set her husband up in an Art Deco house on Doheny Drive, he was in such a paranoid state that he asked her to arrange an exorcism. Had it not been for *The Man Who Fell to Earth*, in which Bowie all but played himself as the spectral alien Newton, the singer might have crossed the thin line between near-dementia and total insanity. Instead, he returned from the New Mexico location of Nic Roeg's film, moved into a house in Stone Canyon, and began preparing the album of slick, thunderous rock-funk that was *Station to Station*. And when it was all over, 'I physically opened a wardrobe door, mentally put all my characters into the wardrobe, and left Los Angeles.' Five years later, describing LA as 'the scariest movie ever written', Bowie declared that 'that fucking place should be wiped off the face of the earth'.

The horror movie of Bowie's year in Hollywood was one in which many other music-industry figures had roles: some of them lead parts, others just walk-on cameos. The spirit of August 1969 seemed to have returned to the city. 'If you walked around Laurel Canyon, you felt this evil *snaking around*,' says Nick Kent. 'When I was living with Iggy and James Williamson just along from the Riot House on the Strip, every night there'd just be these weird people around – people falling apart and

---

* Perhaps it was no wonder that those chubby English glam-rockers the Sweet called their 1975 album *Desolation Boulevard*. On the cover, incidentally, they were pictured in front of the archetypal hard-rock dive Filthy McNasty's. Located at 8852 Sunset, this later became the Viper Room, outside which wannabe-rocker River Phoenix collapsed and died in October 1993.

having nervous breakdowns. Everybody just walked by because they couldn't feel any more.'

One of the people breaking down on the Strip was Iggy himself, whom Bowie visited in the Neuropsychiatric Institute before leaving to do *The Man Who Fell to Earth*. That summer, on weekend leave from the Institute, Iggy and James Williamson convened at a house belonging to Jimmy Webb and – with the help of Scott Thurston and others – recorded the eleven tracks which made up the harrowing *Kill City*. Although the album was only released by Greg Shaw's Bomp label in November 1977 – testimony to the low esteem in which Pop and Williamson were held – *Kill City* was another proto-punk masterpiece, and a haunting cry from the sick heart of Hollywood Babylon '75: 'I live here in Kill City, where the debris meets the sea/It's a playground for the rich but it's a loaded gun to me.'

For James Williamson, songs such as 'Johanna', 'I Got Nothin'' and 'Beyond the Law' comprised the best music he and Iggy ever made together; it was certainly better than *New Values*, their 1979 collaboration for Arista Records. But then Iggy was really a spent force by 1979, his last great music behind him.

IV

Iggy managed to get away from LA, initially moving down to San Diego and later attaching himself to Bowie's *Station to Station* tour. (Like Bowie, he found Berlin to be the perfect cure for the LA blues, reinventing himself as an American artist in Gothic European exile.) The Hollywood he left behind him, meanwhile, was a shattered and fragmented place, ripe for genuine change. If the English Disco scene had been a kind of street reflection/refraction of the more insulated decadence up in the canyons, it had hardly damaged the careers of the established LA superstars. 'By the time I arrived in 1975,' wrote Richard Meltzer, 'there were no more Doors or Byrds or Love ... the last trace of Buffalo Springfield, Neil Young, had pretty much coalesced with a singer-songwriter *zeitgeist* ... glitter-glam fops, unreconstituted hippies and reconstructed Monkees lurked about, as did ageing Brit imports in the canyons and hills.'

To give them their due, it wasn't as if bands such as the Eagles were entirely oblivious to this stagnation. When Don Henley, Glenn Frey and Randy Meisner wrote 'Take It to the Limit', a Top 5 hit in January 1976, they were attempting what Dave Marsh described as 'the heartfelt saga of a wasted generation', taking stock of the burnout – the sense of failed promise – in the LA rock community. Yet by the same token, the Eagles did nothing to convince people that they hadn't been as corrupted by success as any of their peers, especially after they gratuitously denounced the New York Dolls from the stage of Madison Square Garden as a way of giving the finger to their many New York critics. Glenn Frey may have resented the fact that 'we became the symbol for that "laid-back, rich, don't-give-a-shit" California lifestyle', but the band didn't do themselves any favours with their 'SONG POWER' T-shirts and smug putdowns of 'spectacle' bands, particularly when their own shows were regularly being described in terms such as 'loitering onstage'.

By the spring of 1976, moreover, the Eagles had entered a new stratosphere of fame and wealth. Not only was their *Greatest Hits* album perched at No. 1 for five weeks (eventually going on to sell twelve million copies) but with the replacement of Bernie Leadon by Joe Walsh they'd turned themselves into a fully fledged twin-lead stadium rock band. When Don Henley began an affair with Stevie Nicks of Fleetwood Mac, he took to chartering a Lear jet in order either to fly to Mac dates or to bring her to Eagles shows. 'This was simply our way of coping with the absurdity of making so much money and being so famous at such an early age' was his disingenuous disclaimer for such extravagance; more honest was the popular slogan 'Love 'em and Lear 'em' that circulated around the Eagles camp during this heady period.

Along with the excess, of course, came the requisite squabbles. À la Lennon and McCartney and a host of other successful partnerships, the love-hate relationship between Frey and Henley was becoming increasingly fraught. Co-habiting in Dorothy Lamour's old house in the hills, the two men fell out to the point where Henley moved out of the house and into Irving Azoff's place in Benedict Canyon. In addition, the others began to resent Frey and Henley for taking control of the band while continuing to pretend that it was a democracy. 'There was so much turbulence about,' recalled Frey. 'Perhaps a lot of it was bluff, because we were really just a bunch of skinny little guys with long hair and patched pants and turquoise.'

It must have been strange to reflect on the evolution of the LA country rock scene from its comparatively humble origins back in 1968–9. 'When we started out, it was a friendlier business,' recalled Don Henley in 1990. 'It wasn't quite the claw-your-way-into-the-business thing that it is now. The whole country-rock movement – a label I hate – was even connected to environmentalism, to the earth, and everybody was wearing earthy clothes and celebrating the outdoors.' From earthy clothes to designer denim, from the Troubadour to Madison Square Garden: by 1976 'country-rock' was a rather different ballgame, as groups such as Firefall and the Outlaws knew only too well. Firefall, formed by ex-Flying Burritos Rick Roberts and Michael Clarke with Spirit/Jo Jo Gunne bassist Mark Andes, went straight for the Eagles/Ronstadt pop jugular with their insipid Atlantic debut and even had a Top 10 single with the chirpy 'You are the Woman'. This must have been particularly galling to the likes of Poco, who'd been taken on by Geffen-Roberts in 1973 only to have the aspiring mogul lure Richie Furay away to join the Souther Hillman Furay 'supergroup'. Poco weren't the most exciting group in the world, but at least they didn't dress up soft pop-rock in spurious 'country' clothing.

The same could have been said for Emmylou Harris, who kept the flame of Gram Parsons alive with her fine Reprise albums *Pieces of the Sky* (1975) and *Elite Hotel* (1976), both featuring the cream of LA's versatile country/pop sessionmen – James Burton, Glen D. Hardin, Ray Pohlman and company – along with an astute selection of songs old and new. Burton's old boss Rick Nelson, too, had reaffirmed his commitment to country-rock after 'Garden Party', a scathing put-down of rock'n'roll 'revival' shows, was a Top 10 hit in 1972. Determined as ever to prove that he wasn't just another ageing pretty face, Nelson re-emerged in 1973 with a new Stone Canyon Band, only the veteran steel guitarist Tom Brumley remaining from the old lineup. But after releasing the perfectly pleasant *Windfall* album in January 1974, his career began to languish just as that of his old bass player Randy Meisner was taking off with the Eagles.

Equally unjust was the neglect suffered by ex-Monkee Mike Nesmith, whose three superb albums with the First National Band – *Magnetic South* (1970), *Loose Salute* (1971) and *Nevada Fighter* (1971) – stemmed from an intriguing preoccupation with the culture of the old Southwest. Nesmith was sanguine enough about this to call his sixth album *And the Hits Just Keep On Coming*, but when David Geffen later pulled the plug on his Elektra-distributed Countryside label it confirmed that there was no real place for genuinely countrified rock on the LA scene. Among the Nesmith recordings which never saw the light of day were those he made with the Nitty Gritty Dirt Band, who'd had a modest hit back in 1969 with his 'Some of His Shelly's Blues'. The formerly Long Beach-based band were themselves responsible for one of the seminal country-rock projects of the seventies with their Nashville-recorded triple album *Will the Circle be Unbroken?* (1972), featuring such old-time/bluegrass veterans as Doc Watson, Roy Acuff and Mother Maybelle Carter.

The Laurel Canyon elite that had first come together at the Troubadour in 1969 was now firmly entrenched within the Warners-Elektra-Asylum empire. The Glam-rockers from the Rodney's scene may have despised the Lear-jet world of these stars, but it could hardly be said to have kept the Eagles awake nights. 'I remember seeing Glenn Frey standing outside the English Disco, obviously high on coke,' recalls Nick Kent. 'His eyes were like slits looking at these people he detested.' Shoring up the arrogance of such stadium-rock superstars were critics like Robert Hilburn of the *Los Angeles Times*, whose Frank Rich-style stranglehold on the musical taste of the mid seventies virtually established a consensus of mainstream opinion in the music industry. Even *Rolling Stone*, declared foes of the LA scene, hired teenage gunslinger Cameron Crowe to attach himself as a kind of confidant to such leading LA lights as Joni Mitchell and the Eagles.

Along with the giant billboards advertising their albums, the canyon elite now had their own Sunset Strip showcase joint in the form of the

The Roxy on Sunset Strip, in its opening week in 1973. Lou Adler's On the Rox is to the left.

Roxy, founded in 1973 by Whisky owner Elmer Valentine in partnership with Lou Adler and Elliot Roberts. (The idea behind the club, which opened with shows by Neil Young, was to break the Troubadour's monopoly on the non-hard-rock scene.) What they did not have, increasingly, was the sense of community that had sustained them in the late sixties. 'After their success, whether they'll admit it or not,' said Joni Mitchell, 'everybody got much more into their own particular creative process.'

'There was a year or two where we all sort of scuffled and wound up meeting in the same sort of places,' says Jackson Browne. 'Then there was a year or two when we all made our first records. And then after that we saw each other less and less, mainly because we were all working so hard.' For Browne, the loss of 'family feeling' was symbolized by the fact that 'we all stopped passing songs around'. So profitable had the music business become that giving someone else a song you'd written could conceivably mean missing out on hundreds of thousands of dollars. Back in 1969, no one had thought this far ahead. As Section keyboard player Craig Doerge put it, 'the idea that rock'n'roll would be an ongoing lifetime pursuit didn't really sink in till the big CSNY reunion tour.'

'The truth is that the business got more corporate, in the sense that contracts became much more official and the deals got better,' says Peter Asher, then riding high on the continuing success of Linda Ronstadt and

James Taylor. 'See, the freewheeling entrepreneurs who started all those great little labels in the fifties were the same people who screwed you. Now there wasn't so much actual stealing, but at the same time it all became more rigorous and controlled.' The Eagles certainly wouldn't have quibbled with Asher's views of the music industry. As Don Henley admitted, 'everybody's so busy and caught up in their careers and stuff that we all don't hang out much any more ... the old gang's split up.' Glenn Frey claimed that the Geffen-Roberts 'gang' was able to stay in touch up until *On the Border*: 'We spent all of our waking hours together trying to figure out how we were gonna engineer our conspiracy and burst upon the scene. Then, of course, as soon as that happened, it got to the point where J. D. had joined the SHF Band, Jackson had put out three albums, and our careers took over. So we lost, in some ways, our sense of conspiracy. Then I think the Eagles became the centre of *our* conspiracy.'

The Eagles 'conspiracy' to take over the rock'n'roll universe undoubtedly reached its climax with the writing and recording of *Hotel California* (1976). Here truly was the all-bases-covered seventies *pièce de resistance*: from the Joe Walsh-raunchified 'Life in the Fast Lane' to the sweeter-than-sweet Souther/Frey/Henley country-pop balladry of 'New Kid in Town', from the sinister, reggaefied title track to the epic, stringswept finale of 'The Last Resort', *Hotel California* was all things to all men. It was also a grandiose, semi-conceptual statement about LA, a critique of the cossetted, fast-lane world of the entertainment business which itself seemed to epitomize everything that was bogus and overblown about that world. 'We were all middle-class kids from the midwest, and *Hotel California* was our interpretation of the high life of Los Angeles,' said Don Henley. The trouble was, it was difficult to listen to 'Life in the Fast Lane' and not hear the sound of coke-crazed millionaires in Maseratis lording it over the rest of the populace, even if 'Hotel California' – Henley's oblique song about the latent creepiness at the heart of Hollywood hedonism – did seem to redress the balance. 'The Last Resort', seven and a half minutes long, was even more explicit in its denunciation of the false paradise of southern California. Sung in Henley's most sunkissed surf-rock voice, it anticipated the many fine songs he would go on to write as a solo artist in the eighties.

When *Hotel California* spent eight weeks at No. 1 at the beginning of 1977, it confirmed what Peter Frampton's *Frampton Comes Alive!* had hinted the previous spring, and what Fleetwood Mac's *Rumours* would confirm three months later: that melodic Californian rock – even the kind made by exiled Brits – was *the* American sound of the mid seventies. 'There was a time during 1976–7 when the record business went crazy, with *Hotel California*, *Rumours*, *Frampton Comes Alive!*, and then *Saturday Night Fever*,' recalled Glenn Frey. 'That was the decadent zenith of the music business.' Yet Don Henley could see *Hotel California* as a presentiment of the boom's end in exactly the same way that Jackson Browne could present *The Pretender*, a Top 5 album in late 1976, as a statement of social conscience in a climate of relentless self-gratification.*

The darkness and brooding of *The Pretender* – of 'The Fuse', 'Your Bright Baby Blues', 'Sleep's Dark and Silent Gate' and 'The Pretender' itself – had at least something to do with the overdose suicide of Browne's ex-model wife Phyllis Major on 25 March 1976, a mere three and a half weeks after work had started on the album. But it was also the boy wonder's way of dealing with the same sense of 'failed promise' that informed Don Henley's songwriting. Browne told Paul Nelson that the 'capitulation' of 'The Pretender' – 'I'm going to rent myself a house/In the shade of the freeway/I'm going to pack my lunch in the morning/And go to work each day' – was one reaction to the aftermath of the sixties: a way of copping out. Within a couple of years, he'd begun to involve himself in a number of causes, refusing the 'happy idiocy' option in that famous song.

When the *Pretender* sessions began in March 1976, Browne had just finished producing the debut album by new Asylum signing Warren Zevon. The bespectacled Zevon had grown up in San Pedro, paying his dues as one half of the coffeehouse folk duo Lyme and Cybelle. Briefly signed to Imperial Records, he'd recorded *Wanted Dead or Alive* (1969), with a title track penned by Kim Fowley, but had then gone on the road with the Everly Brothers. 'Zevon was like a kid that we could all see a little of ourselves in,' says Elliot Roberts, who welcomed the Jackson Browne protégé into the Asylum family in the late summer of 1975.

What Zevon really did for Asylum was provide a kind of bridge between the old singer-songwriters and the emergent Angry Young Men of new wave rock'n'roll. Although he had one foot in the laid-back Laurel Canyon camp – *Warren Zevon* featured guest spots not only from Browne but from J. D. Souther, the Eagles, Buckingham and Nicks, and even Carl Wilson – his vision of southern California was considerably more acerbic than, say, Browne's or Don Henley's. And *Warren Zevon* was pointedly rooted in the rotting heart of LA: 'Poor, Poor Pitiful Me' namechecked the Rainbow and the Riot House, 'Join Me in LA' the Tropicana, and 'Desperadoes Under the Eaves' the old Hollywood Hawaiian Hotel at Yucca and Grace. 'I used to feel more of a Beach Boys "Be True to Your School" kind of loyalty to southern California,' Zevon said in 1978. 'That's kind of dissolved, and I'm not sure why. I don't know whether LA's changed or whether I have. I suppose I'm an Angeleno, having spent the bulk of my life there ... [but] I'm living in a cave right now – this hotel suite with no windows – and it's not untypical of the way I am.'

---

* *The Pretender* had an interesting cover. With its reference to the album's title track – 'Out into the cool of the evening/Strolls the pretender' – it showed Browne in downtown LA, a solitary WASP in spotless T-shirt and chinos in the midst of shabbier-looking black and Mexican pedestrians. Whether or not it was intended as any kind of statement, it was certainly far removed from the standard iconography of LA album covers.

Zevon's songs were unashamedly derivative of Nathanael West and the *noir* crime writers. Snapshots of the sleazy truth behind the Sunset Strip glitz, tracks such as 'The French Inhaler' and 'I'll Sleep When I'm Dead' had little to do with the fast-lane, mirrored-shades world of Joe Walsh. If Browne and Henley were increasingly uncomfortable with the trappings of their success, Zevon made a body-swerve away from the sunlight, refusing to give the rock'n'roll mythology of California any credence at all. 'With a cold eye, a boozer's humour, and a reprobate's sense of fate,' noted Greil Marcus, 'this California rounder put LA back on the rock'n'roll map and nearly blew the Malibu singer-songwriter crowd right off it.'

True, 'Hasten Down the Wind' became the mellow, melancholy title track of Linda Ronstadt's first platinum album in 1976, but 'Poor, Poor Pitiful Me' was cheekily ironic about the egos of spoiled-brat rock stars, and the Tex-Mexican 'Carmelita' referred to being 'strung out on heroin' as though it was as normal as having a cold. 'Desperadoes Under the Eaves', finally, caught the panicky huddling-together of the rock fraternity, vagabonds living like everyone else with the apocalyptic knowledge of LA's ever-likely destruction:

> Don't the sun look angry through the trees,
> Don't the trees look like crucified thieves
> Don't you feel like desperadoes under the eaves.
> Heaven help the one who weaves…

The influence of *Warren Zevon* on Jackson Browne's *Running On Empty* (1977) is arguable, but *Running On Empty* went even further than *The Pretender* in addressing the malaise and emotional bankruptcy of rock'n'roll – and of America in general – at a time when the record industry was reaching its commercial peak. Recorded on- and off-stage with the 'Section' band during Browne's 1977 tour, this 'anti-live' in-concert album was about waste, self-abuse and 'The Road' itself. The fact that *Running On Empty* sold even better than its predecessor, climbing to No. 3 at the very beginning of 1978, showed how easy it was to take Browne at the level of his anodyne AOR voice and pretty-boy image: Middle America lapped up 'Running' and 'The Load-Out' and 'You Love the Thunder' in exactly the same way it lapped up Peter Frampton.

If it did nothing else, 'Running On Empty' sounded a kind of death-knell for the whole singer-songwriter/Me Generation era: when Browne yelled 'I don't know about anyone but me!', he already knew he'd had enough of navel-gazing, of being in the spotlight as a rock'n'roll confessor. 'At the height of my success I was always being asked to do things like host *Midnight Special*, and I hated TV,' he has said. 'But that's also my brand of conceit: that I don't really need that kind of attention as much as a certain anonymity. Otherwise you wind up writing songs about being a rock star, whether it's Joni Mitchell's brilliant "For Free" or a whole album like *Running On Empty*. Especially if you use that personal narrative form, it's incumbent on you to live a somewhat normal life and sing what other people care about. Otherwise you're sort of recounting your exploits for people who begin to subscribe to the life of another person as being more interesting than their own.'

An Asylum singer-songwriter who quickly made a beeline away from the laid-back confessional style was Tom Waits. A native Californian, Waits had grown up in smalltown Orange County, finding an escape route through fantasies of Kerouac's Beat America. After a long succession of dead-end jobs in laundromats and pizza parlours, Waits made his first forays into the singer-songwriting life, accompanying himself initially on a jumbo acoustic guitar. Following early appearances in tiny folk clubs around San Diego, he came under the influence of Randy Newman and the Broadway/Tin Pan Alley tradition of Gershwin and Irving Berlin, eventually switching to piano as his main instrument.

Gravitating north to LA, Waits began to incorporate the jazz argot and comic monologue style of those legendary Hollywood hipsters Lenny Bruce and Lord Buckley into his stage routine. In the early summer of 1971 he made the acquaintance of Bizarre/Straight boss Herb Cohen, who added the goatee-bearded singer to his management roster and

'Waits was a little different...' Boho Tom in Tinseltown, 1974.

recorded him on demos that veered from the Tin Pan Alley balladeering of 'Little Trip to Heaven' to the C&W spoof of 'Looks Like I'm Up Shit Creek Again'. The following year he became one of the only real links between Herb Cohen's Los Angeles and David Geffen's – between Zappa and Beefheart on the one hand and Browne and the Eagles on the other – after David Blue played Elliot Roberts those demos. 'There were a lot of good writers we felt should have the chance to record, even though we knew they weren't gonna be hugely successful,' says Roberts. 'Waits was a little different, because he'd reinvented himself as a beatnik. He had the luxury of doing that in LA, because it was an empty white canvas.'

If Roberts was right about this 'reinvention', you wouldn't necessarily have known it from Waits' Asylum debut *Closing Time* (1973). The fact that the Eagles could cover 'Ol' 55' on their third album *On the Border* was testament to the way producer Jerry Yester had managed to tone down the fifties jazz element in the man's songs. 'We were pulling against each other,' Waits said of his relationship with Yester. 'If he'd had his way he would have made it a more folk-based album, whereas I wanted to hear upright bass and muted trumpet.' Although Waits got his wish on tracks such as 'Virginia Avenue' and 'Ice Cream Man', as well as patenting his 'drunken schmaltz' style on 'Rosie' and 'Martha', there wasn't enough to distinguish *Closing Time* from the sound of his labelmates. (Never the most diplomatic of artists, Waits later said of the Eagles that 'they're about as exciting as watching paint dry,' adding, 'They don't have cowshit on their boots, just dogshit from Laurel Canyon . . .').

Enter Bones Howe, famous for producing the Association and the Fifth Dimension but a man with a solid grounding in the West Coast jazz of the late fifties. 'David Geffen called me one day and told me about Waits,' says Howe, seated in the plush Wilshire Boulevard office of his Windswept-Pacific production company. 'He said to me, "Waits has a lot of jazz and beat influences that didn't really come out on his first album," and he played me "Martha" and a couple of other things that sounded really unique.' Bones says Waits was 'the first artist I'd worked with who knew anything about the things *I* knew about,' and the empathy between the two men was readily apparent on *The Heart of Saturday Night* (1974). 'Most of our relationship was talk,' recalls Howe. 'Pre-production always took place in some dumpy restaurant, talking about songs and music and people. Then he'd go into a demo studio with lyrics strewn all over the floor, and the songs would come together. The first record we made together was probably the most "produced" album we did, partly because I wanted to take him out of the folk/singer-songwriter thing.'

With their arrangements written by Wrecking Crew stalwart Mike Melvoin, tracks such as 'Diamonds On My Windshield' and 'The Ghosts of Saturday Night' instantly severed any ties Waits might have felt to the pseudo-rustic California of the Eagles, reconnecting instead with the forties LA of Central Avenue and Raymond Chandler. This was Hollywood east of Highland, a *noir* counterpoint to the vapid affluence of mid-seventies Malibu, and it allowed Waits to hide behind a boho-hobo persona that he developed not only in his performances but in his increasingly notorious life as a resident of the Tropicana Motel.

Owned by former baseball star Sandy Koufax, the Tropicana at 8585 Santa Monica Boulevard had become a popular rock'n'roll haunt, thanks to the patronage of such wild-siders as Jim Morrison, Iggy Pop and Alice Cooper. 'When I moved into that place it was, like, nine dollars a night,' Waits said in 1985. 'But it became a kind of stage, and people came looking for me in the middle of the night. I think I really wanted to get lost in it all, so I did. When they painted the pool black, I finally said this has gone too far. It was a pretty heavy place at times.'*

Although he wrote many songs on the battered piano he installed in his bungalow, the Trop was the scene of major depravity, as shared with such drinking cronies as Chuck E. Weiss and Rickie Lee Jones, a runaway wild-child who'd blown into town in 1973 and become Waits' girlfriend. 'The first time I saw Rickie Lee, she reminded me of Jayne Mansfield,' Waits said, recalling the Troubadour 'Hoot Night' at which he first saw her sing. 'I thought she was *extremely* attractive, which is to say that my first reactions were rather primitive – *primeval*, even. Her style onstage was … sorta like that of a sexy white spade.' Within a year or so, both Waits and Jones were drinking fit to drown, Waits claiming that he 'learned a lot about women' by getting smashed with them. But pretty soon she was scaring him to death, dabbling in hard drugs and living a life he'd only ever flirted with. 'She's much older than me in terms of street wisdom,' he confessed. 'Sometimes she seems as ancient as dirt, and yet at other times she's so like a little girl.'

Waits carried his alcoholic/insomniac act to its logical culmination with the somewhat self-indulgent double-album *Nighthawks at the Diner* (1975), seventy minutes of small-hours trio jazz and gravelly Lord-Buckleyisms. The album was like an Edward Hopper painting come to life, confirming Waits' gifts as a writer but paling next to *Small Change* (1976), his first real masterpiece. Here was the same seedy milieu of strippers and Pepto-Bismol, but with the poetry anchored by gemlike arrangements. Recorded in five days in July 1976, *Small Change* achieved the balance between bop monologue routines ('Step Right Up', 'Small Change') and cornball melancholia ('Tom Traubert's Blues', 'I Wish I Was in New Orleans') which had been heard on *The Heart of Saturday Night*, but with a new and almost cinematic feel. 'What happened was that we talked about movies and underscoring and sort of moved away from the idea of *songs*,' says Bones Howe, who hired the veteran jazz drummer Shelly Manne to give the album an extra authenticity. 'We also did the whole thing live to two-

* Recalls writer/scenester Pleasant Gehman: 'The pool was black because it was all rusty from bands throwing lawn furniture in there.' For her, the 'Top Trop' (along with Duke's coffee shop next door) was the West Coast answer to New York's Chelsea Hotel.

track, after talking about how I'd cut jazz records in the fifties. It was just about creating a good climate for him in the studio.' This was Waits' most focused celebration of marginal society yet: Bukowskian lowlife seen through 'the bottom of a bottle of bargain Scotch' but observed with compassion and precision. *Small Change* laughed in the face of detractors and established him as a vital lone voice in the rock wilderness.

V

Tom Waits' studiedly sleazy life at the Tropicana was his way of dealing with the mythological baggage of Hollywood Babylon – a Beat version of the rock'n'roll debauchery occurring nightly on and around the Sunset Strip. By the spring of 1977, the LA scene had reached its moral nadir, one symbolized by the arrest of Roman Polanski on a charge of unlawful sex with a 13-year-old girl in a house belonging to Jack Nicholson. As money poured in from worldwide sales of albums by Peter Frampton, Rod Stewart, the Eagles and Fleetwood Mac – whose *Rumours*, that AOR 'soap opera' about the group's tangled relationships, spent a stupendous thirty-one weeks at No. 1 – the record business went boom-crazy. 'There Oughta Be a Law Against Sunny Southern California', Texan songwriter Terry Allen had protested in a 1975 song, but the antipathy of outsiders couldn't halt the apparently limitless growth. Even at Warner Brothers, bastion of taste through the early and mid seventies, the sheer scale of the success seemed to turn even the most sober heads. 'There was something rotten in the state of Denmark,' says Van Dyke Parks, whose *Clang of the*

An Anglo-Californian alliance: Fleetwood Mac. Left to right: Lindsey Buckingham, Mick Fleetwood, Stevie Nicks, Christine McVie, John McVie.

Yankee Reaper (1975) had sold as unspectacularly as his previous albums. 'I knew that I didn't understand what was happening to music and didn't understand arena rock, so I got out of the studio and into the office.' According to Frank Zappa, whose Discreet label was still being distributed by Warners, 'the company was probably more infested with white powder than just about any other in the business.'

At Elektra-Asylum, too, genuine love for music seemed to have been superseded by avarice and naked ambition. 'I was the only person I could find in the company who actually gave a shit about music,' says Art Fein, who worked in the publicity department in 1977. 'I thought the first Zevon album was the greatest thing in the world, but I felt like a fool talking about it. Most of the guys working there just wanted to smoke dope or talk about football. The last straw was at the company convention, when I said I didn't *want* to have my cock sucked by Donna in Room 103.'

Of all the companies Fein could have picked to move to, he chose Casablanca, where the drug consumption was even more out of control. With the label firing on all cylinders by 1977 – it had merged with Peter Guber's film company the year before – Neil Bogart sold 50 per cent of Casablanca to PolyGram for $10 million and moved his offices to the 8200 block of Sunset Boulevard. From thereon in it was sheer cocaine madness. For promo head Danny Davis, who'd survived the experience of working with Phil Spector and Don Kirshner, Casablanca took the biscuit: he later described the coke-crazed Bogart as a cross between Mike Todd and P. T. Barnum. The spirit of the company was perfectly encapsulated by 'Sunset People', the creepily robotic closing track on Donna Summer's platinum-selling *Bad Girls* (1979): 'Rainbow girl, Whisky man/Spotting every star they can on Sunset, on Sunset...'

Bogart even wrote the original story for the appalling *Thank God It's Friday* (1978), an attempt to repeat the mega-success of *Saturday Night Fever*. The film performed respectably at the box office, helping to put PolyGram up there with the giants, but behind the scenes at Casablanca things were beginning to look pretty rocky. At one point, there were no fewer than a hundred acts contracted to the label, most of them thoroughly disposable disco entities. Even when the inevitable crash came in 1979, Bogart refused to believe the company was in trouble. His way of allaying the fears of PolyGram executives was to put them in Mercedes convertibles and spoon-feed them cocaine. Having lost them millions, he was finally forced out the following year.

At the end of 1977, Linda Ronstadt was at No. 1 for five weeks with *Simple Dreams*, in her own words 'a great statement about California music' that featured not only the Top 5 singles 'Blue Bayou' and 'It's So Easy' but two songs ('Carmelita' and 'Poor, Poor Pitiful Me') from the first Warren Zevon album. Even Randy Newman was getting in on the act, scoring with the huge hit 'Short People' and with *Little Criminals*, an album once again featuring the Eagles on backing vocals. 'I want Shea Stadium!' Newman had shouted self-mockingly during his *Good Old Boys* tour in 1974. Now that he almost had it – at the cost of the controversy whipped up by the 'sizeist' 'Short People' – he claimed he'd have preferred 'quiet money'. 'Randy was one of the funniest people you've ever met in your life,' says Russ Titelman, who was once again co-producing Newman with Lenny Waronker. 'We had so much fun working with him. He was also one of the only singer-songwriters who could write in that style for a big orchestra. He had complete command, in spite of what he thought of himself.'

The Eagles themselves, by their own admission, were 'running out of gas artistically': all the Lear jets and Lafite-Rothschild in the world couldn't make up for the three years of fear and loathing which went into *The Long Run* (1979). (In the meantime, Joe Walsh put his seal on the whole era with 'Life's Been Good', a kind of 'Life in the Fast Lane' Part 2 which made the Top 20 in the summer of 1978.) Although the album stayed at No. 1 for nine weeks and produced three Top 10 singles, it was scant consolation for a band who already had money oozing from every pore and who were now obliged to sit down together again to work on *Eagles Live*. 'As Henley and Frey and the others were getting further and further apart personally,' recalled Elektra-Asylum chief Joe Smith, 'the thought of having to spend more time in an editing room, and maybe even come up with a new song or two, scared them to the point where they were now on the fence about the project.' By the time *Eagles Live* appeared in late 1980, moreover, that rock-god-with-a-conscience Don Henley had been busted in the company of a stoned, naked 16-year-old girl. He was subsequently charged with possessing cocaine, quaaludes and marijuana and contributing to the delinquency of a minor.

Henley got off lightly: a $2,500 fine with two years' probation. Other revellers were less fortunate. Those LA party animals Keith Moon and John Bonham shuffled off their coils after battling booze with Antabuse, while Lowell George keeled over from a coke-induced heart attack the day after performing a Washington DC date on his solo tour in June 1979. Meanwhile, David Crosby sank ever deeper into freebase hell and John Phillips nearly lost his foot to gangrene after repeatedly shooting opiates into it.

It was down to Steely Dan, those other clients of Irving Azoff's formidable Front Line management firm, to sum up the late seventies with their 1980 masterpiece *Gaucho*, its release delayed by legal wranglings with MCA. Becker and Fagen had been in the Top 40 for fifty-one weeks with *Aja*, but now they stood back from the party to dissect the airbrushed world of the Malibu elite in songs like 'Babylon Sisters', 'Glamour Profession', and 'Time Out of Mind'. 'We'll jog with show folk on the sand/Drink kirschwasser from a shell,' Fagen sang on 'Babylon Sisters', while on the withering 'Glamour Profession' he was a coke dealer with 'the LA concession'. That the duo managed to do this while making music intoxicating in its clinical slickness was no mean feat. Sadly, *Gaucho* – a platinum-selling album in early 1981 – marked the end of the decade's most brilliant partnership. 'Writing songs kept us entertained,' reflected Walter Becker later, 'but after a while we became like any married couple. Things built to a head and we had to cool it.'

For his part, Donald Fagen wondered whether the rest of the world might not have finally caught up with the Dan's 'high irony'. No wonder he chose instead to explore the friendlier autobiographical themes of his 1982 solo album *The Nightfly*.

Looking East along Hollywood Boulevard.

8 *The Decline of the West*

I had an interesting experience concerning ageing in Hollywood. A friend of mine and I went to this Beverly Hills party ... and sitting at the table next to us was this kind of last supper of the old Hollywood. They were drinking toasts to Marilyn Monroe, and there were lots of stories flying around about celebrities and people they'd known ... I looked around and thought, 'Is this the way that we must go in this town? Is our hippie philosophy going to surrender to *this*?'

                                                        Joni Mitchell, 1979

You want me to be mellow,
It's just another word for yellow.
You say you want a peaceful boy,
Well, I just wanna destroy...

                                                        The Dils, 1977

I

By the end of 1976, the year of *Hotel California* and *The Pretender* (and *Warren Zevon* and *Small Change*), teen scenesters who a year before had loitered outside the Rainbow or the Hyatt or the Chateau Marmont in hopes of glimpsing Led Zeppelin were instead turning to the new punk rock winging its way over to LA from London and New York.

Fittingly enough, it was Rodney Bingenheimer who in August 1976 began his career as a DJ spinning punk 45s on a tiny radio station called KROQ. 'I was always anti-Eagles, anti-beards,' he says. 'Within a few months I was playing four solid hours of punk.' Fittingly, too, it was Rodney's long-time partner-in-crime Kim Fowley who helped orchestrate the first stirrings of a homegrown punk sound by following up the Hollywood Stars débâcle with an all-girl group he dubbed the Runaways. If Fowley's claims that the girls 'single-handedly relit the Hollywood firmament' now seem a mite far-fetched, there are veterans of the fallout from the English Disco scene who will vouch for the proto-punk power of the original Joan Jett/Sandy West/Mickie Steele trio.

'A lot of the old glitter-rock crowd had gone disco after Rodney's closed,' says Kid Congo Powers. 'Apart from Sparks and a couple of other bands it was sort of limbo time for a while. I wasn't real thrilled

'They look better than the Shangri-Las, and you wanna be the first on your block to start dropping their name': The Runaways, with Kim Fowley (centre, with T-shirt) and Mercury executives Scott Anderson and Denny Rosencrantz.

by the Hollywood Stars, but a bit later I saw the first ever gig by the Runaways – in Phast Phreddie Patterson's living room – and it was *really* exciting.' Pat Smear, guitarist with seminal Hollywood punks the Germs (now with Dave Grohl's Foo Fighters) says the Runaways 'primed kids for punk, even if people don't want to admit it now'.

The Runaways was the perfect name for this jailbait combo, a typically Fowleyan tribute to the endless female strays who annually poured into Hollywood in pursuit of love and fame. Fronted by the androgynous Joan Jett, they were a street-sleaze affront to every laid-back canyon cowboy on the Strip, and the logical end-product of the Rodney's trash aesthetic. 'They're building up a following in beach towns like Huntingdon and Newport Beaches, just like Dick Dale and the Beach Boys did fifteen years ago,' Fowley yelled down a transatlantic line to *Zigzag* magazine. 'They look better than the Shangri-Las, and you wanna be the first on your block to start dropping their name. I'm sending out the photos and the stories of how they came out of the gutters of California. This one is going to turn me into the Brian Epstein/Colonel Tom Parker that my enemies have always been terrified I'd become.'

It didn't turn Fowley into any such thing, but it did kickstart the live scene back into some semblance of life, and in the process gave him the kind of clout in LA for which he'd always longed. 'Everyone loved the idea of 16-year-old girls playing guitars and singing about fucking,' he says. 'I was very powerful.' In addition to producing four Mercury albums by an expanded Runaways lineup fronted by the peroxide-blonde bombshell that was Cherie Curie, Fowley masterminded several other 'punk'/power pop scams, including Venus and the Razorblades' *Songs from the Sunshine Jungle* (1977), Stephen T's *West Coast Confidential* (1978) and his own *Sunset Boulevard* (1978), all of them rooted in the man's vision of himself as the ultimate Hollywood pop hustler.

'There was a real cusp here,' says Rick Gershon, who later ran fan clubs for the Plimsouls and the Long Ryders. 'A lot of this music was on the fringe of the glam thing and simultaneously on the fringe of punk. Rodney opened a club called the Cabaret in a hotel just off the 405 freeway near Westwood, and that was where he and Fowley started introducing their local discoveries. These shows were the real coming-of-age for a lot of people, me included, despite the fact that Fowley was marketing these obviously hand-picked acts as organic punk bands.'

'Kim Fowley wasn't as important as he'd like to think, but he was around a lot because he was an older person with money,' says writer/scenester Pleasant Gehman. 'He and Rodney would come to the Sugar Shack in North Hollywood, which was a kind of missing link between the English Disco days and the punk scene. The Shack would play T-Rex and the *Rocky Horror* soundtrack, and that was where Kim met Cherie Curie and Vickie Arnold of the Razorblades.'

Fortunately, perhaps, the rebirth of the live scene in and around Hollywood didn't hinge entirely on the scams and hustles of Kim Fowley. Equally important in providing alternatives to cheesecloth country rock and meat'n'potatoes boogie was a loose coalition of bands known as 'Radio Free Hollywood', whose prime movers – the Pop!, the Dogs and the early Motels – were each in their different ways militating against the AOR/disco mainstream. The Pop! were a sort of power-pop Faces/Raspberries hybrid, the Dogs a Stooges-influenced trio from Detroit, and the Motels a dark art-rock band fronted by the charismatic Martha Davis. Booking shows at venues such as the Troupers' Hall on north La Brea and printing their own newsletter, the 'Radio Free Hollywood' triumvirate opened doors for bands as seemingly incompatible as the Quick, Van Halen and Tom Petty and the Heartbreakers.

Contemporaneous with the Radio Free Hollywood shows in 1975–6 was the appearance of fanzines such as Phast Phreddie Patterson's *Back Door Man*, which established a canon of anti-mainstream heroes and championed hard-rock/metal of the Aerosmith/Blue Oyster Cult variety. '*Back Door Man* had a very in-your-face, opinionated attitude about these bands,' says Gary Stewart of Rhino Records, 'and it espoused the values of their records over the wimpy, bland, singer-songwriter crowd. That was the magazine which got me to go out and buy the first Runaways album, and it also promoted a lot of the Radio Free Hollywood bands. Along with *Bomp* and *Phonograph Record*, Phast Phreddie and others helped to set the scene for *a music that wasn't popular*, and for the bands who would follow. They were advocating neo-sainthood status for the Stooges and the MC5, and at the same time praising all those bands Lenny Kaye had immortalized on *Nuggets*.'

For Stewart, the final piece of the pre-punk jigsaw was Rodney's Sunday night show on KROQ, on which the diminutive scenester played records by bands from London and New York, and by 'anybody brave or stupid enough to put out a record in Los Angeles'. With 'Rodney on the Roq', as the show came to be dubbed, the nascent LA scene had a print outlet, a live venue outlet and a radio outlet. 'The scene was set for something to happen, and so it did,' says Stewart. 'It all came together around the end of the summer of '76.'

Some date the official birth of the LA punk scene from a Flamin'

LA's very own Sid Vicious: Darby Crash of the Germs.

Groovies/Ramones show at the Roxy that August – a seminal double bill that also came to London's Roundhouse. No one in Hollywood had seen anything like the Ramones, unless it was the shows Iggy and the Stooges had played back in 1974. 'I wasn't a punk fan, but I couldn't believe how great the Ramones were,' says Art Fein. 'I went round to all the journalists before the Groovies came on, and I could tell they didn't know what to think yet. They didn't know whether it was right to like it.'

If ageing journalists weren't prepared to commit themselves, the younger veterans of the English Disco scene seized on to punk as a lifesaver. 'We'd hang out at the Licorice Pizza record store near Uni High and read *NME*,' recalls Pat Smear. 'There was no real ideological programme yet. No one even had an electric guitar.' Rick Gershon concurs with this: 'Although people were doing their homework and reading their *NME*s, clearly it wasn't representative of any sort of economic or political situation in LA. But once they'd grasped the attitude and the aesthetic, a truly organic scene could develop with bands who weren't looking over their shoulders to England.'

In this sense, the really decisive event occurred the following April, when the Damned came to town to play hard-rock stronghold the Starwood and then attended a show at the tiny Orpheum Theater on Sunset that co-organizer Peter Case had dubbed 'Punk Rock Invasion'. Headlined by manic art-terrorists the Weirdos, the 'invasion' bill was made up by the Dils, who played angry agitpop anthems in front of a hammer-and-sickle flag, and by four babyfaced Latinos from San Diego called the Zeros. But it was the Germs, making their chaotic debut appearance, who came closest to the punk spirit of supreme incompetence: although they'd formed a few months earlier (as Sophistifuck and the Revlon Spam Queens, featuring a pubescent Belinda Carlisle), the band as yet had no songs to their name, and scant musical ability. Their short set, instantly greeted by howls and jeers, climaxed with singer Bobby Pyn being smothered in an Iggy-esque blend of peanut butter and licorice whips.

It was the Germs who managed to record the first real LA punk single, a droning, self-deconstructive song recorded on a Radio Shack tape recorder in Pat Smear's garage in June 1977. Released on Chris Ashford's shoestring What? label, 'Forming' presaged a flood which included the vinyl debuts of the Dils ('I Hate the Rich'), the Weirdos (the *Destroy All Music* EP), and the Zeros ('Don't Push Me Around'), the latter pair issued on Greg Shaw's fast-off-the-mark Bomp label. 'LA punk made perfect sense to me,' says Shaw today, reclining in his self-styled 'hippie pad' in Silverlake. 'I think it was a more authentic expression of the real intrinsic spirit of Hollywood than English punk was of England. LA has always been phoney and self-deprecating and goofy and cartoonish and pop-culture-obsessive, and that's what you got with the Germs and the Weirdos.'

When the Germs' Bobby Pyn changed his *nom de Punk* to Darby Crash,

Art-terrorists the Weirdos at the Whisky a Go Go, August 1977.

he became LA's very own Sid Vicious, a dysfunctional Hollywood hooligan chasing a fantasy of Iggy-style self-destruction. 'I always hated the Germs, yet at the same time it was a perfect commentary on LA,' recalled rock writer and Angry Samoans guitarist Gregg Turner. 'Here was some guy who was just regurgitating Bowie and every single rock-star move, and yet it was grotesque and funny.'

Like Sid Vicious, Darby Crash quickly earned the Germs the kind of notoriety that was essential in punk circles, even if it was infused with the contempt felt by observers such as Gregg Turner. The most telling myth surrounding Darby was that of his rich-kid origins, frequently cited by detractors of LA punk. 'We were poor scumbags surrounded by obscenely rich Bel Air kids at Uni High,' says Pat Smear in an effort to set the record straight. 'Darby's mom was raising him alone and working a twelve-hour day.' This information would have made little difference to the likes of *Rolling Stone*'s Ken Tucker, who wrote that 'in the land of sun and money' punk rock merely provided 'the latest excuse to get drunk and wrap the family Merc around a tree on the weekend'. When Kim Fowley staged a 'New Wave Rock'n'Roll' weekend at the Whisky a Go Go in June 1977, Darby and his disciples instigated an *Animal House*-style food-fight riot which almost had them banned from the club. Bannings soon became routine on the Hollywood live circuit, in any case: the Weirdos managed to get punk/new wave acts nixed from the Starwood after setting fire to the American flag on the fourth of July, and the Troubadour closed its doors to punk when fans of the Bags overturned tables in a mini-riot.

The one real refuge for punk was a subterranean establishment in the X-rated heart of Hollywood called the Masque, opened by Scottish-born Angeleno Brendan Mullen in July 1977. For six months, the club served as a nerve-centre for the LA punk scene, providing a venue for such key local bands as the Germs, the Weirdos, the Dils, the Screamers, the Zeros, the Plugz, the Nerves, the Alley Cats and the Bags. 'The Masque was like a funeral and a celebration all at once,' says John Denny of the Weirdos. 'The funeral was for the death of rock music as we knew it, the celebratory aspect for the dawning of a new era.'

By the end of the summer the LA scene was a reality, whether sniffy outsiders liked it or not. 'LA punk was initially an imitative scene,' says Gary Stewart, who was selling all the latest punk releases at Rhino, 'but that doesn't mean it was shallow or that there weren't any good records. Obviously this was a very different environment from London or New York, but people here were craving exciting, angry music and weren't getting it from what they were hearing on the radio. Some of them were people from unhappy suburban families, some were runaways from middle America, and none of them was living the California dream. So I think the charges of LA punk being a pose were unfair.'

Aside from the Masque, the major congregation-point for the Hollywood punk scene was a record collectors' 'swap-meet' held on the first Saturday night/Sunday morning of every month in the parking-lot of Capitol Records. Recalled by former record dealer Jeff Gold as 'an all-night version of the Portobello Market in London', the swap-meet was where every self-respecting punk in LA turned up to mingle with fellow pop deviants and buy singles on What?, Bomp and Dangerhouse. Also on sale at the swap-meet were a multitude of new fanzines, most auspiciously *Slash* and *Search & Destroy*. *Slash* in particular reflected the interest in punk of an older, artier crowd: downtown neo-bohemians who dug the quasi-situationist theatre and iconography of the Weirdos and a Suicide-esque synth/drums trio the Screamers. Founded by Steve Samiof in May 1977, *Slash*'s stance was typified by the writing of French reggae fanatic Claude Bessy (a.k.a. Kickboy Face) and by the drawings of the Texan illustrator Gary Panter. 'If there was a single icon of Los Angeles punk, it was the screaming head that Gary Panter designed for the Screamers,' says *Simpsons* creator Matt Groening, who moved to LA from Oregon in the middle of the punk summer of '77. 'I've seen that head copied and stolen and mutated thousands of times.' (Equally iconic was Panter's punk cartoon hero Jimbo, a regular feature of *Slash*.)

Slash benefit gigs at the Larchmont and Baces Halls were vital punk events in late 1977, as were shows booked at the Whisky by Kim Fowley protégée Michelle Myer and at the Chinatown restaurant Madame Wong's by jewellery designer Paul Greenstein. 'Suddenly there was a scene, and it was becoming really big,' says Kid Congo. 'The Screamers, for instance, were huge, as well as being wild and original and mysterious. They could easily sell out three nights at the Whisky, and yet they never made a record.' For ageing gonzo Richard Meltzer, author of *Gulcher* and *The Aesthetics Of Rock*, bands such as the Screamers were helping to turn his adopted hometown into a place which 'came as close to being a fertile musical oasis as any [shithole] I've stumbled over'. Meltzer even had his own punk aggregation in the form of the short-lived Vom, featuring Gregg Turner and other soon-to-be Angry Samoans. 'All told,' he concluded in *LA is the Capital of Kansas* (1988), '[LA punk] was arguably the most *specifically* anti-totalitarian US rock-roll ever, and the one true Southern Cal "underground music" after Central Avenue bebop of the forties.'

The Screamers outside Gower Gulch, at the corner of Sunset and Gower. Left to right: David Brown, KK, Tomato du Plenty, Tommy Gear, and friend.

Not even the closure by the LAPD of the Masque, after an uproarious Bags show in December, made any appreciable difference to the continuing growth of the scene. The Masque was itself back in action in February 1978, after a series of benefit gigs was staged with the help of *Slash* magazine's Bob Biggs. *Slash* had now joined the ranks of Bomp and Dangerhouse by forming a label which in May 1978 released an excellent Germs EP featuring 'Circle One', 'No God', and the Ramones-meet-the-Pistols blitzkrieg 'Lexicon Devil'.

Besides the Germs, whose followers sported the band's blue circle logo on armbands and burned their wrists with cigarettes, Masque favourites included Mexican trio the Plugz, Valley goofsters the Dickies and a crop of 'second wave' miscreants such as the Deadbeats, the Eyes, the Controllers, the Skulls and house band Arthur J. and the Gold Cups. (The latter named themselves after a pair of singularly unsavoury Hollywood hangouts, both home to punk runaways and hustlers. 'Arthur J. and the Gold Cups were part of a really heavy street scene,' says Kid Congo Powers. 'It was kids off the bus and drag-queen junkies on roller skates.') Like the Zeros, the Plugz injected some long-overdue Mexican rage into what was still predominantly a white scene, particularly with their vicious version of Ritchie Valens' 'La Bamba'. Other classic 45s from this period included the Deadbeats' 'Kill the Hippies', the Weirdos' 'We Got the

Neutron Bomb', X's 'Adult Books'/'We're Desperate', and the Alley Cats'
'Nothing Means Anything Anymore'.

'I'd go see bands like the Alley Cats and realize they had no reverence
whatever for the great rock bands,' says Jeff Gold, who worked at Rhino
Records. 'It was as if they'd come full-born out of nowhere and were
making this really compelling music. There was a lot of activity around
LA at this time, a real DIY ethic and aesthetic that anybody could make
a record or promote a show. At Rhino we would literally take *any* record
on consignment. Every record had distribution, and KROQ would play
a lot of them. The scene was about young kids not making a lot of money
but having a lot of fun. Nobody really thought about not getting paid by
distributors or about being steamrollered: you just did it.'

The Masque punk scene even gave birth to its very own Chelsea Hotel,
in the shape of a gone-to-seed apartment building called the Canterbury
Arms. Living alongside every conceivable species of Hollywood lowlife
from pimps to bikers to junkies, members of the Germs, the Bags, the
Screamers, the Weirdos and the early Go-Gos cohabited in near-harmony.
'The Canterbury Arms was just down the road from the Masque,' says
Kid Congo. '90 per cent of it was punk rockers, and it was a real central
point for all the bands and scenesters. The Go-Gos learned to play their
instruments in the basement.'

Kid Congo was himself just one of the innumerable scenesters who
hung around the Masque and the Canterbury Arms in the same way they'd
hung around Rodney's English Discotheque. By the summer of 1978, the
punk scene had become almost as incestuous as its forebear, with an
oddly McCarthyite paranoia about who was a 'real' punk and who was
just a poseur. 'Many punks had come from social situations where they
had been the outsiders,' wrote Craig Lee of the Bags. 'Having escaped
suburbia . . . they now had their own group from which they could sneer
and deliver visual jolts to the unimaginative, dumb, suburban world.' At
the top of the social hierarchy were the fearsome harpies known as 'The
Plungers', who included Trixie, Trudie, Mary Rat and the wonderfully
named Hellin Killer. Also on the scene were Brit-in-LA Robbie Fields,
owner of the new Posh Boy label, and Pleasant Gehman, whose gossipy
Lobotomy fanzine read like an old issue of *Tiger Beat* with a safety pin
through its nose.

But as it had worn off in 1967 and 1974, so the LA magic began to
wear off towards the end of 1978. Not only was the punk in-crowd
becoming oppressively cliquish, but the Canterbury Arms was soon
suffering the fate which had befallen Haight-Ashbury during the Summer
of Love: girls were raped, fights broke out between punks and bikers, and
harder drugs began to take their toll on the scene. On the musical front
alone, the spirit of camaraderie was gradually fading. The Dickies were
deemed to have 'sold out' by signing to A&M, and a schism of sorts
opened up between punk and its powerpop/'new wave' cousin, as

represented by bands such as the Quick, the Nerves and the Blondie-esque Needles and Pins. Greg Shaw shifted the focus of Bomp (and its Voxx subsidiary) from punk to powerpop and neo-psychedelia, while Esther Wong fired Paul Greenstein and opted to hire bands like the Pop!, 20/20, Code Blue and the Knack. In August 1978, finally, Michelle Myer lost her job as the booker at the Whisky. The bad vibes seemed to culminate in the riot which took place at the Elks Lodge Hall in March 1979, when the LAPD broke up a show by the Alley Cats, the Zeros, the Plugz and the Go-Gos. Thereafter, punk and violence seemed almost inseparable, particularly with the rise of a hardcore punk scene in the beach towns of Orange County.

II

By the time of the Elks Lodge riot, of course, punk had already scared the hell out of the mainstream rock establishment. This was particularly the case in Los Angeles, which had been singled out as a bastion of bloated, out-of-touch superstardom. Predictably, the industry had been slow to take punk (or 'new wave') seriously, so radically uncommercial did it sound to their ears. 'The majors perceived no real threat from punk because their insularity was the same as that of movie companies or TV companies,' says Art Fein. 'I remember this guy at Columbia telling me they'd done some projections and calculated that nothing was going to change for five years. He pointed to this graph and said, "Look, the line is flat"!'*

The artists themselves were less happy about being branded as Old Farts by the new insurgents. Several of them, including Neil Young and Joni Mitchell, had taken part in The Band's 'Last Waltz' concert in November 1976 – a farewell jamboree which looked suspiciously like a kind of 'last supper' of seventies rock'n'roll. (Dave Marsh described The Band and their stellar guests as 'a gang of aesthetic bankrupts trying to hide from a world where there's no future for them'.) Now Neil Young, for one, was sitting up and pondering the implications of punk rock – its anger and its energizing spirit. 'The punk thing is so good and healthy, because the people aren't taking themselves seriously,' he said. 'People like Devo make fun of the established rock scene, and they're much more vital to my ears than what's been happening in the last four or five years.'

* One of the biggest hits to come out of Los Angeles in 1978, Ambrosia's insipid 'How Much I Feel', was taken from an album called *Life Beyond LA*! But it said a great deal about the LA scene that when Hollywood got around to making a movie about an LA radio station refusing to submit to commercial pressures – John Alonzo's *FM* (1978) – the soundtrack was made up entirely of AOR acts. *FM* even featured live appearances by Jimmy Buffett, REO Speedwagon and Linda Ronstadt, whose show in the film was hijacked from a rival station. Only Steely Dan, with their sly theme song, understood the irony of this FM rock being presented as in any way countercultural.

It was Devo, a band enthusiastically embraced by the LA punk scene, who gave Young the 'Rust Never Sleeps' slogan for the title of his 1979 album, and even made a fleeting appearance in his 1979 film of the same name. 'I can relate to "Rust Never Sleeps", you know,' he said. 'The longer I keep on going, the more I have to fight this corrosion.' *Rust Never Sleeps*, divided between acoustic and electric sides, showed that the restless Canadian was clearly winning his war. Opening the solo acoustic side with 'My My, Hey Hey (Out of the Blue)', Young declared that rock'n'roll was here to stay, that although Elvis was gone his spirit lived on in the nihilistic rage of Johnny Rotten. 'Thrasher' was his condemnation of dinosaurs like Crosby, Stills and Nash, 'poisoned with protection' in their 'crystal canyons' but unable to avoid the thrashers of punk rock. 'Pocahontas' and 'Powderfinger' returned the listener to the historical rage of *Zuma*'s 'Cortez the Killer', but 'Sedan Delivery' was punk in all but name, and the closing 'Hey Hey, My My (Into the Black)' was a frenzied, squalling reprise of the album's opener, a defiant refusal of the temptation to rust and 'fade away'.* Reaching No. 7 on the *Billboard* album chart in July 1979, *Rust Never Sleeps* turned out to be Young's best-selling album since *Harvest*.

Young's fellow 'dinosaurs' greeted the dawn of punk with a predictable blend of fear and loathing. Huddled together at Lucy's El Adobe restaurant on Melrose Avenue, the old Asylum gang tried to figure out how to weather the storm. Linda Ronstadt, for example, covered Elvis Costello's 'Alison' on *Living in the USA* (1978), then set about recording a whole 'new wave' album, *Mad Love*, with the help of an outfit called the Cretones. Art Fein says he remembers seeing Ronstadt sitting up in the balcony taking notes during a Clash show at the Palladium. 'It was strange when you heard something you really liked, knowing that these people *hated* you,' says Ronstadt's producer Peter Asher. 'When Costello said Linda's version of "Alison" was the worst thing he'd ever heard in his life, Linda and I both understood that *of course* he had to say that. I've met him since and he was completely charming.' Richard Meltzer savaged *Mad Love*, calling it 'even more corrupt, gawky and anachronistic than such regional stalwarts of sixties-revisionist New Wave as the Pop!, Naughty Sweeties, and 20/20...'

Other Asylum artists fared better in the hands of the critics. Warren Zevon followed up his remarkable debut with *Excitable Boy* (1978), which went gold and even produced a hit single in the ever-popular 'Werewolves of London'. The bespectacled Zevon at least looked the part of the new wave singer-songwriter, as well as possessing lyrical gifts to rival those of Elvis Costello. But he was also wrestling with a very old-fashioned booze problem, one which put him out of action for the best part of two years.

* The phrase took on a certain notoriety when Kurt Cobain used it to conclude his suicide note. Young, appalled by this misapplication, went on to write 'Sleeps with Angels' (1994) about Cobain.

Meanwhile, his mentor Jackson Browne took time out to organize events such as the Madison Square Garden 'No Nukes' extravaganza before re-emerging with *Hold Out*, a No. 1 album in July 1980. Alongside its love songs about Browne's new love, Lynne Sweeney, *Hold Out* featured the epic 'Disco Apocalypse', the moving 'Of Missing Persons' (a tribute to such deceased pals as Lowell George), and a song about Hollywood street life called 'Boulevard'.

Punk left Tom Waits stranded between the new music and the AOR mainstream, not ready to embrace the Masque scene but no longer content with the cosy cultishness of his lot on Asylum. Art Fein, who often hung out with Waits and Chuck E. Weiss in 1977, remembers a well-lubricated Waits getting into a fight over punk rock, 'saying it was all shit'. Yet three years later Waits was telling *NME*'s Kristine McKenna that Asylum 'liked dropping my name in terms of me being a "prestige" artist, but ... they didn't invest a whole lot in me in terms of faith, because their identity was always more aligned with that California rock thing'. Although *Foreign Affairs* (1977) had its share of Waits classics ('Potter's Field', 'Burma Shave'), the album suggested that he was stuck in something of a stylistic rut.

'You get to the point where you can kind of nail the things you hear and see together in a package and call it your own,' Waits told me in 1985. 'I think for a while I had a romance with Tin Pan Alley and that type of thing, and it was actually rather rigid for me, because you write a certain kind of song at the piano. The piano brings you indoors immediately, so those types of song were all a different shade of the same colour.' If Waits took his Ellington/Johnny Mercer obsessions to the limit with his sublime soundtrack to Francis Ford Coppola's atrocious *One from the Heart*, he jolted himself out of Tin Pan Alley with *Blue Valentine* (1978) and *Heartattack and Vine* (1980), albums written for the most part on the guitar. Going one better than *Blue Valentine*'s 'Sweet Little Bullet from a Pretty Blue Gun', 'Heartattack and Vine' was a savage sermonette about Tinseltown's broken dreamers, sounding for all the world like vintage Howlin' Wolf: 'Better off in Iowa against your scrambled eggs/Than crawling down Cahuenga on a broken pair of legs ...' Not long after the album was released, he not only quit Herb Cohen but abandoned Los Angeles itself. Three years later, having signed to Island Records, a totally new Tom Waits would emerge in New York with the brilliant *Swordfishtrombones*.

It took Waits' old flame Rickie Lee Jones (pictured with him on the cover of *Blue Valentine*) to taste the success — at least fleetingly — that he should himself have enjoyed. When Jones recorded a four-song demo for A&M in 1978, her manager took a tape over to Warners, whose interest in her grew after Lenny Waronker and Teddy Templeman learned that Lowell George was planning to cut one of the songs ('Easy Money') on his solo album *Thanks, I'll Eat It Here*. 'Rickie Lee was fairly wild, but you

Rickie Lee Jones at the Grammy awards ceremony in 1980.

knew you were in the presence of something special,' says Russ Titelman, who co-produced her 1979 debut album with Waronker. 'The sessions were spontaneous, explosive: she'd never done this before, she was just a kid with a guitar, but she knew exactly what she wanted. At the end of the session, we played through the album and she sat there and asked, "Is that *me*?" '

It was a valid question, actually, because between them Waronker and Titelman had managed to turn Jones into a kind of beatnik hybrid of Lowell George, Van Morrison, Tin Pan Alley Waits and multi-tracked Joni Mitchell: a Warner Brothers composite, in essence. And when 'Chuck E.'s in Love', Rickie Lee's funky homage to her Tropicana pal Chuck E. Weiss, made it into the Top 5 in May 1979, their approach seemed to have been vindicated. As with Waits, however, Jones received a hefty amount of flak for what were assumed to be her boho affectations, flak which detracted from the power of songs such as 'Company' and the gorgeous 'On Saturday Afternoons in 1963'. It didn't help that the headstrong creature proceeded to diss all the queen bees of the canyon aristocracy, lambasting Joni Mitchell's jazz pretensions and contrasting them with the fact that she and Waits were actually 'living on the jazz side of life'. ('I prefer the nighttime to daytime,' she said of the life she and Waits were still leading in their dilapidated Tropicana apartment. '*You* fill in the darkness, and LA is very quiet and empty at night.') Nor could it have been said that Jones was exactly cut out for the overnight success of 'Chuck E.'s in Love': at most, all she'd ever dreamed about was the cult acclaim accorded Waits. Although she followed *Rickie Lee Jones* with the marvellous *Pirates* (1981), a journey through her troubled childhood, she never again had a hit single, and her career was soon blighted by drug problems.

If Warners lucked out – at least temporarily – with Rickie Lee Jones, they had a harder job to do with such established artists as Randy Newman and Ry Cooder. Mo Ostin must have smiled when the word went out that his old friend Joe Smith at Elektra-Asylum was holding a contest for his promo men on the sales of Joni Mitchell's *Mingus*. 'First prize is they get to keep their jobs,' Smith joked, but it was a joke which made some people wince. The fact was that the record industry had crashed from the giddy heights of its success with the Framptons and Fleetwood Macs, and people were losing their jobs left, right and centre. It was becoming increasingly hard, therefore, to justify the presence of 'prestige artists' on already overloaded rosters. When Elektra-Asylum moved from their famous building on North La Cienega to new offices on Sunset, it seemed to many to mark a symbolic end to the seventies. Already home to Queen and the Cars, Elektra would now become associated with acts such as the Cure, Mötley Crüe and Tracy Chapman.

Even Ry Cooder, whose arcane musical pursuits had reached their high-water mark with *Jazz* (1977), was obliged to make a bid for the big time with the good-humoured, Little Feat-esque *Bop Till You Drop* (1979), trumpeted as 'rock's first all-digital recording' and featuring 'Down in Hollywood', Cooder's very own funked-up tribute to Tinseltown street life. The bid didn't work, but Cooder cleaned up on the live circuit. He also began to make a rather good living in the soundtrack business, in the employ initially of Walter Hill (*The Long Riders*, *Southern Comfort*) and then of Wim Wenders (*Paris, Texas*) and Louis Malle (*Alamo Bay*).

Randy Newman's decision to write movie soundtracks (following in his uncles' footsteps) roughly paralleled that of Cooder, who'd worked with him a decade earlier on *Performance*. Not that Randy didn't try to follow up the success of 'Short People' and *Little Criminals*: *Born Again* (1979) was his most outrageously misanthropic record to date, replete with such black-humoured songs as 'It's Money That I Love', 'Mr Sheep', 'Half a Man' and a hysterically funny 'tribute' to the Electric Light Orchestra called 'The Story of a Rock'n'Roll Band'. Newman himself called it 'a nihilistic, no-human-feeling album ... a comedy record', but the comedy was fiendishly acute. 'The idea was that I'd had some success and been born again as this monstrous, money-grubbing rock'n'roll person,' he said of the album cover, which depicted him in Kiss-style makeup with dollar signs for eyes.

The biggest Warner Brothers act of 1977, Fleetwood Mac, faced a rather harder task than Cooder or Newman when it came to following up the multi-million-selling *Rumours*. The loathing punks felt for the band – which found its snottiest expression in the Rotters' 1979 classic 'Sit On My Face, Stevie Nicks' – narked Lindsay Buckingham, who prided himself on his musical eclecticism and openness to the 'new wave'. In his desire to, in his own words, 'refute the machinery', the obsessive Buckingham masterminded the act of virtual sabotage that was *Tusk*, a double album of wonderfully eccentric sketches and doodlings which caused ripples of panic throughout the Burbank boardrooms. Although the album was in the Top 5 at the end of 1979, it sold a mere fraction of the 25 million units notched up by *Rumours*. Added to this were the ongoing complications in the band's private lives: Mick Fleetwood and the McVies were recovering from divorces and general cocaine mayhem, while Christine McVie was caretaking the impossible Dennis Wilson in Coldwater Canyon.

There was some consolation for the Warners executives in the ongoing success of the Doobie Brothers, whose recruitment of Steely Dan backing-singer Michael McDonald had completely overhauled their musical identity. By the release of *Minute by Minute* (1979), with its No. 1 hit 'What a Fool Believes', McDonald had steered the band away from the space-cowboy posturings of Tom Johnston and towards a keyboard-based 'lite-soul' style which defined the sound of late-seventies LA pop. It was significant that the band's hit singles were collaborations between the dumpy-looking McDonald and outsiders such as Kenny Loggins and Carole Bayer-Sager, rather than compositions emanating from within the

'Van Halen is an attitude.' Left to right: *Alex Van Halen, Michael Anthony, David Lee Roth, Eddie Van Halen.*

group. Much of the credit for the Doobies' success would have to be laid at the door of Ted Templeman, who by the late seventies had established himself as one of the most accomplished record producers in the business.

It was Templeman who was at the helm for the debut Warners album by Van Halen, a hard-rock/metal quartet from Pasadena who at the eleventh hour had decided against becoming a punk band. The very fact that Van Halen had even had to weigh up such a decision to plump for metal says a lot about the status of hard rock at the time. Not that there wasn't still a headbanging circuit on and around the Sunset Strip, but there was nothing hip about bands such as Quiet Riot or Mickey Ratt. When Templeman and Mo Ostin checked out Van Halen at the Starwood one miserable Monday night, they knew that here was something different. Fronted by a comic-strip showman called David Lee Roth and boasting the outstanding musicianship of Dutch-born brothers Eddie and Alex Van Halen, the band had already picked up a loyal following among the party-animal crowd in LA and were capable of pulling in big audiences without ever having released a record. With one foot in the Sunset Strip glam-punk of 1974 and the other in the stadium metal of Led Zeppelin, Van Halen were ready, in John Shearlaw's words, to 'turn a backyard barbecue in the San Fernando Valley into a nationwide party'.

Van Halen, recorded at Sunset Sound in four weeks with minimal overdubbing, showed that the band had been right not to take the 'Radio Free Hollywood' exit from the hard-rock freeway. From the opening blast of 'Runnin' with the Devil' to the streamlined thrash of 'Atomic Punk', it was the most exciting metal album of the year, climbing into the Top 20 in April 1978 and establishing young Eddie as a new axemeister supreme. 'Van Halen is an attitude,' claimed David Lee Roth, whose spangled-rooster, Jim-Dandy-as-Captain-America antics made him an instant groupie groin-throb. 'It's like driving down the Strip with a load of girls, the radio on, and a couple of cases of beer.' Predictably, not one member of the band was a native Californian, while Roth himself, despite coming on like the ultimate Aryan rock god, was Jewish.

Roth eventually proved the undoing of the original unit, since neither the Van Halen brothers nor bassist Michael Anthony shared his ironic vision of what the band represented. 'Ted Templeman and I clicked right away,' Roth later recalled. 'We could sit around and drink beer and toss out tunes till the sun came up. When we were in the studio we'd go,

"Okay, let's steal this little part from the Ohio Players, and then we'll do this little drum feel from that Dave Clark Five song." Whereas Eddie's and Alex's frame of reference in popular music was very limited. For them it was either a twenty-minute Cream jam or Deep Purple or Black Sabbath.' In the studio, Roth claimed, there was always friction between the Van Halens and Templeman, a friction which eventually translated to Roth's own relationship with the brothers. But by that time, Van Halen had chalked up six consecutive platinum albums, Eddie had gotten hitched to soap-opera cutie Valerie Bertinelli, and the band had been paid a whopping $1.3 million to headline the final day at the 1983 US Festival near San Bernardino.

III

While Van Halen veered away from punk in 1977, a number of bands chose to steer a midway course between punk and pop, influenced as much by Blondie as by the post-Flamin' Groovies bands (the Nerves, 20/20) favoured by Greg Shaw. 'The first time we went out to LA in 1977, all the kids were dressed in bellbottoms and stuff,' recalled Blondie's Chris Stein. 'The next time we came, they were all dressed like us, in little suits with narrow lapels.' Predictably, the majors perked up at the more accessible sound of these power-pop/'new wave' bands and began chasing their signatures. Suddenly, everyone seemed to be wearing jackets and skinny ties, whether it was older bands such as the Pop! the Quick, the Motels or newer ones such as the Plimsouls, formed by Peter Case from the ashes of the Nerves at the beginning of 1979.

Even Tom Petty and the Heartbreakers incorporated new wave trappings into the stolid mainstream idiom of their sound, especially after being exposed to the British punk scene in 1977. 'When I got back from London, Denny Cordell came to my house,' Petty recalled. 'I told him how exciting things were getting in England and he said, "You're not going to believe what's happening *here*!"' The ultimate 'skinny tie' band was a quartet called the Knack, whom Petty and Cordell saw at the Troubadour in 1978. Ageing musos riding the retro-pop bandwagon, the Knack were immediately suspect, but it didn't stop Capitol signing them and entrusting them to the care of Brit glam-rock veteran Mike Chapman, who'd just finished work on Blondie's *Parallel Lines* album. Recorded in two weeks for a mere $20,000, *Get the Knack* (1979) proceeded to lodge itself at No. 1 for a phenomenal five weeks, only one week less than the nauseating 'My Sharona' remained at the top of the singles chart. 'The Knack made it because the heterosexual white audience found out that everyone in disco was gay,' says Kim Fowley, who was doubtless miffed that none of his own power-pop charges had the same degree of success.

A Knack backlash had set in even before singer/writer Doug Feiger

Garage heaven: the Plimsouls.

had the gall to quote Jim Morrison in the title of the band's follow-up album, *But the Little Girls Understand*, but meanwhile every other record company was signing its own pet skinny-tie band. Earle Mankey produced a pretty decent Epic album by 20/20, the Pop signed to Arista, and the Plimsouls wound up on Richard Perry's new Planet label for a debut album that showcased Peter Case's gifts as a writer and first-rate John Lennon impersonator. 'It wasn't that they tried to turn us into something we weren't,' Case said in 1983. 'But they expected to have this immediate hit, and when they realized we didn't fit into "the new wave explosion" we were off the label so quick that we were still on the road when they stopped answering our phone calls.'

For Richard Meltzer, who saw Linda Ronstadt's *Mad Love* as the nadir of this retrograde, pseudo-punk rock, Noo Wave was 'the most insidious marketing ploy since the Bosstown Sound, and a thousand times more EVIL, purporting to be "of the new" while effectively camouflaging the goddamn industry's hell-and-gone TERROR of the Real Thing'. Of course, the real 'new wave' was to be found in the cultural backwaters of inland America, particularly in such hotspots as Akron, Ohio, and Athens, Georgia. Coming out of Akron, Devo briefly offered the LA scene a taste of something genuinely quirky and dehumanized, their deadpan, hyper-robotic sound at its best on the Brian Eno-produced *Q: Are We Not Men? A: We are Devo!* (1978). But it wasn't long before Jerry Casale and Mark Mothersbaugh were sucked into the plastic Hollywood ad-world they were satirizing, exemplifying the dangers of avant-gardists straying too close to the citadel of mass entertainment.

Despite the objections of Richard Meltzer and a hundred other scribes, the promise of power-pop was still potent enough to bring such LA veterans as Phil Spector and Jack Nitzsche out of the shadows. Neither man was in terribly good shape, but that didn't stop them pitching up at various studios to oversee albums by the Ramones, Graham Parker and the Rumour and Mink DeVille. After the winding-up of the Phil Spector International label in 1977, the maestro had retreated indoors with his windows blacked out, only re-emerging when Warners persuaded him to produce an album by, of all people, Leonard Cohen. The sessions for *Death of a Ladies' Man* were nothing short of nightmarish, with Spector and Cohen boozing together and Spector pulling guns on engineers, observed all the while by a horrified Doc Pomus. 'Phil couldn't resist annihilating me,' Cohen said of the album, which predictably drowned songs such as 'Paper-Thin Hotel' and 'I Left a Woman Waiting' in a pointlessly over-the-top 'wall of sound'. 'I don't think he can tolerate any other shadows in his own darkness.'

It was the sons of guitarist Barney Kessel who dragged Spector along to see the Ramones at the Whisky a Go Go, paving the way for the Warner-affiliated Sire label to suggest that he produce their next album. It was a curious marriage, to be sure, and one made even stranger by

Spector's apparent desire to turn the gangling Joey Ramone into a punk version of Ronnie Spector – complete with the obligatory version of a Ronettes classic, in this case 'Baby I Love You'. Phil liked the fact that the group stood out against the blanket of corporate AOR rock – in a way, this was *the band* he'd been searching for in the days of the Modern Folk Quartet – but the Ramones themselves were totally spooked by his methods and his need to lock them into the La Collina Drive compound. Held mainly at the old Gold Star studio, the sessions for *End of the Century* (1980) were like a Chinese water torture, with the perfectionist Spector forcing the band to re-do parts until they felt as if they were cracking up. As he'd done on Cohen's album, Spector pulled a gun – this time on Dee Dee Ramone, who was devouring quaaludes by the handful as a way of dealing with Spector's madness.

It was a small miracle that at the end of all this psychosis the album actually sounded pretty good. Respecting the band's CBGBs roots enough to build his sound around them, Spector had turned *End of the Century* into a punk testament to New York pop. Kicking off with the rousing nostalgia anthem 'Do You Remember Rock'n'Roll Radio?' and taking in the Heartbreakers' junkie classic 'Chinese Rocks', the album came close to being a punk/power-pop masterpiece and nearly led to Spector producing Blondie – a plan quickly nixed by Chris Stein after getting the lowdown on the Ramones sessions.

Among the visitors to the La Collina Drive mansion at the time of those sessions was Jack Nitzsche, whom Spector, brandishing a gun from an upstairs window, promptly ordered off his grounds. As it happened, Nitzsche was even more messed up than his old mentor, and had recently been arrested for assaulting his actress girlfriend Carrie Snodgress. Not only had he been drinking heavily for several years, he was now using heroin into the bargain. Which only makes it the more remarkable that he'd recently chalked up such production credits as the soundtracks to Paul Schrader's *Blue Collar* (reuniting Ry Cooder with a rejuvenated Captain Beefheart) and William Friedkin's *Cruising* (featuring the Germs, no less), along with Graham Parker and the Rumour's acclaimed *Squeezing Out Sparks*. Nitzsche had also been co-opted into the Spectoresque fantasies of Mink DeVille, producing Willy DeVille songs ('Spanish Stroll, 'Venus of Avenue D') that harked back to the pop Manhattan of Doc Pomus and Mort Shuman. But things were going from bad to worse for Jack: when he produced Rick Nelson's Capitol album *Playing to Win* (1981), he was nodding out at the console. Only when he was reunited with his old love Buffy Sainte-Marie, penning the sappy Joe Cocker/Jennifer Warnes smash 'Up Where We Belong', did he surface from the depths.

The group which took the LA power-pop dream further than anyone was the all-girl Go-Gos, who jettisoned their punk songs in favour of a bright, bouncy California pop sound. With the chubbily cute Belinda Carlisle on vocals, they came on like a sorority version of the Runaways, as encouraged by manager Miles Copeland, a major new player on the LA scene. But the bounciness was deceptive, and not just because the band was besieged by drug problems. If the big hits came with the Blondie-goes-to-California-style 'Vacation' and 'We Got the Beat', guitarist Charlotte Caffey also wrote songs ('Lust to Love', the B-52s-ish 'This Town') that betrayed the pain and pathos behind the sunny façade. When Belinda sang 'This town is so glamorous/Bet you'd live here if you could/And be one of us', the flaunting of Los Angeles was double-edged. Later in the song she admitted that 'We're all dreamers, we're all whores', adding that 'discarded stars, like worn-out cars/Litter the streets of this town'.

'This Town' was one of the standout tracks on *Beauty and the Beat*, which sat pretty at the top of the American album charts for six weeks in the fall of 1981. 'Seeing the Go-Gos go from the Masque to the Greek Theatre in three years was fairly extraordinary,' says Jeff Gold. 'And then seeing them open for the Police at Madison Square Garden was beyond surreal.' The success of the Go-Gos, like that of his more famous charges the Police, established Miles Copeland as the king of Noo Wave in Hollywood. Having staged the ultimate overground LA punk event – the URGH! 'Music War' at the Santa Monica Civic, featuring a mixture of locals and out-of-towners – he was now building up a roster of 'alternative' rock acts on his IRS label that included the Buzzcocks, the Cramps, Wall of Voodoo and the sub-Devoid Oingo Boingo. In time he would add REM and the Bang(le)s to his trophy cabinet.

IV

One of the principal tenets of the American punk scene in general was that Disco – most obviously the music of *Saturday Night Fever* – 'sucked'. Not surprisingly, perhaps, the 'DISCO SUCKS' backlash against black/gay dance music was particularly rife in Los Angeles, where racism and homophobia lurked in even the hippest quarters. 'In retrospect, the much-vaunted punk/new wave explosion was a very white-male-dominated scene,' says Rhino's Gary Stewart. 'There were some breakthroughs in terms of women, with the Runaways and the Go-Gos, but there was also a racist component to the scene, which was why skinheads and neo-Nazis were attracted to it.' Yet if LA was never a 'disco' metropolis in the way that New York was – never fostering the kind of club culture Manhattan enjoyed in its Studio 54 heyday – it did produce much of the 'dance' music which crossed over from the black to the pop charts in the late seventies, most obviously from the disco conveyor-belt of Casablanca Records but also from Motown and from Dick Griffey's SOLAR (Sound of Los Angeles Records) label. It was no coincidence that the major black icons of the period – Donna Summer, Rick James, Michael Jackson, even the early Prince – were all moulded by the LA entertainment machine.

LA was really a studio city, its black music epitomized by the productions of Quincy Jones. True, it had produced – or at least nurtured – such self-contained 'bands' as War, the Crusaders, Rufus and Earth, Wind and Fire, but by the end of the seventies the sound of black LA bore the same anonymous muso sheen as the countless AOR records pumped out across the nation's airwaves. The fact that Quincy Jones, for example, employed many of the white sessionmen who were playing on hits by Toto, Steely Dan and Boz Scaggs went some way to explaining the homogeneous rock-soul feel of so many 'black' LA records of the period. Even Earth, Wind and Fire used the likes of keyboardist David Foster and guitarist Steve Lukather on *I Am* (1979), an album of cosmic funk'n'roll as dazzling in both conception and execution as Michael Jackson's *Off the Wall* from the same year.

Quincy Jones was already a major figure in the jazz world when he moved out to Hollywood in 1965. By the end of the decade he'd scored four Sidney Poitier films, written the theme for *Ironside* and released his own Grammy-winning *Walking in Space* (1969). After several more albums and soundtracks in the early seventies, Jones discovered a local band called the Brothers Johnson and produced their brilliant 'I'll Be Good to You', a Top 5 hit in May 1976. Three years later, George and Louis Johnson were prominent among the players of *Off the Wall*, that triumph of studio-crafted musical miscegenation. Here was the first real mass-audience black/white album, covering every musical base from hyper-kinetic funk to tear-jerking ballads and beginning the process whereby Jackson turned himself into a kind of sexless white android – the ultimate Hollywoodization of soul. With the aid of Toto, Paul McCartney and Eddie Van Halen, Jackson and Jones then proceeded to make *Thriller*, the best-selling album of all time.

Berry Gordy must have observed the meteoric ascent of Michael Jackson with mixed feelings, particularly since it was at Motown's twenty-fifth anniversary celebrations in 1983 that Jackson, moonwalking through 'Billie Jean', imprinted himself once and for all on global popular consciousness. Motown hadn't fared too well in the disco era: if Smokey Robinson hit with 'Cruisin'' and Diana Ross with the Chic-produced 'Upside Down', Stevie Wonder's eccentric 1979 opus *Journey Through the Secret Life of Plants* (1979) never came close to repeating the success of the magnificent *Songs in the Key of Life* (1976). Marvin Gaye's bizarre *Here, My Dear* (1978) sold even more poorly. The result of a court order to give the royalties from an album to his ex-wife Anna, sister of Berry Gordy, the double LP barely scraped into the Top 30.

For a couple of years, Motown's biggest star was probably Rick James, who as Ricky James Matthews had played with Neil Young in the Mynah Birds some fifteen years earlier. James copped most of his riffs and attitude from George Clinton's P-Funk family, but came on like some Hollywood super-pimp – a male counterpart to the Donna Summer of 'Hot Stuff'

'The entertainment business is ugly, demented and perverted, and you have to be ugly, demented and perverted to cope with it.' Rick James sings his street songs.

and 'Bad Girls'. He had big R&B hits with 'You and I', 'Bustin' Out' and the unsubtly titled 'Mary Jane' before proclaiming himself the king of 'punk funk', a somewhat specious tag given his celebration of everything that was putrid about the LA high life. 'The entertainment business sucks,' James told me some years later. 'It's ugly, demented, perverted, and you have to be ugly, demented and perverted to cope with it. When I have to go into the slime, I crawl into the slime. There's so many plastic people in Hollywood, it's like a walking Disneyland.' James never really recovered from the double-platinum success of his best album *Street Songs* (1981). Drugs all but destroyed him, and in the early nineties he was jailed after torturing a girl for sexual kicks.

It was Rick James who helped turn a petite California Girl called Mary Christine Brockert into Teena Marie, perhaps the unlikeliest star of the Motown stable in the late seventies. One could argue that for Berry Gordy to have signed a blonde Caucasian to the label was the ultimate proof of Motown's desertion of its heritage, but Teena Marie happened to make some of the funkiest 'black' records ever to come out of Los Angeles: records like 'Behind the Groove', 'I Need Your Lovin' ', 'Square Biz' and 'Portuguese Love'. With *It Must be Magic* (1981), moreover, she proved she was more than a token white disco diva. 'The Ballad Of Cradle Rob and Me' sounded like a dancefloor Rickie Lee Jones, and 'Revolution' was an impassioned protest from a girl who 'cried tears in my bedroom when they chased me home from school/Nigger lover this and nigger lover that'.

Rick James complained that Motown thought they were still in the sixties – that they weren't catering to 'the people in the street'. A company which had its finger pressed harder on the pulse of pop radio, if not of 'the street', was SOLAR, which had grown out of promoter Dick Griffey's association with *Soul Train* host Don Cornelius. Between 1978 and 1983, SOLAR enjoyed a run of post-disco crossover hits which included Shalamar's 'The Second Time Around' and the veteran Whispers' 'And the Beat Goes On'. Bubbly and infectious, the SOLAR sound was especially popular in England, where Shalamar had four Top 10 hits in the space of a year.

Given Warner Brothers' comparative lack of commitment to black music,* it remains somewhat surprising that they signed the one-man-band prodigy that was Prince. But sign him they did, and on his own audacious terms, which included having him produce his own debut album. 'We took him into the studio one day,' recalled Lenny Waronker. 'We said, "Play the drums" and he played the drums and put down bass and guitar parts. And we just said "Yeah fine, that's good enough." ' Waronker was bragging, of course, and when push came to shove, Warners assigned one Tommy Vicari to 'oversee' the sessions at Sausalito's Record Plant. When *For You* finally appeared in April 1978, it began with

---

* Though they did sign Funkadelic, George Benson, Al Jarreau and Chaka Khan.

an extraordinary fanfare to Prince's whole career: 'For You', consisting of the boy wonder's seraphic falsetto multi-tracked forty-five times in a shimmering cascade that would have stopped Brian Wilson in his tracks. Eighteen months later, with the fabulously sexy 'I Wanna be Your Lover' in the Top 20, Prince was on the brink of his eighties superstardom. 1980's *Dirty Mind*, recorded as 16-track demos in his hometown of Minneapolis, was the punk-funk album Rick James could only dream of making.

A more typical Warners album was Etta James's *Deep in the Night* (1978), producer Jerry Wexler's attempt to reactivate the career of a West Coast R&B legend. Recorded at the Robb Brothers' Cherokee studio with a red-hot band that included pianist Richard Tee, guitarist Larry Carlton, bassist Chuck Rainey and drummer Jeff Porcaro, the album fell into a kind of Boz-Scaggs-meets-Lowell-George bag and bombed miserably at a time when great singers were expected to debase themselves on 12″ disco mixes. Curiously, only a tempestuous version of the Eagles' 'Take It to the Limit' stood out among the lacklustre rock/soul covers. It was the beginning and the end of Etta's career as a Warners artist.

Warners even attempted to inject new life into what was left of the career of Sly Stone, releasing the ominously titled and painfully dull *Back On the Right Track* in 1979. 'He rebelled, he never thought the album was his,' said manager Ken Roberts. 'Warners assigned people to work with him and changed his music around. After that Sly just went away.' 'Went away' was really a euphemism for Stone's old bad habits. Four years later, while touring to promote a second Warners album, he was arrested for freebasing cocaine in a hotel room in Fort Myers, Florida.

V

When kids from the LA suburbs started getting into punk around 1978, they created an offshoot from the Hollywood scene which became known as 'hardcore'. Musically and demographically, hardcore was very different from the punk rock heard at the Masque (or at the New Masque, which opened in January 1979). It was younger, faster and angrier, full of the pent-up rage of dysfunctional Orange County adolescents who'd had enough of living in a bland Republican paradise. 'Punk was urban, hardcore was suburban,' says Greg Shaw. 'Punk had been arty and conceptual, but then came the kids from the beach, boneheads who'd heard that punk was violence but didn't realize it was metaphorical violence.' For Pleasant Gehman, punk had been about 'doing things and making things and starting bands and magazines': 'We thought the hardcore people were sorta like dumb kids,' she says. 'Some of the bands were great, but it was hell trying to go see them because there'd be a bunch of football jocks with mohicans there.'

Three beach towns in particular were crucial to the development of hardcore punk. In Hermosa Beach, Black Flag began playing shows at a venue known as the Church, while further down the coast at Huntingdon Beach a scene developed around bands such as the Crowd, the Screws and the Outsiders. Finally, the heavy-metal stronghold of the Fleetwood in Redondo Beach began opening its doors to a number of bands from the South Bay area, as well as to more established groups from the original Hollywood scene.

'We were all surfers,' recalled Black Flag guitarist Greg Ginn, who grew up near the Beach Boys' home suburb of Hawthorne. 'We had skateboards, and we rollerskated up and down the Strand. It made sense to revolt eventually.' Black Flag producer Spot, the band's first bass player, remembered Ginn circa 1976 as 'someone totally out of step with the sunshine and surf and skateboards' – a geek at odds even with the usual outcast types. Rehearsing 'deep within the bowels of the Hermosa Bath House', as Spot recalled, Black Flag whipped themselves into shape and recorded the 'Nervous Breakdown' EP in January 1978. Featuring the diminutive Keith Morris on vocals, the title song was a punk classic, all buzzsaw guitars, brain-drilling drums, and a crazed Rotten/Strummer rant of a voice. Not long after its release, Middle Class released the 'Out of Vogue' EP, an equally incendiary blast of hardcore from the 'burbs of Orange County, and Robbie Fields of Posh Boy put out the seminal 1979 compilation *Beach Boulevard*, featuring the Crowd, Rik L. Rik and the Simpletones.

At the Fleetwood, harmony briefly reigned between the twin factions of the LA punk scene. 'We'd play on bills at the Fleetwood with some of the South Bay bands,' recalls Pat Smear of the Germs. 'But it didn't last too long. Pretty soon the Huntingdon Beach scene began to take over.' Perhaps in retaliation for the fact that Hollywood clubs wouldn't book the South Bay bands, the 'beachcore' scene began to develop some alarming tendencies. 'After a while, if you showed up at the Fleetwood with long hair, you'd get stabbed,' says Smear, and Spot, who worked there as a stage manager, remembers the club as 'the epitome of the Hate-Kill-Destroy ethic'.

Ironically, Black Flag were accused of providing an anthem for these disaffected, bigoted sociopaths with 'White Minority', a song intended as satire but seized upon by some as a statement of solidarity. 'Hardcore was overtly negative and nihilistic, and that attracted both ends of the political spectrum,' says Gary Stewart of Rhino Records. 'That's not a dismissal of the music, but at its most extreme it was just as reactionary and right-wing as it was initially left-wing in its ideology.' By the summer of 1980, brawls and stabbings were regular occurrences on the beachcore circuit, and bands such as the Adolescents were taking hardcore nihilism to a brutal extreme.

On their 1981 debut album on Lisa Fancher's Frontier label, the

Adolescents described themselves as 'just a wrecking crew/Bored boys with nothing to do', then proceeded to give vent to their hatred of anyone who wasn't like them: straights, girls, queers, kids. As Greil Marcus noted, 'a wish to exterminate the other is presented here as a rebellion against the smooth surface of American life, but it may be more truly a violent, spectacular accommodation to America's worst instincts.' Unable to attack those in power, these 'bored boys' turned their rage on anyone who could easily be hurt. Fortunately, the violence of the hardcore scene rarely erupted on Marcus's 'smooth surface', even if the *Los Angeles Times* tried to suggest that such an eruption was imminent when they ran Patrick Goldstein's famous piece about 'slamming' in the summer of 1980. Still, it helped Goldstein's case that a full-scale 'riot on Sunset Strip' occurred – almost fifteen years on from the CAFF riots of the mid sixties – when Black Flag invaded Hollywood and played a show at the Whisky a Go Go.

The Hollywood scene itself was in a state of near-disintegration by 1980, although there was a last gasp from the Masque era in the Germs' *(G.I.)*, released late in 1979. Produced by Joan Jett and featuring sixteen surprisingly powerful songs, *(G.I.)* fused Kurt Cobain-style angst with a musical proficiency which had been completely beyond their grasp two

The mosh pit: 'Just a wrecking crew/Bored boys with nothing to do...'

years before.* 'Richie Dagger's Crime' was about a kid who 'sits in his corner like a child despised', while 'Sex God' was about 'the fucking son of a superman', with 'a weapon that's as deadly as life': somewhere between these schizoid poles lay the true Darby Crash. Nicole Panter, who managed the band at the time, remembered that people were shocked by the sophistication of Darby's lyrics on this album.

The Germs were among the bands who featured in *The Decline of Western Civilisation*, Penelope Spheeris's riveting documentary about the LA punk scene shot over the winter of 1979–80. A film-maker who'd pioneered 'music videos' for bands such as Fleetwood Mac and the Doobie Brothers, Spheeris was bored enough of seventies rock'n'roll to follow up a friend's advice and check out some of the bands playing at the Masque. 'Once I'd heard this music, it was like I owned the rights to make a film about it,' recalls the woman who went on to direct *Wayne's World*. 'I'd go up to people who were shooting bands with video cameras and say, "You can't do that, *I'm* the one who's doing this!" That's how obsessed I was with being *the* documentarian of this scene, which was just such a breath of fresh air. Those bands were rocking the boat in such a beautiful way, and there's no one doing that now.'

Darby Crash never saw the finished *Decline*. After a visit to London in the summer of 1980, he came back to LA sporting a mohawk and set about rehearsing a new Darby Crash Band. There were plans to play a 'farewell' Germs gig in December, but in the small hours of 7 December he opted instead to carry out the plan he'd always had of killing himself. Making a suicide pact with his girlfriend Casey in her mother's nondescript Hollywood bungalow on North Fuller Avenue, he administered fatal injections of 'China White' heroin and lay down to die. Casey survived, but Darby achieved the pseudo-martyrdom he'd always craved – even if his death was somewhat overshadowed by the shooting the next day of John Lennon. 'Darby's death was really the signal here in LA for people to say, "Okay, we've pushed it far enough – we're at the edge of the cliff right now,"' says Penelope Spheeris. 'And a lot of the people that were close to him subsequently settled down.'†

If *The Decline of Western Civilisation* turned out to be a kind of epitaph to the Masque scene – thanks to Darby's death – the other bands featured in the film were all pushing punk forward. X had recorded one classic single on Dangerhouse ('Adult Books'/'We're Desperate') before signing to Slash for the critically acclaimed *Los Angeles* (1980). John Doe and Exene Cervenka were the Masque's very own Sonny and Cher, poetry-workshop types who had come out to LA from the East Coast in the

---

* Not long after I interviewed him in the SST store on Sunset Boulevard, the band's guitarist Pat Smear was recruited by Germs aficionado Kurt Cobain as the fourth member of Nirvana. He was still in the group when Cobain killed himself in the spring of 1994.
† A rather lonelier rock death occurred that month when Tim Hardin, one of the original singer-songwriters, overdosed in an apartment on North Orange Drive.

mid seventies. It said a lot about them that they asked Ray Manzarek to produce *Los Angeles*, even going so far as to include a version of the Doors' 'Soul Kitchen' on the album. For what they were really trying to capture in such bleak vignettes as 'Los Angeles' and 'Sex and Dying in High Society' was an outsider's perspective on the vacant desperation of LA's fallen punk angels, taking up where Jim Morrison had left off on *LA Woman*. *Los Angeles* was a new version of the inverted City of Night,

or what Greil Marcus called 'Chandler's LA without Philip Marlowe'.

To Ken Tucker of the *LA Herald-Examiner*, X were 'the only great rock band' to emerge from the LA punk scene, 'wedding Chuck Berry-style rock'n'roll guitar chords to an authentic West Coast poetics that combined Jack Spicer's surreal informality with Charles Bukowski's brutish vulgarity'. But to some of their contemporaries, X were just Jefferson Airplane with a pogo beat. 'They were great before they made records,' says Pat Smear, 'but then they started turning into what they really were, which was older people with roots in "rock'n'roll".' Certainly, neither *Los Angeles* nor *Wild Gift* (1981) packed the punch of the Circle Jerks' *Group Sex* (1980) or Black Flag's *Damaged* (1981), masterpieces of authentic belligerence and near-psychosis by two of the other bands featured in *The Decline of Western Civilisation*. The real sound of LA punk was to be heard not in the productions of Ray Manzarek but in the raw gawkiness of Red Cross and the Descendents, the scuffling Chicano irritation of the Brat and Los Illegals.

The Circle Jerks, formed by Keith Morris after he quit Black Flag in 1978, were the ultimate cartoon punks. Songs such as 'Wasted', 'Operation', 'Beverly Hills' and 'I Just Want Some Skank' suggested a suburban state of mind that lurched precariously between rage and self-mockery. The very idea of choosing Beverly Hills as a target for punk anger was absurd, and Morris knew it. It said everything about the Circle Jerks that they not only entitled their second album *Wild in the Streets*, after a classic AIP exploitation movie, but approached LA veteran David Anderle to produce it for Miles Copeland's Faulty Records subsidiary. 'I found the West Coast punk thing really exhilarating, even with its edge of violence,' says the man who'd been Brian Wilson's right-hand man in 1966. 'It was such a relief after the miasma of disco and all those Styx/Rush/Kansas type bands.' *Wild in the Streets* lacked the pristine runtiness of *Group Sex*, but it showed Morris moving beyond his suburban-slacker apathy and venting some righteous anger about Reagan's America: 'Caviar and limousines/ High finance and jellybeans/Decorate the east wing California modern/ It's great to be the king...'

For Fear, another of the bands featured in Penelope Spheeris's film, it was a little harder to shrug off the violence of the hardcore scene. Early in 1981, after playing the Stardust Ballroom on Sunset and Western, bassist Derf Scratch was attacked by a 6' 3" skinhead and wound up in Canoga Park Hospital with seven broken bones in his face. 'There are all these rich kids, and they have all kinds of money from their parents,' he said afterwards. 'They got into the punk scene, and the only way they can prove to themselves and their friends that they're punks is to beat somebody up. They can't really say, "Yeah, I'm punk, I don't have any morals, fuck the middle class," because that's where they came from.' It was a Fear fan who succeeded in closing down the Starwood that summer after stabbing one of the club's bouncers.*

The fact that Derf Scratch blamed such violence on rich kids trying to prove they weren't 'poseurs' was mildly ironic considering Fear were themselves punk opportunists par excellence. Led by bit-part actor Lee Ving, they were accomplished musos who came late to the party and only tapped into punk's most smarmy and mean-spirited aspects. Their belated Slash debut, *The Record* (1982), was a work of hollow, facile satire, featuring such soulless metal-punk tirades as 'We Destroy the Family', 'I Don't Care About You' and the miserably chauvinistic 'New York's Alright if You Like Saxophones'. By a strange coincidence, they were managed by Danny Hutton, like David Anderle a member of Brian Wilson's *Smile*-era inner court. 'Fear were like a joke band, but they could all play,' the Three Dog Night singer remembers. 'Ving would bait the audience like a wrestler, and if anyone jumped onstage he'd beat them up. I beat my head for a couple of years trying to get them a deal, and everyone wondered why I was sticking with them.'

Next to *The Record*, Black Flag's *Damaged* sounded like the real thing. If the slacker legacy of Keith Morris was still there on 'Six Pack' and 'TV Party', the band had come a long way since 1978, especially with the arrival of psycho-Marine frontman Henry Rollins. Tracks such as 'Rise Above', 'What I See' and 'Life of Pain' burned with a convulsive intensity that scared MCA chief Al Bergamo into vetoing the album's release even after thousands of copies had been pressed. 'It's funny that the people

---

* The Starwood was just one of the clubs owned by Adel Nasrallah, a.k.a. Eddie Nash, a Palestinian who'd fetched up in LA in the sixties and pioneered gay bars in West Hollywood. In the summer of 1981, when the Starwood was closed down, Nash was robbed at gunpoint of drugs, guns, cash and jewellery by three men who lived five minutes away on Wonderland Avenue. The men had previously scored from Nash, with porn star John 'The Wad' Holmes acting as the middleman. The following day they and one of their girlfriends were bludgeoned to death in a horrific killing which became known as 'The Four On the Floor'. For more on this quintessentially Babylonian LA story, see Mike Bygrave, 'Darkness On the Edge of Tinsel Town', the *Guardian*, 9 February 1991.

Life of pain: Black Flag frontman Henry Rollins and slamming fan, 1982.

who hate us most aren't your ultra-conservatives, but your basic liberals,' said Greg Ginn. 'There's a lot of them in the music business, which is why we've come up against so much resistance.' It was significant that Black Flag used Charles Manson as a reference-point in their covert war on the liberal rock establishment, describing their tours as 'creepy crawlies' and drawing on the menacing sense of southern Californian *noir* that was Manson's legacy to rock'n'roll. 'We get an arcane and emotional value from Manson,' claimed bassist and co-founder Chuck Dukowski, who viewed the mainstream music industry as a group of people 'who want to tell you how to behave so they can create this beautiful social dream'.

By the end of 1981, the LA 'alternative rock' scene was starting to splinter into numerous different factions. Notwithstanding the efforts of Posh Boy, Frontier and Black Flag's SST label, the hardcore punk boom was over, with several clubs closing their doors to the skinhead hordes and more than a few of the bands themselves beginning to veer off on different paths. Although there were still some great LA punk albums to come – the Descendents' *Milo Goes to College*, the Angry Samoans' *Back from Samoa*, Red Cross's *Born Innocent* and more – the energy of hardcore had dissipated. New punk bands such as TSOL, China White, Bad Religion and Wasted Youth were promoted by the 'Better Youth Organization', but even they had to find some way of putting a new slant on a musical form which was now old hat. Some groups made a beeline for power-pop, others flirted with Goth-rock or art-noise, and still others returned to the roots music of blues and country and rockabilly. The heterogeneity of the scene was summed up by a ska band called the Boxboys, whose lead singer Betsy Weiss joined metal outfit Bitch and whose drummer was recruited by the 'psychedelic-country' Long Ryders. Predictably, too, Hollywood went 'Noo Romantic' in a big way, with Henry Peck and Joseph Brooks of the Melrose Avenue store Vinyl Fetish sponsoring the 'Veil' night at the Cathay De Grande. KROQ quickly embraced this latest wave from England, along with such homegrown synth-rock permutations as Berlin and Missing Persons.

There was tacit acknowledgement that this new diversity might not be such a bad thing, in a 1981 New Year's Eve show which brought together Fear, Black Flag, roots merchants the Blasters and arty new-wave band Suburban Lawns. But it wasn't long before the likes of Fear began to look pretty redundant, particularly after their little dalliance with the smacked-out, freebase-crazy John Belushi.

It was Derf Scratch who first became pally with the rotund comedian after meeting him in the Guitar Center on Sunset at the end of September 1981. Belushi wanted to know all about the punk scene, and Scratch didn't object too strenuously to being dragged off to Lou Adler's On the Rox club in the star's red Mercedes. Columbia movie executives were appalled when Belushi attempted to shoehorn Fear on to the soundtrack of the dreadful *Neighbors*, but the actor was adamant that 'punk *demands* a response', validating as it did his image of himself as a leather-jacketed Hollywood rebel.

The following February, Belushi returned to LA and checked into one of the infamous Chateau Marmont bungalows. Making contact with Cathy Smith, a drug dealer who at one time had lived the groupie high life with the Rolling Stones, he began a binge that was to last five days, during the course of which he talked of his loathing for movie executives and his desire to make a film about punk rock. On the night of 4 March, after being given a fix by Smith in the On the Rox office, Belushi told Derf Scratch he would drop by later for a jam session. Scratch was still waiting at 4 a.m., by which time the actor was unconscious in his bungalow. Some time after 10.15 the next morning, Belushi died in his sleep.

If Belushi's death was really just one more Hollywood scandal, it didn't say a lot for the punk rock in which he so ardently believed. By the end of that summer, belief in punk was wearing thin, and ex-punks were hamming it up in Horror Rock bands such as the Boneheads, Castration Squad and 45 Grave. Rather less schlocky and theatrical in conception

John Belushi on the town, with actress Meg Foster.

THE DECLINE OF THE WEST 311

were the Gun Club and the Flesh Eaters, who took a more bluesy, hellhound-on-your-trail approach to their subject-matter. With his desperate, haunted voice, the Gun Club's half-Mexican frontman Jeffrey Lee Pierce came on like a Goth-rock Jim Morrison, singing about ghosts and poisons, hexes and voodoo dolls. Pierce had founded the Blondie fan club as a teenage Hollywood scenester, then formed Creeping Ritual with Kid Congo Powers. Minus Powers, Creeping Ritual evolved into the Gun Club and recorded *Fire of Love* (1981), featuring the notorious 'She's Like Heroin to Me'. The concerns of Flesh Eaters mainman Chris D – like Pierce a key figure at *Slash* magazine – ran along roughly the same lines. On *A Minute to Pray, a Second to Die* (1981), he sang of feverish visions, satanic possession, boneyards and bloodletting, backed by a punk/roots band that comprised members of X and the Blasters.

All of these bands owed at least something to the Cramps, so there was a certain logic in the fact that Lux Interior and Ivy Rorschach decided in the fall of 1980 to leave New York for Los Angeles. 'Tell me some good rock'n'roll that's come out of New York besides the Dolls and the Velvets,' Lux fulminated for the benefit of one LA fanzine. 'Tell me how much success *they* had at the time, too. The town is filled with dancers and actors, it really isn't a breeding ground for rock'n'roll.' Moving into a predominantly Chicano East Hollywood neighbourhood, Lux and Ivy quickly created their very own Kenneth-Anger-meets-Frederick's-of-Hollywood version of the city in an apartment on Edgemont Street. For them, LA was the city of Mexican garage bands, Forest Lawn cemetery, and Russ Meyer's *Beyond the Valley of the Dolls* – the Capital of American Trash.

In January 1981, the Cramps went into A&M studios with their new guitarist, Kid Congo Powers, who'd befriended them in New York in 1978 and co-written the Gun Club's tribute song 'For the Love of Ivy'. Kid couldn't really play guitar to save his life, but for the sludgy, wall-of-noise purposes of *Psychedelic Jungle* (1981) it didn't terribly matter. 'I only knew three chords, but I was young and enthusiastic,' he says. 'I think the deciding factor was that I possessed a gold jacket from Lansky Brothers in Memphis.' A mixture of demented originals, *Pebbles* garage rarities and sixties horror novelties such as Nova's 'The Crusher', *Psychedelic Jungle* was a slight departure from the spooked psychobilly of *Songs the Lord Taught Us* but hardly the weak album Lux and Ivy subsequently deemed it to be. For the classic 'Don't Eat Stuff Off the Sidewalk', the band borrowed a crash cymbal from Karen Carpenter, who was often to be seen in the A&M parking lot wearing white bellbottoms that failed to conceal how shockingly skeletal she had become.*

* Carpenter's anorexia had surfaced as early as 1975, when her weight dropped to 85lb. After 'Only Yesterday' that year, the Carpenters never again had a Top 10 single, although 'There's a Kind of Hush' did make it to No. 12 in 1976. Karen had a solo album ready by 1980, but her marriage didn't work out and the anorexia got worse. She finally died of the disease in February 1983, aged 32.

The Cramps were one of the first bands to fall foul of mini-mogul Miles Copeland in the early eighties. Having recorded *Psychedelic Jungle* as quickly and cheaply as possible to extricate themselves from their IRS contract, the group spent most of 1981 and 1982 in a protracted legal suit with Copeland that almost caused them to fold. In addition, Kid Congo was taking Lux and Ivy's penchant for mood-altering substances to an extreme that even they couldn't tolerate. 'After a while they became quite hard taskmasters, and I wasn't very happy,' he remembers. 'They were basically pro-drugs, but they liked the more exciting ones!' After the six-song live EP *Smell of Female* (1983), Powers quit to rejoin Jeffrey Lee Pierce in the Gun Club, allowing the Cramps to return to their mutant-rockabilly roots.

For Kid Congo, the problem with the LA scene in the eighties was that if you didn't fit into certain categories as a band you didn't make it. 'The Gun Club didn't fit into any sub-genre,' he says. 'We were too arty to be in the rockabilly scene, but too rock to be in the arty scene. We could get away with supporting X or the Cramps, but we had a vision of things beyond LA which most bands didn't have and still don't.' Back in 1982, Jeffrey Lee Pierce himself told *New York Rocker* that 'we could easily fit into a little Slash thing with the Blasters and the Flesh Eaters and X,' but something made him 'want to do the opposite of what everybody's doing'. To him, LA was about trendhopping of the most shameless variety. If the city's rockabilly revival had credible roots in the fanaticism of Rockin' Ronny Weisner and his Van Nuys-based Rollin' Rock label – releasing the Blasters' debut *American Music* along with albums by Gene Vincent, Ray Campi, Mac Curtis and others – it still managed to attract a huge number of people who, in Gun Club drummer Terry Graham's words, 'went from David Bowie to Gene Vincent like *that*'.

The Blasters came close to being pegged as a rockabilly band but swiftly redefined themselves as 'roots' traditionalists who could do it all: blues, country, R&B, Tex-Mex and swaggering rock'n'roll. With *The Blasters* (1981), roots rock became the order of the day not only for brothers Dave and Phil Alvin but for their Slash pals Los Lobos, who came out of the barrio of East LA as hip ambassadors for the Mexican music white Angelenos had managed for so long not to hear. Both bands established themselves as darlings of the rock press, despite the fact that their records were actually rather bland. Los Lobos del Este de Los Angeles – 'The Wolves' – had been playing traditional *boleros* and *rancheras* since 1974, but the original songs on their Slash releases ... *And a Time to Dance* (1983) and *How Will the Wolf Survive?* (1984) sounded like a Chicano version of Steve Winwood. They had a No. 1 hit with a version of Ritchie Valens' 'La Bamba' (from the 1987 biopic of the same name) but then returned to their traditional acoustic roots on *La Pistola Y El Corazon* (1988).

The roots-rock reaction to the trauma of hardcore carried over into a mutant retro strain known as 'cowpunk', exponents of which included Rank and File, the Beat Farmers, Blood on the Saddle and Lone Justice.

As he was for the Nudie-suited country rockers of the late sixties, the cowboy was for retired punks a handily mythical ghost who could be used to romanticize punk themes of loneliness and vengeance. If the spectacle of ex-Dils Chip and Tony Kinman in stetsons and bootlace ties was a mite implausible, the music of their band Rank and File was convincing enough: their 1982 Slash debut *Sundown* even retained traces of the old Dils militancy. More authentic as cowpunk *per se* was *Blood on the Saddle* (1984), whose coarse rawhide gnashings made the Kinman brothers sound positively effete.

Tales of the New West was a fitting title for the debut Rhino release by the Beat Farmers, an amiable San Diego outfit who managed to assemble a retro-roots guest-list for the album which included members of the Bangles, the Plimsouls, the Long Ryders, Los Lobos and Rank and File. But the real cowpunk hype was saved for Lone Justice, the five-piece band fronted by young Maria McKee. The half-sister of born-again Love legend Bryan Maclean, McKee had a voice which sounded like Rachel Sweet duking it out with Tanya Tucker, and the band cooked up a fair storm behind her. Unfortunately, Geffen Records had to go and blow it all by giving *Lone Justice* (1985) the full Jimmy Iovine/Tom Petty treatment, robbing them of the chance to establish an identity of their own.

A band who assumed some of the trappings of cowpunk were the Long Ryders, fronted by Gram Parsons devotee Sid Griffin. Their *Native Sons* (1984) was co-produced by Henry Lewy, who'd performed similar duties on the Flying Burrito Brothers' *Gilded Palace of Sin* fifteen years before. Too eclectic to be content with rehashing the country-rock of the Byrds and the Burritos, the Ryders none the less became standard-bearers for the old Gram Parsons dream of 'cosmic American music' and did particularly well in Europe. In LA, meanwhile, they lurked on the fringes of a scene in whose early stages Sid Griffin had played more than a minor part – the 'Paisley Underground'.

Born in Kentucky, Griffin had pitched up in Los Angeles in 1977, briefly playing in a punk outfit called Death Wish before gravitating towards the garage-band power-pop of the Plimsouls and the Rubber City Rebels. Sid claims to have seen the Plimsouls at least forty times, and remembers their shows as 'absolutely devastating'. 'The highlight of that whole period was the Flamin' Groovies coming down to play the Arena in Culver City with the Plimsouls. Everyone in LA who loved power-pop was there.' Early in 1979, Griffin took his sixties psych-punk obsessions one stage further when he formed the Unclaimed with Shelly Ganz, a fellow garage-band fanatic with whom he swapped *Boulders* albums and sat at the feet of Greg Shaw.

Along with the Last, a Hermosa Beach band whose *LA Explosions* album was released on Bomp in 1979, and the Droogs, a neglected LA outfit who'd revived the garage-band sound as early as 1973, the Unclaimed helped pioneer the Vox twelve-string/bowl-haircut/retro-garage aesthetic in America. For Ganz, time had stopped in 1966: he wouldn't even *talk* about Gram Parsons. 'Shelly was so hardcore he wanted to talk about Vietnam and Lyndon Johnson in interviews,' Griffin recalls. 'He'd sit up all night watching *Movies 'Til Dawn* and strumming his guitar, then sleep till 5 p.m.' Ganz's insistence on performing nothing but Misunderstood or Chocolate Watch Band covers ultimately proved too much for the other members of the Unclaimed, but the band's infrequent shows attracted a number of impressionable young musicians who were just discovering the joys of punk psychedelia for themselves. One of them was a kid called Steve Wynn, whom Sid Griffin subsequently approached to play guitar in a new 'psychedelic country band' he was forming with fellow Unclaimed members Barry Shank and Matt Roberts.

Steve Wynn's own band, the heavily Velvets-influenced Dream Syndicate, were at the forefront of the 'Paisley Underground' scene which blossomed in the summer of 1982. A loose coalition of sixties-influenced bands, the Underground was for nine all-too-brief months arguably the healthiest scene LA had produced since the days of the Masque. 'For what it's worth, the original Paisley Underground was the Dream Syndicate, Three O'Clock, the Rain Parade and the Bangs, with the Long Ryders and Green On Red following behind them,' says Sid Griffin. 'All these bands drank beer together and lent each other amps. If one of my strings popped during a gig, I'd just hand the guitar to Karl Precoda of the Syndicate and he'd fix it. Nobody had roadies, and nobody was trying to do each other down. The whole thrust of the thing was more social than musical. Okay, so all the groups were vaguely sixties-influenced guitar-pop bands who'd moved on from punk, but the main thing about the scene was that everybody hung out. I mean, face it – the Bangs were pretty terrible when they started out.'

The Bangs were indeed pretty terrible – four girls-next-door in sixties mini-skirts who could barely play their instruments – but nobody held it against them. As with all the other bands, what mattered was that they were fans, sixties obsessives who, in Greg Shaw's words, had 'sat around all night smoking pot and listening to Emitt Rhodes records'. Slightly more accomplished were the overtly neo-psychedelic bands Three O'Clock and the Rain Parade. As the Salvation Army, Three O'Clock had released a splendidly raw psych-punk album on Frontier before the Army proper demanded they cease using the name. As Three O'Clock, they went into Earle Mankey's Psychedelic Shack to record the altogether more polished *Baroque Hoedown* (1982), featuring tuneful originals and jingly-jangly sixties covers delivered in the winsome teenybop voice of frontman Michael Quercio. The Rain Parade went one better with the exceptional *Emergency Third Rail Power Trip* (1983), an album of baroque trance-rock which stands as possibly the greatest single achievement of the whole Paisley Underground scene.

'The Paisley Underground was the last LA scene I can remember that had any kind of coherence,' says Rhino's Gary Stewart. 'But by the time people realized it was there, it was all over.' Several decisive things happened to the Underground bands in 1983. The Dream Syndicate signed to A&M, following up the wondrous *Days of Wine and Roses* with the disappointing *Medicine Show*. The Bangs became the Bangles and signed to IRS, ready to be groomed for stardom by Miles Copeland. And the Rain Parade's prime mover David Roback quit the band to pursue the various projects which would culminate in the excellent Mazzy Star. But a handful of bands were carrying the Underground torch into previously uncharted areas: the dark, intense Green On Red, whose keyboard player Chris Cavacas lent Dan Stuart's brooding songs an almost Seeds-ish flavour; True West, whose 1983 *Hollywood Holiday* EP was co-produced by Steve Wynn and combined the intensity of Green On Red with the guitar interplay of Television; and the all-girl Wednesday Week, whose excellent *Betsy's House* EP (1983) was released on the Last's Warfrat label. That's without mentioning the Point, with their *Magic Circle* album on Warfrat, or the clutch of post-Paisley bands on the Bomp offshoot label Voxx. This period even saw the re-emergence of such psych-garage legends as Sky Saxon and Roky Erickson, both of whom had releases on the Paris-based New Rose label.

For Rick Gershon, who moved on from running the Plimsouls' fan club to running one for the Long Ryders, the 'sense of community' that had existed within the Paisley Underground scene dissolved the minute the bands began signing to major labels: hardly a novel scenario, but a sad one all the same. Compounding the disappointment was the inability of those labels to market the bands: A&M with the Dream Syndicate, Geffen with the Plimsouls, Island with the Long Ryders. Only Columbia, with the Bangles, got it right, though predictably the group was destroyed in the process. 'By 1986 it had all fizzled out,' says Gershon. 'Peter Case decided he didn't want to be in a band and went off to become this forlorn singer-songwriter. Green On Red sort of moved away, and Steve Wynn all of a sudden didn't belong in LA any more. Saddest of all for me was the Long Ryders, who'd achieved the bottom rung of the ladder but didn't know where to take it from there. I think the rock-bottom point was the Ryders coming back from playing in front of 100,000 people in Spain and barely drawing two hundred at some little club in LA. That really spelled the end of it all.'

VI

For those who chose not to go the Paisley route, there was less of a fall from the fleeting dream of overground success. Post-hardcore bands such as the Minutemen, Saccharine Trust and Red Cross went their own stubborn way, having little truck with the mainstream pop industry. The

Cosmic country rock: the Long Ryders, led by Sid Griffin (second from right).

Minutemen were a combustible trio from San Pedro who grafted sputtering funk riffs and oblique political diatribes on to the punk base of their sound, while Saccharine Trust sounded like a chance collision between Captain Beefheart and the Doors of 'Horse Latitudes'. Both were signed to SST, though the Minutemen also issued records on their own New Alliance label. Red Cross, meanwhile, were teen practitioners of Hollywood trash, their repertoire taking in such topics as cellulite, Linda Blair, the Partridge Family and Russ Meyer, as well as a version of Charles Manson's 'Cease to Exist'.

More of an anomaly on the scene were Savage Republic, a metal-bashing Californian counterpart to the European industrial noise of Test Department and Einsturzende Neubauten. Along with fringe art bands (Monitor, Human Hands, 100 Flowers) and performance-art oddballs (Jimmy Smack, Johanna Went), the Republic often played at the appropriately named Anti-Club on Melrose Avenue, as well as staging 'events' out in the California desert. On the fringes even of *this* 'scene' were the various entities associated with the arcane Los Angeles Free Music Society, together with the eighties spawn of Frank Zappa and Don Van Vliet: deranged weirdos such as Zoogz Rift and His Amazing Shitheads and John Van Zelm Trubee and the Ugly Janitors of America.

As the hardcore virus mutated into the freeform proto-grunge of the Minutemen, the Meat Puppets and that seminal Midwest trio Hüsker Dü, punk itself regressed and became ever more cartoon-like. After all, what did 'punk' mean when Joan Jett could hook up with bubblegum veterans Kenny Laguna and Ritchie Cordell in 1982 and have a No. 1 hit with the brazenly dumb 'I Love Rock'n'Roll'? 'Society made me what I am,' groaned a punk in Alex Cox's hilarious *Repo Man* (1984), an LA-based film featuring the Circle Jerks and Rodney Bingenheimer. 'Bullshit,' sneered Otto (Emilio Estevez). 'You're a white suburban punk just like me.'

The mohican-coiffed punks of *Repo Man* weren't so different from the listless Beverly Hills brats of Bret Easton Ellis's *Less Than Zero* (1985), a vapid but oddly riveting novel permeated by references to X, the Go-Gos and Oingo Boingo. In the final paragraph of the novel, Ellis's hero Clay reflected on the images produced in his mind by X's 'Los Angeles': 'Images of people being driven mad by living in the city. Images of parents who were so hungry and unfulfilled that they ate their own children. Images of people, teenagers my own age, looking up from the asphalt and being blinded by the sun.' In their different ways, both *Repo Man* and *Less Than Zero* confronted the malaise at the heart of LA pop culture in the mid eighties. The strange, apocalyptic quality of the place seemed to be crying out for fresh articulation, and Alex Cox and Bret Easton Ellis were on hand to provide it.

An altogether broader response to life in the City of the Angels was the trilogy of spoken-word collections – *Voices of the Angels* (1982), *English as a Second Language* (1983) and *Neighbourhood Rhythms* (1984) – co-ordinated by former A&R man Harvey Kubernik. Featuring everyone from professional soak Charles Bukowski to Black Flag bassist Charles Dukowski, via Chris D, Henry Rollins, Jeffrey Lee Pierce, Steve Wynn, the Minutemen, Susanna Hoffs, John Van Zelm Trubee, Exene Cervenka, novelist Dennis Cooper and the inevitable Kim Fowley, the trilogy was vinyl proof that no other metropolis on earth inspired such obsessive, self-conscious 'mythography', and in such abundance. 'It's an environmental graphic, an aural mural of the city,' Kubernik said in 1983. 'It's something primordial coming up through the urban garbage. Here you've got the surf punks, the Valley people, the downhome funky bar-blues lingo – you've got a little of everything. It's a wonderful amalgam of voices.'

Like Los Angeles itself, an agglomeration of what contributor Richard Meltzer called 'absolute nowheres', none of the albums had a coherent structure, each flowing with the on/off-ramp freedom of the city's freeways. The hustler sleaze of Walter Lacey's 'Meatrack Man' fed into the Malibu bigotry of Tuff Muffin's 'Beach Rebuttal'; punk scribe Shredder tripped on the heels of black feminist poet Wanda Coleman. Alissa Alvarez's chilling rape poem was followed by Blaster Dave Alvin's low-key vignette 'Old White Women On Vermont', which in turn gave way to Meltzer's anguished elegy to Lester Bangs. 'Harvey's taking the position that each neighbourhood has its own voice,' said the poet Ivan E. Roth, whose 'Beach Party Post' was a highlight of *English as a Second Language*. 'People see LA as a mass, but Harvey's getting down to individuals. It's so factional here, there are so many different groups of people. This at least gives you the opportunity to hear what other people are doing, maybe just get a glimpse or glimmer of their lives.'

VII

One symptom of punk's regression was the 'surf punk' sound of bands such as Agent Orange, the Malibooz, and – yes – the Surf Punks themselves. Even the Cramps tipped a wink to their new locale with the hilarious 'Surfin' Dead', a contribution to the soundtrack of zombie movie *The Return of the Living Dead*. These bands, along with more respectful revivalists like the Wedge and Jon and the Nightriders, were part of a general rekindling of interest in surf culture, suggesting that the LA scene was still haunted by the death of the innocence represented by the early surf scene. 'The basic elements of both eras of music are so similar,' says Mike Palm of Agent Orange. 'They're just so raw, with more emphasis on the emotion, the intensity of playing, than actual technique or arrangements. They fit together so perfectly.'*

In John Milius's 1978 film *Big Wednesday*, an epic and elegiac study of the friendship between three surfers spanning the years of the Vietnam war, Matt Johnson (Jan-Michael Vincent) ends up as a doomed beachbum Adonis hiding behind alcohol and dark glasses. The same pathetic, gone-to-seed quality was captured by Neil Young in 'Surfer Joe and Moe the Sleaze', a track from the 1981 album *re*ac*tor*. With hindsight, both Milius's film and Young's song could almost have been premonitions of the death of Young's old buddy Dennis Wilson. Like Vincent in *Big Wednesday*, Dennis was the California boy who'd had it all, then lost everything. By 1983, with a trail of destructive relationships behind him, he was living like Moe the Sleaze in a tumbledown Venice pad, shacked up with Mike Love's 15-year-old cousin Shawn. When his brief marriage to the girl ended, the pinup rebel of the early sixties virtually became a boardwalk wino. 'The last time I saw Dennis, I was out visiting Peter Asher,' recalled James Taylor, who'd appeared with the Beach Boy in the cult road movie *Two Lane Blacktop* (1971). 'I had had a traffic accident, and Dennis came over looking absolutely wild, in some altered state ... he was green and foaming at the mouth. And a month later he was dead.'

During the last month of his life, as a guest of meat company heir Geordie Hommel Jr, Wilson moved back into the very same Rustic Canyon house where Charles Manson and family had first pitched up in 1968. On 23 December he checked into a detox clinic, walking out on Christmas Day. Two days later, bruised and battered after a binge, he dived off his old boat the *Harmony* at Marina Del Rey to look for some belongings he'd once thrown into the water. Forty-five minutes later, his body was fished up from the bottom of the harbour. 'I still thought of Dennis as all muscle, good looks, and charm,' wrote Brian Wilson, for whom the irony of his brother being swallowed up by the Pacific was almost too hard to bear. Against all the odds, moreover, Dennis had recorded one of the best albums ever to come out of the Beach Boys' camp, the woefully overlooked but aptly titled *Pacific Ocean Blue* (1977). A virtual collaboration between Wilson and his old crony Gregg Jakobson, the album was full of the music the Beach Boys should have been making as a band. Alternately funky ('Dreamer', 'Friday Night') and hauntingly beautiful ('Time', 'Thoughts of You'), it was almost worthy of Brian himself.

* By the nineties, when Agent Orange were playing occasional gigs with the great Dick Dale, the beaches of Southern California were home to the thrash metal/skatecore sound of bands such as Suicidal Tendencies. 'We're a beach band for the nineties,' the latter claimed.

It took no less a figure than Ronald Reagan — whom the Beach Boys had famously entertained in the White House, and whose estranged daughter Patti was one of Dennis's old flames — to grant a special dispensation permitting Wilson to be buried at sea. Thus was the original surf punk, in Brian's words, 'dropped back into the water which had played such an inspirational role in both our lives'.

A predator on the Strip: Ice Cube billboard with Hyatt House behind.

9 *Rituals of the Habitual*

This is no town to be poor in. Every minute someone goes by in their dream car, with their dream life, rubbing your face in it, every minute of the day.

Struggling musician Wallace Moss in Richard Rayner's
Los Angeles Without a Map (1988)

It's so weird, because the West Coast was originally defined by the Beach Boys and the Ventures. But that shit has just evaporated. The beach kids listen to hiphop now.

Hiphop promoter Matt Robinson in Brian Cross's
It's Not About A Salary (1994)

I

With the dissolution of the Paisley Underground scene, the brief sense of community in LA was gone for good. As was happening throughout America and in England, bands were forsaking the indie dream and signing to major labels, while the indies themselves – Slash and Enigma, for example – survived only when they compromised with the mainstream. 'The organic scene was over,' says Rick Gershon, who later became West Coast publicity director for A&M. 'All that was left was the same old Hollywood bullshit.'

In Reagan's new yuppie America, money was no longer a dirty word, least of all in Los Angeles. The 1984 Olympics seemed to symbolize the city's new mood of glitzy affluence, a mood which went hand in hand with the success of the entertainment industry after Michael Jackson's phenomenal *Thriller* album. 'Everyone had started to think corporate, and that creeping mogulism went all the way down the line to the roadies,' says writer Carl Gottlieb. 'By the time Spago opened in 1981, everyone in Hollywood wanted to be a rock'n'roll star, and everyone was doing coke. Doormen would be *tipped* in coke. But the difference this time was people weren't sharing their drugs. In the eighties you were locking the door and keeping it all to yourself. These people were supervising the music and movies of our time. You can't blame the drugs themselves, they were just symptomatic. Someone like Jackson Browne retained some of the hippie ideals, but everyone else lapsed into the yuppie greed of the eighties.'

Yuppie greed: a buzzphrase for a decade dominated by corporate consolidation and summed up by the eventual sale of David Geffen's Geffen label to MCA for a cool half a billion dollars. 'Welcome to the boomtown,' sang David and David, staring into the dark heart of Reagan's California in 1986. 'All that money makes such a *s-s-succulent* sound …' For Richard Meltzer, Californians had money instead of culture – or *as* culture.

'It is a cliché, a joke, something we're past feeling anguished about,' Sara Davidson had written in a 1980 *Esquire* piece about the swanky condo life of Marina Del Rey, 'but the fact is that a considerable number of people have passed through a door and come out wearing different clothes, and this transformation has taken place almost without comment. People who in the flowering of the sixties gave their children names like Blackberry and Veda-Rama have changed them to Suzy and John. The parents are, they say, "getting our money trip together". The successful ones are buying homes, Calvin Klein suits, and Porsches, and sending their kids to private schools to avoid busing.'

David (Baerwald) and David (Ricketts) weren't the only songwriters observing the transformation Davidson was writing about in 'Rolling into the Eighties'. Although their A&M album *Boomtown* came closer to the *noir* slant on California Babylon than any other contemporary rock record, the duo were grappling with the same issues which – to varying degrees – beset Jackson Browne on *Lawyers in Love* (1983), Randy Newman on *Trouble in Paradise* (1983), Don Henley on *Building the Perfect Beast* (1984) and Joni Mitchell on *Dog Eat Dog* (1985). In their very different ways, each of these sixties/seventies veterans was addressing the intrinsic callousness of American capitalism. 'Lawyers in Love' was taken as a swipe at yuppies but was as much about xenophobia and Reagan's new Cold War, and pointed forward to the more explicitly polemical *Lives in the Balance* (1986). Newman's 'I Love LA' was a gloriously tongue-in-cheek celebration of the city, complete with gung-ho backing vocals by most of the city's rockocracy (Henley, Ronstadt, Fleetwood Mac et al.), and was followed on *Trouble in Paradise* by a mordant reflection on another suspect suntopia, Cape Town.

Even Ry Cooder, whose eclectic selection of cover versions contained scant evidence of a radical

'I love LA': Randy Newman, 1983.

conscience, titled his 1982 album *The Slide Area*, after the scathing LA novel by the British screenwriter Gavin Lambert. 'Lambert's idea was that in LA you have all these natural phenomena that make the place unstable,' he told Paul Rambali. 'All these $500,000 homes, totally exclusive, the homes of the sun and surf set, aren't worth spit.' LA, Cooder added, was 'an easy place to live as long as you're white, middle-class and you've got a job'. If you weren't, like the Mexican wetbacks in Tony Richardson's *The Border* (which Cooder scored), the city was far from being a paradise. 'You can stick all the pachucos in the eastern part and all the blacks down in Watts and no one's gonna care so long as they don't see 'em. It's worse now with Reagan in there taking away even the little token amounts of money for people who really need it ... he did more to sell out the state to big business than any other governor in the history of California.'

In 1982, when the Eagles finally called it a day and their manager Irving Azoff became head of MCA Records, few people would have expected Don Henley to emerge from the split as a credible solo artist. But after hooking up with Danny 'Kootch' Kortchmar, a veteran of James Taylor's and Jackson Browne's bands, the drummer-singer released *I Can't Stand Still*, complete with the angry hit single 'Dirty Laundry' and a song about illiteracy called 'Johnny Can't Read'. *Building the Perfect Beast*, recorded with the aid of assorted Macs, Totos and Heartbreakers, was an even more pointed attack on the values of eighties America. From the sublime pop hit 'The Boys of Summer', with its unforgettable image of 'a Deadhead sticker on a Cadillac', to the sinister techno-rock of the title track, the album reflected a level of political engagement which was clearly beyond the reach of his fellow ex-Eagles.

'I wonder what's happened to the sixties generation, the baby-boomers who were going to change the country,' Henley said apropos the album. 'We let it slip through our fingers somewhere along the line. It didn't turn out the way we'd planned. Everybody turned from brotherly love and universal love to self-love somewhere in the seventies. We all went inside ourselves and said, "Well, it's not working, I'm just going to go to work and make a lot of money and take care of *me*" ... that's what I tried to get at in "Boys of Summer".'* On 'Sunset Grill', Henley paid tribute to Joe Froelich's little hamburger stand at 7439 Sunset, describing the track rather portentously as 'a song about accountability in these nameless, faceless times in corporate America'. For Henley, Froelich stood for something personal and local in a city that increasingly felt like 'the twilight zone'.

Don Henley was one of the guest stars on Joni Mitchell's 1985 album *Dog Eat Dog*, the most savage indictment of yuppie America delivered by

---

* Henley claims he really did see a Deadhead sticker on a Cadillac, cruising along the San Diego Freeway one evening. 'It was a Cadillac Seville,' he recalls, 'which in America is a symbol of the bourgeoisie and the right wing generally.'

any elder rock states(wo)man in the mid eighties. Following up *Wild Things Run Fast* (1982), Mitchell's good-humoured return to pop accessibility, *Dog Eat Dog* was a hi-tech assault on greed and materialism produced by English boffin Thomas Dolby. Opening with the brooding, pounding 'Good Friends', graced by the inimitable voice of Michael McDonald, the album cast its withering gaze on the religious right ('Tax Free'), charity rock ('Ethiopia'), and basic avarice ('Dog Eat Dog'). 'I started the eighties by going to a party with the theme "Be Nice to the Eighties and They'll be Nice to You",' she said in 1988. 'Everyone realized at the brink of it that it was going to be a hideous era.'

Mitchell's old compatriot and new Geffen labelmate Neil Young chose a more truculent route through the eighties. Having aligned himself with the punk insurrectionists at the end of the seventies, he spent the first half of the ensuing decade making a series of false starts and volte-faces. *Trans* (1981) was an electronic sci-fi album which verged on the embarrassing, *Everybody's Rockin'* (1983) a pointless rockabilly set. In 1984, in typically ornery fashion, he announced that he was voting for Ronald Reagan: the dismal country album *Old Ways* (1985) was the way he chose to express this reactionary stance. Later it emerged that Young was pre-occupied throughout this period with a gruelling learning programme for his son Ben, who suffered from cerebral palsy, but that didn't stop Geffen Records suing him for deliberately making what they called 'unrepresentative music'. Nor did it do anything except exasperate the majority of his fans. Ironically, it was a brief and fruitless reunion with Crosby, Stills and Nash that triggered the raging electric rock'n'roll of the *Eldorado* EP and subsequent album *Freedom* (1989). By the time Young had reunited with Crazy Horse for *Ragged Glory* (1990), he was back on track at last.

For all the alarm and repugnance expressed by the old guard of singer-songwriters – or by less weatherbeaten figures such as T-Bone Burnett, whose 1983 song 'Hefner And Disney' was a wry reflection on the plastic 'Never Wonderland' of Los Angeles – the eighties continued to unfold with an uneasy mixture of glitz and hypocrisy. In the MTV age of Madonna and new-Brit-in-LA Billy Idol, pop was big business, something highlighted by the guilty-conscience parade of 'Live Aid' and 'USA for Africa'. When Quincy Jones assembled the Great and the Good of the LA pop aristocracy to sing the wretched 'We Are the World' at A&M Studios on 28 January 1985, the gathering summed up the new worthiness of pop in the eighties. As the all-star cast warbled the lines 'There's a choice we're making/We're saving our own lives', they spoke more truth than perhaps they knew: some of them were also trying to salvage their careers.

By the end of the decade – with the sales of CBS to Sony, MCA to Matsushita, and A&M to Polygram, as well as the merger between Time and Warner Brothers – the record industry had become a corporate monster personified by David 'Gekko' Geffen, whose personalized baby of a record label had enjoyed massive sales with the likes of Asia and Aerosmith. Geffen may have kept faith with the Neil Youngs and Joni Mitchells of the world, but he was no longer in the business of providing artistic 'asylum', as the crass power-balladeering of Cher demonstrated. 'David Geffen used to care about music and his artists,' said Don Henley in 1993, 'but he's not in the record business any more. He's in the David Geffen business.'

II

It was Geffen Records who picked up on the latest permutation of bad-boy Sunset Strip metal when the company signed Guns N' Roses in 1986. With the rise and rise of Van Halen, hard rock had been enjoying something of a renaissance in LA, spawning a metal scene in which the likes of Ratt, Quiet Riot and Great White briefly broke out of the Gazzari's/Starwood circuit and tasted stardom. The biggest band to emerge in the wake of Van Halen was Mötley Crüe, whose *Too Fast for Love* was released on their own Leathur label in 1982 and proceeded to sell 20,000 copies in LA alone. By 1985 this sub-Dolls outfit, led by bassist Nikki Sixx, was in the Top 10 with a cover of Brownsville Station's 'Smokin' in the Boys' Room', although their bad-boy habits had led to the conviction for manslaughter of singer Vince Neil after the death in a car crash of Hanoi Rocks drummer 'Razzle' Dingley.

Van Halen themselves reached the pinnacle of their success with the synth-driven, irresistibly Who-esque 'Jump', No. 1 for five weeks early in 1984. The following year, an ugly fight saw David Lee Roth quitting the band and re-emerging with a version of 'California Girls' that was little more than an excuse to shoot a *Boobwatch*-style video starring a bevy of bikini-clad beauties. By then, Van Halen's increasing accommodation of pop had opened the way for a number of bands to offer something more degenerate and dangerous to the metal hordes on the Sunset Strip. 'Within two years, the Strip had gone from lip-gloss to cock-stink,' says Kim Fowley, whom Guns N' Roses approached for advice and direction early in their career. 'Suddenly a lot of cock-stink bands showed up, and everybody had to beat up policemen and shoot heroin in their feet. By 1988, we had to deal with the clones of Guns and Poison. The tits got bigger, the men got dumber, and the music got uglier.'

According to club-owner Cheryl Rixon-Davis, it was Artist Development director Bryn Bridenthal who successively groomed the bad-boy images of Mötley Crüe at Elektra and then Guns N' Roses at Geffen. It's worth noting that when Guns released their debut album, *Appetite for Destruction*, in 1987 they were just one of a hundred identikit LA bands with lion manes, loud guitars and bicep artwork courtesy of Sunset Strip Tattoo. Only when the torrid tales of overdoses and detox centres started

Axl Rose, 1987.

filtering through to the world at large did *Appetite* begin creeping up the charts. The fact that the record was a thoroughly ordinary collection of hard rock/metal songs did not unduly trouble punters thirsting for a little vicarious debauchery.

As with the Crüe, Guns were merely a Xerox of a Xerox of a Xerox: the 1969 Stones via Aerosmith via Hanoi Rocks. 'As amazing as it seems in this drug-free-exercise-and-health age,' said lead guitarist Slash, 'there's a bunch of us still clinging fast to the late sixties and early seventies.' 'Clinging' was about the sum of it, however abjectly the world's media colluded with the age-old Sunset Strip pose. Lead singer Axl Rose was the archetypal messed-up smalltown boy, come to Hollywood to reinvent himself as a junkie rock god, and the others weren't a lot more prepossessing.*

The incredible thing about the Sunset Strip metal and hard-rock scene is simply that all those poodle haircut/Harley Davidson/skull-and-crossbones-tattoo clichés refuse to die. Year in, year out, one sees the same imbeciles unloading their Marshall stacks into crappy pay-to-play dives like the Coconut Teazer or gawping at pink Ibanez axes in the Guitar Center. Boys in leather pants and mirror shades still swarm into Hollywood to hang out at the Rainbow bar, all of them hoping against hope that *their* minor variation on a dead theme is going to propel them into the stadiums. The casualties among those chasing the Guns N' Roses fantasy – no-hope bands living in squalid cubicles like those in the 'Billiards' building on Hollywood and Western – are endless.

'The trouble is, metal was where the money was, as well as the gratuitous sex and drugs,' says Rick Gershon. 'Labels like Geffen moved in to sweep every pretty-boy hairtree, some of whom were just unemployed actors on Harleys. There were even punk veterans who wound up in metal bands. Some of it was interesting, but there was no sense of community there – absolutely the reverse, because there was an intense rivalry between all these bands.' One man who'd seen it all before was Lou Adler, for whom many of the bands trooping in and out of the Roxy were (and are) simply 'imitating a rock'n'roll lifestyle'. 'They all know the script,' he adds, 'and they're following the line that's been laid down for them.'

Almost as incredible as the endless recycling of the clichés is that the same breed of groupies and caretakers continues to come to the aid of these dorks, feeding them, fellating them and procuring the requisite pharmaceuticals for their bad-boy lifestyles. Just as Christine Hinton moved into an apartment behind the Whisky to tend to David Crosby in 1965, and just as Ronnie Haran let Jim Morrison trash her similarly situated pad in 1966, so in 1985 Vicky Hamilton looked after Slash and Axl in her place on North Clark Street.

* For a contemporary account of the fascination which Hollywood sleaze still exerted on provincial American teenagers, see Robert Keating's 1986 *Spin* piece 'To Live and Die in LA'.

Hard-rock landmark: Sunset Strip Tattoo.

If Guns N' Roses wanted simultaneously to be the Rolling Stones and the Sex Pistols, bands like Poison were merely rehashing what Van Halen had done ten years before, with none of the wit or panache. 'Poison represented a kind of safe, icky metal,' says Cheryl Rixon-Davis. 'They were like the Bangles or New Kids of hard rock.' Not that this was enough to stop film-maker Penelope Spheeris documenting the metal scene in exactly the same way she'd documented the later stages of punk. 'I found the whole thing rather comical,' she says. 'I mean, you literally couldn't move for the spandex and big hair on Sunset at weekends, so I thought: we have a surge of another sort here, and it's time to get out with the cameras again. As it turned out, it was even more hilarious than I'd imagined – and more tragic, too.' Fittingly enough, it was *The Decline of American Civilisation, Part Two: the Metal Years* (1989) which led Mike Myers and Lorne Michaels to hire Spheeris to direct the hugely successful *Wayne's World* (1992), about a pair of metal-worshipping drongoes in Aurora, Illinois.

An offshoot from the hard-rock scene which proved to be rather more interesting than Poison and co. was the clutch of bands who fused the relentless drive of metal with the kinetic sexuality of funk. Foremost among these were the Red Hot Chili Peppers, who'd evolved out of a Hollywood HM outfit called Anthym but who'd gradually incorporated the influences of funk and hardcore punk into their sound. Bassist Flea had briefly replaced Derf Scratch in Fear, but by late 1983 his slap-and-pop style of playing was a central pillar in the sound of Anthony Kiedis and Hillel Slovak's Red Hot Chili Peppers. Signed to EMI America, the Peppers quickly acquired a reputation as the most exciting (and possibly the most debauched) live band on the Hollywood circuit, one to which

'The absolute Funk Rock matrix':
Red Hot Chili Peppers, 1989.
Clockwise from top left: Flea,
Anthony Kiedis, John Frusciante,
Chad Smith.

they only did justice after being paired up with their hero George Clinton for *Freaky Styley* (1985). On this, their second album, they included versions of Sly Stone's 'If You Want Me to Stay' and the Meters' 'Africa' (retitled 'Hollywood'), along with such outrageously lewd songs as 'Sex Rap', 'Blackeyed Blonde' and 'Catholic Schoolgirls Rule'. *Interview*'s Glenn O'Brien described the group as 'the absolute Funk Rock matrix', and other writers noted the way the Peppers – by now as influenced by rap as by funk – bridged black and white music in a way no LA band had attempted before.

By the time of the release of *The Uplift Mofo Party Plan* (1988), recorded after heroin had all but rent the band apart, the Chili Peppers were at the forefront of a racially schizoid funk-rock scene that included bands as diverse as Thelonious Monster, sometime ska troupe Fishbone, and ex-Minuteman Mike Watt's fIREHOSE. (Peppers guitarist Hillel Slovak became one of the many casualties of the Hollywood heroin scene when he died from an overdose in June 1988.) Perhaps the most intriguing of this breed – though they were the least indebted to funk *per se* – was Jane's Addiction, a band led by the almost messianic Perry Farrell and described by a Warners A&R man in Richard Rayner's novel *Los Angeles Without a Map* as 'sorta glam-rock, sorta heavy-metal, sorta post-punk'.

Born Perry Bernstein in New York, Farrell had bummed around America and washed up in LA during the last days of the Hollywood punk scene. 'I just freaked out when I got there,' he remembers. 'On my first night I went to this teenage gay club, and then we went on to Oki Dog, where everyone like the Germs were hanging out with green mohawks. I was all glam and *femme* at the time, so they threw beer bottles at us and spat on our car. Then the next night I went up to the Strip and saw all these guys who still had shag haircuts, and I couldn't believe it.' Farrell decided he wanted no truck with either the punk *or* metal crowds, and instead hung out on the periphery of the downtown art/noise scene listening to the likes of Savage Republic and Kommunity FK. By 1983, he'd settled permanently in LA, though home as often as not was the beach or a friend's car.

Jane's Addiction were formed shortly after Farrell left his first band Psi Com in 1985. Taking their cue from the shock-tactic performance artists he'd seen downtown, the group's early shows at the Scream featured transsexual strippers and self-crucifying dancers, providing an art-rock alternative to the Guns N' Roses/Faster Pussycat scene on the Strip. Farrell quickly established himself as a manic Iggy-esque frontman, a libertarian High Priest with a banshee-like voice described perfectly by Simon Reynolds as 'a high-helium peal of petulance'. With Dave Navarro's careening guitar and Stephen Perkins' neo-tribal drumming, the band steered a compelling midway course between primitivism and decadent transgression. 'What I wanted has nothing to do with British music,' Farrell claimed later. 'What I wanted was an LA sound . . . we come from a land of shopping malls and funk and gangs and sunshine. It's up and it's powerful and it's sometimes violent.'

Recorded live at the Roxy, the punk-funk-metal of *Jane's Addiction* (1987) – with songs such as the propulsive 'Pigs in Zen' and the transparently Stooges-derived 'Whores' – led to the band's signing by Warners and the 1988 album *Nothing's Shocking*, with its 'shocking' cover of Siamese twins with their scalps on fire. From the mighty opening of 'Up the Beach'/'Ocean Size', Farrell came on like some demented zen surfer, albeit one with a taste for dresses and dreadlocks and dangerous drugs. This dionysiac guru was a true mongrel, a creature who stood outside even the prevailing norms of rock rebellion. If there was a gleam of madness in his wired eyes, that in itself made him a more potent focus for the new counterculture of crusties and travellers. 'True leaders gone, of land and people,' Perry sang on the epic 'Three Days' from *Ritual De Lo Habitual* (1990); 'We choose no kin but adopted strangers/The family weakens by the lengths we travel ... All of us with wings ...'

Farrell put his tribal theories into practice when he launched the travelling multi-media rock festival Lollapalooza in 1991. With its heterogeneous assembly of acts – Henry Rollins, Ice-T, Nine Inch Nails and others – Lollapalooza was a huge success at a time when giant stadium bands were having trouble filling modestly sized arenas. It also provided a swansong of sorts for Jane's Addiction themselves, whose drug problems were only one of the reasons why Farrell chose to commence a new phase of his life with a band called Porno for Pyros. 'Nothing I do will ever last more than five years,' he'd claimed, and he seemed to be keeping to his word. 'I'm taking alternative music and commercializing it,' he said. 'What's more exciting is the undergrowth of that, the *bottom buds*. It's all becoming very widespread, eclectic and fresh – you don't know *what's* coming next.'

III

Jane's Addiction and the Peppers were part of a wave of white rock in LA that acknowledged for the first time the power of black and Mexican cultures, cultures which were increasingly hard for whites to ignore as the eighties drew to a close.* It's true that rap, like punk before it, came comparatively late to Los Angeles, but that it came at all was remarkable in a city where authentic black expression had been more or less stifled

---

* The most interesting LA artist to emerge since the first draft of this book was completed, a strange white boy called Beck, has fused hiphop, folk and blues in a uniquely unholy alliance. Even rave culture made it to LA: the largest rave in America took place in 1992 at the Knott's Berry Farm family amusement park! As R. J. Smith put it in a piece charting the post-riots decline of the scene, 'the rave became home to a new vision of Los Angeles.' See R. J. Smith, 'Paradise Lost', *Details*, November 1994.

since the release of the Watts Prophets' *Rappin' Black in a White World* in 1971. And once it was in full bloom, it was as though fifty years of pent-up fury had erupted on the streets of South Central LA.

Just as it was hard for the rest of the world to take the LA punk scene seriously, so West Coast rap suffered from the invidious notion that this radical new musical form was inseparable from the South Bronx. The first rap records to come out of LA – sub-Sugarhill offerings produced by the likes of father-and-son team Jerry and Duffy Hooks – were pointedly ignored by local black radio and East Coast rappers alike. Only with the increasing popularity of breakdancing in 1982 – specifically the West Coast phenomena of 'popping' and 'locking', as seen in films like *Breakin'* and *Wild Style* – did the LA sound attain any kind of credibility. At a trendy downtown club called Radio, local DJs Chris the Glove and the Egyptian Lover worked alongside such East Coast visitors as Afrika Islam and Grandmaster DST. By 1983, the Egyptian Lover had recorded the electro-rap classic 'Egypt, Egypt'.

As important as Radio and the slightly later Radiotron were the huge dances staged throughout LA by a group of DJs (including the Egyptian Lover) who called themselves Uncle Jam's Army. Featuring East Coast acts like Whodini and Run DMC, these dances also provided showcases for such local heroes as Ice T, whose 'The Coldest Rap' (1983) fell into the same Kraftwerk-meets-Pacman electro-rap bag as the Lover's records. Held in venues as large as the LA Coliseum and the Sports Arena, the Uncle Jam's Army events were the ultimate proof that West Coast rap was no passing fad, which was doubtless why in 1984 the radio station KDAY finally sat up and paid attention to it.

It is hard to overestimate the importance of KDAY programmer Greg Mack's decision to embrace rap, sponsoring the Friday night roller-rink 'battles' between young MCs and employing a seminal group of DJs calling themselves the Mixmasters (and including future NWA members Yella and Dr Dre). The Mixmaster radio shows became hugely popular around Los Angeles, helping to make KDAY the No. 1 black station in the city. 'Dre and Yella were the first ones, and their careers just skyrocketed,' Mack told Brian Cross. 'I couldn't keep DJs 'cause we were losing them right and left to rappers.' Dre and Yella were themselves part of the World Class Wrekin' Cru, whose manager Lonzo Williams had promoted rap shows at a club called Eve's After Dark. 'I hired Kurtis Blow to come to the club, and he brought Davy D,' Williams recalled. 'Davy taught Yella how to scratch, and that brought scratchin' to the West Coast. A few months later, I brought in Run DMC with Jam Master Jay, and he also taught some of my boys.'

Although the World Class Wrekin' Cru had a big local hit with 1985's 'Slice', distributed by the vitally important Macola label, they quickly tired of the old-school dance moves and the matching leather-and-lace outfits that Lonzo Williams insisted they wear. Like Ice T, they were moving slowly but surely towards the harder, more underground style which would come to be known as 'gangsta' rap – music which made more sense as a street soundtrack booming from boxes and car speakers than it did in clubs. When Dr Dre hooked up with a rapper called Eazy E in 1987, he took the Wrekin' Cru off on a completely new tangent.

Although gangsta rap was already established on the East Coast with Schoolly D, Just Ice and Boogie Down Productions, Ice T had named himself after the legendary pimp writer Iceberg Slim long before Schoolly D's debut album was released in 1986. When Ice recorded his classic 'Six in the Morning', he wasn't simply hopping on to the new bandwagon, he was reconnecting with the ghetto life of his upbringing. 'I'm a self-made monster of the city streets/Remotely controlled by hard hiphop beats,' he sang, and the fearsome boast encapsulated the mindset of the new rap gangsta, on the run from the LAPD and its terrifying 'batteram'. After five years of house-rocking rap anthems by such inoffensive acts as the LA Dream Team, it was time for a dose of stone cold reality. Records like 'Six in the Morning', Todd Terry's 'Batteram', and Ice Cube's 'Boyz n the Hood' took the message of 'The Message' into the age of crack, AIDS and gang-banging. Gone were the fast electro beats and synths of the early eighties, and in their place came the slower, more insidious grooves of seventies funk.

If West Coast gangsta rap had an official birth, it was probably at a Run DMC show in Long Beach in 1986, when a large contingent of Crips and Bloods showed up with firepower in tow and six people were killed. 'That was the worst I've ever seen in my life,' said Greg Mack, who was MC'ing the show. 'They let a lot of gangs in from different areas, because security wasn't hip to colours … next thing you know, a whole section was running, gangs were hittin' people, grabbing gold chains, beating people. As we were leaving I saw cop cars and helicopters, and on the news people were leaving all covered with blood. It was the last rap show ever in Long Beach, and Run DMC of course got blamed even though they didn't even get to play.' By the beginning of 1987, gang-related killings (most of them to do with the burgeoning crack trade) were averaging one a day, and white LA was starting to get panicked. For Mike Davis, the gangs 'transmuted self-hatred into tribal rage' while simultaneously embodying, with their gold and Gucci fixations, the materialist values of Reagan's America. For the outside world, the fact that these horrors were being played out against a backdrop of palm trees and barbecues on sunny suburban streets, rather than in a post-holocaust wasteland of gutted Bronx tenements, made them all the more fascinating.

It was the release of Dennis Hopper's *Colors* in April 1988 that brought LA's gang problem to boiling point. The original screenplay set the film in Chicago, but Hopper had stipulated that he wouldn't direct it unless the action was moved to South Central LA. He also made crack-dealing central to the film's plot and recruited a large number of real-life gang

Ice-T, gangsta godfather.

members to appear as extras. During location shooting, a massive security cordon protected the actors and technical team from spectating gang members, among whom fights regularly broke out. *Colors* was hardly the *Easy Rider* of gang culture that Dennis Hopper (a veteran slummer on the radical-chic circuit) wanted it to be, but it did produce the chilling theme track by Ice T, a song which took 'Six in the Morning' one menacing step further: 'Sucker dive for your life when my shotgun splatters/Because the gangs of LA will never die, just multiply...'

Having abandoned the secondhand hiphop style of the early-to-mid-eighties, Ice T was now at the forefront of the West Coast gangsta-rap sound. 'I was really fakin' it back then,' he told Brian Cross. 'I was listening to New York rap and attempting to rap about that particular shit, but it wasn't me ... I thought you had to rap about rockin' a party, but in true fact I had never rocked a party. We weren't living in hiphop culture, but hiphop started in New York. They had graffiti artists, break dancers ... we had gangs.' If 'Six in the Morning' established Ice as the true voice of South Central, 'Colors' and his Sire debut *Rhyme Pays* made South Central itself the new epicentre of American rap. 'From that point on, LA was really considered something,' Ice recalls. 'I put the nail in the wood and NWA just came and was like "Boom", just drove that shit in with *Straight Outta Compton* and it was on.'

It was Ice Cube's brilliant 'Boyz n the Hood' – a collaboration between Eazy E, 16-year-old Cube and the ex-Wrekin' Cru DJs Yella and Dr Dre – which really gave birth to the gang-style aggregation known notoriously as Niggaz With Attitude. After it was a major hit on KDAY in the summer of 1987, Dre, Cube, Eazy and Yella teamed up with MC Ren and recorded the early NWA classics 'Dopeman' and '8 Ball'. But it was *Straight Outta Compton* (1988) which hit the rap world with the explosive force of Public Enemy on the East Coast. 'NWA ... shook the shit out of East Coast rappers and fans alike,' wrote Greg 'Ironman' Tate in the *Village Voice*. 'That record not only put listeners within point-blank range of the LA gang mentality, but it did so non-judgementally, without any sense of moral distance, going so far on some tracks as to use black-on-black violence as the metaphoric base for some of the group's boasting ... what they put to the test was the argument that rap was the voice of black Americans who had no voice elsewhere.'

Straight Outta Compton was as exciting as it was shocking and taboo-smashing. Built on ruff funk beats and deep bass grooves, it had the same visceral texture and immediacy as Chuck D's sound on the Public Enemy records. From the opening title track, an enraged Cube tirade namechecking Charles Manson and AK-47s, through the fearless 'Fuck tha Police' and the cold-blooded 'Dopeman', the record swept you up in its urgent, insistent beats. 'I think we just took rap out of its simplicity and put in a lot more time and effort because we knew we had to come back that much flyer,' said Cube. 'You know, New York had a grip on it, so we knew we had to work that much harder. I think by doin' that, our music found its fullest, we used a lot more live instruments and put a lot more effort into our breaks.'

Straight Outta Compton also had the effect of galvanizing the whole West Coast rap scene, putting Compton on the map as Rap Central and leading to the proliferation of gangsta groups like Above the Law and Compton's Most Wanted. While Ice T formed Rhyme Syndicate and Eazy E launched Ruthless with NWA manager Jerry Heller, over in Hollywood white boys Matt Dyke and Mike Ross were starting to enjoy some success with their Delicious Vinyl label. 'Delicious started with Matt and Mike selling records out of the trunk of their car at swap-meets,' says Paul Moshay, who joined the label as marketing manager in late 1988. 'It was a really exciting period, and it was amazing to see independent records selling wildly.' 'Selling wildly' is almost an understatement: Tone Loc's 1988 hit 'Wild Thing' was the biggest-selling rap single to date, and Young MC's 'Bust a Move' wasn't far behind it. As a DJ, Matt Dyke had been instrumental in mixing up rock and hiphop, turning white punks on to rap in such clubs as Power Tools; now he and Mike Ross were functioning almost as a kind of rap Leiber and Stoller.*

In addition to the success of black hiphop acts, the galvanizing impact of *Straight Outta Compton* was registered by other minorities, particularly in the Chicano and Latino communities. With the help of DJs Tony G and Skatemaster Tate, rappers such as Kid Frost and the Cuban-born Mellow Man Ace began incorporating the twin influences of sixties 'oldies' and of seventies bands like War and Malo into hiphop, creating a Latin sound (complete with 'Spanglish' barrio slang) which paralleled black hiphop in precisely the way Mexican lowrider gangs in East LA had paralleled black gangs in South Central. 'You play rap for some of the hardcore Chicanos, even some of my homeboys, and they say "Why you wanna rap ese, fuckin' blacks' homes, fuckin' *mietas*?"' said Frost, whose 'La Raza' was a big Chicano rap hit. 'And I say my rap is gonna be for the Chicanos' homes about *raza* and shit and they're like, oh, *orale* and when they heard my shit come out they were, like, dang. So I incorporated the oldies into my sound 'cause I know how deep the oldies are. People like "Thin Line Between Love and Hate" and "Smilin' Faces Sometimes", Bill Withers.

---

* The fact that Dyke and Ross were Jewish – like Leiber and Stoller before them – was significant, given the explicit anti-semitism of such rap stars as Public Enemy's Professor Griff. On Ice Cube's second solo album, *Death Certificate*, there was a track ('No Vaseline') pronouncing the death sentence on the Jewish Jerry Heller, the controversy surrounding which was further fuelled by Cube's endorsement of a bilious Nation of Islam tract called *The Secret Relationship Between Blacks and Jews*. 'The notion that the Jewish race had a major part in the African slave trade has become popular again,' Jewish rap publicist Bill Adler told *NME*'s Gavin Martin. 'That this and other anti-Semitic canards should be championed by a leading member of the hiphop community was very upsetting to me.' With Harold Brackman, a professor in Black–Jewish relations, Adler published a comprehensive refutation of the Nation of Islam's claims called *Jew on the Brain*.

We used them because we knew it would be a lot easier for Chicanos to listen to the stories, like I did with "Ain't No Sunshine".'

By 1991, when Kid Frost brought together assorted Chicanos, Cubans, Puerto Ricans and Dominicans for the *Latin Alliance* project, the LA hiphop scene had become a good deal less stratified along racial lines. Blackness was now a rap state of mind as accessible to Latinos as it was to the fearsome Samoan gang the Boo Yah T.r.i.b.e. Cross-pollination was the order of the day, with all the LA minorities influencing each other's taste and music. 'We feel the niggas, the Mexicans, the Chinese, white kids, it don't matter,' said DJ Muggs of Cypress Hill, a South Gate trio comprising an Italian (Muggs), a Cuban (Sen Dog) and a Cuban-Mexican (B Real) who by late 1993 were almost the biggest rap group on the planet. Epitomizing the multi-ethnicity of the LA hiphop scene of the early nineties – what David Toop called 'the Fourth World in progress' – Cypress Hill were part of a confederation known as the Soul Assassins, whose other charter members included the Irish/Latvian House of Pain and the Mexican/Sioux Indian/Puerto Rican Funkdoobiest. They were also as prone to eulogizing violence and misogyny as any of rap's official gangstas, partly because by 1993 it was hard to get anyone's attention unless you were rapping about guns, blunts and bitches (or unless you were Arrested Development).

Violence and misogyny continued to dominate records by Ice T, Ice Cube and the other principal exponents of West Coast hiphop. In 1989, Cube split from NWA and teamed up with Public Enemy's production arm, the Bomb Squad, to record *Amerikkka's Most Wanted* (1990), an album even more exhilaratingly apoplectic than *Straight Outta Compton*. Like Ice T, Cube complemented his records with movie appearances, notably in the acclaimed *Boyz n the Hood*, and both Ices appeared in the disappointing *Trespass* (1992). NWA themselves encountered a new tide of censorship when thousands of copies of their *Efil4Zaggin* album were seized in Britain, but by then they could look around them with pride at the numerous acts they'd helped along the way: Michel'le, the DOC, Da Lench Mob, Above the Law and many others. In 1993, Dr Dre's multi-million-selling album *The Chronic* introduced the world to the notorious Snoop Doggy Dogg, just one of several rappers to be arraigned on murder or accessory-to-murder charges in 1993–4. If rap nationwide had been made more palatable by artists as different as MC Hammer and De La Soul – by the whole culture of *Yo! MTV Raps* – the LA gangstas persisted in upping the transgression stakes. As R. J. Smith wrote in the *LA Weekly* in 1993: 'How many bullets have been shot since Ice T triggered West Coast gangsta style with "Six in the Morning" in 1986? We've had seven years of gunplay, and the world still isn't getting any better.'

Only the new 'freestyling' hiphop scene, centred around a South Central healthfood store called the Good Life, provided any alternative to the unrelenting nihilism and braggadocio of gangsta rap. Performing and recording under the aegis of the umbrella-like Freestyle Fellowship (subsequently the Heavyweights), groups such as Urban Props, Menace II Society and the Fellowship themselves congregated at the Good Life on Thursday nights and delivered themselves of the unrehearsed, on-the-spot raps which became known as 'freestylin''. Not only were the freestylers less intimidating than the gangstas, but they were exploring the same mellow jazz-rap sound which had inspired the likes of the Goats, Gang Starr and Digable Planets. One of the biggest influences on the Fellowship was that legendary trio the Watts Prophets, who'd formed in the wake of the 1965 uprising and were still active on the scene. At the time that the Fellowship's *Inner City Griots* was being released by Island in the spring of 1993, the Watts Prophets were touting demos around which they'd recorded with LA producers the Dust Brothers. West Coast rap had effectively come full circle.

IV

Aside from giving vent to an explosion of black and brown voices from the LA ghettos, West Coast hiphop made mainstream Californian rock sound thoroughly redundant. Alongside Ice Cube's 'The Nigga Ya Love to Hate' or Cypress Hill's 'How I Could Just Kill a Man', Cher and Michael Bolton and the remodelled Belinda Carlisle were the sound of corporate lobotomization – or what Brian Eno, in 1992, termed 'Hollywoodization'. Nor were Guns N' Roses and their ilk much better, for all their meticulously publicized flirtation with 'danger'. Above all, the eighties ushered in a new era of rehabilitation, of professional survivors such as Tina Turner and Eric Clapton, David Crosby and Bonnie Raitt. Every washed-up soak and junkie on the block came back for another stab at the bigtime, and some of them cashed in all over again.*

By 1987, even Brian Wilson was deemed to be capable of a comeback. After six years of abusive 'therapy' at the hands of the outrageous Dr Eugene Landy, Brian managed a passable imitation of a functional human being – passable enough, at any rate, to convince Seymour Stein of Sire Records that he could make a record. The only catch was that Eugene Landy was part of the package, coming in on the project as executive producer and sharing in the writing credits on several songs. A power struggle quickly ensued between Landy and Warners producer Russ Titelman, who objected to Brian's 'surf Nazi' assistant Kevin Leslie and remembers the whole experience as a nightmare. 'When Brian was on it

* One 'survivor' who didn't survive long enough to make a comeback was Rick Nelson, whose dilapidated 1944 DC-3 aeroplane caught fire and crashed on New Year's Day 1986. Rumours that the fire started as a result of Nelson freebasing have never been substantiated, although the former teen idol was definitely partial to cocaine. Two years after his death, Rick's twin sons signed to Geffen as the pop-rock act Nelson.

in the studio, he'd come to life,' says Titelman. 'But then he'd immediately be squashed by Landy.' The friction wasn't helped by the fact that Lenny Waronker also wanted a say in the proceedings, bringing in Jeff Lynne and Lindsay Buckingham without even consulting Brian.

For all the aggravation suffered by Titelman during the sessions for the album, his experience was nothing compared to that of Brian Wilson's old songwriting partner Gary Usher, who'd begun working with him again in May 1986. Usher was so astounded by Landy's behaviour over the succeeding months that he kept a daily journal of the events surrounding the collaboration, later turning it over to the attorney general's office as evidence against Landy. In February 1988, shortly before the release of *Brian Wilson*, Eugene Landy was charged with ethical and licensing code violations by the California Department of Justice.*

Given all this, it was perhaps hardly surprising that *Brian Wilson* proved to be a colossal disappointment. There was something grotesque about a grown man singing such idiotic ditties as 'Walkin' the Line' and 'Little Children', songs which recalled the more inane tracks on, say, *The Beach Boys Love You*. If there were redeeming moments on 'Let it Shine', 'There's So Many' and 'Rio Grande', they couldn't make up for the paucity of genuine ideas on the record. How cruel, therefore, that the Beach Boys themselves should be enjoying an unexpected and unmerited piece of good fortune with the dire 'Kokomo', a song co-written by Mike Love, John Phillips and Terry Melcher that rose all the way to No. 1. Two years later, moreover – by which time Seymour Stein and Lenny Waronker had refused to give him an advance for his second album – Brian's own estranged daughters, Carnie and Wendy, were topping the charts as two thirds of the group Wilson Phillips.

The very name Wilson Phillips betrayed a curious sort of LA nepotism. These were the names of the men (Brian Wilson, John Phillips) who'd neglected their daughters and generally fucked up their lives, but they were also names which gave the trio the cachet of Californian pop legend. Not that Carnie and Wendy and Chynna Phillips shrank from airing their dirty laundry in public. If the irresistible chorus of 'Hold On' could have been a mantra for a Beverly Hills CODA meeting, the group's second album, *Shadows and Light*, was a more sustained exploration of their dysfunctional childhoods. 'It was Wendy who said, "Let's write a song about Dad,"' said Carnie Wilson after the album was released. 'But once we'd come up with "Flesh and Blood" she got scared. She said she didn't want to put it on the album because it was exposing too much. I said, "No, he's gotta hear it because it's good for us, it's good for him, and it's good for anyone else out there who's feeling the same way."'

Hiphop made little impact on Brian Wilson or his Grammy-winning daughters, but it continued to stamp itself on the alternative/underground

* Usher's journal was quoted substantially in a special issue of the magazine *Beach Boys Australia*, subsequently reprinted in 1992 as *The Wilson Project*.

rock scene, interfacing with metal, punk and grunge in the early nineties. The Red Hot Chili Peppers, for example, recorded their breakthrough album *Blood Sugar Sex Magick* with Rick Rubin, the former Def Jam supremo who'd moved to LA from New York in 1991. ('I really have gone Hollywood,' said the man who'd forged the original rap-metal hybrid with the Run DMC/Aerosmith classic 'Walk This Way'; 'I used to make fun of people like me.') An equally significant relocation was that of Rubin's former protégés the Beastie Boys, brat-rappers who'd ruled the world in '86 and then re-emerged in Los Angeles with the excellent Dust Brothers-produced *Paul's Boutique* (1989). Although it took five more years for the trio to haul themselves back to the top of the pop pile with *Ill Communication*, the Beasties were instrumental in paving the way for such LA rap-rock outfits as the mighty Rage Against the Machine.

The Beasties: Mike D, Ad Rock, MCA.

The Beastie Boys of 1986 had been symptomatic of a desire on the part of suburban white teenagers to emulate the B-boy lifestyles of their black counterparts. By the time *Paul's Boutique* was released, the *Los Angeles Times* could report that the affluent sons of Westlake Village and Agoura Hills were wearing bleepers in imitation of crack runners, although the only people who ever bleeped them were their parents. For white hiphop promoter Matt Robinson, the Beasties' Muggs-produced *Check Your Head* (1992) was part of a new West Coast sound – part sampled, part live-performed – which embraced the Pharcyde, the Freestyle Fellowship and Cypress Hill themselves. If some black hiphoppers dissed the trio, others accorded *Check Your Head* the respect it fully deserved. Dr Dre admitted that it 'tripped me out, bugged me the fuck out' when he discovered white kids were buying his records, while Ice T claimed optimistically that 'the injection of black rage into white American youth' was 'the last stage of preparation for revolution'.

The influence of rap on rock was mirrored by the influence of metal and hardcore punk on rap. When Ice T put together his metal/hardcore offshoot Body Count in 1991, he was aiming for a sound which combined 'the attack of Slayer, the impending doom of Sabbath, [and] the drive of Motorhead ... to come up with what I call consumable hardcore music'. It's debatable whether Ice succeeded in his aim, but the very existence of Body Count – featured as part of Ice T's set in the first Lollapalooza tour – was remarkable.

One could argue that grunge itself was a white response to hardcore rap, or at least a tacit acknowledgement that hiphop had laid waste to the pop mainstream, and that it was time for a fresh punk onslaught on corporate rock. Certainly, the grunge scene in the Pacific northwest had severe implications for all the Guns and Poison clones still infesting the Sunset Strip. 'Seattle killed the Strip,' opined one struggling hard-rock guitarist in 1993. 'There were all these bands here that for all these years thought it was all right to still be Poison, and then these bands came along and made all the fake, shallow LA bands look totally ridiculous.'

(Particularly ridiculous were LA Guns, a band formed by original Guns
N' Roses member Tracii Guns, whose two Vertigo albums included such
asinine tracks as 'Hollywood Tease' and 'Riot on Sunset'.) Even when LA
bands made a bid to be as scuzzy as the grungemeisters of Seattle, they
invariably ended up regurgitating all the nihilistic, drug-addled clichés of
English Disco-era Hollywood. As Andy Cairns of Irish band Therapy?
put it, 'the worst thing you can do is defend the LA rock lifestyle, but
once you're there you have to live it, you have to be in detox and be
leathertrousertastic.'

Although Hole's Courtney Love and Inger Lorre of the Nymphs were
happy to cash in on the Riot Grrrl phenomenon of 1992, both of them
were true daughters of Babylon. A veteran of the LA punk/new wave
scene, Love sang of teenage whores and garbage men on *Pretty in the Inside*
(1991), then threw in her lot with grunge by marrying the doomed Kurt
Cobain. Meanwhile, Nymphs songs such as 'Sad and Damned' and 'Death
of a Scenester' were narcissistically self-obsessed paeans to a drug scene
of which even Guns N' Roses had begun to tire. 'We come from the land
of sunshine to bring you darkness,' announced Inger Lorre when the band
played London's Marquee, but the old *noir* schtick had started to ring
pretty hollow.

Only L7, whose bassist Jennifer Finch had once played with Courtney
Love in the Bangles-style Sugar Baby Doll, declined to glamorize the
sleaze of Tinseltown. Like the evergreen Redd Kross, still going strong
after twelve years as the monarchs of retro trash, they were saved by their
sense of humour. 'We laugh at our city,' said guitarist/vocalist Donita
Sparks when the band's Slash debut *Bricks Are Heavy* was released in 1992.
'If you like to see bad TV actors walking down the street putting money
into parking meters, like we do, then LA's the place to be. And if you like
to see your neighbours look just like Guns N' Roses, then it's a good
place to be. Cos your neighbours *do* look like Guns N' Roses. LA is so
fake and phoney, but that's why we like it here.' Singing about anorexia
and the Gulf War over supercharged metal riffs, L7 refused to succumb
to the stoned myopia of the Sunset Strip.

With a poignant Hollywood irony, it was the brat-pack movie stars of
the early nineties who took the 'sad and damned' death trip to its logical
conclusion. Tiring of the save-the-rainforest worthiness that was rife in
movieland at the turn of the decade, LA's brightest young things began
consorting with the new superstars of the Sunset Strip – assorted
grungesters and funk/metal icons like Blind Melon and those trusty
troopers the Red Hot Chili Peppers. Archetypal wannabes, these actors
also began consorting with dealers who peddled everything from crack
and heroin to GHB, a steroid-like drug which renders its users virtually
catatonic. At clubs such as Maxx, the Gate and the Dragonfly (and
restaurants such as the aptly named Babylon), a new and furtive hedonism
began to take root, bringing musicians and thespians together in a mutual

admiration society. 'You see these healthy, famous people at Erewhon, shopping for beet juice,' one TV actor told *Entertainment Weekly*. 'In the light they look great, but when the sun goes down, LA is a different place. The Sunset Strip – that says it all.'

The hippest place of all was the Viper Room, the club at 8852 Sunset co-owned by *Edward Scissorhands* star Johnny Depp. Here Depp and fellow wannabes Keanu Reeves and River Phoenix acted out their rock'n'roll fantasies, playing with their own bands and jamming with *bona fide* rock stars. River Phoenix was due to play the Viper Room with his band Aleka's Attic the night he rolled up stoned out of his mind on smack and coke in late October 1993; Depp himself was jamming with Flea of the Chili Peppers, Al Jourgensen of Ministry, and Gibby Haynes of the Butthole Surfers as Phoenix made his unsteady way out of the club. The shocking death minutes later of the beautiful boy whom everyone deemed to be the cleanest-living kid in Hollywood was not so very different from the death a decade earlier of that other rock'n'roll wannabe John Belushi.

A week after Phoenix's death, the Viper Room reopened for business, but now it was full of tourists and rubberneckers. 'It's like the fucking Hard Rock Café,' sneered one Strip regular. By then, in any case, the shock had been superseded by the next Hollywood scandal on the menu: the story of Michael Jackson and a 13-year-old boy called Jordan Chandler.

BEWARE
OF
DOG

westec
W
COMMUNITY
WATCH

ARMED PATROL

SECURITY
W
westec

ARMED RESPONSE

Epilogue:
Slipping into Darkness

Folks ain't safe a minute in this town. When I come here twenty-two years ago we didn't lock our doors hardly. Now it's gangsters and crooked policemen fightin' each other with machine guns, so I've heard.

Mrs Morrison in Raymond Chandler's
Farewell, My Lovely (1940)

I sit here in California, writing these reminiscences in a heavy rain, thinking of the fires and mud slides, and it does seem as if the magic sunny land I knew has been 'struck', like the movie sets it built, and has disappeared overnight, all its genius gone back into bottles, leaving skyscrapers where the orange blossoms used to scent the wind.

Johnny Mercer, 1976

It has been simultaneously disturbing and gratifying to find one's theories about LA confirmed by what has happened there in the last five years. There was plenty of horror and insanity in LA through the eighties, when the idea for *Waiting for the Sun* was constantly in my mind, but there was nothing to match the sequence of events in the nineties, from riots to brush fires to drought to sex scandals to earthquakes to celebrity murders. I have begun to wonder whether it really is all coming to an end – whether the apocalyptic climax everyone has always predicted is actually about to happen.

Los Angeles had already taken over from New York as the main locus of American fears and tensions when I began work on this book. In the twelve years between Walter Hill's preposterous New York gang movie *The Warriors* (1979) and John Singleton's highly accomplished *Boyz n the Hood* (1991), everything had shifted westwards, and Europeans who were completely *au fait* with Crips and Bloods knew nothing about gangs in Harlem or the Bronx. The whole paradox of 'gang war in paradise' – or more accurately, the eruption of black reality on to white Californian consciousness – had given Los Angeles a dimension it had lacked while the rest of the world still equated the city with Hollywood and Disneyland.

Laurel Canyon, 1993.

'It's really dangerous there in a way it doesn't feel dangerous in New York,' Nora Ephron could say in late 1993. 'It's a strange thing, but a city built like New York feels safer in the midst of crime than those cities that are all little houses next to one another with backyards.' The fact is that everything which had always been intrinsically flawed in the southern Californian dream came to a head during the Reaganite eighties, when whites took increasing fright at the ever-swelling numbers of immigrants, and when vested business interests did their best to keep the city's underclass cordoned off from its bourgeoisie.

In May 1992, the warnings and premonitions of West Coast rap were borne out by five days of 'rioting' on the streets of Los Angeles, mainly in South Central but encroaching much further into the white Westside than the Watts 'riots' of 1965 had done. (I use quotation marks because the 'rioters' themselves, who included members of every LA minority, chose with some justification to see their burning and looting as an 'uprising' or 'rebellion'.) Warnings and premonitions had also come from a variety of sources pointing to the increasing fragmentation of the city and the growing fortification of its wealthier areas. Mike Davis's *City of Quartz* (1992), for example, was rightly lauded as a searing attack on Reagan-era public policy in a metropolis he described as 'a post-modern city of secessionist suburbs and burgeoning barrios'. In a chapter entitled 'The Hammer and the Rock', Davis examined the demonization of LA's supposedly 'unrehabilitable' black youth, 45 per cent of whom were unemployed in the late eighties. If for him there was an alarming 'synergy' between gangsta rap and the 'fantasy power-trips' of Hollywood movies, he understood how the drug-dealing gangs of South Central were a 'power resource of last resort for thousands of abandoned youth'. (An estimated 100,000 of them, in fact.)

Naturally, it didn't take long for rap to respond to the 'rebellion'. Most famously, Ice T recorded a song called 'Cop Killer' with his thrash metal band Body Count, only for the song to create a furore six months down the line. $150 million and several death threats to Warners executives later – despite the fact that the song hadn't led to the death of a single police officer – Ice took the track off the album and later quit Warners for the independent Priority label. His first Priority release was *Home Invasion*, the cover of which depicted a white teenager listening to rap on his Walkman, with Malcolm X and Iceberg Slim books lying open beside him and Ice T's own giant head firing lightning bolts into the boy's brain.

Not only did black hiphop continue to give vent to the rage within LA's black and brown communities, but Ice T's vision of rap's revolutionary impact on white suburbia was partly borne out by bands such as the multi-ethnic Rage Against the Machine, whose rap/metal/hardcore fusion epitomized the tribal eclecticism and political commitment of the new 'Lollapalooza Nation'. (Fittingly, Ice had played the first Lollapalooza tour, while Ice Cube had featured in the second.) If Rage Against the

Machine were rather more PC in their outlook than either of the Ices – they quite rightly abhorred the virulent misogyny of gangsta rappers – guitarist Tom Morello could still claim that it was 'a political act that Ice T and Ice Cube crossed over ... giving white suburban kids a glimpse into a different life'.

A year after the Rodney King rebellion, little had changed in Los Angeles. If there were signs of hope in a new, heavily guarded metro system connecting the city's 'zones' and challenging the dominant autotopian dream, there was also a distinct sense of white panic in the LAPD helicopter-filled air. The night I arrived in LA in the summer of 1993 to do some interviews for this book, the city had just elected a new mayor in the form of Republican Richard Riordan, a millionaire lawyer and investor whose slogan was 'Tough Enough to Turn LA Around'. The crisis he and every Angeleno faced was a grave one, summed up by the *Guardian*'s Mike Bygrave as 'the crisis of modernity, of how you maintain a multiracial, multiethnic society [that is] also fractured between wealth and poverty'. 'We are all Los Angelenos now,' Bygrave concluded.

As if acting out the sickness at its heart, LA proceeded to engross the rest of the world through the series of natural catastrophes and man-made outrages with which most of us are only too familiar: the Menendez killings, the floods and brush fires, the Heidi Fleiss, Michael Jackson and Hugh Grant scandals, the blatantly racist Proposition 187, the O. J. Simpson trial and of course a major earthquake, measuring 6.6 on the Richter scale. (Perfectly mirroring the tangled confusion of LA's sprawling life, Robert Altman's panoramic *Short Cuts* climaxed in a massive 'quake prefaced by the Iggy Pop/Terry Adams song 'Evil California'.) Hollywood Babylon was turning into Hollywood Armageddon, and the ghosts of Nathanael West and Gavin Lambert looked on with cruel amusement.* 'The notion of general devastation had for Maria a certain sedative effect,' Joan Didion had written in her LA novel *Play It as It Lays* (1973). '[It] suggested an instant in which all anxieties would be abruptly gratified.' But Didion herself had already abandoned the city for which she had earlier left New York: when she wrote of LA in the early nineties, the city was merely one of the destinations of her fatigued *Sentimental Journeys* (1992). Other Angelenos – some of them fleeing like Didion, others hunkering down for some grim finale – talked in the same quasi-apocalyptic terms of the city that L7 could still describe as a 'Freak Magnet' for cranks and cultists the world over.

It goes without saying that LA remained as much of a 'magnet' for Brits as it had been when I lived there in the early eighties. Among them were the enterprising young bucks who began running 'Death Tours' of

---

* 'One wonders what Nathanael West would have made of Hollywood Boulevard today,' wrote J. G. Ballard in 1992; 'tacky and faded, the haunt of hookers, drug dealers and edgy tourists, waiting for Tod Hackett's great fire to surge up from the wastelands of central LA and at last destroy the city of dreadful night.'

Hollywood during the recession of the early nineties – as reported by a thoroughly odious Englishman called William Cash, a sort of Waugh-correspondent-in-Lotusland who, when the 'riots' broke, was safely ensconced within the *Playboy* mansion in Bel Air. (The 'riots' even produced a bizarre sub-Reyner Banham tome by British architectural theorist Charles Jencks called *Heteropolis: Los Angeles, the Riots, and the Strange Beauty of Hetero-Architecture!*) Yet at the same time, Brits continued to feel a profound ambivalence about LA, one which Bryan Ferry had defined back in the seventies: 'They said, "Go west, young man, that's best, it's there you'll feel no pain"/Bel Air's okay if you dig the grave, but I want to live again.' Richard Rayner, who quoted Ferry's lines in his celebrated Brit-in-LA saga *Los Angeles Without a Map*, concluded his novel with this mordant reflection: 'I'd prostrated myself before the looping freeways, the creepy mansions, the renegade swimming pools that turned to blood, the 128 assorted varieties of palm trees, the stories of mass murders and fence-post slayings, the beach brains, the surf Nazis, the dedicated careerists and religious fruitcakes, the psychos on the bus. I'd just lain back and LA had fucked me up.'

'LA is now so completely out of hand it isn't even believable to me any more,' said James Ellroy, whose feverish *White Jazz* was his parting shot to the city; 'You can't even write about it today.' Gung-ho Republican Bruce Johnston claimed that 'the Los Angeles and southern California we sang about in the Beach Boys just doesn't exist any more,' while Henry Rollins stated simply that LA was 'a death culture' after watching his best friend being gunned down on a Venice boardwalk in December 1991.

As we move into the second half of the nineties – always assuming the city still exists as this book goes to print – so Los Angeles seems to be increasingly detached from the rest of America. (The symbolism of LA and San Francisco being on a different tectonic plate from the rest of the country – separated by the notorious San Andreas Fault – is of course irresistible.) The more we look to it as a kind of Fourth World 'laboratory of the future', the more it becomes, in Carey McWilliams's haunting phrase, 'an island on the land'. 'Here, in fact, was all America,' McWilliams had written; 'America in flight from itself, America on an island.' Reyner Banham echoed McWilliams's words when he wrote that 'in one unnervingly true sense, Los Angeles is the Middle West raised to flash-point, the authoritarian dogmas of the Bible belt and the perennial revolt against them colliding at critical mass under the palm trees.'

'Maybe we're already living in *Terminator* society,' says David Anderle. 'Maybe it's already *Mad Max*. What I'm nervous about is the possibility that it's harder now to try to change things back than it is to carry on as we are.' Peter Asher, who still manages Joni Mitchell and Randy Newman, admits that he's as much a part of the problem as anyone. 'I'm like everyone else at this level of the industry,' he says. 'I retreat back to Malibu, behind gates, and I don't think about it. I mean, we all gave it thought when the riots happened, but otherwise we assume somebody'll work it all out for us.' Novelist Walter Mosley, finally, argues that 'there has to be a commitment to *include* people in Los Angeles': '*Society itself* has to want to include people.'

Back down on the Hollywood streets, far from the closed gates of Malibu, that old myth-mongering hustler Kim Fowley couches the problem in his preferred pop-apocalyptic terms. 'Just as rock'n'roll died with Elvis and became an attitude, so Hollywood is now simply an attitude. The people who make up Los Angeles now, who've moved here from other countries, are not interested in perpetuating these foibles that Nathanael West wrote about. In thirty years, the people in your book will be pissing and bleeding into a bedpan, getting mugged by interplanetary exchange students. Third World people will have taken over the entire situation, and why shouldn't they?

'Satan has a coffin, and he has LA in the coffin, and he's almost finished hammering it shut, and the coffin's gonna go down the gutters of Hollywood like a glass-bottomed boat, and it'll roll over the memories of Jimmy Cagney and Fatty Arbuckle, and Hollywood will finally end for the same reason that the Roman and British empires ended – for the same reason that all movies and symphonies end. Because there has to be an end.'

Appendix:
Los Angeles in Songs

Joe Turner: Blues on Central Avenue (1941)
Crown Prince Waterford: LA Blues (1947)
Ricky Nelson: Lonesome Town (1958)
Eddie Cochran: Summertime Blues (1958)
The Beach Boys: Surfin' (1961)
The Penguins: Memories of El Monte (1963)
Jan and Dean: Surf City (1963)
The Beach Boys: I Get Around (1964)
The Beach Boys: California Girls (1965)
The Rolling Stones: The Under Assistant West Coast Promotion Man (1965)
The Mamas and the Papas: California Dreamin' (1966)
The Mothers of Invention: Trouble Every Day (The Watts Riot Song) (1966)
Love: Maybe the People Would Be the Times, or Between Clark and Hilldale (1967)
The Doors: Moonlight Drive (1967)
The Leather-Coated Minds: Trip Down Sunset Strip (1967)
The Monkees: Pleasant Valley Sunday (1967)
The Byrds: So You Wanna Be a Rock'n'Roll Star (1967)
The Fifth Dimension: California Soul (1967)
The Mamas and the Papas: Safe in My Garden (1968)
HMS Bounty: Drivin' Sideways on a One-Way Street (1968)
Richard Harris: MacArthur Park (1968)
Dionne Warwick: Do You Know the Way to San Jose? (1968)
Van Dyke Parks: Vine Street (1968)
Cass Elliott: California Earthquake (1968)
John Mayall: Laurel Canyon Home (1968)
Van Dyke Parks: Laurel Canyon Boulevard (1968)
Jackie DeShannon: Laurel Canyon (1969)
The Byrds: Bad Night at the Whisky (1969)
The Flying Burrito Brothers: Sin City (1969)
Firesign Theatre: How Can You Be in Two Places at Once When You're Not Anywhere at All?
  (1970)
Joni Mitchell: Ladies of the Canyon (1970)
John Phillips: Malibu People (1970)
John Phillips: Topanga Canyon (1970)
The Doors: LA Woman (1971)
The Byrds: Precious Kate (1971)
Joni Mitchell: California (1971)

America: Ventura Highway (1972)
David Ackles: Oh! California (1972)
Albert Hammond: It Never Rains in Southern California (1972)
Thelma Houston: Black California (1972)
Todd Rundgren: Sunset Boulevard (1973)
Neil Young: LA (1973)
Steely Dan: Show Biz Kids (1973)
Joni Mitchell: People's Parties (1974)
Neil Young: On the Beach (1974)
Neil Young: Revolution Blues (1974)
War: Low Rider (1975)
Ronnie Spector: Say Goodbye to Hollywood (1975)
Terry Allen: There Ought To Be a Law Against Sunny Southern California (1975)
The Sweet: Desolation Boulevard (1975)
John Cale: Mr Wilson (1975)
Guy Clark: LA Freeway (1975)
The Eagles: Hotel California (1976)
The Eagles: The Last Resort (1976)
Warren Zevon: Join Me in LA (1976)
Warren Zevon: Poor, Poor Pitiful Me (1976)
Warren Zevon: Desperadoes Under the Eaves (1976)
Iggy Pop and James Williamson: Kill City (1977)
Dennis Wilson: Pacific Ocean Blues (1977)
Bob Seger: Hollywood Nights (1978)
David Ackles: Surf's Down (1979)
Donna Summer: Sunset People (1979)
Ry Cooder: Down in Hollywood (1979)
The Rotters: Sit On My Face, Stevie Nicks (1979)
Steely Dan: Babylon Sisters (1980)
Jackson Browne: Boulevard (1980)
Tom Waits: Heartattack and Vine (1980)
John Stewart: Hollywood Dreams (1980)
X: Los Angeles (1980)
The Circle Jerks: Beverly Hills (1980)
Black Flag: White Minority (1981)
Neil Young: Surfer Joe and Moc the Sleaze (1981)
The Go-Gos: This Town (1981)
Randy Newman: I Love LA (1983)
T-Bone Burnett: Hefner and Disney (1983)
True West: Hollywood Holiday (1983)
Frank Sinatra: LA is My Lady (1984)
Don Henley: The Boys of Summer (1984)
Red Hot Chili Peppers: Out in LA (1984)
Red Hot Chili Peppers: Hollywood (1985)
David Lee Roth: California Girls (1985)

Sonic Youth: Death Valley '69 (1985)
David and David: Welcome to the Boomtown (1986)
Ice T: Six in the Morning (1986)
GunsN'Roses: Paradise City (1987)
Jane's Addiction: Up the Beach/Ocean Size (1988)
NWA: Fuck tha Police (1988)
Randy Newman: Red Bandana (1988)
LA Guns: Riot On Sunset (1989)
Public Enemy: Burn Hollywood Burn (1990)
Elvis Costello: The Other Side of Summer (1991)
Cypress Hill: How I Could Just Kill a Man (1991)
The Nymphs: Sad and Damned (1991)
The Nymphs: Death of a Scenester (1991)
Tom Waits: Goin' Out West (1992)
Body Count: Cop Killer (1992)
that dog: Westside Angst (1993)
Annie Ross: Evil California (1993)
Pavement: Unfair (1994)
L7: Freak Magnet (1994)
Wax: California (1995)

Bibliography

Amis, Martin, *The Moronic Inferno* (Viking Penguin)

Anger, Kenneth, *Hollywood Babylon* (Dell, 1981)

    Hollywood Babylon II (NAL-Dutton, 1985)

Anson, Robert Sam, *Gone Crazy and Back Again: The Rise and Fall of the Rolling Stone Generation* (Doubleday, 1981)

Babitz, Eve, *Eve's Hollywood* (Delacorte, 1974)

    Slow Days, Fast Company: The World, the Flesh, and LA (Knopf, 1977)

    'Jim Morrison is Alive and Well and Living in Hollywood', *Esquire*, March 1991

Balfour, Victoria, *Rock Wives* (Quill, 1986)

Bangs, Lester, *Psychotic Reactions and Carburetor Dung: An Anthology* (Random House, 1988)

Banham, Reyner, *Los Angeles: The Architecture of Four Ecologies* (Penguin, 1971)

Baxter, John, *Hollywood in the Sixties* (Tantivy Press, 1972)

Bell, Max, 'Tim Buckley: The Fantastic Voyage of a Starsailor', *NME*, 22 December 1979

Belsito, Peter, and Bob Davis (eds.), *Hardcore California: A History of Punk and New Wave* (Last Gasp, 1983)

Berman, Connie, *Linda Ronstadt* (Proteus, 1979)

Bing, Leon, *Do or Die* (HarperCollins, 1991)

Blaine, Hal, *Hal Blaine and the Wrecking Crew* (H. Leonard, 1990)

Bowie, Angie, *Backstage Passes* (Putnam Publishing Group, 1993)

Brook, Stephen, *LA Days, LA Nights: A Journey Through America's City of Dreams* (St. Martin's Press, 1993)

Brown, Mick, 'Stuff of Dreams: Look Back With Anger', *Sunday Correspondent*, 14 January 1990

Bugliosi, Vincent, *Helter Skelter* (Norton, 1994)

Burdon, Eric, *I Used to be an Animal but I'm Alright Now* (Faber, 1986)

Burns, Jim, 'Let the Good Times Roll', *Jazz and Blues*, February 1972

Burt, Rob, and Patsy North, *West Coast Story* (Chartwell, 1977)

Burt, Rob, *Surf City/Drag City* (Blandford, 1986)

Bygrave, Mike, 'Naked City', *Guardian*, 13 February 1993

Callender, Red, with Elaine Cohen, *Unfinished Dream: The Musical World of Red Callender* (Quartet, 1991)

Capote, Truman, *Music for Chameleons* (Random, 1980)

Carr, Roy, and Fred Dellar, 'Earth Angel: Jesse Belvin', *Vox*, December 1990

Chandler, Raymond, the novels (Random House, various dates)

Claxton, William, *Jazz West Coast* (Books Nippan, 1993)

Cohn, Nik, *Awopbopaloobop Awopbamboom* (Paladin, 1970)

    Ball the Wall (Picador, 1989)

Compo, Susan, *Life After Death and Other Stories* (Faber & Faber, 1991)
  Malingering (Faber & Faber, 1993)
Conrad, Peter, *Imagining America* (Routledge & Kegan Paul, 1980)
Cooper, Alice, with Steven Gaines, *Me, Alice: The Autobiography of Alice Cooper* (G. P. Putnam's Sons, 1976)
Crosby, David, *Long Time Gone* (Dell, 1990)
Cross, Brian, *It's Not About a Salary* (Routledge, Chapman & Hall, 1993)
Dannen, Fredric, *Hit Men: Power Brokers* (Random House, 1991)
Davidson, Sara, 'Rolling into the Eighties', *Esquire*, February 1980
Davis, Clive, *Clive: Inside the Record Business* (Routledge, Chapman & Hall, 1993)
Davis, Mike, *City of Quartz* (Random, 1992)
Dawson, Jim, *Nervous Man Nervous: Big Jay McNeely and the Rise of the Honking Tenor Sax!* (Big Nickel, 1994)
Dawson, Jim, and Steve Propes, *What Was the First Rock'n'Roll Record?* (Faber & Faber, 1992)
Dellar, Fred, *The NME Guide to Rock Cinema* (Hamlyn, 1981)
Densmore, John, *Riders On the Storm* (Dell, 1991)
Des Barres, Pamela, *I'm With the Band: Confessions of a Groupie* (William Morrow, 1987)
Didion, Joan, *Slouching Towards Bethlehem* (Farrar, Straus & Giroux, 1990)
  The White Album (Farrar, Straus & Giroux, 1990)
  Play it as it Lays (Farrar, Straus & Giroux, 1990)
  Sentimental Journeys (HarperCollins, 1993)
Diltz, Henry, *The Innocence Age* (Tokyo: Switch, 1990)
Dr. John (Mac Rebennack), with Jack Rummell, *Under a Hoodoo Moon: The Life of Dr. John the Night Tripper* (St. Martin's Press, 1994)
Dolenz, Mickey, with Mark Bego, *I'm a Believer* (Hyperion, 1993)
Draper, Robert, *The Rolling Stone Story* (Mainstream, 1991)
Editors of Rolling Stone, *Neil Young: The Rolling Stone Files* (Hyperion, 1994)
Eisen, Jonathan (ed.), *The Age of Rock: Sounds of the American Cultural Revolution* (Vintage, 1969)
Ellis, Bret Easton, *Less Than Zero* (Viking, 1987)
Ellroy, James, *The Black Dahlia* (Warner Books, 1988)
  The Big Nowhere (Warner Books, 1988)
  LA Confidential (Warner Books, 1989)
  White Jazz (Random House, 1994)
Epstein, Dan, 'The Oracle of Del-Fi: Bob Keane', *Los Angeles Reader*, 6 January 1995
Fawcett, Anthony, and Henry Diltz, *California Rock, California Sound* (Los Angeles: Reed, 1978)
Fein, Art, *The LA Musical History Tour* (Faber & Faber, 1991)
Finnis, Rob, *The Phil Spector Story* (Rock On, 1974)
Flanagan, Bill, *Written in My Soul: Candid Interviews With Rock's Great Songwriters* (Omnibus, 1990)
Foege, Alec, *Confusion is Next* (St. Martin's Press, 1994)
Fong-Torres, Ben, *Hickory Wind: The Life and Times of Gram Parsons* (Pocket, 1991)
  (ed.) *The Rolling Stone Rock'n'Roll Reader* (Bantam, 1974)
Frame, Pete, *The Complete Family Trees* (Omnibus, 1993)
Friedrich, Otto, *City of Nets: A Portrait of Hollywood in the 1940s* (Headline, 1986)
Gaines, Steven, *Heroes and Villains: The True Story of the Beach Boys* (New American Library, 1986)
Gallagher, Larry, 'Rock'n'Roll High', *Details*, July 1993

Gehman, Pleasant, liner notes to *We're Desperate: The LA Scene 1976–1979* (Rhino Records, 1993)

George, B., *Volume* (Omnibus Press, 1982)

George, Lynell, *No Crystal Stair* (Doubleday & Co. Inc., 1994)

George, Nelson, *The Death of Rhythm and Blues* (Dutton, 1989)

Gibson, William, *Virtual Light* (Bantam, 1993)

Gillett, Charlie, *The Sound of the City* (Da Capo Press, Inc., 1996)

   Making Tracks (Publishers Group, 1995)

Gioia, Ted, *West Coast Jazz: Modern Jazz In California 1945–1960* (Oxford, 1992)

Gleason, Ralph J., *Jefferson Airplane and the San Franciscan Sound* (Ballantine, 1969)

Gold, Jeff, and David Leaf (eds.), *A&M Records: The First 25 Years* (A&M Records, 1987)

Goldman, Albert, *Sound Bites* (Abacus, 1993)

Goldstein, Richard, *Goldstein's Greatest Hits* (Prentice-Hall, 1970)

Gordon, Robert, *Jazz West Coast* (Interlink Publishing group, 1990)

Gourse, Leslie, *Unforgettable* (St. Martin's Press, 1992)

Gray, Michael, *Mother: The Frank Zappa Story* (rev. edn, Plexus, 1993)

Grein, Paul (ed.), *Capitol Records: 50th Anniversary 1942–1992* (Capitol Records, 1992)

Griffin, Sid, *Gram Parsons: A Music Biography* (Sierra Records and Books, 1985)

Grushkin, Paul D., *The Art of Rock: Posters from Presley to Punk* (Abbeville Press, 1987)

Guralnick, Peter, *Sweet Soul Music* (Virgin, 1987)

Hale, Dennis, and Jonathan Eisen (eds.), *The California Dream* (Collier, 1968)

Hawes, Hampton, *Raise Up Off Me* (Da Capo Press, Inc., 1979)

Herman, Gary, *Rock'n'Roll Babylon* (Plexus, 1982)

Hitchens, Christopher, 'It Happened on Sunset', *Vanity Fair*, April 1995

Hockney, David, *David Hockney* (Thames and Hudson, 1976)

Hopkins, Jerry, *Bowie* (Macmillan, 1985)

Hopkins, Jerry, and Danny Sugerman, *No One Gets Out of Here Alive* (Warner Books, 1995)

Horn, Paul, with Lee Underwood, *Inside Paul Horn: The Spiritual Odyssey of a Universal Traveller* (Harper San Francisco, 1990)

Hoskyns, Barney, 'Hotel California Goodbye', *NME*, 25 December 1982

   'Black Flag in the Warm California Scum', *NME*, 20 November 1982

   'The Life and Grimes of Kim Fowley', *LA Reader*, 3 June 1983

   'Riding the Freeways of Language', *NME*, 13 August 1983

Humphries, Patrick, *Small Change* (St. Martin's Press, 1990)

Ice T, with Heidi Sigmund, *The Ice Opinion* (St. Martin's Press, 1993)

Johnston, Ian, *The Wild, Wild World of the Cramps* (Omnibus, 1990)

Jones, LeRoi, *Blues People* (William Morrow, 1971)

Kaufman, Phil, with Colin White, *Road Mangler Deluxe* (White-Boucke, 1993)

Kent, Nick, *The Dark Stuff* (Penguin, 1994)

   'The Mighty Pop Vs. The Hand of Blight', *NME*, 3 May 1975

Lahr, John, *Automatic Vaudeville* (Methuen, 1984)

Leaf, David, *The Beach Boys and the California Myth* (Grosset & Dunlap, 1978)

Lees, Gene, *Singers and the Song* (Oxford, 1987)

Lipton, Lawrence, *The Holy Barbarians* (W. H. Allen, 1960)

Loza, Steven, *Barrio Rhythm: Mexican–American Music in Los Angeles* (University of Illinois, 1993)

Lurie, Alison, *The Nowhere City* (Avon Books, 1992)

Maclean, Hugh, and Vernon Joynson, *An American Rock History, Part One: California, the Golden State 1963–1985* (Telford: Borderline Productions, 1987)

McEwen, Joe, *Sam Cooke: The Man Who Invented Soul* (Chappell, 1977)

McWilliams, Carey, *Southern California* (Gibbs Smith, 1973)

Malone, Bill, *Country Music USA* (University of Texas, 1968)

Marcus, Greil, *Mystery Train: Images Of America in Rock'n'Roll Music* (3rd edn, Omnibus, 1990)

(ed.) *Stranded: Rock and Roll for a Desert Island* (Knopf, 1979)

In the Fascist Bathroom: Writings on Punk 1977–92 (Viking, 1993)

Marsh, Dave, *The Heart of Rock and Soul* (Penguin, 1989)

Louie Louie (Hyperion, 1993)

Martinez, Ruben, *The Other Side: Fault Lines, Guerilla Saints, And the True Heart of Rock'n'Roll* (Verso, 1992)

Meltzer, Richard, *The Aesthetics of Rock* (rev. edn, Da Capo, 1987)

LA Is The Capital Of Kansas (Harmony, 1988)

Millar, Bill, *The Coasters* (Star, 1974)

Miller, Jim (ed.), *The Rolling Stone Illustrated History of Rock'n'Roll* (Random House, 1980)

Mingus, Charles, *Beneath the Underdog* (Knopf, 1971)

Morthland, John, *The Best of Country Music* (Doubleday/Dolphin, 1984)

Mosley, Walter, *Devil in a Blue Dress* (Norton, 1990)

A Red Death (Pocket Books, 1992)

White Butterfly (Pocket Books, 1993)

Black Betty (Norton, 1994)

Muirhead, Bert, *The Record Producers File: A Directory of Rock Album Producers 1962–1984* (Blandford, 1984)

Nelson, Paul, and Lester Bangs, *Rod Stewart* (Sidgwick & Jackson, 1981)

Nilsen, Per, and Dorothy Sherman, *The Wild One: The True Story of Iggy Pop* (Omnibus, 1988)

Nolan, Tom, 'The Frenzied Frontier of Pop Music', *LA Times WEST Magazine*, 27 November 1966

Nolan, Tom, and David Felton, 'The Beach Boys: A California Saga', *Rolling Stone*, 28 October/11 November 1971

O'Day, Anita, *High Times, Hard Times* (Limelight Editions, 1989)

Otis, Johnny, *Listen to the Lambs* (W. W. Norton, 1968)

Upside your Head! Rhythm & Blues on Central Avenue (Wesleyan University Press, 1993)

Pearlman, Sandy, 'Excerpts from the History of Los Angeles: 1965–1969', in Jonathan Eisen (ed.), *Twenty-Minute Fandangos and Forever Changes: A Rock Bazaar* (Vintage, 1971)

Pelissero, Ellen, and Stan Cornyn, *What a Long, Strange Trip it's Been: An Authorized History of Warner Bros Records* (unpublished, 1980)

Pepper, Art, *Straight Life* (Da Capo Press, Inc.)

Phillips, John, with Jim Jerome, *Papa John* (Doubleday, 1986)

Phillips, Michelle, *California Dreamin': The True Story of the Mamas and the Papas* (Warner Books, 1986)

Pollock, Bruce, *In Their Own Words* (Collier, 1975)

Priore, Dominic (ed.), *Look! Listen! Vibrate! Smile!* (Surfin' Colours Prod., 1989)

Propes, Steve, and Galen Gart, *Recorded in Hollywood: Glory Years of LA Rhythm & Blues* (Big Nickel, 1995)

Pynchon, Thomas, 'A Journey into the Mind of Watts', *New York Times Magazine*, 12 June 1966
   The Crying of Lot 49 (HarperCollins, 1986)
   Vineland (Viking Penguin, 1991)

Rambali, Paul, 'Standing Up for the Small Man: A Conversation With Randy Newman', *NME*, 8 December 1979

Rayner, Richard, *Los Angeles Without a Map* (Paladin, 1989)

Reed, Tom, *The Black Music History of Los Angeles: A Classical Pictorial History of Black Music in Los Angeles from the 1920s to 1970* (Black Accent on LA Press, 1992)

Ribowsky, Mark, *He's a Rebel: The Truth About Phil Spector* (Dutton, 1989)

Rieff, David, *Los Angeles* (Simon & Schuster)
   Timeless Flight (Hallenbook, 1990)

Rogan, Johnny, *Neil Young: The Definitive Story of His Musical Career* (Proteus, 1982)
   Timeless Flight: The Definitive Biography of the Byrds (2nd edn, Square One, 1990)

Rollins, Henry, *Get in the Van: On the Road with Black Flag* (2.13.61, 1994)

Roxon, Lillian, *Rock Encyclopaedia* (Grosset & Dunlap, 1969)

Ruscha, Ed, *Every Building on the Sunset Strip* (Wittenborn, 1966)

Russell, Ross, *The Sound* (Dutton, 1961)

Sanders, Ed, *The Family* (Dutton, 1990)

Scoppa, Bud, *The Byrds* (Scholastic Book Services, 1971)

Sculatti, Gene, and Davin Seay, *San Francisco Nights: The Psychedelic Music Trip 1965–1968* (Sidgwick & Jackson, 1985)

Selvin, Joel, *Ricky Nelson: Idol for a Generation* (Contemporary, 1990)
   Summer of Love: The Inside Story of LSD, Rock and Roll, Free Love, and High Times in the Wild West (Dutton, 1994)

Selvin, Joel, and Jim Marshall, *Monterey Pop* (Chronicle, 1993)

Shaw, Arnold, *Honkers and Shouters* (Macmillan, 1986)

Shearlaw, John, *Van Halen: Jumpin' for the Dollar* (Zomba, 1984)

Siegel, Jules, 'Goodbye Surfing, Hello God!: The Religious Conversion of Brian Wilson', *Cheetah*, October 1967

Smith, Joe, *Off the Record* (Warner Books, 1989)

Smith, Joseph, *The Day the Music Died* (Evergreen, 1981)

Smith, R. J., 'The View from Cypress Hill', *LA Weekly*, 11–17 June 1993
   'Paradise Lost', *Details*, November 1994

Snowden, Don, 'Johnny Otis: An R&B Pioneer Looks Back On a Lifetime in Music', *New York Rocker*, February 1982

Spector, Ronnie, *Be My Baby* (Crown, 1990)

Spurrier, Jeff, 'California Screaming', *Details*, December 1994

Staehling, Richard, 'From Rock Around the Clock to the Trip: The Truth About Teen Movies', in *Kings of the Bs*, ed. Todd McCarthy and Charles Flynn (Dutton, 1975)

Sugerman, Danny, *Wonderland Ave* (Plume, 1990)

Sweet, Brian, *Steely Dan: Reelin' in the Years* (Omnibus, 1994)

Talbot, David, and Barbara Zheutlin, 'Jack Nitzsche: Expecting To Fly', *Crawdaddy!*, November 1974

Taylor, Derek, *It Was Twenty Years Ago Today* (Bantam, 1987)

Theroux, Peter, *Translating LA* (Norton, 1995)

Thompson, Dave, *Red Hot Chili Peppers* (St. Martin's Press, 1993)

Toop, David, 'Surfin' (Death Valley) USA', *Collusion*, Feb/April 1982
   Rap Attack 2: African Rap to Global Hip Hop (Serpent's Tail, 1991)
Tosches, Nick, *Unsung Heroes of Rock'n'Roll* (Crown Publishing, 1991)
Turner, Tina, with Kurt Loder, *Tina: My Life Story* (Avon Books, 1987)
Various, 'California Dreamin' – LA in the '60s', *Goldmine*, 6 September 1991
Various, 'The LA Episode' issue, *Raygun* No. 12, Dec/Jan 1993/4
Various, *The Rolling Stone Interviews 1967–1980* (St. Martin's Press, 1981)
Ward, Ed, *Rock of Ages* (Penguin UK, 1987)
Warhol, Andy, and Pat Hackett, *POPism: The Warhol '60s* (Harcourt Brace Jovanovich, 1980)
Waters, John, 'John Waters' Tour Of LA', in *Crackpot* (Fourth Estate, 1988)
Waugh, Evelyn, *The Loved One* (Little Brown, 1977)
Webb, C. W., *Captain Beefheart: The Man and His Music* (Kawabata, 1989)
Welding, Pete, 'The Rolling Stone Interview: Johnny Otis', *Rolling Stone*, 9 December 1971
West, Nathanael, *Complete Works* (Picador Classics, 1988)
Whitcomb, Ian, *Rock Odyssey* (Limelight Editions, 1994)
   'Art Rupe: The Specialist', *Blues Unlimited*, Oct/Nov 1973
White, Timothy, *Rock Lives* (Henry Holt & Co., 1991)
   The Nearest Faraway Place: Brian Wilson, the Beach Boys and the Southern California Experience (Henry Holt and Co., 1994)
   'Lenny and Mo: How Two Execs Taught Bugs Bunny to Rock', *Billboard*, 12 November 1994
Williams, John, *Into the Badlands* (HarperCollins, 1993)
Williams, Richard, *Out of His Head: The Sound of Phil Spector* (Abacus, 1974)
   'A Little Whiter than Black', *Independent on Sunday*, 17 November 1991
Wilson, Brian, with Todd Gold, *Wouldn't it be Nice: My Own Story* (Bloomsbury, 1986)
Wincentsen, Edward, *Denny Remembered: Dennis Wilson in Words and Pictures* (Virgin Press, 1991)
Wolfe, Tom, 'I Drove Around Los Angeles and it's Crazy etc.', *Los Angeles Times*, 1 December 1968
Wolff, Daniel, *You Send Me: From Gospel to Pop – The Life and Times of Sam Cooke* (William Morrow, 1995)
Woodward, Bob, *Wired* (Pocket Books, 1986)
Young, Gavin, 'LA: A City Lost and Beaten', *Observer*, 28 March 1993
Zappa, Frank, *The Real Frank Zappa Book* (Simon & Schuster, 1990)

I am also indebted to the authors of numerous articles from the following publications: *NME, Melody Maker, Rolling Stone, Billboard, Zigzag, Let it Rock, Musician, Dark Star, Goldmine, Record Collector, Crawdaddy!, Village Voice, Hot Wacks, New York Rocker, Spin, Strange Things Happening, LA Weekly, LA Reader, Creem, BAM, Blues and Rhythm, Who Put the Bomp?, Los Angeles Free Press, Back Door Man, Slash* and too many more to mention.

Index